SELECTIVE ENFORCEMENT AND INTERNATIONAL CRIMINAL LAW

Series Supranational Criminal Law: Capita Selecta, Volume 20

Published in the series:

1. *Supranational Criminal Law: a System Sui Generis,* Roelof Haveman, Olga Kavran and Julian Nichols (eds.)
2. *Double Jeopardy Without Parameters: Re-characterization in International Criminal Law,* Olaoluwa Olusanya
3. *Harmonization of Criminal Law in Europe,* Erling Johannes Husabø and Asbjørn Strandbakken (eds.)
4. *Sentencing and Sanctioning in Supranational Criminal Law,* Roelof Haveman and Olaoluwa Olusanya (eds.)
5. *Application of International Humanitarian and Human Rights Law to the Armed Conflicts of the Sudan: Complementary or Mutually Exclusive Regimes?,* Mohamed Abdels alam Babiker
6. *Supranational Criminology: Towards a Criminology of International Crimes,* Alette Smeulers and Roelof Haveman (eds.)
7. *Individual Criminal Liability for the International Crime of Aggression,* Gerhard Kemp
8. *Collective Violence and International Criminal Justice –An Interdisciplinary Approach,* Alette Smeulers (ed.)
9. *International Criminal Law from a Swedish Perspective,* Iain Cameron, Malin Thunberg Schunke, Karin Påle Bartes, Christoffer Wong and Petter Asp
10. *The Implementation of the European Arrest Warrant in the European Union: Law, Policy and Practice,* Massimo Fichera
11. *The Principle of Mutual Recognition in Cooperation in Criminal Matters,* Annika Suominen
12. *The European Public Prosecutor's Office,* Martijn Willem Zwiers
13. *Victimological Approaches to International Crimes: Africa,* Rianne Letschert, Roelof Haveman, Anne-Marie de Brouwer, Antony Pemberton (eds.)
14. *The United States and International Criminal Tribunals,* Harry M. Rhea
15. *EU Sanctions: Law and Policy Issues Concerning Restrictive Measures,* Iain Cameron (ed.)
16. *Whose Responsibility?* Malin Thunberg Schunke
17. *Genocidal Gender and Sexual Violence,* Usta Kaitesi
18. *Addressing the Intentional Destruction of the Environment during Warfare under the Rome Statute of the International Criminal Court,* Steven Freeland
19. *Individual Criminal Liability for the International Crime of Aggression,* Gerhard Kemp

SELECTIVE ENFORCEMENT AND INTERNATIONAL CRIMINAL LAW

The International Criminal Court and Africa

James Nyawo

intersentia
Cambridge – Antwerp – Portland

Intersentia Ltd
Sheraton House | Castle Park
Cambridge | CB3 0AX | United Kingdom
Tel.: +44 1223 370 170 | Fax: +44 1223 370 169
Email: mail@intersentia.co.uk
www.intersentia.com | www.intersentia.co.uk

Distribution for the UK and Ireland:
NBN International
Airport Business Centre, 10 Thornbury Road
Plymouth, PL6 7 PP
United Kingdom
Tel.: +44 1752 202 301 | Fax: +44 1752 202 331
Email: orders@nbninternational.com

Distribution for Europe and all other countries:
Intersentia Publishing nv
Groenstraat 31
2640 Mortsel
Belgium
Tel.: +32 3 680 15 50 | Fax: +32 3 658 71 21
Email: mail@intersentia.be

Distribution for the USA and Canada:
International Specialized Book Services
920 NE 58th Ave. Suite 300
Portland, OR 97213
USA
Tel.: +1 800 944 6190 (toll free) | Fax: +1 503 280 8832
Email: info@isbs.com

Cover illustration: Francisco DE GOYA (1746–1828), Etching, Plate 21 from 'Los desastres de la guerra'

ISBN 978-1-78068-387-4
D/2017/7849/33
NUR 828

British Library Cataloguing in Publication Data. A catalogue record for this book is available from the British Library.

To my parents Veronica and Garikai Nyawo

PREFACE

A major controversy that has arisen during the International Criminal Court's first decade has been the issue of selective enforcement of international criminal law. This has been prompted by the Court failing to open investigations or prosecutions outside Africa. This book assesses the claims of this nature made against the Court – primarily by some African leaders and ruling elites – and how the criticism has impacted on the role of the Court as a mechanism for promoting the international rule of law. The assumption is that if the claims that the Court, based in The Hague, the Netherlands, focuses selectively on Africa are valid, then the Court's role as an effective mechanism for promoting the international rule of law could be called into question.

The book analyses three key components of the Court's legal framework – the mechanisms that trigger the Court's jurisdiction, admissibility rules and the independence of the Office of the Prosecutor – in order to establish how the Court became engaged in Africa and its problems. It argues that the Court's broad, yet not universal, jurisdiction means that it is expected to intervene in other regions apart from Africa. However, when African politicians and members of the ruling elite claim that the Court is selectively focusing on Africa, they mean that it is targeting sitting heads of state and other government officials, to the exclusion of their political rivals or ordinary citizens.

The underlying theme that emerges from this analysis is that the Court is a victim of realpolitik both at the global and state levels. At the global level, powerful states, particularly the permanent members of the United Nations (UN) Security Council, seek to utilise the Court to further their own interests against those states that they consider to be against their own hegemonic interests. At the state level, the ruling elites tend to be comfortable with the Court as long as it targets their political competitors, but are willing to mobilise state apparatus to frustrate the Court if they become the focus of the Court's interventions. Still, since there is no contestation on the principle of ending impunity for atrocity crimes which the Court stands for, perhaps African states have to first play their primary role through their domestic jurisdictions and deny the 'politicised Court' any room for intervention. In other words, if African states could demonstrate that they are willing and capable of addressing the impunity gaps within their boundaries, there would be no need for the Court or the UN Security Council's intervention. If African states could act proactively, they could actually boost their own empirical sovereignty.

Key findings of the research include that the timing of African leaders' criticisms of the Court usually corresponds with the Court's decisions to investigate/issue warrants of arrests or summons to the aforementioned leaders. However, the fact that African states that have referred situations in their own territories to the Court have not challenged the admissibility of the cases suggests that they agree that the Court is the best and most effective forum for delivering justice. The role of the UN Security Council in referring situations to the Court, and in not acting on the African Union's requests for deferrals of proceedings in Darfur and Kenya, has been the main source of African leaders' dissatisfaction with the Court. This book links African leaders' early support for the Court to their distrust of the UN Security Council's handling of African issues, especially with regard to the Lockerbie crisis in Libya and the situation in Rwanda before and during the genocide against the Tutsi.

The book argues that the political dynamics that led to the establishment of the Court – especially the early opposition of the US to the Court and the emergence of the European Union (EU) as the political and financial supporter of the Court – complicated the Prosecutor's ability to use his powers to initiate investigations in areas where he was likely to confront either the US or national interests within the EU. Although the codification process of the substantive and procedural law of the Court was heavily influenced by the legal positivism philosophy of international law, which was necessary if the Court was to gain universal acceptance, the evidence in this book suggests that politics (at both the global and domestic levels) played a crucial role in the application of the international criminal law by the Court. In this regard, the findings in this book are oriented towards the assertion made by critical legal studies that the application of law is not neutral, but follows the political structure of any given society.

Practically speaking, the Court and the proponents of international criminal law need to acknowledge that politics is the Achilles' heel for effective enforcement of international criminal justice and should begin to work within such a reality to devise mechanisms to engage politics in a positive and constructive manner. This could include encouraging domestic prosecutions and the Prosecutor should be free to exercise his power to push back on UN Security Council referrals unless certain guarantees are given, including sustained political and financial support throughout the proceedings.

ACKNOWLEDGEMENTS

Writing and completing this book would not have been possible without the guidance, support and encouragement I received from various people, most of whom I will not be able to mention by name. I would, however, like to express my sincere gratitude to Professor William Schabas who accompanied me throughout the research that led to the material used to write this book. His attention to detail and knowledge of the subject matter was crucial in refining not only the research process but also my ideas and views. I am also indebted to the academic staff with whom I worked closely at the Irish Centre for Human Rights (Republic of Ireland) and Middlesex University (UK); Professors Vinodh Jaichard and Ray Murphy, and Dr Shane Darcy and Dr Nadia Bernaz for their support and encouragement and informative discussions that we had at different stages of my research and writing process. I owe the confidence and desire to write this book to the first opportunity presented to me by Professor Vincent Nmehielle (University of the Witwatersrand) who agreed to publish a chapter I had written in his publication on *Africa and The Future of International Criminal Justice*. During the process of researching and writing this book I also drew inspiration from Professor Charles Jalloh (Florida International University), Professor Setondji Ronald Adjovi (Arcadia University) and Professor Mohamed Abdelsalam Babiker (Khartoum University), who have always been available to listen to my views and provide feedback. A special mention is reserved for Professor Reolof Haveman, who believed in the publication of my research by encouraging me to submit the first draft manuscript to the publishers; since that moment of encouragement he has been a provider of consistent support in order to see this book completed and published.

Dr Aimie Muyoboke Karimunda (Rwanda), Dr Godfrey Mupanga (Zimbabwe), Dr Everest Benyera (South Africa), Dr Josepha Close (Belgium), Dr Giulia Pecorella and Dr Alphonse Muleefu, all of whom started as my fellow colleagues and peers, provided me with much needed support throughout the process. They provided companionship that made the journey towards publication manageable.

Finally, I would like to thank my wife, Mara, and our three children Garikai, Sigona and Pepukai, for providing the moral support and space that I needed to focus on this publication.

CONTENTS

'Before considering double standards on the international level you should confront double standards at home'

Navanetham Pillay,
former United Nations Commissioner for Human Rights
and Judge of the International Criminal Court, 2015

CHAPTER 1
INTRODUCTION

On 18 July 1998, representatives attending a United Nations (UN) Diplomatic Conference of Plenipotentiaries on the Establishment of a Court in Rome, Italy, from states and governments around the world, adopted the Rome Statute – a treaty that established the International Criminal Court ('the Court'). The Conference and the adoption of the Rome Statute were the conclusion of a protracted process that was started by the UN General Assembly Resolution 44/39 of 4 December 1989. The Resolution had requested the International Law Commission 'to address the question of establishing an international criminal court'.[1]

A total of 120 states voted in favour of its adoption, 21 abstained and 7 voted against, including the US, Israel and China.[2] The Court was established on 1 July 2002 when the Rome Statute was ratified by 60 states,[3] giving the Court the mandate to end impunity for the perpetrators of the most serious crimes of concern to the international community.[4]

Prior to the adoption of the Rome Statute and the subsequent establishment of the International Criminal Court, there was growing concern among the proponents of international criminal justice regarding the haphazard creation of tribunals that were primarily focused on single conflicts and hence were selective in nature.[5] Theodor Meron, the Former President of the International Criminal Tribunal for the former Yugoslavia and Presiding Judge of the Appeals Chambers of the International Criminal Tribunal for Rwanda, notes that what was missing – and needed – was a 'uniform and definite corpus of

1 UN Doc. A/44/39, 4 December 1989.

2 Michael Scharf, 'Results of the Rome Conference for an International Criminal Court' (1998) 3 *ASIL Insights* https://www.asil.org/insights/volume/3/issue/10/results-rome-conference-international-criminal-court accessed 22.05.2012.

3 Rome Statute of the International Criminal Court (2002) 2187 UNTS 90, Art. 1 stating that: 'This Statute shall enter into force on the first day of the month after the 60th day following the date of the deposit of 60th instrument of ratification, acceptance, approval or accession with the Secretary-General of the United Nations', (hereinafter referred to as the Rome Statute); see also William A. Schabas, *An Introduction to the International Criminal Court* (4th edn, Cambridge University Press, 2011).

4 International Criminal Court, 'About the Court' (2012) https://www.icc-cpi.int/about accessed 16.05.2012.

5 Theodor Meron, 'International Criminalization of Atrocities' (1995) 89 *American Journal of International Law* 554, p. 555.

international humanitarian law that could be applied apolitically to internal atrocities everywhere, and that recognises the role of all states in the vindication of such law'.[6] Louise Arbour, a Canadian lawyer who was Chief Prosecutor of the Tribunals for the former Yugoslavia and Rwanda at the time, spelt out the role that these claims of selective enforcement played in the establishment of a permanent international criminal court when she stated that:

> Irrationally selective prosecutions undermine the perception of justice as fair and even-handed, and therefore serve as the basis for defiance and contempt. The *ad hoc* nature of the existing Tribunals is indeed a severe fault line in the aspirations of a universally applicable system of criminal accountability ... Not that the impunity of some makes others less culpable, but it makes it less just to single them out. It therefore runs the risk of giving credence to their claim of victimisation, and even if it does not cast doubt on the legitimacy of their punishment, it taints the process that turns a blind eye to the culpability of others. The broader the reach of the International Criminal Court, the better it will overcome these shortcomings of *ad hoc* justice.[7]

Justice Richard Goldstone, the former South African judge and former Chief Prosecutor of the UN Criminal Tribunal for the former Yugoslavia and Rwanda, also recounts how when he was appointed the prosecutor for the International Criminal Tribunal for the former Yugoslavia, one of the early questions that he was asked was: 'Why the Security Council had established a war crimes tribunal for the former Yugoslavia and had not done so in the case of Cambodia or Iraq or Iran, or any other equally serious conflicts in Africa or Asia.'[8] In addition to the prevailing concerns about the *ad hoc* nature of responses to atrocities, 'tribunal fatigue' was developing within the UN Security Council.[9]

The future of the Court is at a critical juncture. At 14 years old, the Court, just like any child in its teens, is likely to be yelled at or belittled and probably suffers from problems of attention and anxiety. Its resilience will continue to be tested, especially its ability to appreciate that states are likely to react strongly whenever it intervenes because, when it does, the stakes are usually very high.

The debate in the UN General Assembly over the Court's 2015 annual report indicated that since its establishment in 2002, the Court has become an enigma in the global governance system. During the debate, every state's assessment and

---

6 Ibid.

7 Cited in Caroline Fehl, 'Explaining the International Criminal Court: A "Practice Test" for Rationalist and Constructivist Approaches' (2004) 10 *European Journal of International Relations* 357, p. 374.

8 Richard Goldstone, *For Humanity: Reflections of a War Crimes Investigator* (New Haven, Yale University Press, 2002), p. 78.

9 The term 'tribunal fatigue' was first coined by David Scheffer to describe the Security Council's weariness of building more *ad hoc* tribunals or expanding the two that existed; see David Scheffer, *All the Missing Souls: A Personal History of the War Crimes Tribunals* (Princeton, Princeton University Press, 2012), p. 118.

perceptive was reflective of its experience with the Court and how they prefer it to function. The perspectives varied from state to state. On the one hand, representatives from some states called for close cooperation between the Court and the UN Security Council and urged more states to ratify the Rome Statute. On the other hand, some states viewed the calls for a closer link between the Court and the UN Security Council as improper and a back-door move to merge the Court with the UN system, which was not the intention of the drafters of the Rome Conference in 1998.

The representatives from Algeria, Kenya and Sudan raised concerns that the Court's activities had focused exclusively on Africa while ignoring other parts of the world.[10] The debates and the various issues raised underscored how the community of nations seems to be struggling to come to terms with the new institution within the global governance system – the International Criminal Court. As the Court navigates its way in order to fulfil the promise and determination of states parties to 'put an end to impunity for the perpetrators of these crimes (war crimes, crimes against humanity and genocide) and thus to contribute to the prevention of such crimes',[11] it has inevitably shaken up and questioned the usefulness of some well-established rules and norms of international law in the pursuit of justice for the millions of victims of atrocities committed primarily by those in control of the state apparatus.

In response, states, instead of demonstrating that humanity can actually strike back when crimes are committed, no matter by whom, and can hold those responsible accountable, have shifted their attention and efforts into defending the fundamental principles of international law, such as state sovereignty and immunity.[12] These principles tend to insulate those with political power on their side from either national or international accountability when they are accused of committing atrocities. States want to ensure that such principles are not overridden, even if it is in the pursuit of the enforcement of international criminal justice. Some states have turned these principles into solid, concrete blocks that they have used to build walls against the effective fulfilment of the aspirations and hopes of the victims of unimaginable atrocities. Consequently,

---

10 See remarks by Mehdi Remaoun (Algeria), Macharia Kamau (Kenya) and Omer Dahab Fadal Mohamed (Sudan), UN Doc. GA 11720 Debating Report of International Criminal Court, Delegates Stress Need for Court's Adequate Funding, Accession by Member States to Rome Statute, Meetings Coverage and Press Releases, General Assembly Seventieth Session 49th Meeting, 6 November 2015.

11 Rome Statute, Preamble, para. 5.

12 See Kenya's proposed amendment to Art. 27 of the Rome Statute for the Serving Heads of States, their deputies and anybody acting or is entitled to act as such to be exempted from prosecution during their current term of office, UN depositary notification, C.N.1026.2013 Treaties XVIII.10 of March 2014 (Proposal of Amendments by Kenya to the Statute) and Senator Jess Helms's testimony, where he stated that the Rome Treaty is irreparably flawed and that the US must be aggressively opposed to the Court: *Testimony of Senator Jesse Helms, to the Sub Committee on International Operations on*, 23 July 1998.

it seems that as long as controlling the state apparatus, combined with the benefits that come with state immunity proves to be an effective way of escaping accountability, perpetrators of atrocities might invest in trying to gain access and control of such apparatus.

Those already in control appear to be unwilling to relinquish their power, as doing so is likely to expose them to the long arm of international criminal justice, as was the case with the former President of Liberia, Charles Taylor, Iraq's Saddam Hussein, Laurent Gbagbo of Cote d'Ivoire and Chadian dictator Hissène Habré. All of these men faced trial for the crimes they committed as state officials – in these cases as sitting heads of state. This is primarily because once they leave power, they lose their immunity *ratione personae* and even their immunity *ratione materiae* can be open for scrutiny if their acts while in office would not fall into official functions associated with their duties and responsibilities.[13] Leaders are simply learning very fast that outside the edifice of the State House and state immunity, the world is becoming relentlessly unforgiving of those who commit atrocities during their term in office. As such, those in power and whose reign is associated with or suspected of atrocities and gross violations of human rights are critical of the Court and perhaps would prefer to weaken it.

At the same time, some of the criticisms appear to be a result of a clear misunderstanding of the functions and the mandate of the Court. As such, the Court could be actually being criticised due to a misconception of its operation. There is a possibility that it is also intentionally misunderstood by those whose agenda is to effectively push it aside and belittle it. For example, there are those who accuse it of disregarding state sovereignty, yet, it is up to states to either ratify a treaty or not. The Court operates on the principle of complementarity, upon which it was built, which ensures that sovereign states are given the primary role to investigate and prosecute those responsible for international crimes.[14] The Court only intervenes as the last resort. In addition, there appears to be a tendency to criticise the entire Court as if it acts in unison, when in fact it has different and independent organs – the Presidency, the Judicial Divisions, the Office of the Prosecutor and the Registry.[15] The Judicial Division, which consists of the Chambers of judges, acts as the control or checking mechanisms to ensure

13 See *Arrest Warrant of 11 April 2000 (Democratic Republic of the Congo v. Belgium)*, Judgment (2002) ICJ, para. 51 for the list of state officials who have enjoy these immunities.

14 The Office of the Prosecutor, 'Policy Paper on Preliminary Examinations', November 2013, pp. 11–14; and for an in-depth study, see Mohamed M. El Zeidy, *The Principle of Complementarity in International Criminal Law: Origin, Development and Practice* (Leiden, Martinus Nijhoff, 2008).

15 Article 38(3)(a) of the Rome Statute states that the Presidency is responsible for the proper administration of the Court, with the exception of the Office of the Prosecutor; Art. 39 provides for how the judiciary of the Court is constituted of three different chambers (the Pre-Trial Chamber, the Trial Chambers and the Appeals Chamber), and Art. 40(1) and requires

that the Office of the Prosecutor does not misuse some of its authority, such as initiating investigations *proprio motu.*[16]

There is considerable evidence that these organs do not always agree and, in fact, are not expected to do so in the interests of justice and safeguarding the credibility of the Court. In fact, the Court was designed that way in order to ensure that there are checks and balances in place. We have already witnessed cases where the Appeals Chamber overturned Trial Chamber decisions or the Pre-Trial Chambers requested additional evidence from the Office of the Prosecutor before authorising an investigation or confirmation of charges. In most cases when the Court is being criticised, it is usually the Office of the Prosecutor's actions that have triggered the criticisms.

For its part, the Court, and the Office of the Prosecutor in particular, which is mandated under the Rome Statute to receive referrals and information on crimes within the jurisdiction of the Court, appears to have been gullible and uncritical of the intentions and motives of states parties and the UN Security Council when they made referrals to the Court. This was possibly driven by the needs of and pressure from the proponents of international criminal justice who wanted the Court to have begun its work at the earliest time possible. As a result, the Office of the Prosecutor rushed into accepting and opening investigations in a way that prompted accusations that its enforcement of international justice was politicised. In some cases, the meticulousness of the investigations was actually put into question. The accusations that the Court had been politicised were made both with regard to referrals made by the UN Security Council and also by the states parties. To augment the challenges for the Office of the Prosecutor, the charges it brought to the Court against a considerable number of suspects could not be confirmed during the Pre-Trial Chamber phase of the proceedings.

Furthermore, a lack of predictable and consistent cooperation from states parties, including those that had referred situations to the Court, complicated the work of the Court. The UN Security Council seems to be completely uninterested, at least in public, in following up the implementation of its own resolutions and referrals to the Court. This means that the Court ended up being isolated to the extent of not having the political will necessary for the

that all judges in these chambers perform their functions independently; Art. 42(1) clearly states that the Office of the Prosecutor shall act independently as a separate organ of the Court; and finally Art. 43 provides for the Registry of the Court, which shall be responsible for the non-judicial aspects of the administration and servicing of the Court.

16 *Situation in Georgia* (ICC-01/15), Decision on the Prosecutor's request for authorisation of an investigation, 27 January 2016, para. 3, stating the following concerning Art. 15(3) of the Rome Statute, which requires that the Office of the Prosecutor must seek authorisation from the Pre-Trial Chamber before opening an investigation and that 'this procedure has the object and purpose of ensuring judicial control over the Prosecutor's exercise of her *proprio motu* power to open an investigation in the absence of a referral by a State Party or by the Security Council of the United Nations'.

effective accomplishment of its mandate. Perhaps the Office of the Prosecutor could have proceeded wisely and slowly. There is an African saying in Swahili that goes 'Haraka haraka haina baraka', which advises doing things slowly and with caution.

The African Union (AU), together with a few, influential and vocal states, have put the Court under immense pressure and criticism lately. They claim that the Court has become a political instrument targeting Africa and Africans. This is because, until recently, the Office of the Prosecutor had only officially opened investigations and prosecutions in Africa.[17] It was only in 2015 that the Office of the Prosecutor requested, and was granted by Pre-Trial Chamber I authorisation, the opening of investigations in Georgia.[18] Authorisation was granted in 2016, making Georgia the first situation outside Africa that has been investigated by the Court. It is not clear whether such diversity would quell Africa's accusations – only time will tell.

That said, there are several African states that support the Court, although they seem to be reluctant to do so publicly. In general, the Court has become a divisive institution in Africa. It has provided a practical test for African states and their collective governance institutions, such as the AU, to demonstrate their sincerity towards ending the global impunity of prosecution for atrocity crimes and compliance with the principles of the international rule of law.

Both the Court and the AU share a common objective in rejecting impunity.[19] However, instead of a common and shared objective being employed to nurture unity of purpose between the two institutions, the indications so far suggests otherwise. Some of the positions taken by the AU decision-making organs, combined with pronouncements made by individual African head of states regarding the work of the Court, indicate that there has been a sharp fallout between the Court and Africa – at least for now. This has negatively impacted the Court's capability to play a meaningfully and timely role in the global fight against impunity as it continues to struggle to gain crucial political support from the continent.

The AU is not, and cannot, be a state party to the Rome Statute as only sovereign states can do so. However, African states tend to coordinate part of

---

17 The first investigation to be officially opened by the Office of the Prosecutor was in the Democratic Republic of the Congo on 23 June 2004. The other African situations where the Office of the Prosecutor opened investigations are Uganda (2004); Darfur, Sudan (2005); the Central African Republic (2007); Kenya (2010); Libya (2011); Cote d'Ivoire (2011); and Mali (2012).

18 *Situation in Georgia* (ICC-01/15) Corrected version of 'The Request for Authorisation of an Investigation Pursuant to Art. 15', 17 November 2015.

19 In paragraph 5 of the Preamble to the Rome Statute it is noted that the states parties are 'Determined to put an end to impunity for the perpetrators of these crimes and thus to contribute to the prevision of such crimes', and the Constitutive Act of the African Union identifies the rejection of impunity as one of its guiding principles in Art. 4(o) where it is stated that the Union shall function in accordance with the following principles: 'Respect for the sanctity of human life, condemnation and rejection of impunity and political assassination, acts of terrorism and subversive activities'.

their international relations through the AU, the objectives of which include defending sovereignty, territorial integrity and the independence of its member states, and to promote and defend African common positions.[20] The fact that the AU cannot be a state party to the Rome Statute does not mean that the Court cannot ask it for cooperation and assistance as the Rome Statute anticipates that the Court may require cooperation from intergovernmental organisations in the course of its work.[21]

Under the Rome Statute, only regional organisations and other international governmental organisations, including the UN or the European Union (EU), can sign cooperation agreements with the Court. For example, on 10 April 2006, the EU became the first regional organisation to sign an agreement of cooperation and assistance with the Court.[22] The purpose of the agreement was to establish predictable cooperation and assistance between the EU and the Court and to promote the regular exchange of information and documentation that could be of common interest. That said, the general obligation to cooperate between the EU and the Court established under the agreement does such supplant bilateral cooperation obligations between individual EU Member States and the Court.

Similarly, the Court has been trying to establish a Liaison Office at the AU headquarters in Addis Ababa in order to enhance the relationship between the two institutions and to facilitate communication. However, such efforts have yet to bear fruit and are complicated by the tension and deterioration of relations between the AU and the Court. The state of affairs between the Court and the AU prompted the latter to make a decision in 2010 temporarily rejecting the Court's request to establish a Liaison Office in Addis Ababa.[23] This is despite the fact that African States Parties have always supported the opening of such an office in Africa.

During the establishment of the Court, African states played a crucial and supportive role, which makes it inconceivable that after such early support and enthusiasm the AU appears to have opted for an arm's length relationship with the new permanent Court. African states' initial support (see Chapter 2) had demonstrated the continent's general viewpoint in international affairs, which is to favour multilateralism in addressing global collective problems, including impunity.[24] Multilateralism, which is the collective search for common solutions

---

20 See Constitutive Act of the African Union (2000) Art. 3(b) and (d).

21 Article 87(6) of the Rome Statute states that: 'The Court may ask any intergovernmental organization to provide information of documents. The Court may also ask for other forms of cooperation and assistance which may be agreed upon with such an organization and which are in accordance with its competence or mandate.'

22 *Official Journal of the European Union*, Agreement between the International Criminal Court and the European Union on Cooperation and Assistance L 115/50-57, 28.04.2006.

23 Decision on the Progress of the Commission on the Implementation of Decision Assembly/AU/Dec.270 (XIV) on the Second Ministerial Meeting on the Rome Statute of the International Criminal Court (ICC) Doc. Assembly/AU/10(XV), Item 8.

24 Constitutive Act of the African Union (2000), Art. 3(e).

to common problems, resonates well with the indigenous African political philosophy that is based on consensus-seeking behaviour or *indaba*. *Indaba* refers to a process that involves a circle of elders gathering to resolve, through consensus, important societal issues.

In addition to the general support for multilateralism, another possible argument behind the African states' overwhelming support for the Court is that it was purely a self-serving gesture for a continent that realised that in a post-Cold War era, it was increasingly being marginalised in global political and economic affairs. The former Egyptian-born UN Secretary-General Boutros Boutros-Ghali put it crudely when he said Africa was risking sliding into being a 'lost continent'. Perhaps a combination of African states' weak economic and political institutions and a lack of influence in the UN Security Council and other international financial and trade institutions was the main motivation for the African states to push for another institution in the global governance system that was independent of the UN Security Council. They wanted an international criminal court to be an institution that was beyond the realm of old centres of diplomatic and economic power out of concern that such powers would turn the Court into an organ for political witch hunting.

Furthermore, the legacy of injustices and brutal conflicts suffered by Africa was another motivating factor behind the early support by the African states for the establishment of the Court. In 1960, Kwame Nkrumah had outlined the extent of such injustices while addressing the UN General Assembly:

> For years, Africa has been the foot-stool of colonialism and imperialism, exploitation and degradation. From the north to the south, from the east to the west, her sons languished in the chains of slavery and humiliation, and Africa's exploiters and self-appointed controllers of her destiny strode across our land with incredible inhumanity without mercy, without shame, and without honour.[25]

The desire to put an end to such injustices had driven the nationalist movements across Africa to fight for self-determination and freedom from foreign interferences and rule. Such struggles culminated in the attainment of political independence and, to some extent, the restoration of equality of men, which Tanzania's first President, Julius Nyerere, referred to in 1967 as 'the basic principle of human intercourse'.[26]

The same theme of historical injustices was raised during the opening sessions of the Rome Conference in 1998. Professor Tiyanjana Maluwa – legal advisor to the Organisation of African Unity (OAU), now the AU – pointed out that Africa

---

25 *UN General Assembly Fifteenth Session Official Records*, 869th Plenary Meeting, 23 September 1960, para. 2.

26 Julius Nyerere, 'Address by President, Mwalimu Julius K. Nyerere at the Tanganyika African National Union National Conference', 16 October 1967.

was interested in the establishment of a permanent international criminal court because its population had endured violations of its human rights for centuries. In the 1970s and in the context of international pressure against apartheid in South Africa, independent African states played a crucial role at the UN General Assembly in the criminalisation of organisations, institutions and individuals committing the crime of apartheid. On 28 October 1971, Guinea, which was under the leadership of Touré Ahmed Sékou one of the founding fathers of the OAU, together with the Soviet Socialist Republics, submitted a draft convention to the UN General Assembly for states on the suppression and punishment of the crime of apartheid.[27] Mention was made of a possible international criminal court as a forum for punishing those accused of apartheid. However, the proposal was dropped during the subsequent discussions. Still, Guinea did not relent. It brought the need to have a court within the frame of drafting the African Charter on Human and Peoples' Rights in the early 1980s. Its proposal was to have a Court established to prosecute violations of international crimes and human rights, and the chances are that its undeclared interest was to ensure that those practising apartheid in South Africa were to be held accountable. However, fellow African states might have thought that this was a bridge too far to cross in terms of having a regional criminal court, so they settled for an African Commission on Human and Peoples' Rights. The African Commission has the mandate of the protection and promotion of human rights and does not have criminal jurisdiction.[28] Therefore, when the UN General Assembly revisited the discussion of the establishment of an international criminal court, it was *pas de nouvelles* (not news) for African states. It seems that in the mid-1990s, African states were ready for the Court. Perhaps during that period, the Court was viewed as a useful tool to defy foreign domination and injustices, and a demonstration by smaller and middle powers' of their ability to push back superpowers'uncontrolled supremacy and dominance in the global governance system.

At the time of writing, 14 years have passed since the establishment of the Court and it seems that the shifting sands of international affairs and geopolitics have left Africa with extreme conflicting emotions, resulting in a love–hate relationship towards the Court. Some African leaders consider the behaviour of the Court and in particular the Office of the Prosecutor to be unruly. The critics of the Court claim that it has changed into something different – into a tool of imperialism. It is hard to establish with absolute certainty what was in the minds of the African states when they embraced the establishment of the

---

27 UN General Assembly, A/C.3/L.1871 Guinea and Union of Soviet Socialist Republics draft of a Convention on the suppression and punishment of the crime of apartheid, 28 October 1971. See also a draft protocol proposed by Nigeria, Pakistan and the United Republic of Tanzania for a Separate Protocol on the Suppression and Punishment of the Crime of Apartheid to be annexed to the International Convention on the Elimination of All Forms of Racial Discrimination, UN Economic and Social Council; E/CN.4/L.1189, 14 March 1972.

28 African Charter on Human and Peoples' Rights, Art. 30.

Court and at the same time to understand why they are now claiming that this Court is not what they had signed up for. However, it can be said with some degree of certainty that they did not sign and ratify the Rome Statute knowing that it was likely to investigate and prosecute them. They did not expect to be the target of an instrument that they had created. Perhaps their thinking was that the chances of them being investigated or even prosecuted was remote, such that when it became a reality, they began to experience nightmares and sought ways of ending or frustrating what they viewed to be the Court's crusade to promote accountability within the continent. Kenya's President Uhuru Kenyatta, who was indicted by the Court at one stage before his charges were dropped, summed up the sentiments that the Court was betraying African states to fellow African leaders during an AU extraordinary summit to discuss the regional body's relationship with the Court:

> As has been demonstrated quite thoroughly over the past decade, the good-faith subscribers had fallen prey to their high-mindedness and idealism. I do not need to tell your Excellences about the nightmare my country in particular, and myself, and my Deputy as individuals, have had to endure in making this realisation.[29]

The message was tailored to rally the support of African states that were also states parties to the Rome Statute by reminding them that if Kenya, a fellow state party and supporter of the Court, could be targeted, then no one was safe, hence the need for a collective pushback. The trick seemed to have worked as Kenya's diplomatic offensive against the Court gathered momentum and support in African corridors of power, perhaps more support compared to Sudan, whose president had also been indicted, but whose offensive against the Court had been overtaken by Kenya.

The main source of AU frustration with the Court and the UN Security Council is what it perceives to be the politicisation of international criminal justice. The UN Security Council is authorised by the Rome Statute to refer situations where international crimes, under the jurisdiction of the Court, are suspected of being committed to the Court. The authority and the referrals by the Security Council extends the Court's jurisdiction to non-states parties and was first exercised in 2005 and then in 2011, when the UN Security Council referred the situations in Darfur, Sudan and Libya to the Court.

What is exasperating to the AU, and some individual African states, about these referrals is that the majority of UN Security Council members – China, Russian and the US – are non-states parties, although they can refer other non-states parties. However, the power of the veto-wielding permanent members

[29] African Union Extraordinary Session of the Assembly of Heads of State and Government of the African Union, 'Speech by His Excellency Hon. Uhuru Kenyatta, C.G.H., President and Commander in Chief of the Defence Forces of the Republic of Kenya, Addis Ababa', 12 October 2013.

of the UN Security Council makes it impossible for them to be referred to the Court. They can simply veto such resolutions. This is purely a matter of a double standard, having one set of rules that are applicable to the permanent members of the Security Council and another for the rest of the world.

In addition, some members of the UN Security Council have used their veto power to protect their key allies from any referral to the Court. Having referred Sudan and Libya, the UN Security Council could have also referred situations in Syria, Sri Lanka or the Occupied Territories of Palestine, where all the preconditions for referrals were present. In all these countries, there was evidence that atrocity crimes that come under the jurisdiction of the Court were being committed and that the situations posed a threat to international peace and security. For example, the situation in Syria triggered events that have further destabilised the Middle East, almost resulting in armed conflict between Russia and Turkey following the downing of a Russian warplane and in terror attacks in France and Belgium in 2015. It has also produced one of the worst refugee and humanitarian crises in the Middle East and Europe. The failure of the UN Security Council to refer these cases, yet to refer Sudan and Libya, has led to genuine claims that the Court is being used to target Africans.

Linked to the AU's frustration that the Court appears to be used by the world's powerful states on the UN Security Council to punish their enemies in Africa is its disappointment in how the UN Security Council has treated its request for the deferral of proceedings against President Omar al-Bashir. Soon after the indictment of President al-Bashir in 2009, the AU asked the UN Security Council to exercise its authority under the Rome Statute to defer the proceedings for 12 months. From the AU's perspective, such a period was necessary for the facilitation and conclusion of the peace negotiations between the Sudanese government and the Darfur rebels.

One scholar claimed that the indictments were disruptive to the peace negotiations for Darfur and equated them to 'arresting Martin McGuinness during the negotiations that were about to end the thirty-year Northern Ireland civil war'.[30] McGuinness was the chief negotiator for Sinn Fein in the Northern Ireland peace process that led to the Good Friday Agreement.

The claims that the indictment affected the peace process sounds to be far-fetched, but there is no doubt that in 2008/2009, the AU was the regional body that was most engaged with the Darfur crisis, so the intervention of the Court was viewed as an encroachment upon its territory. It appears that the real challenge that the peace talks were facing during that period was that the rebels did not view either the AU or the Arab League as impartial peace brokers, but that they were seen as being closer to Khartoum. In fact, linking the Darfur peace process to the deferral request fails to explain the conclusion of the Doha

---

30 Paul Moorcraft, *Omar al-Bashir and Africa's Longest War* (Barnsley, Pen & Sword Military, 2015), p. 168.

Peace Agreement. The Agreement was concluded in 2011 in the absence of the UN Security Council deferral. This suggests that the earlier obstacles to a peace agreement could not have been the Court's proceedings in Darfur.

Still, it can be argued that the UN Security Council could also have treated the AU's request with prudence by giving an official response or by deferring the proceedings for the requested 12 months. This would have been unlikely to have had made any difference anyway, apart from that now the failure by the UN Security Council to act has become a justification for the AU to ask its member states to stop cooperating with the Court, which, as we shall see, has created considerable diplomatic rows between African states and the Court.

The UN Security Council's inaction has not only confirmed the earlier concerns of African states that it would use the Court for its own purposes, but has also made the AU and its member states feel marginalised from the global governance system. Post-colonial African states have always been preoccupied and afraid of being sidelined or not respected when it came to finding solutions to collective global problems. This African preoccupation was highlighted as early as the late 1950s, when Ethiopia, Liberia, Egypt, Libya, Sudan, Morocco, Tunisia and Ghana where the only independent African countries. Haile Selassie, Emperor of Ethiopia, used every opportunity he had at the international level to stress that 'many small powers should be heard and accorded equal opportunities for consultation and deliberation on major international problems'.[31] Similarly, as early as the 1960s Ghana's Kwame Nkrumah started the campaign for a permanent seat for an African nation to be created on the Security Council. His justification was that Africa was increasingly becoming an important actor in global affairs.[32]

The sequencing of peace and justice is also another source of tension between the Court and the AU. The tension even extends to non-state actors such as religious group in Northern Uganda.[33] There is a view in African states that at times peace or conflict resolution should be prioritised over the pursuit of justice. This perspective formed the bases for the AU's request for the deferral of proceedings against President al-Bashir and also its support to extricate Kenyan President Uhuru Kenyatta and his Deputy President, Samoei Ruto, from the Court proceedings over crimes committed during the 2007 post-election violence. In both situations, the Court and its main supporters, the majority of whom are European states remained rigid and insisted on justice to take its course. Despite a lack of consensus on how justice and peace should be sequenced, the approach

---

31 See Angelo Del Boca, *The Negus: The Life and Death of the Last King of Kings* Second Edition (Addis Ababa, Arada Books, 2015), p. 245.

32 Above note 25, para. 6.

33 In 2005, just before the Office of the Prosecutor issued an arrest warrant for the LRA's leadership, the Acholi traditional leaders went to The Hague to ask him not to issue the arrest warrants. They wanted the Prosecutor to know that the Court's intervention in Northern

of the Court and its supporters has been for justice at all costs – *Fiat justitia, et pereat mundus.* Such an approach has led to a total disregard of the views of the leaders of the AU and the Acholi. This perhaps created the perception within the AU and its member states that the Court was eroding their independence and self-determination.

Such a perception is explicable coming from a continent where people still carry the scars and vivid memories of European colonialism. Perhaps the denial of a chance to decide when and when not to pursue justice brings back bad memories of colonisation when Africans were forced to put their destiny in European hands. As a result, they view Africa as being reduced to being simply consumers of policies and decisions created elsewhere. This thinking is often reflected when African leaders critical of the Court evoke the history of colonisation into the discourse of international criminal justice, especially in order to justify their positions and policies against the Court.

At that level, the discourse on the enforcement of international criminal justice shifts from being a debate of pure legal principles and accountability into the politics of self-determination. The majority of African leaders have ceased to view the Court as a legal institution, but rather a neo-colonial tool used by the powerful nations that have a long-term interest in exploiting and having access to African resources.

In this regard, those leading the AU's pushback against the Court's intervention view themselves as the champions of the total emancipation and liberation of Africa. Their two-prong approach to achieve such liberation seems to be: first, the reaffirmation of Africa's independence and voice within the global governance system, hence the push for UN Security Council reform, and in their support for African candidates for key positions at international institutions such as the Chief Prosecutor of the Court; and, second, through threatening their withdrawal from some of the global institutions and building or revitalising African institutions based on Africa's own history, tradition and culture. This possibly explains the AU's decision taken in Malabo, Equatorial Guinea, to speed up the establishing of an African Court of Justice and Human and Peoples' Rights and also the emergence of traditional justice systems such as *Gacaca* in Rwanda, *Mato Oput* in Northern Uganda and *Palavra* in Liberia as alternatives.

The reality so far is that none of these approaches has materialised, which raises questions as to the amount of support that the anti-Court rhetoric might have among the African states. It seems that the rhetoric comes from a few very vocal critics. Although such critics might enjoy and exercise their democratic right to publicly air their views on the performance of international institutions such as the UN Security Council or the Court on the international plane, they are usually not ready to accommodate similar criticism from their own citizens. This is common in a few states where the leaders use every international forum to admonish the injustices in the international governance system, yet in their own countries, any voices of dissent or opposition are silenced. This creates a gulf between the ideas of African leadership and the people that they claim to represent, which in turn affects the credibility of the leaders' positions.

Still, the prospect of Africa coming up with its own home-grown institutions is appealing. It would be a perfect response to the call made to the Third World by Frantz Fanon, a Martinique born Afro-Caribbean psychiatrist and philosopher:

> So, comrades, let us not pay tribute to Europe by creating states, institutions and societies which draw their inspiration from her. Humanity is waiting for something other from us than such an imitation, which would be almost an obscene caricature. If we want to turn Africa into a new Europe and America, into a new Europe, then let us leave the destiny of our countries to Europeans. They will know how to do it better than the most gifted among us.[34]

In fact, African leaders have been investing in building Africa's own institutions. Still, such institutions simply replicate the EU models, with the exception of a very few, such as the Africa Union Panel of the Wise[35] and the African Peer Review Mechanism.[36] The African institutions need to be built based on progressive African values and norms, and to be reflective of its diverse heritage. Above all, ordinary Africans must be at the centre of such institutions.

However, the Regional Economic Committees (RECs) limit the influence that the AU and its structures might have on issues that occur at a sub-regional level. The AU has to coordinate with these committees, which are very territorial and not quick to invite AU interventions. The AU and the RECs do not always share the same common position, and this weakens the AU position at an international level. A prime example is when the Economic Community of West African States (ECOWAS) recommended that Mali refer its situation to the International Criminal Court at a time when the AU was accusing of targeting Africa.

The other challenge facing the AU regarding establishing its own independent institution is the reliance on foreign donor funding. For example, the AU approved budget for 2016 was US$416,867,326 and a total of US$247,033,986 (59 per cent) was expected to be secured from the AU international partners.[37] The amount from international partners is almost equivalent to the amount that

Uganda would seriously jeopardise efforts to the conflict through peaceful means; *IRIN*, 'Acholi Leaders in The Hague to Meet ICC over LRA Probe', 16 March 2005, see http://www.irinnews.org/news/2005/03/16/acholi-leaders-hague-meet-icc-over-lra-probe.

34 Frantz Fanon, *The Wretched of the Earth* (Harmondsworth, Penguin, 1963), p. 83.

35 The African Union Panel of the Wise was established in 2007 and is a key pillar of the African Peace and Security Architecture (APSA) as a conflict prevention mechanism; see Joao Gomes Porto and Kapinga Yvette Ngandu, *The African Union's Panel of the Wise: A Concise History* (Durban, ACCORD 2015).

36 See Adebayo Adedeji 'NEPAD's African Peer Review Mechanism: Progress and Prospects' in John Akokpari, Angela Ndinga-Muvumba and Tim Murithi(eds.) (eds.), *The African Union and its Institutions* pp 241–269 (Johannesburg, Fanele, 2002).

37 Decision on the Budget of the African Union for the 2016 Financial Year, 14–15 June 2015, Johannesburg, South Africa, Doc. Assembly/AU/Dec.577(XXV).

the AU had budgeted for its 2016 programmes – US$266,363,451. In practice, this means that if the international partners fail to honour their pledges, some of the AU's programmes might not be implemented. The AU is already looking for appropriate fundraising mechanisms to offset its overreliance on donors. However, at least until such alternative forms of funding are established and are functioning well, the claims for African solutions for African problems remain fanciful.

In the meantime, the AU has maintained its campaign to at least have a voice in relation to how the Court operates and also to have its interests taken into account, especially regarding the indictment of sitting heads of state. The Ethiopian Foreign Minister, Tedros Adhanon Ghebreyesus, made this clear while delivering concluding remarks during the Fourteenth Session of Assembly of States Parties in 2015. He was speaking on behalf of the AU when he concluded his speech with a stern warning to both the Court and the UN Security Council that they should stop ignoring the voices of Africa. He went on to make an unspecified threat, couched in classical wording common in international diplomacy, that the continent 'may be left with no other choice than to reserve its rights to take any measures necessary in the interest of preserving and safeguarding peace'.[38] No specifics were provided on what 'any measures necessary' entailed, yet in the past there were media reports and statements by heads of state indicating that the AU had threatened to reject the Court and to ask for the withdrawal of its member states that are states parties to the Rome Statute.

The former Libyan leader, Colonel Muammar Gaddafi, made this known during a rare appearance at the UN General Assembly in 2009. He highlighted what he considered to be the double standards in the prosecution of those who commit atrocity crimes:

> It is easy for Charles Taylor to be tried, or for Bashir to be tried, or for Noriega to be tried. That is an easy job. Yes, but what about those who have committed mass murder against the Iraqis? They cannot be tried? They cannot go before the ICC? If the Court is unable to accommodate us, then we should not accept it. Either it is meant for all of us, large or small, or we should not accept it and should reject it.[39]

During the 2016 Ugandan presidential debate, President Yoweri Museveni repeated his call that Uganda should withdraw from the Rome Statute.[40] President

---

38 Assembly of States Parties to the Rome Statute of the International Criminal Court, Fourteenth Session, 'Statement of H.E. Dr Tedros Abhanon Ghebreyesus, Minister of Foreign Affairs of the Federal Democratic Republic of Ethiopia on Behalf of the African Union', 18–19 November 2015, The Hague, the Netherlands.

39 UN General Assembly, Statement by Colonel Muammar Gaddafi, Leader of the Revolution General Debate of the 64th Session (2009), 23 September 2009.

40 Jill Craig, 'A First: Uganda's Museveni Takes Part in Presidential Debate', *Voice of America* (13 February 2016).

Uhuru Kenyatta also views the Court as dysfunctional and in need of reform.[41] He suggested that the AU ministerial committee, tasked with paving the way for a constructive engagement between the AU and the Court, should also look into the development of a road map for an African withdrawal from the Rome Statute.

In 2013, Kenya submitted proposals for the Amendment of the Rome Statute in accordance with Article 121(1) of the Rome Statute. One of the proposals is to amend Article 27 on the irrelevance of official capacity. Kenya's proposals is that 'serving Heads of State, their deputies and anybody acting or [who] is entitled to act as such may be exempted from prosecution during their current term of office'.[42] This reflects the fact that Kenya is ready and committed to follow the set legal procedures to reform the Rome Statute. However, the substance of the amendment caused some raised eyebrows among the victims of atrocity crimes, as the majority of these crimes are committed by, but not limited to, those in control of the state security apparatus. Of course, the amendment does not guarantee impunity for state authorities, but in the unlikely event that it is approved, it would delay justice for the victims. It even limits the possibility of state officials being held accountable considering that in some Africa countries, regimes are not easily changed and terms of office are elastic. In fact, it gives sitting head of states who are suspected of committing atrocity crimes motivation to remain in power. It also raises questions about the preservation of evidence and protection of witnesses during the period during which a suspect who is a head of state or official remains in office.

At the same time, it is curious to know whether any possible *en masse* withdrawal by African states would actually harm the Court. Much is said about the Court suffering if African States Parties were to withdraw from it. These claims can be misleading as they give the impression that as Africa has the largest number of states parties, such a numerical advantage can easily be turned into power to influence the Court. We already know from the UN system that numerical advantage does not necessarily translate into power and influence. In addition, it seems that those who peddle such fears ignore the fact that the African states' support for multilateralism – including the support for the Court – could be rooted in the continent's self-preservation needs, considering the fragility the majority of the African states.[43] The reality is that the interwoven nature of domestic and foreign challenges that African states face – such as terrorism, epidemics like

41 Uhuru Kenyatta, 'Statement by His Excellency Hon Uhuru Kenyatta, C.G.H., President and Commander in Chief of the Defence Forces of the Republic of Kenya, on the Status of the Kenyan Situation at the ICC', 30 January 2016.

42 UN, 'Submission by the Republic of Kenya on Amendments to Rome Statute of the International Criminal Court for consideration by the Working Group on Amendments', para. 2, Reference: C.N. 1026.2013. Treaties-XVIII.10 (Depositary Notification), 14 March 2014.

43 According to Fragile State Index, between 2010 and 2015, there were between 6–7 African states in the top 10.

Ebola, climate change and humanitarian catastrophes – are usually beyond their national capacity to handle.

Such challenges, combined with the fragility of African states, could be linked to their desire for multilateralism both at the regional and the global levels. This might explain why it was October 2016 before at least three African state parties – Burundi,[44] South Africa[45] and Gambia[46] – either took concrete steps or announced publicly their intention to withdraw from the Rome Statute. Still, three states represents a small number to warrant the description of '*en masse*' withdrawal. There are even indications that, following elections in Gambia, the new leadership may reverse the decision for Gambia to withdraw. Furthermore, if we were to accept the predications, made by the US National Intelligence Council in its publication *Global Trends 2025: A Transformed World* that 'Sub-Saharan Africa will remain the region most vulnerable to economic disruption, population stresses, civil conflict and political instability',[47] then disengaging from the Court, one of the global governance institutions that contributes towards peace and security, would signal a lack of foresight.

The relationship between the Court and Africa is a complicated one and there appears to be no one single, straightforward explanation for the complex dynamic between the two. It is this relationship that this book seeks to explore, looking specifically at the allegation that the Court is selectively focusing on Africa and assessing the validity of such claims as they are presented by Africa's political leaders and its ruling elites against the Court. The book attempts to assess how the Court has implemented international criminal law since its establishment. Discourse on this subject seems to be increasingly shaped and dominated by African political leaders and ruling elites. The book covers the Court's formative phase between 2002 and 2016.

In this regard, the book focuses on the components of the Court's statutory regime that are directly related to how it became engaged in African situations. The components include the role of the Office of the Prosecutor, the referral systems and the admissibility rules under the Rome Statute. For each component, the book will analyse its provisions in the Rome Statute and how it has been interpreted and applied by the Court. It is hoped that a picture will emerge that contributes to our understanding of both the relationship between the Court and Africa, and how the Court actually functions.

---

44 'Burundi notifies U.N. of International Criminal Court Withdrawal', Reuters 26 October 2016 http://www.reuters.com/article/us-burundi-icc-idUSKCN12Q287 accessed 3.12.2016.

45 South Africa, 'Instrument of Withdrawal signed by the Minister of International Relations and Cooperation of the Republic of South Africa' 19 October 2016; see also 'Declaratory statement by the Republic of South Africa on the decision to withdraw from the Rome Statute of the International Criminal Court', United Nations, Reference: C.N.786.2016.TREATIES-XVIII.10 (Depositary Notification).

46 'Gambia announces withdrawal from International Criminal Court' Reuters 26 October 2016 http://www.reuters.com/article/us-gambia-icc-idUSKCN12P335?il=0 accessed 3.12.2016.

47 US National Intelligence Council, 'Global Trends 2025: A Transformed World', November 2008.

1.1. STATUTORY RULES AND THE COURT'S ENGAGEMENT OR SELECTION OF SITUATIONS OR DEFENDANTS

The Court does not have universal jurisdiction;[48] however, its jurisdictional regime is broader than those of the *ad hoc* tribunals that were established to address atrocities in specific states such as the former Yugoslavia and Rwanda.[49] According to Article 12 of the Rome Statute, the Court can exercise its jurisdiction for crimes committed by nationals of states parties and over atrocities committed in the territory of a state party.[50] This means that the Court can exercise its jurisdiction in the territories of at least 123 states, all of which have signed and ratified the Rome Statute. Yet, it must be kept in mind that the nationals of the most powerful and populous states (such as Russia, the US, China, Indonesia and India) remain outside the jurisdiction of the Court, as they have not ratified the Rome Statute. They can, however, be taken to the Court in the event that they commit international crimes in the territory of a state party or through a referral by the UN Security Council. As already highlighted, the chances that nationals of three permanent members of the UN Security Council that have not ratified the Rome Statute be brought to the Court through the UN Security Council referral process are slim, mainly due to their veto powers.

It is worth noting that Article 12 of the Rome Statute underwent some modifications following the 2010 Review Conference in Kampala. The modifications linked to the two amendments were made to the subject-matter jurisdiction of the Court during this conference and these had a knock-on effect on the Court's jurisdiction with regard to the crime of aggression. The Kampala Amendments expanded the list of prohibited weapons[51] and provided conditions for the exercise of jurisdiction and the elements of crime of aggression.[52] The amendments pertaining to the crime of aggression provide for a narrower

---

48 Universal jurisdiction entails that states can prosecute specific crimes regardless of the place of commission, the nationality of the perpetrator and the nationality of the victims; see Bruce Broomhall, *International Justice and the International Criminal Court: Between Sovereignty and the Rule of Law* (Oxford, Oxford University Press, 2003); M. Cherif Bassiouni, 'Universal Jurisdiction for International Crimes: Historical Perspectives and Contemporary Practise' (2002) 42 *Virginia Journal of International Law* 81; and Charles C. Jalloh, 'Universal Jurisdiction, Universal Prescription? A Preliminary Assessment of the African Union Perspective on Universal Jurisdiction' (2010) 21 *Criminal Law Forum* 1.

49 Robert Cryer, *Prosecuting International Crimes: Selectivity and the International Criminal Law Regime* (Cambridge, Cambridge University Press, 2005), p. 223.

50 Rome Statute, Art. 12.

51 The ICC Review Conference, 'Part II Resolutions and Declarations adopted by the Review Conference Resolution RC/Res.5' (Adopted at the 12th plenary meeting, on 10 June 2010, by consensus).

52 The ICC Review Conference, 'Part II Resolutions and Declarations adopted by the Review Conference and Resolution RC/Res.6' (Adopted at the 13th plenary meeting, on 11 June 2010, by consensus).

personal (*ratione personae*) jurisdiction in comparison to that applicable to other crimes under the jurisdiction of the Court: war crimes, crimes against humanity and genocide. Article 15 *bis* provides that the Court's jurisdiction over the crime of aggression extend only to nationals of states parties and not their territories.[53] This means that leaders and other nationals of a non-state party may not be prosecuted under the Rome Statute if they invade a state party.[54] The formulation somehow established the jurisdictional regime that the US had proposed during the Rome Conference when it wanted the nationals and territories of non-states parties to be exempted from the Court's jurisdiction.[55] That said, it is possible that nationals of non-states parties could be prosecuted by the Court as a result of a UN Security Council referral, in the same way that the UN Security Council referred Sudan and Libya.

The Court can also exercise jurisdiction over nationals of non-states parties, under two conditions. First, the non-state party has to accept the jurisdiction of the Court.[56] It is under this provision that the Court investigated the situation in Côte d'Ivoire and subsequently opened cases against former President Laurent Gbagbo, his wife Simone and Charles Bié Goude. Gbagbo was transferred to the Court in November 2011.[57]

Second, the Court can exercise its jurisdiction over nationals of non-states parties if a situation is referred to it through a UN Security Council resolution passed within the framework of Chapter VII of the Charter of the United Nations.[58] During the negotiations leading up to the adoption of the Rome Statute in 1998, the role of the UN Security Council in the referral of situations was very controversial. States were divided, and on one side stood the states that belonged to the Like Minded Group, a temporary and improvised caucus

---

53 Rome Statute, Art. 15 (4). *Bis*.

54 William Schabas, *Unimaginable Atrocities: Justice, Politics, and Rights as the World Crimes Tribunals* (Oxford, Oxford University Press, 2012), p. 203.

55 Compare David Scheffer, 'The United States and the International Criminal Court' (1999) 93 *American Journal of International* 12, at p. 18, who notes out that 'Under Article 12, the ICC may exercise such jurisdiction over anyone anywhere in the world, even in the absence of a referral by the Security Council, if either the state of the territory where the crime was committed or the state of nationality of the accused consents. Ironically, the treaty exposes non-parties in ways that parties are not exposed' to the analysis of the outcome of the Review Conference in the report to the Committee on Foreign Relations International Criminal Court Review Conference, Kampala, Uganda, May–June 2011, which states that: 'The most significant aspect of the outcome for the United States is its elimination of any risk that U.S. officials will be subject to prosecution for aggression by the ICC absent U.S. consent. The decision of the Assembly of States Parties exempts from key aspects of the ICC's aggression jurisdiction actions committed by the nationals or on the territories of countries, including the United States, that are not parties to the ICC.'

56 Rome Statute, Art. 12(3).

57 *Situation in the Republic of Côte d'Ivoire* (ICC-02/11-01/11-1), Warrant of Arrest for Laurent Koudou Gbagbo, 23 November 2011.

58 UN Charter, Chapter VII.

of governments that shared similar positions during the negotiations[59] and opposed any role for the UN Security Council in the judicial work of the Court. Sudan is one of the states that have been consistent in their opposition to the role of the UN Security Council in the affairs of the Court, dating back to 1996. At that time, the Sudanese representative was very clear about his country's opposition to any role for the UN Security Council, saying:

> His delegation had great difficulty in accepting that the Security Council, which had a political role, should play any part in the work of the international criminal court. Accordingly, the draft statute of the court should not vest in the Council any powers over and above those, which it enjoyed under the Charter of the United Nations.[60]

The basis for this argument was the fact that the UN Security Council is primarily a political body and is not representative of the international community.

On the other hand, members of the UN Security Council – in particular, the US, China and Russia – had preconditioned their support for the Court on the role that the UN Security Council was to be given in its proceedings.[61] In the end, a compromise was reached permitting the UN Security Council to refer situations while still being restricted to its Chapter VII powers. Later on in this book, the main controversies that this compromise has caused between the Court and Africa will be discussed in greater detail. The first of these is linked to the fact that the majority of the members of the UN Security Council did not ratify the Rome Statute, hence their own citizens are beyond the Court's reach, yet they can refer other nationals to the Court. Second, the referrals appear to be one-sided, focusing on situations in Africa, and also lack clarity on the status of the immunity of sitting heads of state. Third, the UN Security Council has not provided funding and political support to the Court to ensure the smooth implementation of its referrals. All these issues have taken a toll on the Court's performance and credibility.

There are three ways that the Court's jurisdiction can be triggered. The first of these is that states parties can refer situations to the Court.[62] Some scholars argue that the concept of a state referring itself to the Court was never contemplated during the drafting of the Rome Statute in 1998.[63] William Schabas, a leading

---

59 The Group was primarily formed by European powers who are neither great powers nor small powers yet they have considerable influence in global affairs, before joined by some African and South American states. The general view is that the group's influence was boosted when France and the United Kingdom – a Member of the UN Security Council joined in.

60 UN General Assembly Official Records, 'Agenda Item 147: Establishment of an International Criminal Court, Sixth Committee Summary Record of the 29th Meeting', 1 November 1996, para. 91.

61 Bruce Broomhall, 'Toward U.S Acceptance of the International Criminal Court' (2001) 64 *Law and Contemporary Problems*, p. 79.

62 Rome Statute, Art. 13(a).

63 William A. Schabas, 'Complementarity in Practice: Some Uncomplimentary Thoughts' (2008) 19 *Criminal Law Forum* 5.

academic in the field of international criminal and human rights law, views self-referrals as an invention of the Office of the Prosecutor,[64] motivated by the Court's desire to generate activity for itself.[65] The second trigger mechanism is that of the UN Security Council acting under Chapter VII of the UN Charter, as already discussed. The third trigger mechanism is the Office of the Prosecutor initiating investigations *proprio motu*.

As of 2016, all the triggering mechanisms had been used to put the Court's wheels of international justice into motion. Notably, in the majority of cases when investigations were opened and prosecutions were authorised, it was not the Office of the Prosecutor that selected or chose them. The Office of the Prosecutor was directed to such situations either by the UN Security Council or the states parties, while the Office of the Prosecutor only triggered the jurisdiction of the Court in situations involving Kenya, Cote d'Ivoire and recently Georgia. It is therefore curious as to why the Court as a collective seems to be on the receiving end of criticism that it is selectively focusing on Africa since the criticism could well be directed at the UN Security Council and the states parties that have invited the Court to investigate in the first place. Of course, the Office of the Prosecutor could open investigations through its own initiative and could thus have taken the Court to other regions; however, pragmatism played a key role in the Prosecutor's strategy, as shall be discussed in Chapter 3. The strategy was to wait for referrals. Even in Kenya, where the Prosecutor had to eventually resort to his own initiative, there are official records that he had inquired 'whether or not Kenya would refer the situation to the ICC, in terms of Article 14 of the Rome Statute'.[66] The Kenyan government's response was in the negative. It seems that the Prosecutor's assumption was that referrals would bring with them the much-needed state cooperation and political support.

The strategy might have been sound, but the outcome has not been very encouraging as state cooperation was not readily available and, where it came, it had unintended costs on the credibility of the Office of the Prosecutor. It compromised the ability of the Office of the Prosecutor to investigate the international crimes committed by the state security apparatus, as doing so would have likely jeopardised the state cooperation. In addition, the level of state cooperation simply changed with the shifting political events in the states parties, and this applies to Kenya, Uganda and even Cote d'Ivoire.

The Court's admissibility regime (which will be discussed in Chapter 5) is a pivotal feature that governs the Court's engagement with or selection of

---

64 William A. Schabas, *The International Criminal Court: A Commentary on the Rome Statute* (Oxford, Oxford University Press), p. 309.

65 William A. Schabas, 'Prosecutorial Discretion v. Judicial Activism at the International Criminal Court' (2008) 6 *Journal of International Criminal Justice* 731, 761; and Darryl Robinson, 'The Controversy over Territorial State Referrals and Reflections on ICL Discourse' (2011) 9 *Journal of International Criminal Justice* 355.

66 *Kenya National Assembly Official Record (Hansard)*, 18 November 2009, p. 17.

situations and defendants. The admissibility regime has two main limbs: the complementarity principle and gravity.[67] The rationale behind the regime is that the national criminal justice systems have primacy over the Court, with the Court being the last resort. It distinguishes the Court from *ad hoc* tribunals that, in the case of Rwanda and the former Yugoslavia, did enjoy primacy over national criminal justice systems.[68] Under the Rome Statute, the Court can only open investigations in a state if the national criminal justice system in that particular state is either unwilling or unable to investigate or prosecute those suspected of committing international crimes.[69]

The Rome Statute provides states with jurisdiction, the accused persons and also the pre-trial chambers using *proprio motu* (of its own accord) with powers to challenge the admissibility of cases under the Court.[70] Admissibility can be challenged at any stage of the proceedings as long as the trial has not started.[71] States with jurisdiction can successfully challenge admissibility if they can demonstrate that they themselves can genuinely investigate and prosecute the suspects wanted by the Court. This is why it would make sense for African states to focus on investigating and prosecuting international crimes within their domestic jurisdiction as a way of safeguarding their sovereignty and avoiding having to deal with the Court, which they claim is politicised.

The complementarity principle reflects the sovereignty principle within international law that acknowledges the right of a territorial state to exercise criminal jurisdiction over its nationals or those who violate its national laws.[72] The rationale behind the inclusion of a complementarity principle in the Rome Statute was the need to safeguard state sovereignty and to ensure that suspects faced trial in their own national criminal jurisdictions. There were also practical reasons, such as the fact that national authorities are generally closer to the evidence and potential witnesses than the International Criminal Court.[73]

---

67 See Jo Stigen, *The Relationship between the International Criminal Court and National Jurisdictions: The Principle of Complementarity* (Leiden, Martinus Nijhoff, 2008); and El Zeidy, *The Principle of Complementarity in International Criminal Law*, note 14.

68 Markus Benzing, 'The Complimentarity Regime of the International Criminal Court: International Criminal Justice between State Sovereignty and the Fight against Impunity' (2003) 7 *Max Planck Yearbook of the United Nations* 591–632.

69 Rome Statute, Art. 17.

70 Morten Bergsmo, 'The Jurisdictional Regime of the International Criminal Court (Part II, Articles 11–19)' (1998) 6 *European Journal of Crime, Criminal Law and Criminal Justice* 345.

71 William W. Burke-White and Scott Kaplan, 'Shaping the Countours of Domestic Justice: The International Criminal Court and an Admissibility Challange in the Uganda Situation' (2009) 7 *Journal of International Criminal Justice* 257.

72 Ian Brownlie, *The Principles of Public International Law* (7th edn, Oxford, Oxford University Press, 2008).

73 Benzing, 'The Complementarity Regime of the International Criminal Court', note 65, p. 592; see also Antonio Cassese, 'The Rationale for International Criminal Justice' in Antonio Cassese (ed.), *The Oxford Companion to International Criminal Justice* (Oxford, Oxford University Press, 2009).

1.2. SELECTIVE ENFORCEMENT IN INTERNATIONAL CRIMINAL LAW

The legitimacy of institutions and agencies that enforce international criminal justice[74] is often measured based on the principles of coherence and consistency.[75] It is suggested that if institutions uphold these principles, they will increase compliance levels. According to Thomas M. Frank, 'a rule is coherent when its application treats like cases alike'.[76] In the case of institutions that implement international criminal justice, coherence and consistency determine levels of state cooperation in, for example, gathering evidence and arresting and surrendering those suspected of committing international crimes. This is because international criminal justice institutions such as international tribunals and the Court do not have their own enforcement mechanisms and rely heavily on state cooperation to ensure the enforcement of their decisions and judgments.[77] However, the situation with the Court and the non-execution of some of the arrest warrants by the states parties, suggests something was broken between the Court and some parts of the community of nations that the Court is supposed to depend on for the fulfilment of its mandate. The AU actually passed decisions adopting a non-cooperation position with the Court following the Pre-Trial Chamber 1 decision to issue an arrest warrant for President al Bashir and the subsequent inaction of the Security Council on the deferral request.

An overview of the historical development of the international criminal justice regime reveals that the system has repeatedly been found wanting in terms of

---

74 Throughout this chapter and the study overall, the term 'international criminal justice' is used to refer to the application of the principle of judicial accountability to international crimes through either national, criminal or civil courts exercising both territorial jurisdiction and universal jurisdiction or international criminal tribunals; see M. Cherif Bassioni, 'International Criminal Justice in Historical Perspective: The Tension between States' Interests and Pursuit of International Justice' in Cassese (ed.), *The Oxford Companion to International Criminal Justice*, note 70.

75 Legitimacy in this context refers to what Thomas M. Frank said is 'a property of a rule or rule making institution which itself exerts a pull toward compliance on those addressed normatively because those addressed believe that the rule or institution has come into being and operates in accordance with generally accepted principles of right process'; see Thomas M. Frank, *Fairness in International Law and Institutions* (Oxford, Oxford University Press, 1995), p. 24.

76 Frank, *Fairness in International Law and Institutions*, note 72, p. 38.

77 For the International Criminal Justice's reliance on state cooperation see Antonio Cassese, *International Law* (2nd edn, Oxford, Oxford University Press, 2005), p. 461, who points out that although international criminal justice agencies have the power to issue warrants for the seizure of evidence or the searching of premises, and to issue subpoenas or arrest warrants, they cannot address the acts resulting from the exercise of those powers. This is due to a lack of enforcement agents empowered freely to enter the territory of sovereign states and exercise enforcement there. National and international tribunals are 'giants without arms and legs who need artificial limbs to walk and work. These artificial limbs are the State authorities. If the cooperation of States is not forthcoming, these tribunals are paralysed'.

coherence and consistency. This is one of the main problems facing international criminal justice and is the main focus of this book, having led some scholars to conclude that: 'Each war crimes trial is an exercise of partial justice to the extent that it reminds us that the majority of war crimes remain unpunished. If Yugoslavia, why not Somalia, if Rwanda, why not Guatemala?'[78]

The selective enforcement of international criminal law refers to situations where an enforcement agency, which could be a national court, an *ad hoc* tribunal or the international criminal court, has discretionary power and does nothing when enforcement would clearly be justified.[79] Scholars such as Tim McCormack have suggested that there is dual selectivity in the enforcement of international criminal law.[80] The first form of selectivity can be said to be closely associated with the question: 'Whose law and whose justice counts?' This relates to the acts that the proscribing authority (in the case of the Court, the delegates who participated in the drafting of the Rome Statute) was prepared to characterise as international crimes. In other words, it is selective enforcement based on what is codified as an international crime or the subject-matter jurisdiction (*ratione materiae*) of international criminal tribunals. The second branch of selectivity is linked to the enforcement agencies' decision to prosecute some atrocities – those committed by certain parties – and not others. This is the selective enforcement that the Court is being accused of by some African states and the AU.

Selective enforcement contravenes the principle of equality before the law, enshrined in Articles 14 and 16 of the International Covenant on Civil and Political Rights.[81] It also violates Article 21(3) of the Rome Statute, which provides that:

> The application and interpretation of law pursuant to this article must be consistent with internationally recognised human rights, and be without any adverse distinction founded on grounds such as gender as defined in Article 7, paragraph 3, age, race, colour, language, religion or belief, political or other opinion, national, ethnic or social origin, wealth, birth or other status.

It also violates the principle of sovereign equality under the UN Charter.[82] In addition, and with regard to those offences that go unpunished, it simply means that there are wrongs that are not righted, which translates to impunity, which is what the Court purports to fight.

---

78 Gerry J. Simpson, 'War Crimes: A Critical Introduction' in Gerry J. Simpson and Timothy L.H. McCormack (eds.)(eds.), *The Law of War Crimes: National and International Approaches* (Dordrecht, Kluwer Law International, 1997), pp. 8–9.

79 Cryer, *Prosecuting International Crimes*, note 46, p. 192.

80 Timothy L.H. McCormack, 'Selective Reaction to Atrocity: War Crimes and the Development of International Law' (1997) 60 *Albany Law Review* 681.

81 International Covenant on Civil and Political Rights (adopted 16 December 1966, entered into force 23 March 1976) 999 UNTS 171 (ICCCPR), Arts 14 and 16.

82 UN Charter, Art. 1(2).

At the same time, selective enforcement in some form is almost inescapable. This is because enforcement agencies lack the capacity (both human and financial) to prosecute all international crimes, no matter how serious the crimes may be.[83] This was confirmed by the Appeals Chamber of the International Criminal Tribunal for the former Yugoslavia in the *Čelebići* appeal case when it observed that:

> [In] many criminal justice systems, the entity responsible for prosecutions has finite financial and human resources and cannot realistically be expected to prosecute every offender which may fall within the strict terms of its jurisdiction.[84]

Generally, selective enforcement of the law is not considered to be inherently wrong. In fact, it is promoted in certain domestic legal systems, particularly those following common law and French-style civilian systems in their concept of prosecutorial discretion,[85] which refers to the power accorded to the prosecutor to choose between two or more permissible courses of action.[86]

Daniel Nsereko, a former International Criminal Court Appeals Chamber Judge (2008–12) from Uganda, notes that the choice must not be arbitrary, but rather must be made in the context of the relevant circumstances and what seems just, right, equitable and reasonable in those circumstances.[87] That said, the conundrum of selective enforcement in contemporary international criminal law is that, although it is not intrinsically wrong, it is at times unacceptable, especially when applied in an arbitrary and discriminatory manner.[88] At an international level, selective enforcement can have negative consequences for the legitimacy of the enforcing institution and it can also undermine the retributive purposes of the entire international criminal law system. It is precisely for this reason that the Court's credibility is now being questioned from several angles, including by those who initially supported it.

Although selective enforcement is considered a reality in international criminal law, it is necessary to attempt to understand why the Court, which was

---

83 For a detailed discussion on the selectivity and international criminal law, see Cryer, *Prosecuting International Crimes*, note 46.

84 *Prosecutor v. Delalic, Mucic, Delic and Landzo 'Celebici* Case', Appeals Judgement, International Criminal Tribunal for the former Yugoslavia, IT-96-21-A (20 February 2001), para. 602.

85 Daniel D. Ntanda Nsereko, 'Prosecutorial Discretion before National Courts and International Tribunals' (2005) 3 *Journal of International Criminal Justice* 124; Allison Marston Danner, 'Enhancing the Legitimacy and Accountability of Prosecutorial Discretion at the International Criminal Court' (2003) 97 *American Journal of International Law* 510; Luc Cote, 'Reflections on the Exercise of Prosecutorial Discretion in International Criminal Law' (2005) 3 *Journal of International Criminal Justice* 162.

86 Marston Danner, 'Enhancing the Legitimacy and Accountability of Prosecutorial Discretion at the International Criminal Court', note 82, 518.

87 Nsereko, 'Prosecutorial Discretion before National Courts and International Tribunals', note 82, 124.

88 Cryer, *Prosecuting International Crimes*, note 46, p. 193.

essentially designed to have a universal reach, appears to have focused on opening investigations in one region – Africa. It is not yet clear whether this focus in fact proves the allegations that the Court is a tool of neo-colonialism or whether it is merely a reflection of the genuine need for international criminal justice in Africa due to the high frequency of armed conflicts during which atrocity crimes are committed, combined with the lack of political and institutional capacity to investigate and prosecute those responsible. It is also possible that there are other reasons that have yet to surface. Examining some of the claims as to why the Court has focused on Africa is one of the purposes of this study.

1.2.1. BOOK HYPOTHESIS

When selective enforcement is carried out in an arbitrary and less transparent manner, it puts both the legitimacy and credibility of the Court at risk. The claims against the Court need to be taken seriously, otherwise they risk destroying the hopes, aspirations and enthusiasm that welcomed its establishment in 2002. The awkward relationship that has developed between the Court and the African states threatens to reverse the gains that have already been made towards building a universal system to end impunity for international crimes. Renewed calls for African States Parties to withdraw from the Rome Statute were made in mid-2016 by the Open-Ended Ministerial Committee of Ministers for Foreign Affairs on the ICC ('the Committee'). The Committee was established following the 25th AU summit decision in Johannesburg, South Africa. At the summit the AU Assembly recommended 'the formation of an open-ended Ministerial Committee of Ministers of Foreign Affairs'.[89] The purpose of the Committee is to maintain dialogue with the Security Council in finding solutions to issues affecting Africa's relationship with the ICC. The Committee consists of twelve AU member states, six of which are state parties to the Rome Statute; Burundi, Kenya, Madagascar, Namibia and Senegal. The remaining six are non-party states; Ethiopia, Eritrea, South Sudan, Libya, Sudan and Zimbabwe. When the Committee met on 11 April 2016 in Addis Ababa, it called for the African States Parties to collectively withdraw from the Rome Statute unless the following African demands were addressed; a) to give immunity to sitting Heads of State and Government b) recognition for primacy of African judicial mechanisms and AU decision-making organs over the ICC and c) a reduction of the powers of the Prosecutor.[90] The Committee also agreed to meet the United Nations Security Council before the July 2016 AU

---

89 Decision on the Update of the Commission on the Implementation of Previous decisions on the International Criminal Court, 14–15 June 2015 Johannesburg, South Africa, Doc. Assembly/AU/Dec.586 (XXV).

90 Ministry of Foreign Affairs Kenya, 'African Union Open-Ended Ministrial Committee on International Criminal Court (ICC) attended by Cabinet Secretary Amb. Amina Mohamed' 11 April 2016.

Summit which was to be held in Kigali, Rwanda. By the end of 2016, the meeting with the United Nations Security Council had not taken place. The last attempt to have the meeting, in the form of informal interactive discussions between the UN Security Council and the AU on the 23 September 2016, was cancelled as the Committee was not satisfied with the level of representation from the Security Council members. The Committee would have preferred to have permanent representatives and not junior officers from the Security Council attending the meeting. The failure of dialogue at this level may have been the final straw leading to the decision by Burundi, South Africa and Gambia to announce their withdrawal from the Rome Statute. There is probably a sense that the permanent members of the UN Security Council do not adequately respect African states. Naturally one would expect that if African countries are represented at a high ministerial level, a similar level of representation should be expected from the other side, rather than sending note takers to attend such a crucial meeting. Of course there could be some domestic factors that contributed to the decisions by the three African States Parties to announce and take steps to withdraw from the Rome Statute. However, the timing of such action suggests that Africa's treatment by the UN Security Council is at the heart of the tension between the Court and the AU.[91] On 5 September 2013, the Kenyan parliament voted to withdraw from the Court.[92]

In any case, the Court demonstrated considerable resilience in the face of opposition initially from the US and then the AU. However, the concerns expressed by African states raise questions about the new international criminal justice system as regards its ability to effectively enforce the international rule of law and deliver justice to all victims of international crimes.

The Court's focus on Africa, combined with the opening of criminal proceedings against African government officials under the principle of universal jurisdiction, gives the inaccurate impression that Africa has a monopoly on international crimes. It makes one wonder whether the claims that the Court has become an imposition or a plot by the industrialised West to maintain their domination of Africa are justified.

The manner in which Africa appears to have been targeted by the Court raises a number of questions, such as: how did the Court end up opening investigations

---

91 Dire Tladi, 'The African Union and the International Criminal Court: The Battle for the Soul of International Law' (2009) 34 *South African Yearbook of International Law* 57, 60. Tladi points out that in June 2009 during the Ministers of Justice of African States Parties to the ICC Statute, a number of African States Parties called for the withdrawal of support for the Court, while others defended the court against attacks. See also 'African Countries Back away from ICC Withdrawal Demand' *Sudan Tribune* (10 June 2009); and also Bill Corcoran, 'Days of Reckoning for Criminal Court as African Union Members Convene: Kenya is Pushing for Mass Withdrawal from the Court, But Plenty Disagree' *Irish Times* (9 October 2013); and Desmond Tutu, 'In Africa, Seeking a License to Kill' *New York Times* (10 October 2013), who criticised the reports that the AU leaders were planning to withdraw from the Court at an extraordinary summit in 2013.

92 *Hansard National Assembly of Kenya Official Report*, 5 September 2013.

in situations involving only African states? Does this mean that there are no international crimes being committed outside Africa or is it that the crimes in Africa are the worst? If so, what is it that makes them the worst? Could it be that the Court is designed in such a way that it targets weak states that are found in regions such as Africa? These are very complex, broad questions and it would be overly ambitious for this study to attempt to provide conclusive answers to all of them.

This book considers the issues relating to the selective enforcement of international criminal law by the Court in the light of some of the questions raised above and from a critical legal studies perspective. While the traditional theoretical perspectives of naturalism and positivism fall outside the scope of this research, some references to these will be made – primarily when analysing the decisions made by some judges and the Office of the Prosecutor of the Court. The hypothesis for this thesis is that politics is central to the claims of selective enforcement of international criminal law by the Court, not only with regard to the targeting of situations at an international level, but also the targeting of individuals within certain situations, and that this threatens the status of the Court as a mechanism for promoting the international rule of law.

The book argues that the Western-powers-versus-Africa debate has dominated the discourse on selective enforcement, essentially missing how African national politics have also contributed to selective enforcement. The words of South African judge Navanethem Pillay, who sat on the International Criminal Tribunal for Rwanda and the International Criminal Court, captured this when she told the Kenyan Senator in 2015 that: 'Before considering double standards on the international level, you should confront double standards at home.'[93]

Taking all the evidence into account, it seems that the majority of the African ruling elite are not ready to be held accountable for their actions, whether domestically, regionally or internationally. They prefer to see their opponents being brought to justice rather than themselves. This is reflected in both the proposals to amend the Rome Statute in order to protect heads of state from investigations and prosecutions during their terms of office and also in the Malabo Protocol for the establishment of the African Court with the jurisdication over international crimes. It seems that there is a lack of appreciation that at the heart of international principles of state sovereignty and associated immunities was the wish to promote the welfare and protect citizens, and not to shield state officials.

Still, there is no doubt that selective enforcement undermines the principle of the international rule of law, which is the bedrock of the liberal legalism upon which the international criminal justice system is anchored. The alleged

---

93 Mark Kersten, 'Kenya Gambled and Lost at the ICC's Yearly Conference – But it's Not Game Over Yet', *Justicehub blog*, https://justiceinconflict.org/2015/12/04/kenya-gambled-and-lost-at-the-iccs-yearly-conference-but-its-not-game-over-yet/ 4 December 2015.

failure of the Court to officially open investigations and prosecutions in other parts of the world, such as the Occupied Territories of Palestine, Sri Lanka, Iraq, Afghanistan and Syria, raises questions about the usefulness of liberal legalism as a philosophical paradigm for international criminal justice. At a global level, liberal legalism posits that the international community should operate under an international rule of law; in other words, legal institutions should keep order and solve disputes by relying on legalistic procedures that are objective and independent of the society that they regulate. This seems to be what the Court is failing to achieve, but the question is should we blame the Court or the international systems within which it exists?

1.2.2. BOOK OUTLINE

This book is presented in eight chapters.

Following on from the Introduction, chapter 2 theorises about the establishment of the International Criminal Court. It discusses the rationalist and constructivist perspectives in explaining the establishment of the Court. It also examines the role that African civil society has played, and continues to play, in terms of how the Court functions on the continent.

Chapter 3 discusses the role of the Office of the Prosecutor. It argues that the emergence of a bi-polar system – the US opposing the Court on the one hand and the EU and its Member States occupying the role of political and financial provider for the Court on the other – influenced the prosecutorial strategy of the Court. The Prosecutor had to avoid confrontation with the US and avoid upsetting the Court's benefactors in the EU. Consequently, the Prosecutor preferred for either states or the UN Security Council to refer situations to the Court in lieu of using his power to open investigations. The assumption was that referrals of this type brought with them political support and cooperation. Despite this, the Office of the Prosecutor did not receive the political support it needed when it came to apprehending suspects. Apart from being let down by the political actors failing to arrest and surrender suspects, the internal challenges within the Office of the Prosecutor are also discussed as a contributory factor to the dissatisfaction with the Court's performance.

Chapter 4 focuses on the referral mechanisms of the jurisdiction of the Court, focusing on how some have been manipulated both at the global level and within specific countries, leading to claims of selective enforcement. It begins by highlighting the state complaint systems as used in international human rights regimes in order to expose the weaknesses and strengths of the state referral system within the international criminal justice system. The chapter points out that self-referrals have become synonymous with state referrals, although this was not the primary intention of the drafters. It discusses self-referrals from Uganda, the Democratic Republic of the Congo, the Central African Republic,

Mali and the Comoros. The UN Security Council referrals of Sudan and Libya are also discussed.

Chapter 5 examines the admissibility rules of the Court. It argues that since the majority of the cases that were taken to the Court were self-referrals, few states have challenged the admissibility of their cases. The fact that none of the states that referred their cases to the Court has challenged their admissibility could be an indication that these states still view the Court as the effective forum for prosecuting their political rivals.

Chapter 6 focuses on the fallout between the Court and the AU, primarily after the indictment of the President al-Bashir and the subsequent inaction by the UN Security Council to the request for the proceedings to be suspended. It also analyses how the Court's relationship with other African States Parties such as Kenya and Uganda became complex. It is argued that in Kenya, the relationship deteriorated immediately after the naming of the suspects. Prior to that, there was some support, including from some of the would-be suspects, for the Court to intervene in Kenya. One of the reasons for this was that there were some Kenyans who felt that the Kenyan judiciary systems lacked the necessary integrity to investigate and prosecute high-profile suspects.

Chapter 7 discusses how the AU reacted to falling out with the Court, especially over the decision on non-cooperation with the Court in the arrest and surrender of President al-Bashir. The decision created diplomatic chaos between several states parties – Kenya, Chad, Nigeria, the Democratic Republic of the Congo and South Africa. It raised the fundamental questions about whether there is a hierarchy of obligations between the AU and the Court. In addition, the decision ignited a fundamental question on the immunity of heads of state for non- states parties at the Court. So far, the judiciary of two African states, Kenya and South Africa, seem to suggest the application of a restricted theory of immunity; hence, President al-Bashir is likely to be arrested if he were to travel to those two countries. Also discussed are alternative and African-based measures of addressing impunity on the continent as proposed by the AU. These include the Darfur hybrid tribunal and the African Court of Justice and Human and Peoples' Rights.

Chapter 8 is divided into two parts. The first part highlights some of the key lessons that could be learned from the relationship between the AU and the Court. The second part focuses on possible future developments for the Court. One of the main lessons is that it seems that the Court, and the Office of the Prosecutor in particular, underestimated the complexity of the African political terrain when the Office of the Prosecutor acted on the states' referrals without a clear understanding of the political dynamics in each of the states. This complicated the work of the newly established institution as it appeared to have been driven into political minefields. The other major lesson that could be learned is how Africa is actually taking the lead in terms of clarifying and refining the Rome

Statute system through its proposed amendments. This demonstrates that despite the challenges that the two institutions could be facing, the African States Parties still have faith in engaging with the Court with the aim of reforming it to reflect certain realities on the ground. The problem, however, is the Kenyan proposal to grant immunity to heads of state and government functionaries until they leave office – such a proposal sends the wrong message about the commitment to end impunity for international crimes.

The chapter urges African states to seek alternative mechanisms to the Court and to the existing accountability mechanism from its own cultural, historical heritage and traditions, and to avoid mimicking European states and models. It points out that the main challenge that Africa faces is that it was created in the image of Europe; hence, the trend for African policy leaders is to copy European models and try to apply them in Africa. Africa is invited to dig deep into its pre-colonial institutions and progressive values in order to shape its accountability mechanisms. The establishment of the African Peer Review Mechanism in 2003 is given as a good example of African states coming up with mechanisms rooted in African values of mutual respect and a non-adversarial approach to addressing problems. On the future of the Court, the chapter ties it to the ability of the EU to maintain its dominance as the main political and financial provider to the Court. It argues that resemblances between Europe and African and their historical link through colonialism make it hard to imagine that African States Parties will leave the Court in large numbers. The EU and European states are likely to use their carrot and stick to ensure that Africans remain in the Rome Statute system. This would change in the event that the EU's common market experiment crumbles or if the region focuses on other priorities in its neighbourhood, such as the rise of Russia, immigration and an economic meltdown. Such developments would weaken the Court greatly, which will consequently affect the African membership and support for the Court.

CHAPTER 2

THE ESTABLISHMENT OF THE INTERNATIONAL CRIMINAL COURT, AND AFRICA'S ROLE AND EARLY SUPPORT

The architects of the Court had to agree upon the appropriate method to establish a court that would be universally accepted, effective and independent. The draft Statute of the Court, prepared and adopted by the International Law Commission in 1994, indicates that three proposals were contemplated initially:[94] (a) through a UN Security Council or General Assembly resolution; (b) by amending the UN Charter, which would have made the international criminal court an integral part of the UN and hence create binding obligations for all its members; and (c) through a multilateral treaty.[95]

Although the third proposal – that of establishing the Court through a multilateral treaty – was eventually adopted, commentaries on the Draft Statute indicate that the method was initially considered unsatisfactory.[96] There was a concern that such a statute would only be signed and ratified by states where atrocities were unlikely and would be shunned by those states where atrocities would occur.[97]

However, as the negotiations progressed, the option of establishing the court through a multilateral treaty became widely accepted. This is because doubts were cast about the binding effect of the UN General Assembly resolutions, and the legitimacy and legality of UN Security Council resolutions in establishing a permanent international court were also discussed. It is not clear whether amending the UN Charter would have resulted in the creation of a court with universal reach and acceptance, given that the Charter reserves some rights for the five permanent members of the UN Security Council. Some delegates felt that amending the UN Charter would be a complex exercise. A multilateral treaty was preferred because, unlike a declaration, a treaty creates binding obligations for its parties. When a treaty is accepted and ratified by a state, that

---

94 Report of the International Law Commission on the Work of its Forty-Sixth Session, UN GAOR, 49th Sess., Supp. No. 1 0, UN Doc. A/49/10 (1994).

95 Ibid, pp. 27–28.

96 Ibid.

97 Ibid.

treaty – pursuant to its constitutional procedures – has force of law to facilitate cooperation, especially in transferring suspects. In the end, the International Law Commission's report to the UN General Assembly recommended the organisation of an international conference of plenipotentiaries where a convention on the establishment of an international criminal court was to be concluded: the Rome Conference.[98]

During the Rome Conference, a legal positivism philosophical approach dominated the negotiations on both the substantive and procedural law of the Court. One commentator pointed out that this was because the drafters of the Rome Statute 'wished to hem in the discretion of the judges, hence (unlike in the ICTY) there was, *inter alia* a closed list of war crimes' and 'to apply a strict understanding of the legality principle of *nullum crimen sine lege*'.[99] The Draft Statute that was adopted by the International Law Commission in 1994 avoided defining the crimes under the jurisdiction of the Court.[100] The expectation was that the definitions and contents of the crimes were to be found in general international law. According to James Crawford, the Statute was supposed to be conceived of as primarily procedural and adjectival, with the substantive law that the Court applies being derived from other sources.[101]

Certain states were not comfortable with the draft and pushed for the definition of crimes in the Statute with clarity and precision – they did not want to leave room for the judges to have a legislative role in defining crimes. The preference of these states for a written law – a positivist approach – was evident in debates surrounding the attempt to define the crime of aggression.[102] Although aggression is a crime in customary law, the drafters failed to agree on its definition during the Rome Conference, they included Article 5(2), which had made it clear that any conditions under which the Court exercised jurisdiction with respect to the crime of aggression were to be consistent with the relevant provisions of the UN Charter. This wording was removed after a definition was reached in 2010 at the Kampala Review Conference.[103] This had effectively prevented the Court from prosecuting aggression based on customary law. As regards war crimes, the drafters came up with a 'closed list of war crimes',[104] to which the judges are required to abide, probably to avoid a repetition of the judicial law-making process that had been witnessed in the *Tadić* case.[105]

---

98 Ibid, para. 90.

99 Robert Cryer, 'The Philosophy of International Criminal Law' in Alexander Orakhelashvili (ed.), *Research Handbook on the Theory and History of International Law* (Cheltenham, Edward Elgar, 2011), p. 254.

100 James Crawford, 'The ILC Adopts a Statute for an International Criminal Court' (1995) 89 *American Journal of International Law* 404, 411.

101 Ibid.

102 Cryer, 'The Philosophy of International Criminal Law', note 94, p. 256.

103 Cryer, *Prosecuting International Crimes*, note 46, p. 245.

104 Ibid, p. 268.

105 Schabas, *An Introduction to the International Criminal Court*, note 3, p. 124.

A move that is considered to have cemented the positivist influence in the Rome Statute is the inclusion by the drafters of Article 21(1) (a) "Applicable law"[106] and Article 22 "*Nullum crimen sine lege*".[107] Article 21is exclusive and hierarchical in its identification of the Court's sources of law. The article identifies The Rome Statute, Elements of Crimes and the rules of Procedure and Evidence to be the first sources of the Court's applicable law. In fact, the "Elements of Crimes" which assist the Court in the interpretation and application of the crimes under the jurisdiction of the Court, were introduced and added into the Rome Statute following their proposal by the US delegations. One commentator pointed that the US was concerned that the "Elements of Crimes" could give teeth to the concept of *nullum crimen sine lege*.[108]

Comparatively, the drafters of previous statutes or charters establishing international tribunals had not shown the same level of inclination towards legal positivism or written laws as was witnessed during the negotiations for the Rome Statute. Cryer attributes this difference to the trend that when those responsible for making laws, the creators of tribunals, are not subjected to the jurisdiction of the established tribunal, they tend to adopt a relaxed approach to the clarity and precision of the laws they make.[109] This was the case with the London Charter, the Statute for the former Yugoslavia, where the creators of such tribunals were in theory not under their jurisdiction. However, the situation was different with the Rome Statute - the nationals of the states involved in drafting the Statute were likely to become defendants, hence they wanted to know what they were signing up to beforehand.

2.1. ATTEMPTING TO UNDERSTAND AFRICA'S EARLY ENTHUSIASM AND SUPPORT FOR THE COURT

Any attempt to understand why the majority of African states initially embraced the establishment of a permanent international criminal court is a complex endeavour as there is no straightforward explanation. Perhaps a good starting point is to try and answer the question of why states create international criminal tribunals in the first place. The key question with regard

106 Article 21 (1) of the Rome Statute provides that, 'The Court shall apply: (a) In the first place, this Statute, Elements of Crimes and its Rules of Procedure and Evidence.'

107 Article 21 of the Rome Statute provides that: '(1) A person shall not be criminally responsible under this Statute unless the conduct in question constitutes, at the time it takes place, a crime within the jurisdiction of the Court. (2) The definition of a crime shall be strictly construed and shall not be extended by analogy. In case of ambiguity, the definition shall be interpreted in favour of the person being investigated, prosecuted or convicted.'

108 Machteld Boot, *Genocide, Crimes against Humanity and War Crimes: Nullum Crimen Sine Lege and the Subject Matter Jurisdiction of the ICC* (Cambridge, Intersentia, 2002), p. 82.

109 Cryer, *Prosecuting International Crimes*, note 46, p. 233.

to understanding international criminal justice is 'why would states ever bother to create institutions that might end up turning against them or at least be invoked against them as precedents towards a purported moralisation of the international order?'[110] The literature that attempts to explain why states establish international tribunals has been dominated by two main orientations: rationalism and constructivism.[111]

2.1.1. RATIONALISM THEORY AND AFRICA'S EARLY SUPPORT FOR THE COURT

The underlying assumption behind rationalism is that states are rational, unitary actors that create international institutions in order to alleviate strategic cooperation problems that arise in the anarchical international system.[112] In other words, this explains the multilateral approach in the global governance system. In the context of international criminal law, the two strategic cooperation problems that needed to be addressed were, first, the lack of enforcement of international criminal law through the national courts[113] and, second, the high transaction costs – either financial (in the case of the *ad hoc* tribunals) and in terms of the severing of diplomatic ties in the event that a state moves to prosecute a national of another independent state.[114]

In order for international institutions such as the Court to address, or minimise, these enforcement challenges, they are designed with particular features. These include the centralisation and standardisation of monitoring states' compliance. This also brings with it some challenges for the institutions, especially with regard to sovereignty costs. Sovereignty costs here involve the

---

110 Frederic Megret, 'The Politics of International Criminal Justice' (2002) 13 *European Journal of International Law* 1261, p. 1267.

111 See Caroline Fehl, 'Explaining the International Criminal Court: A "Practice Test" for Rationalist and Constructivist Approaches' (2004) 10 *European Journal of International Relations* 357.

112 Duncan Snidal, 'International Political Economy Approaches to International Institutions' in Jagdeep S. Bhandari and Alan O. Sykes (eds.)(eds.), *Economic Dimensions in International Law: Comparative and Empirical Perspectives* (Cambridge, Cambridge University Press, 1997), pp. 477–512.

113 See Timothy L.H. McCormack, 'Their Atrocities and Our Misdemeanours: The Reticence of States to Try Their "Own Nationals" for International Crimes' in Mark Lattimer and Philippe Sands (eds.)(eds.), *Justice for Crimes against Humanity* (Oxford, Hart Publishing, 2003) for a historical review of national prosecutions of international crimes, which concludes that states tend to prosecute 'them' and not 'us', 'them' being enemies and other nationals.

114 For an example of diplomatic fallout between states, see *Arrest Warrant of 11 April 2000 (Democratic Republic of the Congo v. Belgium)*, Judgment, 15 February 2002; and also between the AU and the EU over the exercise of universal jurisdiction – see AU-EU Technical Ad Hoc Expert Group Report on the Principle of Universal Jurisdiction, April 16, 2009. On the financial costs of *ad hoc* tribunals, see Scheffer, *All the Missing Souls*, note 9, p. 168.

loss of some part of independence by the states, so there is a requirement for the designed institutions to have some form of flexibility to accommodate states' sovereignty. This explains the inclusion of provisions allowing states to challenge admissibility in the Rome Statute. States are given the first chance to exercise their right to investigate and prosecute international crimes before the Court intervenes.

In the context of Africa, it should be recalled that the drafting of the Rome Statute also coincided with the Lockerbie debacle, which pitted Libya against the three permanent members of the UN Security Council (the UK, the US and France). The issue at hand was the extradition of two Libyan nationals suspected of bombing Pan Am Flight 103 over Lockerbie, Scotland, killing more than 250 people.

The then OAU disapproved of the manner in which the UK and the US used their positions as permanent members of the UN Security Council to impose economic sanctions on Libya as punishment for its refusal to hand over the two suspects. UN Security Council Resolution 748, regarding the imposition of sanctions on Libya, was adopted on 31 March 1992 – after Libya had sought the resolution of the problem through a legal framework.[115] Prior to this, on 3 March 1992, Libya had filed an application with the International Court of Justice contending that neither the UK nor the US had the right to compel it to surrender its nationals for prosecution in their jurisdictions.[116] Libya's refusal to extradite the two nationals to either the US or the UK had sound legal justification. It was based on the provisions of the Convention for the Suppression of Unlawful Acts against the Safety of Civil Aviation (1971), which allows a state party to either prosecute or extradite. Libya indicated that it was ready to investigate and prosecute the two suspects, and was even prepared to invite international observers to the trial.

The US and the UK were not ready to accept and trust a Libyan-led trial. This was a classic example of a lack of strategic cooperation, as the parties could not agree on the location for the trial.[117] The US and the UK reverted to the UN Security Council and imposed crippling economic sanctions on Libya. For both the US and the UK, the fact that Libya had made an application to the International Court of Justice was simply considered to be inconsequential. Their move to take the issue to the Security Council was criticised and opposed

---

115 UN Doc. Res/748, 31 March 1992.

116 *Questions of Interpretation and Application of the 1971 Montreal Convention Arising from the Aerial Incident at Lockerbie (Libyan Arab Jamahiriya v. United Kingdom)* (Instituting Proceedings) 1992 ICJ Application Instituting Proceedings Filed in the Registry of the Court on 3 March 1992.

117 A.V. Lowe and Colin Warbrick, 'The Lockerbie Affair' (1992) 41 *International and Comparative Law Quarterly* 907.

by the African states occupying the temporary seats in the Security Council at the time – Cape Verde, Morocco and Zimbabwe – as well as India and China.[118]

During the UN Security Council session leading up to the adoption of Resolution 728 on 31 March 1992 (10 in favour and five against), representatives from Zimbabwe and Cape Verde voted against. The representative from Zimbabwe, Mr Mumbengegwi, stated that his delegation did not believe that it was necessary for the UN Security Council to resort to Chapter VII before peaceful diplomatic means had been exhausted.[119] He warned that 'by taking the Chapter VII route while this case was still pending before world court, the Security Council was risking a major institutional crisis'. He went on to stress that, since the Security Council was acting on behalf of 175 states (in 1992), it was of 'crucial importance that every decision taken by the Security Council be able to withstand the careful scrutiny of the 160 Member States on whose behalf the Council is expected to act'.[120]

The Lockerbie debacle was also raised during the UN Sixth Committee's 41st meeting in 1994 during the discussions on the establishment of the International Criminal Court. George Odartey Lamptey, from Ghana, introduced the subject as he explained to the Committee his delegation's amendments to the draft Resolution A/C.6/49/L.24.[121] The amendments included an inclusion in the resolution of specific operative paragraphs, one of which stated that the Sixth Committee had decided to 'convene a United Nations conference of plenipotentiaries for a period of 4 to 6 weeks in the spring of 1996, to elaborate and adopt the statute of an international criminal court'. The majority of the amendments from Ghana made reference to the urgent need for UN plenipotentiaries.

In explaining his delegation's amendments and their urgency, Mr Lamptey referred to the Lockerbie crisis when he pointed out that:

> [Had] such a court already been in existence, the problem that had soured relations between the Libyan Arab Jamahiriya and the United States of America, the United Kingdom and France would not have arisen. As it was, the Libyan people were suffering because they would not let their nationals go on trial before jurisdictions in which they had no confidence.[122]

Ghana's amendments were supported by the Nigerian and Malaysian delegations, but were opposed by France and India. The French representative noted that although his delegation was in favour of establishing the Court, 'to lay down a

118 UN Doc. Res/748, 31 March 1992.
119 U. N. Doc S/PV.3063, 31 March 1992, p. 52.
120 Ibid, p. 54.
121 Summary Record of the 41st Meeting of the Sixth Committee, U.N Doc A/C.6/49/SR.41, 12 December 1994, para. 22.
122 Ibid, para. 22.

time-scale in advance would waste time rather than gain time'.[123] When the issue was put to a recorded vote, the motion to adjourn the debate on the Ghanaian amendments received 58 votes in favour, 29 against and 38 abstentions. None of the African states voted in favour of the motion to adjourn – they either voted against or abstained, as they clearly wanted the amendments to be approved. The Libyan Arab Jamahiriya was against the adjournment of the debate, which perhaps indicates that the Court was seen as a possible solution to its impasse with the three super-powers (the UK, the US and France).

In short, the joint political move made by the UK and the US to impose economic sanctions in what was viewed as a purely legal dispute was not received well by several states. It angered both the then OAU and the League of Arab States, which felt that sanctions should have been used as a last resort. Together, these groups suggested several alternative actions that the UN Security Council could have taken to resolve the issue, including establishing a special criminal tribunal at the International Court of Justice headquarters in The Hague to prosecute the two suspects.[124] In 1998, that is, when 10 years had passed without a solution being reached, Colonel Muammar al-Gaddafi told a Dutch television interviewer that 'an international court is the solution with judges from America, Libya, England and other countries'.[125]

The OAU expressed its frustration at the UN Security Council's handling of the conflict – and its refusal to remove the sanctions on Libya in particular – by adopting a resolution where it:

> DECIDE[D] not to comply any longer with Security Council Resolutions 748 (1992) and 883(1993) on sanctions, with effect from September 1998, if the United States of America and the United Kingdom refuse that the two suspects be tried in a third neutral country pursuant to the verdict of the International Court of Justice by July 1998, date on which the sanctions will be due for review, owing to the fact that the said resolutions violate Article 27 paragraph 3, Article 33 and Article 36 paragraph 3 of the United Nations Charter, and the considerable human and economic losses suffered by Libya and a number of other African peoples as a result of the sanctions.[126]

This resolution was passed at the time when the Rome Conference was about to begin the process of establishing the International Criminal Court. The entire

---

123 See ibid, para. 28, remarks by Mr Legal (France).

124 Declaration of the Thirty-Third Ordinary Session of the Organisation of African Union Assembly of Heads of State and Government on the Dispute between the Libyan Arab Jamahiriya and the United States of America and Great Britain, AHG/Dec.127 (XXXIV), 8–10 June, 1998 Thirty-Fourth Ordinary Session/Second Ordinary Session of the African Economic Community Ouagadougou, Burkina Faso.

125 Barbra Crossette, '10 Years after Lockerbie, Still No Trial' *New York Times* (22 December 1998).

126 The Crisis between the Great Socialist People's Libyan Arab Jamahiriya and the United States of America and the United Kingdom, AHG/Dec.127 (XXXIV).

Lockerbie debacle provides insight into what may have influenced the positions taken by African states during the Conference – especially with regard to the role of the UN Security Council and why it supported the establishment of an independent international criminal court. The OAU's call for its member states to stop complying with the UN Security Council resolution in the Lockerbie debacle mirrors the non-cooperation resolutions adopted by the AU since 2009 urging member states not to cooperate with the Court in relation to the arrest of President al-Bashir after the UN Security Council failed to respond to its deferral request.

Linked to the rationalist explanation is also a realist perspective on the establishment of the Court. The two are linked insofar as they view states as being rational actors that establish international institutions to serve or address specific interests. Realists simply argue that 'states create international criminal tribunals to legitimise their goals and because they think or know they can control them'.[127] They argue that political authorities, including political entities such as the UN Security Council, should be in charge of the judicial process. In other words, the Court should be seen as a product and projection of the power and self-interest of political actors, and not necessarily of a genuine interest in ending impunity. Certain commentators and critics of the Court's focus on Africa tend to argue from this theoretical perspective – that the Court was established by the Western powers to serve their imperial interests in Africa. However, this seems flawed considering that more than 40 African states participated in the negotiations involved in establishing the Court and then went on to ratify it in large numbers. On the flip side, it could be argued that the African leaders' frustration with the Court is linked to the fact that they prefer to control its judicial work and determined whom it should investigate and when it could open investigations and prosecutions. This was similar to the desire of the US to have a court that it could control through the Security Council.

2.1.2. CONSTRUCTIVIST THEORY AND AFRICA'S EARLY SUPPORT OF THE COURT

The constructivist approach attributes the establishment of the Court and the international tribunals to the development within the international community of a common identity based on the need to respect human rights, rules and values as the basis for governing state behaviour. One of the key assumptions behind this development is that international criminal justice is a product of those policies that are most associated with the promotion of the human

127 Megret, 'The Politics of International Criminal Justice', note 105, p. 1267.

rights movement.[128] Accordingly, international criminal justice is viewed as a product of the hope and faith that states have in international tribunals that such institutions do good. These sentiments date back to the period immediately after the Second World War.[129] International criminal justice is linked to the strong belief that legal institutions such as the Court have the ability to keep order and peace, and to prevent and deter future conflicts.[130]

In this regard, the establishment of and states' support for the Court is linked to the emergence of a new political culture based on human rights and legalism, as opposed to military power and unilateralism. So even though the negotiations for the establishment of the Court stalled for almost five decades, the new world order that followed the end of the Cold War (what Francis Fukuyama described as the end of history and the universalisation of Western liberal democracy as the final form of human government)[131] rejuvenated the process, leading to the adoption of the Court. Human rights norms had reached a 'prescriptive status' that garnered a level of universal acceptance.[132] They had become defining values and a unique identity of the communities of liberal states. In this regard, the support for the establishment of the Court was a mere reflection of the changing times and attitudes towards taking concrete steps to promote human rights and accountability.

When looking to explain the African states' early support for the establishment of the Court, one must be careful not to make sweeping generalisations. It is possible that the theoretical orientations outlined here complement each other, as individually they are inadequate. A statement made by representative of the OAU, Professor T. Maluwa, at the beginning of the five weeks of the Conference in Rome, is worth repeating here:

> Africa had a particular interest in the establishment of the Court, since its peoples had been the victims of large-scale violations of human rights over the centuries: slavery, wars of colonial conquest and continued acts of war and violence, even in the post-colonial era. The recent genocide in Rwanda was a tragic reminder that such atrocities were not yet over, but had strengthened OAU's determination to support the creation of a permanent, independent court to punish the perpetrators of such acts.[133]

---

128 *Ibid*, p. 1268.

129 Carsten Stahn, 'Between "Faith" and "Facts": By What Standards Should We Assess International Criminal Justice?' (2012) 25 *Leiden Journal of International Law* 251, p. 256.

130 M. Cherif Bassiouni, 'Combating Impunity for International Crimes' (2000) 71 *University of Colorado Law Review* 409, p. 410.

131 Samuel P. Huntington, *The Clash of Civilizations and the Remaking of World Order* (New York: The Free Press, 2002), p. 31.

132 Fehl, 'Explaining the International Criminal Court', note 106, p. 371.

133 U.N Doc A/CONF.183/SR, 17 June 1998, para. 115.

This statement reveals how history is indeed indispensable in tracing the fortunes of international criminal justice.[134] The history of atrocities in Africa appeared to have been a major contributing factor in the African states' support. History is crucial here, because it also seems to have shaped how some African commentators and state officials have evaluated the Court's performance since its establishment, with some viewing it as having been turned into a neo-colonialist agent.[135]

The majority of the post-colonial generation of African state leaders and ruling elites would have had first-hand experience of living under colonial rule – some would have even been put on trial and prosecuted for fighting for the independence of their people. They would have been aware that the majority of the 'large-scale violations of human rights' during the colonial era were not accounted for.[136] As such, the establishment of the Court was perhaps an opportunity for them to ensure that the rule of law was to be applied universally to any future atrocities committed. However, the fact that the Court is now targeting some of them and not perpetrators in other parts of the world, especially the UK and the US, for atrocities committed in Iraq and Afghanistan has left Africa's ruling elite with the impression that the Court is there to perpetuate the imbalances of the colonial period.

The statement also reflects a forward-looking (teleogical) approach to international criminal law, in that it recognises the continuation of atrocities in Africa and the need for punishment in order to deter future crimes. This desire to end impunity is reflected in the AU Constitutive Act, which suggests that there is some confluence of values between the AU and the Court.

It is possible that the events that followed the aftermath of the Rwandan Genocide, especially the establishment of the *ad hoc* tribunal, were viewed by some as an afterthought,[137] and this could have played a key role in generating

---

134 Megret, 'The Politics of International Criminal Justice', note 105, p. 1265.

135 See Mahmood Mamdani, *Saviors and Survivors: Darfur, Politics and the War on Terror* (New York, Verso, 2009), p. 286; and also remarks made by the Uganda Deputy Foreign Minister Asuman Kiyingi to a journalist: 'It's a really colonial context. We were a dominated people. For a very long time we have been taking directives from these people.' See Barry Malone, 'Africans Push UN to Call off "Racist" Court' *Al Jazeera* (15 November 2013).

136 Some of the specific atrocities suffered by Africans include the abuses committed in the Belgian Congo by King Leopold II recorded in Adam Hochschild, *King Leopold's Ghost: A Story of Greed Terror and Heroism in Colonial Africa* (Boston, Mariner Books, 1998) and in Arthur Conan Doyle, *The Crime of the Congo* (4th edn, London, Hutchinson & Co, 1909), against the Herero people of Namibia, then South West Africa, by the German settlers, as noted in Jan-Bart Gewald, 'Imperial Germany and the Herero of Southern Africa: Genocide and the Quest for Recompense' in Adam Jones (ed.), *Genocide, War Crimes and the West* (London, Zed Books, 2004), and in Algeria by the French, as noted in Shiva Eftekhari, 'France and the Algerian War: From a Policy of "Forgetting" to a Framework for Accountability' (2003) 34 *Colombian Human Rights Law Review* 413.

137 Makau Mutua, 'From Nuremberg to the Rwanda Tribunal: Justice or Retribution' (2000) 6 *Buffalo Human Rights Law Review* 77, p. 85.

African support for the Court. There is a suggestion that the Rwandan Tribunal was established as a result of a sense that the UN Security Council was embarrassed at the suggestion of double standards that had been raised against it. This suggestion was based on the fact that in 1993, the Security Council established a tribunal for the former Yugoslavia. It was difficult for the Security Council to reject a tribunal for Rwanda when it had set one up for the former Yugoslavia.[138] That said, the attribution of the establishment of the Rwandan tribunal to the precedential effect of Yugoslavia is too simplistic to be convincing, because it fails to explain why similar tribunals were not established in neighbouring Burundi or the Democratic Republic of the Congo, which at that time were also facing atrocity crimes.[139]

At the time of the negotiations for the establishment of the Court, the OAU was also undergoing major changes in order to build its capacity in peacekeeping and to respond to conflicts.[140] The new values that emerged from the transformation of the OAU into the AU were congruent with those of the proposed Court – the commitment to end impunity and favour intervention in cases of genocide, war crimes and crimes against humanity.

In this regard, it can be argued that the Africa states' support for the establishment of the Court was a rationally calculated manoeuvre aimed at minimising the marginalisation of the continent within the international community by the UN Security Council in particular, whose record of addressing African problems was found wanting – particularly in Rwanda and Sierra Leone. A permanent international criminal court meant a reduction in *ad hoc* diplomatic efforts to establish tribunals to respond to many conflicts in Africa. In addition, there was no guarantee that such diplomatic efforts could lead to a solution that would be favourable to Africa, as Africa does not have a permanent member on the Security Council.

In this case, an international and permanent Court could have been seen as a solution – at least as a counterweight to the dominance of the permanent members of the UN Security Council – as African states would not have to pass through the Council to take issues to the Court. This link was acknowledged

---

138 See ibid; William A. Schabas, 'The Banality of International Justice' (2013) 11 *Journal of International Criminal Justice* 545; and Payam Akhavan, 'The International Criminal Tribunal for Rwanda: The Politics and Pragmatics of Punishment' (1996) 90 *American Journal of International Law* 501, p. 501, who points out that it could be possible that in 1994, the plight of African victims could not have generated the same outcry as the suffering Europeans, and that the Rwandan Tribunal was established because of the precedential effect of the Yugoslav Tribunal.

139 Stef Vanteginste, 'Bypassing the Prohibition of Amnesty for Human Rights Crimes: Lessons Learned from the Burundi Peace Process' (2011) 29 *Netherlands Quarterly of Human Rights* 189.

140 See Solomon Gomes, 'The Peacemaking Role of the OAU and the AU: A Comparative Analysis' in John Akokpari, Angela Ndinga-Muvumba and Tim Murithi (eds.)(eds.), *The African Union and its Institutions* (Johannesburg, Fanele, 2002).

by, and angered, US officials after the Rome Conference. The US, which had campaigned for a Court under the total control of the UN Security Council, was not impressed first by the ultimate design of the Court and second by those opposed to what the US proposed. Senator Rod Grams told a hearing after the Rome Conference that 'it is ironic that the same countries which look to the United States to be the global enforcer have created a court which inhibits our ability to project force'.[141]

From the African states' perspective, the Court 'appeared genuinely egalitarian in structure and profoundly fair in conception'.[142] Their desire for an institution independent of the UN Security Council is reflected in the majority of the AU's concerns and resistance to the proposal linking the Court to the Security Council in referring situations. The active involvement of the Security Council was inevitable, but probably was not what the African states wanted. The problem is that over the last decade, their worst nightmare – the double standards of the UN Security Council in handing ongoing and prospective Court situations – has come to pass.

With the benefit of hindsight, a realist perspective could be useful in understanding why conflict-prone states such as Burundi, the Democratic Republic of the Congo, Uganda and Nigeria might have supported the Court. As already pointed out, from a realist perspective, states are said to establish or support tribunals to advance their goals because they think that they can control such institutions.[143] It can therefore be argued that the majority of states around the Great Lakes that are prone to conflicts considered the Court to be an extra tool to employ against their political enemies. After all, they had seen how in Rwanda – where Hutu–Tutsi struggles for control of the state were common and led to the catastrophic and rapid genocide in 1994 – the Rwandan Tribunal had focused on one side (the enemy of the Rwandan government in a post-genocide Rwanda). Some commentators argue that the Rwandan government requested the establishment of the Rwandan Tribunal partly because it had also hoped to directly influence and control its operations, including determining the jurisdictional limits of the Tribunal.[144] When it became apparent within the UN Security Council that the Rwandan government's demands were untenable, the members went on to establish the Tribunal – although Rwanda voted against the resolution.[145] In response, the Rwandan government was very critical of the work of the Tribunal.

---

141 'Is a UN International Criminal Court in the U.S. National Interest?' Hearing before the Subcommittee on International Operations of the Committee on Foreign Relations, S. HRG. 105–724, 23 July 1998, p. 2.

142 Schabas, 'The Banality of International Justice', note 133, p. 247.

143 Megret, 'The Politics of International Criminal Justice', note 105, p. 1267.

144 Scheffer, *All the Missing Souls*, note 9.

145 Ibid.

In the context of Africa, the influence of common shared values as a motiving factor for the establishment of the Court is conflated by the inconsistencies in the approach adopted by the African states towards the Court. For example, Botswana, which is considered to be a solid democratic state and a defender of the Court on the continent, signed a bilateral agreement with the US prohibiting any transfer of US suspects to the Court. In fact, many of the African states that ratified the Rome Statute also signed bilateral agreements with the US. Such double standards by African states indicates how hard it is to wholly accept the proposition that those countries that welcomed and ratified the Rome Statute were purely driven by their commitment to human rights and fighting impunity.

2.2. ROLE OF THE AFRICAN CIVIL SOCIETY/NGOS IN PROMOTING THE ROME STATUTE AND COOPERATION WITH THE COURT IN THE CONTINENT

African and international human rights non-governmental organisations (NGOs) played a key role before, during and after the Rome Conference in ensuring that states (including African states) embraced the new Court.[146] It seems that the first time that NGOs became involved in the negotiating process for the Rome Statute was back in 1994 after six organisations, including the World Federalist Movement, sensed that they could influence the proceedings at the Sixth Committee regarding the establishment of the Court. This led to the formation of the Coalition for the International Criminal Court aimed at the creation of a just, effective and independent Court. The Coalition's websites states that:

> The Coalition for the International Criminal Court (CICC) includes 2,500 civil society organisations in 150 different countries working in partnership to strengthen international cooperation with the ICC; ensure that the Court is fair, effective and independent; make justice both visible and universal; and advance stronger national laws that deliver justice to victims of war crimes, crimes against humanity and genocide.[147]

During the negotiations leading up to the Rome Conference, the Coalition members were active both within and outside the Preparatory Committee

---

[146] Charles C. Jalloh, 'Regionalizing International Criminal Law?' (2009) 9 *International Criminal Law Review* 445, p. 450; see also Marlies Glasius, *The International Criminal Court: A Global Civil Society Achievement* (Abingdon, Routledge, 2006) for a detailed discussion on the role of NGOs in the establishment of the Court.

[147] Coalition for the International Criminal Court, 'About the Coalition', <http://www.iccnow.org/?mod=coalition> accessed 17.10.2016.

sessions as they tried to push their agenda for an independent and effective Court. For example, No Peace Without Justice, an Italian-based human rights organisation with offices in Rome, Brussels and New York, and a founding member of the Coalition for the International Criminal Court, supported African-based organisations. The group held the Dakar Conference in Senegal on 5–6 February 1998, which was organised at the behest of the President of Senegal and was attended by representatives from 25 African states – few of whom had previously followed the Preparatory Committee sessions.

Those who attended the conference in Dakar included Emma Bonino, the founder of No Peace Without Justice; George Soros, Chairperson of the Open Society Institute; Louise Arbour; Chief Prosecutor of the Tribunals for the former Yugoslavia and Rwanda and Cherif Bassiouni, Vice President of the United Nations Preparatory Committee. At the end of the conference, the states adopted the Dakar Declaration for the establishment of the International Criminal Court, which supported the establishment of an independent court. This became Africa's common strategy during the Rome Conference.[148]

Before the Rome Conference, African-based NGOs took part in Preparatory Committee sessions, during which they had fruitful interactions with representatives of the Coalition.[149] The European Commission made a significant financial contribution to the UN Trust Fund to support the establishment of the International Criminal Court in pursuance of UN General Assembly Resolution A/Res/51/2007. The fund assisted African states and NGOs in being actively involved in the preparatory work leading to the Rome Conference. The individual countries that made generous contributions to the Trust Fund included Belgium, Denmark, Finland, the Netherlands, Norway, Sweden and the UK. Upon returning to their home countries after several preparatory sessions or seminars, the NGOs were expected to push issues related to the Court to their domestic constituencies and educate other organisations. Generally the work of the Coalition was facilitated by the effective use of the internet, which had just become widely available.[150] Ugandan academic Dr Daniel Nsereko is given the credit for single-handedly managing to advance the agenda for the establishment of the Court in Botswana, where he was based.[151] As already highlighted, he later became an Appeals Judge at the International Criminal Court.

After the adoption of the Rome Statute, the Coalition shifted its focus to campaigning for the universal acceptance of the Court through ratification. In this quest for recognition, it worked closely with the prominent members of the

148 A/CONF.183/SR.4, para. 16.

149 Regional Reports, Africa, *ICC Monitor*, 6 November 1997.

150 William R. Pace and Rik Panganiban, 'The Power of Global Activist Networks: The Campaign for an International Criminal Court' in Peter I. Hajnal (ed.), *Civil Society in the Information Age* (Aldershot, Ashgate, 2002).

151 Glasius, *The International Criminal Court*, note 131, p. 29.

Like Minded Group mainly from the EU, which became the main sources of the Court's funding. The support of the Court had become one of the EU's symbolic external policy anchors, fully in line with its defining values of human dignity, freedom, democracy, equality, the rule of law and respect for human rights.[152] One of the main channels through which the European Commission supported NGOs working towards the acceptance of the Court was through the European Initiative for Democracy and Human Rights (EIDHR).[153]

Still, the role of NGOs in Africa should not be overly romanticised or exaggerated. Their efforts to influence the national and foreign policies of their state authorities do not seem to have yielded significant results in Africa, especially when state interests and political stakes are high. Part of the problem is the perception that NGOs lack financial independence and are mere extensions of the former colonial powers that seek to maintain influence in the affairs of their former colonies. This perception is not helped by the fact that, in the majority of situations, human rights actors from developing countries seem to religiously follow policies and positions set by Western international NGOs. It is rare that African-based NGOs come up with original propositions that are reflective of African values or indigenous knowledge systems. The majority tend to follow, at times uncritically, what is pushed upon them by often Western-based human rights organisations. Perhaps this could be due to their profound lack of in-depth knowledge, appreciation and pride in progressive African values that could benefit the entire human rights movement. Makau W. Mutua, a Kenyan academic on international human rights and international law, notes that in most situations there is no vigorous and fundamental disagreement between NGOs from Africa and Western international NGOs on the issues involved.[154] Some would even argue that NGOs in developing countries have become more or less 'alternative career paths to offices of the state' for many Africans.[155]

2.2.1. CIVIL SOCIETIES/NGOS ARM-TWISTING THE AFRICAN GOVERNMENTS INTO COOPERATING WITH THE COURT

However, there are few examples where NGOs appear to have played a huge role in ensuring that state authorities complied with their obligations under

---

152 See Statement by Herman Van Rompuy, President of the European Council on 10 September 2010, cited in Luc Reydams and Jan Wouters, 'The Politics of Establishing International Criminal Trbunals' in Luc Reydams, Jan Wouters and Cedric Ryngaert (eds.)(eds.), *International Prosecutors* (Oxford, Oxford University Press, 2012), p. 77.

153 Martijn L.P. Groenleer and Louise G. Van Schaik, 'United We Stand? The European Union's International Actorness in the Cases of the International Criminal Court and the Kyoto Protocol' (2007) 45 *Journal of Common Market Studies* 980.

154 Makau Mutua, *Human Rights: A Political and Cultural Critique* (Philadelphia, University of Pennsylvania Press, 2002), p. 37.

155 Pierre Englebert, *Africa Unity, Sovereignty, and Sorrow* (Boulder, Lynne Rienner, 2009), p. 257.

the Rome Statute – or at least kept the fire of international criminal justice burning when everything looked doomed. Civil societies in Kenya, Nigeria, South Africa and Uganda have played, and continue to play, a pivotal role in the global struggle against impunity. On 18 November 2011, the Kenyan Section of the International Commission of Jurists (an NGO) and the national section of the International Commission of Jurists filed an application with the High Court of Kenya seeking the issuance of a provisional warrant of arrest against President al-Bashir.[156] President al-Bashir had previously visited Kenya without the Kenyan authorities arresting and surrendering him to the Court, despite Kenya being obligated to do so under the Rome Statute.

On 28 November 2011, the High Court of Kenya issued an order to the Attorney General to secure an arrest warrant for President al-Bashir under Kenya's International Crimes Act.[157] The order, and the ensuing diplomatic row between Kenya and Sudan, prevented al-Bashir from travelling to Kenya to attend an Inter-Governmental Authority on Development summit. The venue of the summit had to be moved to Ethiopia. In retaliation, and signifying the sovereignty cost of enforcing international criminal justice, on the next day the Sudanese government expelled the Kenyan ambassador and ordered the Sudanese ambassador in Kenya to return to Khartoum.[158] In other words, the NGOs assisted Kenya in keeping the promise that it had made to the people of Kenya and the international community when it ratified the Rome Statute.

From an optimistic perspective, the role of NGOs here is commendable. However, since the ultimate objective of the Court is to end impunity through investigations and prosecutions, celebrating Kenyan High Court decisions would be premature – particularly in a context where such judicial decisions are often overruled and not upheld by the executive branch of the government, as will be discussed in the case of South Africa. After all, Kenya's relationship with the Court has deteriorated since the Office of the Prosecutor indicted some key Kenyan political figures. In fact, the relations between Sudan and Kenya have improved, as they view the Court, which at one stage was targeting the leaders of both states, as a common enemy.

However, as things stand, the High Court decision means President al-Bashir cannot travel to Kenya freely as he is likely to be arrested.

After the election of President Uhuru Kenyatta and his Deputy Samoei Ruto, who were indicted by the Court over the post-election violence in 2007, the stakes became too high for Kenya's ruling elite to take any chances by dealing with the Court. The relationship between human rights NGOs and the Kenyan

---

156 *Kenya Section of the International Commission of Jurists v. Attorney General and another* [2011] eKLR, 28 November.

157 Ibid.

158 'Sudan to Expel Ambassador after Kenya's Bashir Warrant' *BBC News* (29 November 2011).

authorities became strained as a consequence. At least in Kenya, civil society has remained resolute in its support for justice and accountability to victims over the post-election violence. During the Assembly of States Parties Session in 2015 in The Hague, the Kenyan NGOs acted as a counterweight to the Kenyan government, reminding the Assembly of States Parties that Kenya had not investigated or prosecuted a single individual for the 2007 atrocities.

In South Africa, the Southern Africa Litigation Centre's exigency on the government to honour its international and domestic obligations by enforcing international criminal law exemplifies how civil society can play a crucial role in ending the impunity gap through domestic systems. In the Zimbabwe torture case, the Southern Africa Litigation Centre challenged the South African authorities to investigate Zimbabwean officials for torture committed in Zimbabwe as crimes against humanity in accordance with Article 4(3)(c) of South Africa's Implementation of the Rome Statute of the International Criminal Court Act 27 of 2002.[159] The article authorises South African prosecuting authorities to prosecute any person committing a crime (or crimes) under the jurisdiction of the Court if found in South Africa – or at least this is how the South African legislators understood when they debated the Rome Statute Act in Parliament in 2002.

On 11 June 2002, during the parliamentary debate on the Implementation of the Rome Statute of the International Criminal Court Bill, Advocate J.H. De Lange of the African National Congress (ANC), while offering his party's unconditional support for the Bill, stated:

> Fourthly and more importantly, if the perpetrator is present in the Republic after the commission of the crime, our courts in the instance of these three crimes will from now on have jurisdiction. If there is some person somewhere who thinks that he or she can commit genocide or war crimes and hide in this country, this legislation will not allow that.[160]

The Democratic Alliance (DA) representative Advocate H.C. Schmidt concurred. He was even definitive that the Bill was not contemplating granting the South African authorities some form of absolute universal jurisdiction: 'This Bill does not attempt to provide unlimited or so-called universal jurisdiction to the South African High Court.'[161] This is the position that the South African authorities maintained in arguing their case not to investigate and prosecute Zimbabwean officials. The authorities argued that they could not open investigations if the suspects were not on South African territory.

---

159 *National Commissioner of the South African Police Service v. Southern African Human Rights Litigation Centre* (485/2012) (2013) ZASCA 168 (27 November 2013).

160 *South African Proceedings of the National Assembly*, 11 June 2002, p. 154.

161 Ibid, p. 165.

However, the Southern Africa Litigation Centre, the Gauteng High Court Judge Fiburius and the South African Supreme Court of Appeals have taken an elastic approach and have argued that preliminary proceedings and the conduct of investigations should be conducted independently of the suspects being in South Africa or *in absentia*. This is obviously a different approach from the one being adopted by other national jurisdictions such as Germany, which has narrowed down its application of universal jurisdiction to when there is a direct link between the crimes committed and Germany.

The Zimbabwe case, which was still at the South African Constitutional Court at the time of writing, is likely to have profound implications on how South Africa will implement the Rome Statute and to clarify whether it is ready to apply absolute universal jurisdiction – the investigating of international crimes even when the suspect is not present in the territory of the investigating state as opposed to universal jurisdiction with presence. It also underscores the existing controversy surrounding the preconditions for the application of the universal jurisdiction principle. There is a possibility that the case will generate more heat than fire as it is unfortunate that political considerations usually come into play. Still, the South African Litigation Centre has demonstrated how civil societies in Africa have been innovative and ready to ensure justice and accountability beyond the Court.

In conclusion, it is hard to identify one single explanation for the African states' early support for the Court. It appears that there was a confluence of many factors: the historical context, the political realities that African states found themselves in at the time of the negotiations (the Lockerbie debacle), the sense that Africa was being marginalised by the UN Security Council and to some extent the role of NGOs with heavy financial support from the EU. At the same time, the fact that the majority of the African states that ratified the Rome Statute – with the exception of only a few – also signed bilateral agreements with the US government adds to the complexity of the African approach towards the Court. In any case, the reality is that more than 30 African states ratified the Rome Statute and it is fair to say that, in theory, based on the AU Constitutive Act and several resolutions, the continent has an unflinching commitment to end impunity, at least in theory as more practical evidence is still lacking – apart from the successful establishment of Extraordinary Chambers in the Senegalese judiciary system to put the former Chadian President Hissène Habré on trial for torture.[162]

---

162 See Constitutive Act of the African Union (2000), Art. 4(o), which states that the Union shall function in accordance with the following principles: "Respect for the sanctity of human life, condemnation and rejection of impunity and political assassination, acts of terrorism and subversive activities".

2.3. THE COURT IN THE GLOBAL GOVERNANCE SYSTEM

The Court is an independent institution in the context of the UN system.[163] The relationship between the UN and the Court is governed by the 2004 Negotiated Relationship Agreement,[164] and affirms that the UN recognises the Court as an independent, permanent judicial institution, and that the Court recognises the responsibility of the UN under the UN Charter. Article 6 of the agreement provides for the Court to submit reports on its activities to the UN through the Secretary-General; however, the language of the article in the Negotiated Relationship Agreement indicates that the Court is not obliged to do so: 'The Court may, if it deems it appropriate, submit reports on its activities to the United Nations through the Secretary-General.' As such, the Court can use its discretion. It is allowed to suggest certain items for the General Assembly or Security Council agenda. The underlying principle of the agreement between the Court and the UN is 'mutual respect' between the two organisations.[165]

As we have seen in Chapter 1, the Rome Statute does not provide for regional organisations (such as the EU or the AU) to be parties to the Rome Statute. It is primarily a state-oriented institution. Non-state actors are also not allowed under the Rome Statute to be states parties – this right is reserved for states. Nonetheless, the Court can enter into cooperation agreements with such institutions across the globe and, as discussed in Chapter 1, the EU has an agreement with the Court. During the Rome Conference, the position of the EU regarding the Court was made ambiguous by the presence of two permanent members of the UN Security Council – France and the UK – that supported proposals favourable to the permanent members of the Security Council during much of the conference.[166] This made it difficult for the EU to have a common position until the end of the conference, when the UK changed its position and joined the Like Minded Group of states. The shift was connected to the change in leadership in the UK in 1997 when the Conservative Party lost the election to the Labour Party under Tony Blair. France changed its position just before the final day of the conference, and only after obtaining concessions on the scope of the Court's jurisdiction.[167]

---

163 Article 2 of the Rome Statute provides that: 'The Court shall be brought into relationship with the United Nations through an agreement to be approved by the Assembly of States Parties to this Statute and thereafter concluded by the President of the Court on its behalf.'

164 UN Doc. A/58/318, 2004.

165 Richard J. Goldstone and Adam M. Smith, *International Judicial Institutions: The Architecture of International Justice at Home and Abroad* (Abingdon, Routledge, 2009), p. 111.

166 Groenleer and Van Schaik, 'United We Stand?', note 148, p. 977.

167 Scheffer, *All the Missing Souls*, note 9, p. 221; see also Fanny Benedetti and John L. Washburn, 'Drafting the International Criminal Court Treaty: Two Years to Rome and an Afterword on the Rome Diplomatic Conference' (1999) 5 *Global Governance* 1.

The different position between the EU and the US towards the Court was evident in 2001 and it complicated the role of the Office of the Prosecutor, as we shall see in the next chapter. When US Senator Jesse Helms was introducing a bill that led to the American Service-Members' Protection Act in 2001, the other side of the Atlantic was adopting an official common position in support of the Court. On 11 June 2001, the Council of the European Union adopted a common position whose objectives included 'to support the effective functioning of the Court and to advance universal support for it by promoting the widest possible participation in the Rome Statute'.[168] To this end, the EU adopted a variety of strategies to achieve the objectives of this common position. These included the provision of substantial financial support to the Court as a voluntary contributor.[169] Before Japan's ratification of the Rome Statute in 2007, the EU Member States were among the main funders of Court. The EU also mainstreamed the Court in its external policies. It included provisions related to the Court in the agreements it negotiated and entered into with third countries. For example, both the preamble and Article 11 of the 2005 revised Cotonou Agreement, the partnership agreement that was signed between the EU and more than 75 African, Caribbean and Pacific states, refer to the Court and require the third parties 'to take steps towards ratifying and implementing the Rome Statute and related instruments'.[170]

In 2009, Sudan refused to sign the revised Cotonou Agreement due to the clause that made reference to the ratification of the Rome Statute.[171] Consequently, it lost approximately €300 million pledged at the May 2008 Sudan Consortium for the period 2008–13 under the European Development Fund.[172] There are other African states that have managed to maintain their status as recipients of the European Development Fund despite having not ratified the Rome Statute. Mozambique is an example: it signed the Rome Statute in 2000, and the EU has been encouraging it to go a step further and ratify. Several recommendations for ratification have also been made through

---

168 Council Common Position 2003/444/CFSP on the International Criminal Court of 16 June 2003.

169 In 2009, the European Commission provided €879,020, in 2011 €1,037,639 and in 2012 €1,049,694; see International Criminal Court Status of Voluntary Contributions as at 31 December 2009, Schedule 6, ICC-ASP/9/13, p. 44; International Criminal Court Status of Voluntary Contributions as at 31 December 2011, Schedule 6, ICC-ASP/11/12, p. 38; and International Criminal Court Status of Voluntary Contributions as at 31 December 2012, Schedule 6, ICC-ASP/12/12, p. 38.

170 The Cotonou Agreement signed in Cotonou on 23 June 2000; revised in Luxembourg on 25 June 2005; revised in Ouagadougou on 22 June 2010, Art. 11(7).

171 European Commission (Com[2010])195 Final 2010/0104/NLE 'Proposal for Council Decision Concerning the Allocation of the funds decommitted from projects under the 9th and previous European Development Funds (EDF) for the purpose of addressing the needs of the most vulnerable population in Sudan (Brussels 3 May 2010).

172 Ibid.

the UN Universal Periodic Review process. Those who have been monitoring Mozambique's steps towards the ratification process note that the Mozambican authorities have been arguing that there are 'a number of legal obstacles needed to be clarified before ratification could took place, such as extradition, maximum prison sentences and amnesty polices'.[173] The fact that Mozambique continues to receive its share of the European Development Fund suggests that the EU is content with its steps towards ratification. Perhaps the major difference between Sudan and Mozambique is that the former completely discarded the possibility of signing the Cotonou Agreement. In general, the reality that the EU and its Member States are the main financial supporters of the Court, host the Court and act as the *de facto* public relations arm of the Court has often been construed as diluting the Court's ability to be objective and independent when selecting possible targets for investigations.

The Assembly of States Parties, which is made up of all states that have ratified the Rome Statute, is the primary administrative body of the Court. It meets annually to address administrative issues, which include the adoption of the annual budget for the Court, and is also a forum for the adoption of amendments to the Statute and Rules of Procedure and Evidence.[174] For example, on 28 November 2013, it adopted (by consensus) a series of resolutions to amend Resolution ICC-ASP/12/Res 7 of the Rules of Procedure and Evidence. The preamble to the resolution points out that the amendments are to enhance the efficiency and effectiveness of the Court. The adopted amendments cover three areas: first, the place of proceedings; second, the use of prior recorded testimony; and, third, permitting those accused and subjected to summons to attend trial through the use of video technology.

The Court has been criticised for both a lack of efficiency and effectiveness. For example, there is a growing a perception that its proceedings are deliberately lengthy to complete a full judicial cycle. By 2016, only three cases – Lubanga, Katanga and Ngudjlo – had completed the full judicial cycle.[175] On efficiency and the measure of how economically the resources (both financial and human) that are available to the Court have been converted to results, the Court has been found wanting and has come under pressure to improve. This is primary because, between 2004 and 2016, its accumulated budget reached €1.3 billon, and yet the only concrete results it could show for this were three completed cases.

173 Email exchange with EU delegate in Mozambique, 17 February 2016.

174 Schabas, *An Introduction to the International Criminal Court*, note 3, p. 390.

175 Lubanga was convicted on 14 March 2012 and sentenced to 14 years' imprisonment on 10 July 2012; in 2015, the Appeals Chamber unanimously decided against a reduction of his sentence pursuant to the review conducted under Art. 110(3) of the Rome Statute. See *Lubanga* (ICC-01/04/01/06), Decision on the Review Concerning Reduction of Sentence of Mr Thomas Lubanga Dyilo, 22 September 2015.

In response to the call for increased efficiency and effectiveness, the Court and the Assembly of States Parties have taken several steps, including, as we have seen, amending the Rules of Procedure and Evidence. More proposals for amendments are in the pipeline, including a reduction in the number of judges who preside over Article 70 offences at the pre-trial, trial and appeals states. The President of the International Criminal Court, Judge Fernández de Gurmendi, considers such amendments to be critical in addressing the shortage of judges to oversee other cases.

Article 70 offences, which are primarily offences of contempt of court, appear to be on the increase and are putting a strain of the available judges, as well as taking up judicial time.[176] The discussion on the Court's efficiency and effectiveness reflects the crisis of expectations that the Court is facing. The Court seems to be ready to embrace the challenge for it to increase its efficiency and effectiveness, as is evident from the proposed amendments regarding victim participation and the time that the Trial Chamber should take to render its verdict on guilt or innocence. Still, these efforts seems to be geared towards achieving internal accountability, perhaps with the assumption that once there is efficiency and effectiveness, the Court will gain political support for its work. If so, it is hard to imagine how the claims of selective enforcement would be resolved by focusing solely on efficiency and effectiveness.

As such, an additional criterion might be necessary. For instance the impact that the Court is having in the fight against impunity could be added, as this would give the outsiders a view of its work and the transformation that it might be causing. The criterion, which focuses on both the positive and negative changes produced by the Court's interventions, whether directly or indirectly, intended or unintended, could be useful in establishing some form of accountability towards the broader international community, including the victims of international crimes. At the same time, those critical of the Court's efficiency and effectiveness should take into consideration the fact that over the past decade, the Court was in its formative stages and the focus was on opening field bases in situation countries, establishing new systems including new premises, hence the financial costs were inevitably high. Second, there is also need to acknowledge that external factors such as the level and quality of state cooperation have a direct impact on the Court's performance, especially in terms of delivering proceedings in an expeditious manner.

---

176 *Situation in the Republic of Kenya* (ICC-01/09-01/13), *In the Case of the Prosecutor v. Walter Osapiri Basara*, Warrant of Arrest for Walter Osapiri Basara. 2 August 2013 [Wanted for allegations concerning Art. 70 (1)(c) offence of Corruptly influencing a witness and also *Situation in the Republic of Kenya* (ICC-01/09-01/15*). In the Case of the Prosecutor v. Paul Gicheru and Philip Kipkoech Bett*; Decision on the Prosecutor's Application under Art. 58(1) of the Rome Statute, 10 March 2015.

2.4. THE SEAT OF THE COURT

The Hague is the 'seat of the Court', although it may sit elsewhere in the territory of any state party or by special agreement in the territory of any other state.[177] Article 62 of the Statute provides that 'unless otherwise decided, the place of the trial shall be the seat of the Court'. The provision under Article 62 is primarily concerned with the place of trial, while Rule 100 provides additional guidance on its application. Rule 100 has already been amended to add clarity on its practical application by the Trial Chamber, a subject that will be discussed later in this book.[178]

In The Hague, the Court joins the family of other international justice institutions such as the International Court of Justice, the International Criminal Tribunal for the former Yugoslavia, the Appeals Chamber of the International Criminal Tribunal for Rwanda and the Special Tribunal for Lebanon. In 2015, the Court shifted from its temporary premises into permanent premises, which cost an estimated €204 million. This is expected to give the Court permanency and is perhaps a clear signal and confirmation to its distractors that it is, in fact, a permanent institution that is going to be a part of the global governance system.

There is little doubt that the presence of such a magnitude of international justice institutions in The Hague has some historical significance, considering that it is where the Hague Peace Conference was held in 1899 and subsequently where the Permanent Court of Arbitration was established. Still, one would have thought that for an institution purely established for international criminal law, either Nuremburg or London would have also been fit to be the seat of the Court, considering their role in the early development of international criminal jurisdiction after the Second World War. It was in London that the London Conference was held between June and August 1945, which adopted the Charter of the International Military Tribunal, and the Nazi leadership was put to trial in Nuremburg, 'The City of the Nazi Party Rallies', where the Palace of Justice is located. Perhaps a seat in either of these two cities would have reinforced the didactic role of the Court and international criminal law. However, the government of the Netherlands demonstrated its commitment to international justice by offering The Hague, known as the city of peace and justice, as the seat for the Court.[179] Schabas notes that the decision to make The Hague the seat of the Court was not hard to make since the Netherlands was the only state that offered to take it.[180]

---

177 Rome Statute, Art. 3.

178 *Official Records*, Assembly of States Parties to the Rome Statute of the International Criminal Court, Twelfth Session The Hague (ICC-ASP/12/20), 20–28 November 2003, *Amendments to the Rules of Procedure and Evidence*, Resolution ICC-ASP/12/Res 7.

179 Schabas, *An Introduction to the International Criminal Court*, note 3, p. 369.

180 Schabas, *The International Criminal Court: A Commentary on the Rome Statute*, note 61, p. 87.

CHAPTER 3

THE OFFICE OF THE PROSECUTOR AND THE POLITICS OF SELECTING TARGETS FOR PROSECUTION

The Chief Prosecutor of the Court heads the Office of the Prosecutor and is elected by the Assembly of States Parties for a nine-year term; the first to hold the office was Argentine lawyer Luis Gabriel Moreno Ocampo (2003–12). Initially Moreno Ocampo was nominated by the US to be the chief prosecutor for the International Criminal Tribunal for the former Yugoslavia. The Argentine government opposed him because at the time of his nomination, he belonged to the opposition party.[181] In 2011, the Assembly of States Parties unanimously elected Moreno Ocampo's deputy, Fatou Bensouda, a Gambian lawyer, to take over from her former boss.

The Office of the Prosecutor is responsible for receiving referrals and any substantiated information on crimes within the jurisdiction of the Court, before examining them for conducting investigations and prosecutions before the Court.[182] Its role is also to initiate investigations *proprio motu*, on the basis of information on crimes within the jurisdiction of the Court,[183] and this role is subject to judicial review by the Pre-Trial Chamber. Article 53(1) states that the Office of the Prosecutor shall, having evaluated the available information, initiate an investigation unless it determines that there is no reasonable basis upon which to proceed under the Statute.[184] The underlying assumption is that once a situation has been triggered by either a state party or the UN Security Council, the Chief Prosecutor is obliged to initiate an investigation and prosecution.

The factors that the Office of the Prosecutor has to consider when determining whether or not to open investigations are: (a) whether there is a reasonable basis to believe that a crime within the jurisdiction of the Court has been, or

---

181 David J. Scheffer, 'Symposium on "The ICTY 10 Years on: The View from Inside" – Three Memories from the Year of Origin, 1993' (2004) 2 *Journal of International Criminal Justice* 353, p. 353.

182 Rome Statute, Art. 42.

183 Marston Danner, 'Enhancing the Legitimacy and Accountability of Prosecutorial Discretion at the International Criminal Court', note 82, 515.

184 Rome Statute, Art. 53(1). See also Schabas, *The International Criminal Court: A Commentary on the Rome Statute*, note 61, pp. 655–71.

is being, committed;[185] (b) whether the case is, or would be, admissible under Article 17;[186] and (c) the gravity of the crime, the interests of victims and whether there are substantial reasons to believe that an investigation would not serve the interests of justice. These factors constitute the legal framework that the Office of the Prosecutor is expected to apply during its preliminary examinations.[187]

In a keynote address at an international conference, 'Building a Future on Peace and Justice', held in Nuremberg in June 2007, Moreno Ocampo stressed: 'I was given a clear judicial mandate. My duty is to apply the law without political considerations.'[188] He went on to say that 'there can be no political compromise on legality and accountability'.[189] There can be no doubt that at this conference, he came across as a true high priest of the legal positivist philosophy of international criminal law. He attempted to place the law above politics and all other objectives of the international community, such as establishing peace and security, providing humanitarian assistance, promoting political dialogue between the parties to the conflict and preparation for reconstruction and development.

The positivist approach Moreno Ocampo showed in his speech is also reflected in the Office of the Prosecutor's Policy Paper, issued in September 2007, which states that the broader matter of international peace and security is not the responsibility of the Prosecutor, but rather falls within the mandate of other institutions.[190] This is rather curious because the Preamble of the Rome Statute states that the drafters recognised that grave crimes threaten the peace and security, and the wellbeing of the world. The rationale behind the UN Security Council being given a role to refer situations to the Court under Chapter VII was that the Court could contribute to the maintenance of international peace and security.

By denying the link or the potential influence of politics in the functioning of the Court and the Office of the Prosecutor in particular, the Prosecutor

---

185 In *Situation in the Republic of Kenya* (ICC-01/09-19-Corr) Decision Pursuant to Articlr 15 of the Rome Statute on the African Union authorization of an Investigation into the Situation in the Republic of Kenya, 31 March 2010, para. 35, the Pre-Trial Chamber interpreted 'reasonable basis' to mean 'a sensible or reasonable justification for a belief that a crime falling within the jurisdiction of the Court has been or is being committed'.

186 In the context of a preliminary examination or investigation phase, the Court would have not yet identified a single case, hence commentators and the Office of the Prosecutor have interpreted the phases as situations and not cases, for detailed discussion see Schabas, *The International Criminal Court: A Commentary on the Rome Statute*, note 61, p. 660; and also Office of the Prosecutor, 'Policy Paper on Preliminary Examinations', November 2013, p. 10.

187 Office of the Prosecutor, 'Policy Paper on Preliminary Examinations', November 2013.

188 Luis Moreno Moreno Ocampo, 'Building a Future on Peace and Justice: The International Criminal Court' in Kai Ambos, Judith Large and Marieke Wierda (eds.)(eds.), *Building a Future on Peace and Justice Studies on Transitional Justice, Peace and Development The Nuremberg Declaration on Peace and Justice* (New York, Springer, 2007), p. 11.

189 Ibid, p. 12.

190 Office of the Prosecutor, 'Policy Paper on the Interests of Justice', September 2007, p. 5.

misjudged the context in which he was operating and perhaps this left him less prepared for the challenges he later encountered. A simple reflection on the debates at the Rome Conference should have provided the Prosecutor with some basic cues that his role was not to be taken lightly and was, above all else, political. The states' political diversity and religious cultures, combined with a lack of consensus on certain elements of the Rome Statute, meant that from the onset, the presence of politics in the enforcement of international criminal law was inescapable. The Office of the Prosecutor had to work with that reality, considering that, by their nature, the crimes under the jurisdiction of the Court are political and are different from those handled by domestic criminal justice systems.

Against this background, this chapter seeks to explore whether or not there is an interaction between politics and prosecutions in the context of the claims that the Court's criminal justice mission has been politicised and favours the politically powerful. It seeks to evaluate whether it is helpful to deny the link between politics and international criminal justice or whether it is better to accept it as a reality and explore ways in which the two can be faithful partners to each other in the struggle against impunity.

This chapter attempts to argue that the fact that the Court is itself a mechanism that was established following political compromises made by more than 100 states and NGOs means that it is inevitable that the actions of the Office of the Prosecutor and the entire Court will either be influenced by politics or will generate political debates. Since the overall thrust of this book is the selective enforcement of international criminal law by the Court, the focus in this chapter will be limited to the role of the Office of the Prosecutor in the selection of situations for investigation and prosecution, and not necessarily the specific cases themselves. The Court has been criticised for playing a covert game of politics both when exercising jurisdiction and when it has chosen not to do so.[191]

Jean Ping, a Gabonese diplomat, speaking in 2011 in his capacity as the Chair of the AU Commission, said that the court is 'discriminatory' because it only goes after crimes committed in Africa, while ignoring crimes by the Western powers in Iraq, Afghanistan and Pakistan.[192] The claim reflects the the saying attributed to an ancient Greek philosopher, Solon, that 'Written laws are like spiders' webs, and will like them only entangle and hold the poor and weak, while the rich and powerful will easily break through them.'[193]

---

191 See Diane Marie Amann, 'Politics and Prosecutions: Form Katherine Fite to Fatou Bensouda' in Elizabeth Andersen and David M. Crane (eds.)(eds.), *Proceedings of the Fifth International Humanitarian Law Dialogs, American Society of International Law Chautauqua Institution 28–30, 2011*, vol 44 (Washington DC, American Society of International Law, 2012), p. 34.

192 Scott Stearns, 'African Union Says ICC Prosecutions are Discrimintatory' *Voice of America* (4 July 2011).

193 *Hoyt's New Cyclopedia of Practical Quotations*, Funk & Wagnalls, New York, London, 1922; Bartleby.com, 2009. www.bartleby.com/7).

3.1. THE US'S PARANOIA OVER THE POLITICISATION OF THE COURT AND ITS POSSIBLE IMPACT ON THE PROSECUTORIAL STRATEGY

The inclusion in the Rome Statute of an independent prosecutor with the power to commence investigations *proprio motu* was celebrated as a salutary development in the global fight against impunity.[194] In general, expectations were high that, when unleashed, the Prosecutor's powers would ensure that the impunity gap for powerful rulers and military juntas everywhere in the world would be closed. The Prosecutor could act as long as there was evidence of crimes within the jurisdiction of the Court being committed.[195] This decision was considered to be 'the only truly effective method to ensure that all cases which should be brought before the court be brought'.[196]

What was perhaps overlooked was that the divisions that were manifested during the negotiating process of the Rome Statute somehow had a knock-on effect in terms of how the Office of the Prosecutor was to carry out its mandate. As will be discussed in this section, on the one hand, the opposition of the US to an independent prosecutor and the subsequent anti-court crusade it launched under President George W. Bush meant that the Prosecutor had to try to quietly avoid any confrontation with the US, as this would have threatened the very existence of the then-embryonic Court. Therefore, the strategy was primarily to ensure that the Court survived the onslaught from the US. However, it was probably a more cordial relationship than one might expect as the US had previously supported Moreno Ocampo when he was in line for a job at the International Criminal Tribunal for the former Yugoslavia.

The contribution of the US towards the establishment of international criminal jurisdiction that made it possible to prosecute international criminals is evident in the role it played in the establishment of the International Criminal Tribunal for the former Yugoslavia, the International Criminal Tribunal for Rwanda, the Special Court for Sierra Leone and the Special Tribunal for Lebanon. However, all these tribunals are what some commentators would consider to be 'safe tribunals',[197] in that they were designed in such a way that they were unlikely to end up investigating or prosecuting the nationals of those states that had designed them as they were not given the jurisdiction to do so.

The US played a pivotal role in the negotiations leading to the adoption of the Rome Statute. In fact, during the Rome Conference, its 50-member

---

194 Marston Danner, 'Enhancing the Legitimacy and Accountability of Prosecutorial Discretion at the International Criminal Court', note 82, 515.

195 Rome Statute, Art. 15.

196 Amnesty International, 'The International Criminal Court: 16 Fundamental Principles for a Just, Fair and Effective International Criminal Court', 1 May 1998, IOR 40/012/1998.

197 Robert Cryer, *Prosecuting International Crimes*, note 46, p. 233.

delegation – which included career diplomats, lawyers, scholars and military personnel – made it the one of the largest groups at the Rome Conference. However, throughout the negotiating process, the US took issue with one aspect of the jurisdiction of the Court – a completely independent prosecutor who could open investigations on nationals of non-states parties. David Scheffer, an American lawyer and diplomat who served as the first US Ambassador-at-Large for War Crimes Issues under President Bill Clinton, headed the US delegation. He noted in his memoirs that as early as March 1995, there were debates unfolding in Washington over whether or not the US should insist that the consent of the state of nationality of the accused should be obtained before the Court could prosecute him or her.[198] In the end, the US delegation settled for the requirement that the consent of state of nationality of the accused be obtained, unless the situation was referred to the Court by the UN Security Council. The US was alone on this issue. In fact, France had submitted the so-called state consent regime proposal to the Preparatory Committee in August 1996.[199] The regime required that all states affected by the core crimes under the jurisdiction of the Court had to give their consent in every individual case and regarding every suspect. The states in question included the territorial state where atrocities are committed, the state of nationality of the victim, the state of nationality of the suspect and the custodial state.

Hans-Peter Kaul, a German international law scholar and former diplomat who attended the Rome Conference and in 2003 was elected as the first German judge of the Court, found this approach to be sovereignty-oriented and restrictive. Although the proposal was no longer relevant by the time of the Rome Conference in 1998, the US still insisted on its demand that in the event of a state party referral or the Office of the Prosecutor commencing investigations *proprio motu*, the consent of the state of nationality of the suspect was required. The failure of the Conference to grant this demand formed the basis for the US opposition to the Court. The rationale behind the opposition of the US is incomprehensible and contradicts the existing rules of international treaty law and state practice. For example, there is international rule that permits states other than the state of nationality of the accused to investigate and prosecute terrorists and also core crimes, which are under the jurisdiction of the Court. In addition, succumbing to such demands would have eroded the philosophical underpinnings behind the establishment of the Court, which was to counter the inherent scepticism over the willingness of member states to prosecute their nationals for international core crimes.[200]

198 Scheffer, *All the Missing Souls*, note 9, p. 176.

199 Hans-Peter Kaul, 'Precondition to the Exercise of Jurisdiction' in Antonio Cassese, Paula Gaeta and John R.W.D. Jones (eds.)(eds.), *The Rome Statute of the International Criminal Court: A Commentary*, vol. 1B (Oxford, Oxford University Press), p. 594.

200 Ibid, p. 590; and McCormack, 'Their Atrocities and Our Misdemeanours', note 108, (eds.) pp. 107–47.

The US maintained its position throughout the negotiations and justified it on the basis of 'exceptionalism'. Kaul links this exceptionalism to the fact that the US considers itself to have worldwide responsibilities to help maintain international peace and security; therefore, it needs to protect its forces against politically motivated accusations, frivolous or arbitrary charges and other forms of investigation undertaken without its explicit consent.[201] Alongside this vision of the Court, the US wanted the UN Security Council to be the sole entity with referral power, contingent on the possible veto of one of the permanent members,[202] thus, in effect, allowing it to veto any referrals likely to affect US national interests – a position also shared by the other permanent members.

In general, the permanent members of the UN Security Council were concerned that the new court would impede their collective duty to take action to maintain world peace and order. Therefore, their vision of the new court was 'closer to a permanent *ad hoc* tribunal of the Security Council than to an independent international judicial institution'.[203] This vision led them to oppose giving power to the Prosecutor to trigger the jurisdiction of the Court.

Until the final day of the Rome Conference, the US maintained its position that Article 12 which governs the necessary preconditions for the exercise of jurisdiction should be worded in such a way that both the state of the territory where the crime is committed and the state of nationality of the accused would need to be party to the Statute before the Court could exercise jurisdiction. Scheffer told the delegates at the conference that 'we have a simple and reasonable proposal for [Article 12]. In Section 2 of [Article 12], we propose deleting the four words, "one or more of," in the second line'.[204] The four words that the US wanted deleted were ones that gave the Court jurisdiction over nationals of non-states parties if they committed international crimes in the territory of a state party. Their removal would have meant that the Court could only exercise its jurisdiction when both the territorial state and the state of which the suspect was a national were states parties.

In one of the last attempts by the US to achieve the accommodation of its concerns, it submitted a proposal seeking the exclusion from the jurisdiction of the Court of all acts committed in the course of official duties and acknowledged by the sending state as such.[205] The proposal was defeated resoundingly with 113 delegations supporting no action, 17 delegations opposing no action and 25 delegations abstaining. Commentators pointed out that agreeing to the US proposals seeking to allow the states of nationality of the accused to decide whether its nationals would be prosecuted would have been a regression from

---

201 Kaul, 'Precondition to the Exercise of Jurisdiction', note 194, p. 601.

202 Scheffer, *All the Missing Souls*, note 9, p. 178.

203 Benedettii and Washburn, 'Drafting the International Criminal Court Treaty', note 162, p. 18.

204 Scheffer, *All the Missing Souls*, note 9, p. 223.

205 UN Doc. A/CONF.183/C.I/L.90, 16 July 1998.

the Nuremburg principle that an individual cannot find immunity behind the veil of the state.[206]

A group of states, which also shared the US's opposition to Article 12, resisted the idea of an independent prosecutor on the grounds that it would be unwise to grant the Prosecutor the right to initiate investigations as this would make the Prosecutor a human rights ombudsman, who could respond to complaints from any source.[207] The US felt that such a decision was premature and that it would be better for the Prosecutor to have 'maximum independence and discretion in prosecuting cases referred by States Parties or the U.N. Security Council'.[208] What the US wanted was a court under the control of the UN Security Council.[209] This would have ensured that, through the Security Council, the US would be able to influence how the Court exercised its jurisdiction – just as it had done with the *ad hoc* tribunals.

At the end of the Rome Conference, the Rome Statute was adopted, but through a vote rather than by general consensus, majoritarian democracy winning the day. The assumption was that the Rome Statute reflected the will of the 120 states, and perhaps that the views and values of the minority states that had either voted against or abstained need not be considered. The lack of consensus exposed divisions within the delegations and, as it turned out, was to have a significant impact on how the Court was to function. The US delegation felt that the Statute had flaws and it 'represented a political compromise of fundamental issues of international criminal law and international peace and security'.[210] It objected to the Court exercising jurisdiction over the nationals of non-states parties without the consent of those states.

In the aftermath of the Rome Conference, in the US there was bipartisan opposition to an independent prosecutor for the Court. For example, during a hearing before the Sub-Committee on International Operations of the Committee on Foreign Relations, Republican Senator Rod Grams of Minnesota submitted that the International Criminal Court was not only bad, but also dangerous to the national interests of the US. He was concerned that giving the Prosecutor the power to initiate prosecutions without referral from the UN Security Council or states parties would mean that there would 'be no effective screen against politically motivated prosecutions from being brought forward'.[211] At the same

---

206 Bruce Broomhall, *International Justice and the International Criminal Court: Between Sovereignty and the Rule of Law* (Oxford, Oxford University Press, 2003), p. 143.

207 UN Doc. A/Conf.183/SR.5, para. 60.

208 Ibid.

209 David Scheffer, 'The United States and the International Criminal Court' (1999) 93 *Journal of International Law* 12, p. 13.

210 Ibid, p. 17.

211 See the remarks by Senator Rod Grams in 'Is a UN International Criminal Court in the U.S. National Interest?', US Senate Hearing 105–724 (S. Hrg.105-724) Hearing before the

hearing, Scheffer added that an independent Prosecutor 'would embroil the Court in controversy political decision making, and confusion'.[212]

The first review of the Statute came in 2010 at the Kampala Review Conference, where many of the initial concerns of the US were accommodated. For example, in the case of the crime of aggression, the Prosecutor cannot exercise his powers to initiate investigations against the nationals of non-states parties – including the US. The implication here is that although US nationals could be investigated for crimes such as genocide, war crimes and crimes against humanity if they were to commit such crimes in the territory of a state party, none of its nationals would be prosecuted for aggression so long as it remains a non-state party. It seems that the main cause of the friction between the US and the Court was not the independent powers of the prosecutors to initiate investigations, but the extension of this to non-states parties.

The US came away from the Kampala Review Conference with its concerns satisfied. In 2010, US Ambassador-at-Large for War Crime issues, Stephen Rapp, said:

> Thus far, this court had been appropriately focused. The cases that it has taken up in Northern Uganda involving Joseph Kony and the crimes of the Lord's Resistance [Army] in the DRC, the various militia groups that have engaged in campaigns of mass atrocities in Darfur, Sudan and in the Central African Republic were cases that cried out for justice and accountability and for the protection of the victims.[213]

It is hard to see how it could be said that the Court's focus was appropriate when it focused on Africa to the apparent exclusion of Afghanistan and Iraq, where the US and the UK were accused of committing atrocity crimes. Such discrepancies in the Prosecutor's prosecutorial strategy have invited the accusation that it is discriminatory. However, given the general friction between the US and the Court, it is highly likely that political considerations were factored into the Prosecutor's failure to officially open investigations in Afghanistan. It can be argued that, by focusing on Africa and not immediately doing so on Afghanistan, the Prosecutor made a political decision – the exact issue the US had highlighted during the negotiation process – but this time was acting in favour of US interests.

Subcommittee on International Operations of the Committee on Foreign Relations, United States Senate, One Hundred Fifth Congress, Second Session, 23 July 1998.

212 See the statement by David Scheffer in ibid.

213 Council on Foreign Relations, 'Koh and Rapp's Remarks on U.S. Engagement in the International Criminal Court and the Outcome of the ICC Assembly of States Parties Conference' (Harold Hongju Koh, Legal Advisor US Department of State; and Stephen J. Rapp, Ambassador-at Large for War Crimes Issues, Remarks at a Press Conference (Washington, DC, 15 June 2010).

3.2. THE EU, THE PROVISION OF POLITICAL LEADERSHIP AND FINANCIAL STABILITY TO THE COURT, AND THE IRAQ PROBLEM

On the other side of the Atlantic, Western European governments, with their dynamic international human rights organisations, had worked tirelessly to ensure that the Prosecutor was independent and could open investigations as necessary. In addition, the EU had supported the Court in the face of the onslaught from the US. This created situation where, in effect, the Court and the Office of the Prosecutor were indebted to both the EU and the global civil society and may have wished to either avoid upsetting them by recklessly opening investigations or to demonstrate quickly that their support was not in vain. In view of all these competing pressures, the Prosecutor ended up having a soft landing in Africa, where the Court was initially received with much enthusiasm.

If the Prosecutor made the decision to prolong the official opening of investigations *proprio motu* in Afghanistan was to avoid a possible confrontation with the US, a similar analogy is possible with regard to the Court's failure to intervene and open investigations into the allegations that British troops committed war crimes in Iraq. The difference is that in Iraq, those involved did not threaten to invade the Netherlands in order to liberate their nationals from the Court, as the US did. As this brief section will discuss, the Prosecutor appears to have developed cold feet with regard to opening investigations in Iraq out of pragmatism – doing so would have antagonised the UK, one of the key supporters of the Court. This avoidance strategy may not hold up under the considerable and persistent pressure to officially open investigations for torture crimes committed during the 2003 invasion of Iraq.

In the history and politics of the establishment of the Court, the role and influence of the EU – or more specifically the Western European states – is crucial. To some extent, the EU's support of the Court contributed to its rapid creation and subsequent resilience, especially in the face of aggressive attacks from the US and then later the AU. One commentator pointed out that the success of the Court and the Prosecutor depends heavily on their 'core constituency (Western European states and international human rights non-governmental organisations), while at same time avoiding confrontation with the United States and – to a lesser degree – Russia and China'.[214] With the US pleased with the Prosecutor's avoidance of areas where it was vulnerable, the next issue was how to please the Western European states, either individually or collectively. It can be argued that the Prosecutor managed to do this by avoiding opening investigations in Iraq against the British military for alleged torture crimes.

214 Luc Reydams and Jan Wouters (eds.)(eds.), *International Prosecutors* (Oxford, Oxford University Press, 2012), p. 72.

The inaction in this case has been repeatedly highlighted by those critical of the Court as reflecting double standards and the discriminatory enforcement of international criminal law.

First, it is important to highlight that the majority of the Western European states – especially those that are members of the EU – campaigned tirelessly for the establishment of an effective and independent permanent international criminal court. During the negotiations, the majority were at the core part of what Schabas describes as a geographically heterogeneous caucus of states, the Like Minded Group,[215] which by the end of the Rome Conference comprised more than 60 of the 160 participating states, including Belgium, Italy, Germany, Ireland, Liechtenstein, the Netherlands, Portugal, Spain and the UK.[216]

Although the members of the group did not agree on every issue that was under negotiation, its members remained committed to the success of the Rome Conference. However, on a few occasions, its position clashed with those of the five permanent members of the UN Security Council, such as its call for the Court to have a jurisdictional regime based on some form of universal jurisdiction, whereas the permanent members of the UN Security Council wanted the Security Council to be given a central role in the filtering or blocking of cases.[217] The US evaluated the proposal to grant the Prosecutor the right to initiate investigations as 'unrealistic, unwise and likely leading to politically motivated prosecutions',[218] while the Like Minded Group (with the enthusiastic support of NGOs) considered such a proposal to be a cornerstone of the independence of the Court.[219]

Some of the common positions of the Like Minded Group included support for the full cooperation by states with the Court, the prompt creation of an independent and effective court, and the power of the Court to make the final decision regarding whether to proceed with a case.[220]

One theory put forward to explain the EU's interest in the establishment of the Court and its success was that the region desired for 'international actorness'[221] – in other words, for the EU to be seen as a global actor. The Court is one of the few issues within the EU's Common Foreign Security Policy on

---

215 Philippe Kirsch and John T. Holmes, 'The Rome Conference on an International Criminal Court: The Negotiating Process' (1999) 93 *American Journal of International Law* 2, 4.

216 See Schabas, *An Introduction to the International Criminal Court*, note 3, p. 18.

217 Hans-Peter Kaul, 'Preconditions to the exercise of Jurisdiction' in Cassese et al. (eds.), *The Rome Statute of the International Criminal Court: A Commentary*, note 94, vol. 1B, p. 585.

218 Statement by Bill Richardson, on Behalf of the United States, to the Rome Conference, 17 June 1998.

219 Philippe Kirsch and Darryl Robinson, 'Initiation of Proceedings by the Prosecutor' in Cassese et al. (eds.), *The Rome Statute of the International Criminal Court: A Commentary*, note 94, vol. 1A, (eds.)659.

220 See Schabas, *An Introduction to the International Criminal Court*, note 3, p. 19; and Benedettii and Washburn, 'Drafting the International Criminal Court Treaty', note 162, p. 21.

221 Groenleer and Van Schaik, 'United We Stand?', note 148, p. 970.

which its Member States agree and can demonstrate cohesion.[222] In addition, the support is attributed to the fact that the guiding principles and interests of the Court correspond with those of the EU, which is founded on the values of freedom, democracy, respect for human rights and an international agenda that emphasises international institutions and multilateralism.[223] The Court was a good tool that the EU could use to shape globalisation in the interests of all its citizens, based on its own common values and principles.

This commitment to the Court can be seen through the fact that the EU, along with Canada, provided the bulk of the funds to the Trust created by the UN Secretary-General that enabled the participation of 50 of the least developed countries in the work of the Preparatory Committee and the Rome Conference.[224] After the Conference, the EU and its Member States adopted a dual strategy of diplomacy and advocacy to promote the Statute and the Court, unanimously adopting a Common Position on the International Criminal Court, concluding an agreement on cooperation and assistance with the Court, and making reference to the ratification of the Rome Statute in bilateral agreements with third parties.

Finally, the EU ensured that the Court could not easily be outlawed by advocating that the UN Security Council implement the recommendations contained in the Cassese Inquiry, which was set up to address the accountability problems in Darfur, Sudan. The recommendations included referral of the situation in Darfur to the Court. As will be discussed later, the US had preferred and supported the establishment of an African tribunal to investigate and prosecute those suspected of committing crimes in Darfur. This was an expression of its discomfort with taking any steps that could have been viewed as supporting or legitimising the Court. The US was not ready to back a UN Security Council resolution referring Sudan to the Court.[225] However, in the end, the UN Security Council referred the situation in Darfur to the Court, thereby officially acknowledging and legitimising the Court as an international player. Since then, the Security Council has made another referral, in the case of Libya, to the Court, thus making it hard for the Court to be marginalised.

---

222 Ibid, p. 977.

223 Salla Garsky, 'Strong, Independent, and Effective: The European Union's Promotion of the International Criminal Court' in Astrid Boening, Jan-Frederik Kremer and Aukje van Loon (eds.)(eds.), *Global Power Europe, Vol 2: Policies, Actions and Influence of the EU's External Relations* (New York, Springer, 2013), p. 4.

224 Report of the Preparatory Committee on the Establishment of an International Criminal Court, UN Doc. A/CONF.183/2, 14 April 1998, para. 17, which names the following European states as the main contributors to the Trust Fund: Belgium, Canada, Denmark, Finland, Netherlands, Norway, Sweden and the United Kingdom of Great Britain and Northern Ireland. See also ibid, p. 7.

225 John P. Cerone, 'US Attitudes Towards International Criminal Courts and Tribunals' in Cesare P.R. Romano (ed.), *The Sword and the Scales the United States and International Courts and Tribunals* (Cambridge, Cambridge University Press, 2009).

In 2015, the EU Council welcomed the AU's decision to establish a hybrid court in South Sudan to investigate and prosecute atrocity crimes committed during the civil war that broke out in 2013.[226] The decision suggests that there is a shift in the stance of the EU towards its preference for the Court as the primary key player for international accountability of atrocity crimes. The shift could be attributed to the realisation that the Court is overwhelmed or that the chances of a UN Security Council referral for South Sudan were slim. It could also be the case that the EU has come to realise that the UN Security Council referral resolutions, if they do come, lack the legal clarity to make any constructive contribution to ending impunity and the preservation of international peace and security in Darfur and Libya.

A combination of the EU's and its Member States' vigorous diplomatic defence of the Court and their provision of financial resources through NGOs has led some commentators to view the Court as a European Union Court.[227] Such a view might not be completely accurate considering that states' contributions to the Court are made based on 'an agreed scale of assessment, based on the scale adopted by the United Nations'.[228] The scale of assessment is calculated based on the capacity to pay which is reflected in the Gross National Income of states. As a result, there is a minimum amount set for the low-income states and maximum amount set for high-income states. This funding system differs from the multi-unit class systems, which as Schabas pointed out 'is a voluntary scheme by which States themselves determine the appropriate level of contribution that they wish to make'.[229] Still, one cannot rule out the fact that states that contribute the most are likely to use their economic power to influence either the decisions of the Court or to influence public opinion on their status as global actors. The US is usually accused of using its position as a state that contributes 22 per cent (the highest percentage) of the UN's budget in order to influence its policies. The graph below shows financial contribution of the four leading European financial supporters of the Court from 2005 to 2013 and confirms compliance with the United Nations scale of assessment adopted in the Rome Statute.

[226] *Council of the European Union*, Outcome of Proceedings South Sudan, Doc. 12886/15, Luxembourg, 12 October 2015.

[227] Groenleer and Van Schaik, 'United We Stand?', note 148, p. 978; and also David Hoile, '*The International Criminal Court' - 'Europe's Guantanamo Bay?*' (Africa Research Centre, 2010) p. 98.

[228] Rome Statute, Art. 117.

[229] Schabas, *The International Criminal Court: A Commentary on the Rome Statute*, note 61, p. 1153.

Figure 1. Four major European financial contributors to the Court (2005–13)

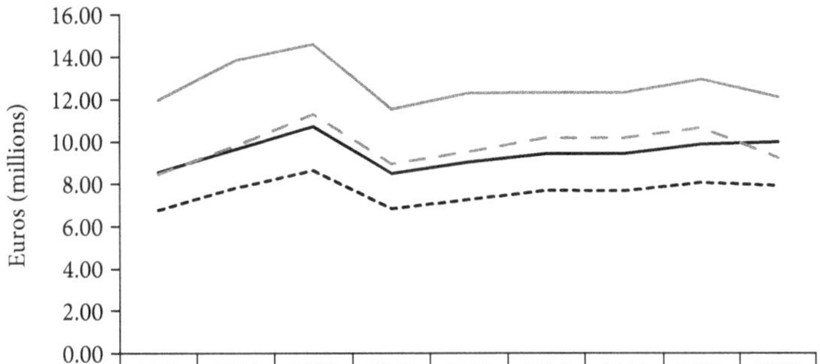

	2005	2006	2007	2008	2009	2010	2011	2012	2013
France	8.55	9.64	10.69	8.48	9.03	9.42	9.42	9.87	9.96
Germany	11.98	13.85	14.60	11.54	12.29	12.33	12.33	12.93	12.12
Italy	6.76	7.81	8.62	6.83	7.27	7.69	7.67	8.06	7.92
UK	8.47	9.80	11.27	8.94	9.51	10.16	10.16	10.65	9.22

Source: Annual Reports of the Committee on Budget and Finance.

The graph shows Germany is the highest contributor. In 2008, due to the effects of the global economic downturn, all the contributions significantly dropped.

Figure 2. Three major African financial contributors to the Court (2005–13)

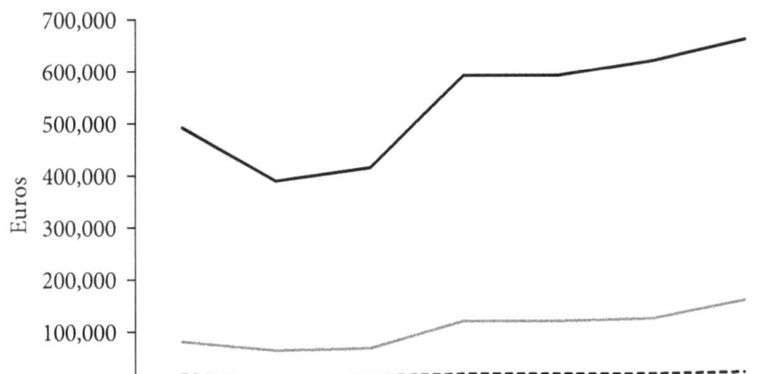

	2007	2008	2009	2010	2011	2012	2013
South Africa	491,923	390,212	415,436	592,423	592,200	620,738	662,378
Nigeria	81,422	64,586	68,762	120,023	119,978	125,160	160,217
Kenya	16,963	13,456	14,325	18,458	18,458	19,348	23,192

Source: Annual Reports of the Committee on Budget and Finance.

The graph shows African's major economic powerhouse and regional powers – South Africa, Nigeria and Kenya – maintained their contributions to the Court while the relationship between the Court and the AU was strained. Kenya has been notably consistent in its contributions and the controversy over the Court's investigation into and subsequent trial of Deputy President Ruto does not appear to have affected Kenya's contributions in the 2007–13 period.

While the Court exists and operates in such a divided world, Prosecutor Moreno Ocampo's suggestion that it is apolitical in relation to the enforcement of international criminal justice invites scepticism and even suggests some naïvety. In fact, other prosecutors have acknowledged that international criminal law is inherently political, warning: 'It is a naïve Chief Prosecutor who plans for, and executes, his prosecution plan (if he or she has one) without keeping in mind the bright, red thread of politics that permeates the entire existence of a tribunal or court.'[230] It is hard to deny that the establishment of the Court was in itself a politically complex diplomatic act.

3.2.1. MINDING THE BRIGHT RED THREAD OF POLITICS IN IRAQ

Indeed, although Prosecutor Moreno Ocampo claimed that his actions (including the selection of possible defendants) were apolitical and guided by purely judicial considerations, the reality suggests otherwise – particularly in relation to Iraq. By 2009, the Office of the Prosecutor had received more than 200 communications concerning the situation in Iraq, which had been invaded by the UK and the US. There was at least a convincing legal argument against launching investigations on the US that the Prosecutor explained in a letter issued on 9 February 2006 responding to the communications and explaining the decision not to launch any investigations. In brief, both Iraq and the US were, and still are, non-states parties; hence, the Court did not have straightforward jurisdiction.

That said, classified documents exposed by WikiLeaks suggest that Moreno Ocampo wished to 'dispose of Iraq issues' – in other words, 'not to investigate'.[231] A classified 2003 report by Clifton M Johnson, a Legal Counselor with the US Department of State, claims that:

> In semi-private forums and in private conversations reported to Embassy legal officers, Moreno Ocampo has indicated consistently that his initial investigative interests will focus not on Iraqi but on the situation in the Congo, including the potential involvement of Belgians with financial interests in the diamond industry, and Colombia.[232]

---

230 David M. Crane, 'The Bright Red Thread: The Politics of International Criminal Law – Do We Want Peace of Justice? The West African Experience' in Leila Nadya Sadat (ed.), *Forging a Convention for Crimes against Humanity* (Cambridge, Cambridge University Press, 2011), p. 59.

231 'ICC: A Cautious Beginning with Mixed Signals from the Prosecutor' WikiLeaks (15 July 2003), para.9.

232 Ibid.

Chief Prosecutor Moreno Ocampo was not the only one who preferred to dispose of the Iraq issues. Bruno Cathala, the first Registrar of the Court (2003–08), is reported to have told the US legal officer that it was important for the Court to dispose easily of 'silly things like Iraq'.[233] It is not clear how the situation was considered silly in comparison with the one in the the Democratic Republic of the Congo. Perhaps the fact that the remarks were made to a US official, the silliness of the situation in Iraq referred to here, was linked to the fact that the Court did not have jurisdiction over the US conduct in Iraq.This made the issue a non-starter hence 'silly' for the Court. It is worth noting that in private, the Prosecutor indicated his intention to focus on the Democratic Republic of the Congo, Belgium and Colombia. These situations belong to three different continents, an important fact if he had achieved this aim, thereby possibly showing some level of equality in the geographical distribution of investigations. This might have helped to create the impression that the Court was not focusing on just one specific geographical area: Africa.

Turning to the allegations made against the US, the Prosecutor's letter stated that: 'In accordance with Article 12, acts on the territory of a non-state party fall within the jurisdiction of the Court only when the person accused of the crime is a national of a State that has accepted jurisdiction (Article 12(2)(b)).'[234] In this regard, the Prosecutor applied the Rome Statute in a way that demonstrated his loyalty to the legal positivist perspective. Both the US and Iraq were, and are still, non-states parties to the Rome Statute, so the Court had no legal basis upon which to intervene. The Prosecutor reaffirmed that his position was not to make law, but rather to apply the law as outlined in the Rome Statute so as not to be seen as overly threatening to states. He adopted the same approach in his response to the initial 38 complaints concerning aggression in Iraq, noting that the Rome Statute prohibited him from exercising jurisdiction over aggression:

> Thirty-eight communications express the view that a crime of aggression took place in the context of the war in Iraq. The Court cannot exercise jurisdiction over alleged crimes of aggression until the crime is defined and the conditions for the exercise of jurisdiction are set out. The Assembly of States parties of the International Criminal Court may adopt such a provision at a review conference to be convened in 2009. Thus, the alleged crime to which these communications refer does not fall within the jurisdiction of the Court.[235]

The controversy seems to be linked to the Prosecutor's determination not to officially launch investigations on the basis of allegations of the wilful killing

233 Ibid.

234 Letter of Prosecutor dated 9 February 2006 (Iraq).

235 Press Release by the Prosecutor 'Communications Received by the Office of the Prosecutor of the ICC', 16 July 2003, p.2. See, https://www.icc-cpi.int/NR/rdonlyres/B080A3DD-7C69-4BC9-AE25-0D2C271A9A63/277502/16_july__english.pdf.

or inhuman treatment of civilians by British troops during the invasion and occupation of Iraq. After analysing the allegations, he concluded that it was reasonable to believe that crimes within the jurisdiction of the Court had been committed;[236] however, he suggested that the crimes did not meet the admissibility threshold in relation to gravity. In assessing gravity, he made reference to the number of victims (quantitative analysis), suggesting that the number of victims was far fewer than those of the long-running conflicts in Northern Uganda, the Democratic Republic of the Congo and Darfur. This approach has been criticised and we will undertake a detailed analysis of admissibility issues in Chapter 5.

In any case, the Prosecutor left the door open for the determination to be revisited when he stated:

> I wish to remind you, in accordance with Rule 49(2) of the Rules of Procedure and Evidence, that should you have additional information regarding crimes within the jurisdiction of the Court, you may submit it to the Office of the Prosecutor.

Indeed, on 10 January 2014, the European Centre for Constitutional and Human Rights (ECCHR) (an independent, non-profit legal and educational organisation based in Berlin, Germany), along with the Public Interest Lawyers, Birmingham (an international and domestic public law firm based the UK), responded to this invitation and provided the Office of the Prosecutor with additional information, requesting that the Prosecutor formally open investigations into the allegations that the British troops tortured civilians in Iraq.[237]

The 200-page communication dismisses the Prosecutor's previous determination and analysis of gravity as a criteria for not opening investigations. It also attempts to demonstrate that there is a chronic sense of impunity within the British army over torture crimes because they have either avoided or undergone less rigorous trials dating back to colonial times. They detailed additional cases to support their claim.[238]

In response, on 13 May 2014, the new Chief Prosecutor, Bensouda, issued a statement that her Office would reopen 'the preliminary examination of the situation in Iraq'.[239] The justification for reopening the case was that the 2014 communication contained additional information that 'was not available to

---

236 Letter of Prosecutor dated 9 February 2006 (Iraq).

237 European Center for Constitutional and Human Rights (ECCHR) and Public Interest Lawyers (PIL), *Communication to the Office of the Prosecutor of the International Criminal Court – The Responsibility of Officials of the United Kingdom for War Crimes Involving Systematic Detainee Abuse in Iraq from 2003–2008* (2014).

238 Ibid, p. 208.

239 Statement by the Prosecutor 'Prosecutor of the International Criminal Court, Fatou Bensouda, Re-opens the Preliminary Examination of the Situation in Iraq', 13 May 2014. See https://www.icc-cpi.int//Pages/item.aspx?name=otp-statement-iraq-13-05-2014.

the office in 2006'.[240] In September 2015, the Office of the Prosecutor received additional Article 15 communications from Public Interest Lawyers International, which included an expanded list of alleged crimes, such as the denial of fair trial and rape and sexual violence.[241] Based on the two communications, the Office of the Prosecutor has started the preliminary examination focusing first on establishing whether the crimes under the jurisdiction of the Court were committed in Iraq. According to the Office of the Prosecutor, it has been conducting: 'A thorough factual and legal assessment of the information received in order to establish whether there is a reasonable basis to belief that the alleged crimes fall within the subject-matter jurisdiction of the Court.'[242]

One would have expected that Office of the Prosecutor to follow up the preliminary examination conducted by the former Prosecutor and establish the gravity of the crimes, as that is why the investigation was suspended in the first place. That said, it seems that two possible factors influenced the Prosecutor to start the analysis anew.

The Prosecutor pointed out that the two new communications might have provided detailed information that was not available before and she has to ascertain the reliability of the information in the communications and the credibility of the sources that provided them. This was because the information presented by Public Interest Lawyers International was not generated through first-hand accounts by the victims, but was transmitted to the group through a third party, an agent who is based in Iraq. This presents a risk that false statements may be recorded, a situation not helped by the fact that the UK has paid compensation in previous torture cases. One cannot rule out that this compensation might have encouraged more Iraqis to come forward and have their testimonies recorded, some of which could be mere fabrications in an attempt to get a settlement from the UK – hence the need for the Office of the Prosecutor to proceed cautiously.

While avoiding being too speculative, the two separate communications are likely to land the Office of the Prosecutor in a legal and political minefield. Legally the communications are likely to test how the Office of the Prosecutor will interpret the complementarity principle, as the British government had demonstrated and maintains that it would seek to have the first bite of the apple through its own domestic proceedings.[243]

The primacy of the British justice system over the Court was debated in the UK House of Commons and was affirmed by the then Foreign Secretary, Robin

---

240 Ibid.

241 Office of the Prosecutor, 'Report on Preliminary Examination Activities', 12 November 2015, p. 7.

242 Office of the Prosecutor, 'Report on Preliminary Examination Activities', 12 November 2015, para. 39.

243 'William Hague Rejects Iraq "Abuse" Complaint to ICC' *BBC News* (12 January 2014).

Cook, during the Second Reading of the International Criminal Court Bill in 2001. At the time, Cook urged the Commons to have robust confidence that the British legal system would be able to satisfactorily demonstrate to the Court that any allegations were properly investigated: 'In short, British service personnel will never be prosecuted by the International Criminal Court because any *bona-fide* allegations will be pursued by the British authorities.'[244] When the issue was brought up again in 2005 in the House of Lords, the Labour government suggested that it would take a catastrophic failure within the UK justice systems for the Court to assume jurisdiction of British cases.[245] In 2016, during the second reading of the Armed Forces Bill in the Lords, Lord Thomas of Gresford a legal practitioner and the Chairman of the Association of Military Court Advocates, alluded to the same sentiments when making reference to the Office of the Prosecutor's preliminary examinations in Iraq. He told the Lords:

> Your Lordships should appreciate that it would be a terrible insult and slight upon our system if the International Criminal Court were to declare that this country is incapable of dealing with war crimes within our system.[246]

The communications have potentially set the Prosecutor on a collision course with the UK and have again raised the question of selective targeting. If the Prosecutor decides not to officially open investigations and does not provide a convincing legal basis for such a decision, then the critics of the Court will have more ammunition with which to attack the Court as biased against Africans and other politically weak states. In accordance with Article 17, the Prosecutor will have to demonstrate that the UK is unwilling and unable to prosecute potential suspects. Aware of its legal vulnerabilities and obligations under the Rome Statute, the UK invested a considerable amount of financial and human resources into addressing allegations against its service personnel in Iraq.

The UK efforts have included setting up commissions of inquiry such as the Baha Mousa Inquiry to investigate and report on the circumstances surrounding the death of Baha Mousa, an Iraqi national, and the treatment of those detained with him, which between 1 August 2008 and 31 January 2012 cost an estimated £12,900,000.[247] The UK government also set up the Al Sweady Inquiry, which investigated allegations of unlawful killing and ill-treatment of Iraqi nationals by British troops in Iraq in 2004. It also conducted investigations and prosecutions under the Army Act 1955 in the case *R v. Payne and others* through the military justice system and the establishment of the Iraq Historic Allegations Team in 2010,

---

244 Hansard HC vol. 366, col. 222 (3 April 2001).
245 Hansard HL vol. 673, col. 1262 (14 July 2005).
246 Hansard HL Deb. 2368 (11 February 2016).
247 The Baha Mousa Public Inquiry Report, 8 September 2011.

which operates within the Ministry of Defence. In this regard, the Prosecutor's task is likely to involve reviewing the outcomes of all these efforts before making a determination on the UK's unwillingness (or inability) to genuinely investigate and prosecute those responsible. This might include reviewing the exercise of the UK's prosecutorial discretion in previous unprosecuted cases – a highly sensitive area in many states and one usually addressed by the executive and not the judiciary.

As one commentator put it: 'The nature of the unwillingness and inability tests will in many cases demand greater resources ... than proving the guilt of the alleged perpetrator.'[248] Although it seems inconceivable that the British justice system could be found wanting in terms of complementarity rules, it might even have more financial resources to conduct investigations than the Office of the Prosecutor. Still, the European Court of Human Rights found some irregularities that could deem some cases admissible. One clear example of this is *Findlay v. United Kingdom*, where the British military justice system was found to not be adequately independent and impartial to guarantee a fair trial – a violation of Article 6(1) of the European Convention on Human Rights.[249] The British justice system has been reformed since then to accommodate the European Court of Human Rights.[250]

In 2006, British military justice came under scrutiny again when seven soldiers were court-martialled under the International Criminal Court Act 2001 and charged with offences including inhuman treatment, manslaughter and negligence.[251] Although the trial led to the conviction of Corporal Donald Payne, who pleaded guilty to the charges of inhuman treatment and was sentenced to a year's imprisonment, commentators found irregularities pertaining to the charges pressed against the suspects and the selection of suspects (low-ranking soldiers were targeted instead of those with the greatest responsibility).

Amnesty International was critical of the process, concluding that many questions remained unanswered and that further action was required to ensure justice. There seems to be general lack of trust in the court-martial in the UK to the extent that in the current debates on the Armed Forces Bill, Lord Thomas of Gesford, had to suggest that 'serious offences of murder, manslaughter and rape, and serious sexual offences, should be tried in ... ordinary Crown Courts and no longer by court martial – the system that is under attack'.[252] There is also a

---

[248] Bergsmo, 'The Jurisdictional Regime of the International Criminal Court', note 67, p. 359.

[249] *Findlay v. United Kingdom* [1997] 24 EHRR 221.

[250] See Simon P. Rowlinson, 'The British System of Military Justice' (2002) 52 *Air Force Law Review* 17.

[251] See *R. v Payne* [2007], Proceedings of a General Court-Martial held at Military Court Centre Bulford in the case of Corporal Donald Payne and others; Gerry Simpson, 'The Death of Baha Mousa' (2007) 8 *Melbourne Journal of International Law* 340.

[252] Hansard HL Deb. 2368 (11 February 2016).

possibility that if the Prosecutor decides to apply the theory of complicity and superior responsibility in determining unwillingness, some cases could be found admissible by the Court.

Politically, the UK is one of the only two members of the UN Security Council that has from the start – or at least after the Labour government came to power in 1997 – been supportive of an independent Court. It is also one of the main financial contributors to the Court, as shown in the graph below.

Figure 3. Graph 3 UK annual contributions to the Court

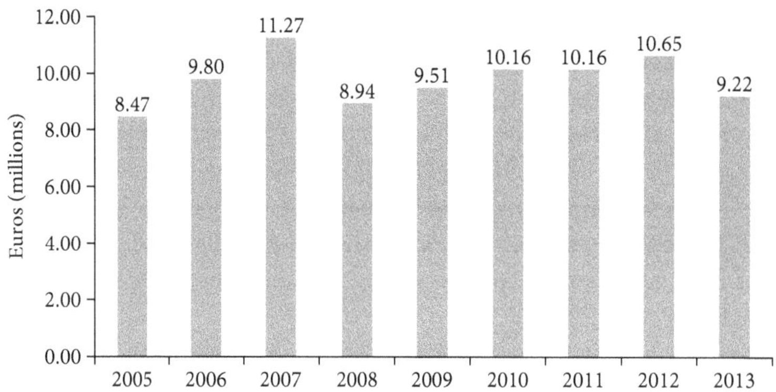

Source: Annual Reports of the Committee on Budget and Finance.

In 2014, the UK's financial contribution the Court increased to €9,773,195.[253]

However, if the relationship between the UK and the European Court of Human Rights is anything to go by, the International Criminal Court will have to be cautious in its approach to possible investigations or prosecutions of war crimes in Iraq. As regards the European Court of Human Rights, Conservative Party politicians and some parts of the media have been critical of the Court's decisions against the UK. The former Prime Minister, David Cameron, is on record criticising the Court for becoming a glorified small-claims court buried under a mountain of 'trivial' claims. He stated that Britain would withdraw from the Convention if it were necessary to 'keep our country safe'.[254] In 2011, the President of the European Court of Human Rights expressed the dismay and concern felt by the Strasbourg judges at the often intemperate and inaccurate criticism that had been levelled against them.[255]

---

253 Assembly of States Parties, 'Financial Statements of the International Criminal Court for the Year Ended 31 December 2004', ICC-ASP/14/12, 4 August 2015.

254 Jon Henley 'Why is the European Court of Human Rights Hated by the UK Right?' *The Guardian* (22 December 2013). For an example of a newspaper article critical of the European Court, see James Slack, 'Europe's War on British on British' *Daily Mail* (11 January 2012).

255 See Nicolas Bratza, 'The Relationship between the UK Courts and Strasbourg' (2011) 5 *European Human Rights Law Review* 505.

In this respect, the significance of political realities in international justice cannot be underestimated. Schabas acknowledged the thin line between justice and politics when he said: 'At [the] international level, policy and politics seem to sit much closer to the centre of the justice agenda.'[256] The central feature of international criminal law is that it sets one party, the Prosecutor, acting on behalf of international society, against another, the defendant. The assumption is that there is a shared vision and understanding of international justice within the international community, which is not always the case. The international community is divided and, as already discussed, finding common ground was not easy at the Rome Conference. This makes the job of the Prosecutor challenging, whether it be in deciding to act (as in Libya or in Northern Uganda) or not to act (as in Iraq in 2006). The next section focuses on the questions that were raised when the Prosecutor decided to act and demonstrates that claims that the Court is selectively focusing on Africa are in themselves reflective of the desires of different actors to have the Prosecutor and the Court play their game of politics.

3.3. CHALLENGES AND PROSPECTS OF THE OFFICE OF THE PROSECUTOR

The global minefield of justice and politics, combined with the failure by the majority of permanent members of the UN Security Council to ratify the Rome Statute, have complicated the function of the Prosecutor from the outset. The success and survival of the Court is primarily dependent on how it navigates this minefield and deals with the global powers – especially the US, which indicated that it was ready to unleash its diplomatic and military capabilities to stop the 'dangerous court' from interfering with its interests and its allies around the globe. At the same time, the rise of the EU, in the absence of the US, created a potential alternative source and centre of political and financial support. With the helping hand of the EU, the Court managed to get its first UN Security Council referral in the form of Darfur, Sudan, in 2005. Six years later, the UN Security Council unanimously referred Libya to the Court, prompting Bensouda to state:

> I would quickly quote the unanimous decision by the UNSC referring Libya, to the ICC. I think this has shown the ICC to be a player, not only for the international criminal justice, but also one of the solutions to bring peace and security to the conflict-torn societies. It has become a relevant player.[257]

---

256 See Schabas, *Unimaginable Atrocities*, note 51, p. 3.

257 Cited in Amann, 'Politics and Prosecutions' (eds.), note 186, p. 25.

As one commentator observed, the 'player' concept introduced by Bensouda is a loaded one that prompts many questions.[258] The 8th edition of the *Oxford Advanced Learner's Dictionary* identifies five possible applications for the noun 'player'. It could refer to a: person who takes part in a game; a company involved in a particular area of business or politics; a machine for reproducing sound; a person who plays a musical instrument; and, in old-fashioned English, an actor.[259] The meanings could be relevant when referring to the Court. If the Court is involved in a game, the follow-up question is: what game is it playing and is it winning? If it is in business, what value is it adding and is the final product marketable? If it is producing sound, who are its audience and are they satisfied? If it is acting, who is directing and is the audience content? In other words, the implication common to all these definitions is one of expectation – something is bound to happen now that the Court is a player.

Based on the understanding that the Court, and the Office of the Prosecutor in particular, is now a player and is expected to impact the global effort to end impunity, some would argue that the Prosecutor is losing, or failing to add, value. Part of the Court's audience are no longer interested and are even contemplating withdrawing, claiming that its directors are biased.

Finally in this chapter, I want to examine how African states have attributed the selective enforcement of the Court to the Office of the Prosecutor. This frustration and claims of selectiveness is understandable, yet at the same time exaggerated; it fails to appreciate that the playing field for the Prosecutor is not even – as the Rome Statute was itself a major political compromise. In addition, the Court relies on the cooperation of states that do not necessarily have a common approach to the obligation to prosecute international crimes. This is because states are often caught in a dilemma 'marked by the twin pathologies of wanting justice yet being "sick of giving it"',[260] especially when it involves their nationals.

In Africa, the Office of the Prosecutor appears to only come under attack when it fails to play the game to the liking of certain political elites. The point of highlighting this is not to exonerate the Prosecutor from his or her hesitation to act when it could have actually added value to the Court's work by broadening its geographical reach, but rather to suggest that a broader analysis of the Prosecutor's operational field would be useful.

3.3.1. APPEARANCE AND REALITY: POLITICS AND THE LIMITS OF PROSECUTORIAL DISCRETION IN THE ROME STATUTE

Theory around the appropriate balance of power between states and international war crimes tribunals has influenced how international criminal law has

---

258 *Ibid*, p. 25.
259 *Oxford Advanced Learners Dictionary*, (Oxford, Oxford University Press 2011 8th edn).
260 Simpson, 'The Death of Baha Mousa', note 246, p. 341.

developed since the end of the Second World War. From the International Military Tribunal at Nuremberg to the Special Tribunal for Lebanon, states and international criminal justice institutions have competed to gain an advantage in the balance of power so as to have more control over the enforcement of international criminal law. As discussed earlier, in the Rome Statute, the balance of power was evened out and credit for this must be given to the Like Minded Group and the legion of NGOs that successfully campaigned to secure independent powers for the Prosecutor. This was not taken lightly by other state delegations (the US in particular), who had wanted a Prosecutor controlled by the either the UN Security Council or states parties.

States, no matter how liberal, seek to preserve their sovereignty wherever possible.[261] In some cases, states have even attempted to use the international war crimes tribunals to further their national interests.[262] The fierce competition for power between states and international war crimes tribunals centres on the role of the Prosecutor. The role of an international war crimes tribunal prosecutor involves investigating and selecting objects of prosecutions and their performance is seen as the measure of the international tribunal's success.[263] In this regard, and as Schabas noted, the Court has been found wanting. Schabas put the average acquittal rate of the Court at 60 per cent, which is much higher than the average acquittal rate of other international criminal tribunals (14 per cent).[264] Questions have also been raised about the selection of targets within specific situations – the Prosecutor is accused of targeting certain sides in certain conflicts.[265] However, it is the failure of the Court to officially

---

261 See Gary Jonathan Bass, *Stay the Hand of Vengeance: The Politics of War Crimes Tribunals* (Princeton, Princeton University Press, 2000), who notes that liberal states such as the US face serious constraints when it comes to complying with the principles of war crimes tribunals.

262 Some scholars argue that the International Military Tribunal at Nuremberg also served as a battleground for an intense political and ideological struggle among the Allied states about the meaning of the Second World War and the shape of the new international order. See Francine Hirsch, 'The Soviets at Nuremberg: International Law, Propaganda, and the Making of the Postwar Order' (2008) 113 *American Historical Review* 701.

263 Luc Côté, 'Independence and Impartiality' in Jan Wouters, Luc Reydams and Cedric Ryngaert (eds.), *International Prosecutors* (Oxford, Oxford University Press, 2012).

264 Schabas, 'The Banality of International Justice', note 133, p. 546.

265 Mamdani, *Saviors and Survivors*, note 130, p. 284, although the Court is criticised for charging Sudanese government officials for the crimes in Darfur, the reality is that it also summoned rebels leaders to The Hague. Bahar Idris Abu Garda, the Chairman and General Coordinator of Military Operations of the United Resistance Front, was summoned to appear on 7 May 2009 (*Idris Abu Garda* (ICC-02/05-02/02/09) Situation in Darfur, 7 May 2009); however, on 8 February 2010, the Pre Trial Chamber refused to confirm charges. See also Abdullah Banda Abakaer Nourain, Commander-in-Chief of Justice and Equality Mouvement Collective-Leadership, one of the components of the United Resistance Front: *Abdullah Banda Abakaer Nourain* (ICC-02/05-03/09), Situation in Darfur, 27 August, 2009.

open investigations in other parts of the world where international crimes are suspected that has had the most damaging impact on its image.

All of the Court's shortcomings are seen as a reflection of the function of the Office of the Prosecutor. Schabas questioned how the disappointing performance of the Court could be attributed to the Office of the Prosecutor, which he claimed is 'staffed and led by experienced professionals, most of whom have proved their abilities at the ad-hoc tribunals'.[266] However, some commentators see the challenges of the Office of the Prosecutor in broader terms. Barbara Lochbihler, a Member of the European Parliament for the German Greens and an active member of the Parliamentarians for Global Action, said:

> [T]he work of the OTP is very difficult and that her room for manoeuver is considerably constrained both by budget restrictions as well as by political support yielded to the Court. Funding is crucial and we all know that money provided to the OTP is by far not enough to efficiently and effectively carry out her work.[267]

On political support, she added:

> The political support given by states and organisations like the EU is not in any way less important, notably due to the ICC's high reliance on cooperation for referrals, execution of arrest warrants, the collection of evidence and the more general support to fight for the Court's integrity.

Indeed, Chief Prosecutor Bensouda confirmed in her remarks during the Fourteenth Session of Assembly of States Parties that her work has suffered from inadequate funding.[268] She specifically singled out her office's inability to investigate both sides to the conflict in Côte d'Ivoire due to, she claimed, financial constraints. Consequently, the Office of the Prosecutor has been accused of not investigating the anti-Gbagbo forces who were supporting Alassane Quattara, the internationally recognised President of Côte d'Ivoire following the elections in 2011. The forces were accused of committing human rights violations as they pushed for Gbagbo to concede electoral defeat and surrender power to Quattara. It was the failure of the Prosecutor to investigate such violations that prompted an outcry and accusations of bias. In her defence, Prosecutor Bensouda called such an outcry an 'erroneous perceptions of bias'. She said that her office had started investigating the anti-Gbagbo forces, but on a shoestring budget. It has to be remembered that during the tenth Session of

---

266 Schabas, 'The Banality of International Justice', note 133, p. 546.

267 Email exchange with Lochbihler Barbarar, 5 February 2016.

268 Fatou Bensouda, 'Tenth Plenary Meeting: Discussions on the Efficiency and Effectiveness of Court Proceedings Strategic Vision of the Office of the Prosecutor on Achieving Efficiency and Effectiveness', Fourteenth Session of the Assembly of States Parties, 24 November 2015.

the Assembly of States Parties, the Assembly had to approve a supplementary budget due to the financial implications related to the situation in Côte d'Ivoire. The Assembly of States Parties had initially approved an overall budget of €111,000,000 with €108,800,000 for the Budget and €2,200,000 for the replenishment of Contingency Fund for 2012, out of which the Office of the Prosecutor was earmarked to receive €27,723,700 (25.4 per cent).[269] The situation in Côte d'Ivoire and other financial commitments led the revision of the budget to €123,065,300 for 2012.[270]

The Court's financial resources are low compared with those of the two *ad hoc* tribunals. The UN General Assembly has a record of approving very high budgets for each of the *ad hoc* tribunals, unlike the Assembly of States Parties, which gives less. In 2008, the UN General Assembly decided to approve a total of US$376,232,900 (€278,638,205) for the International Criminal Tribunal for the former Yugoslavia and US$305,378,600 (€226,163,487) for the International Criminal Tribunal for Rwanda's 2008–09 biennial budgets.[271] In the case of the International Criminal Court, the total of the budgets approved for 2008 (€90,382,100) and 2009 (€101,229,900) gives a biennial budget of €191,612,000, which is low compared with that of each of the *ad hoc* tribunals.

The discrepancy in the available financial resources for the *ad hoc* tribunals and the Court is staggering considering that the *ad hoc* tribunals were just established to focus on specific territory (the former Yugoslavia and Rwanda). In this case, it sounds rather ambitious to expect the Court, and especially the Office of the Prosecutor, to be ready to investigate each and every situation where atrocity crimes are committed. One can only hope that as the *ad hoc* tribunals complete their mandates and following the implementation of the exit strategies, more financial resources and political support will be freed up so that the Court can be efficient and effective.

---

269 Official Records of Assembly of States Parties to the Rome Statute of the International Criminal Court, Resolution ICC-ASP/10/Res.4 Adopted at the 9th Plenary Meeting, 21 December 2011.

270 *Official Records of Assembly of States Parties to the Rome Statute of the International Criminal Court*, Draft Resolution of the Assembly of States Parties on the Proposed Programme Budget for 2012, the Working Capital Fund for 2012, scale of assessments for the apportionment of expenses of the International Criminal Court, financing appropriations for 2012 and the Contingency Fund.

271 See UN General Assembly, Doc. A/Res/63/255, Resolution adopted by the General Assembly on 24 December 2008, 'Financing of the International Tribunal for the Prosecution of Persons Responsible for Serious Violations of International Humanitarian Law Committed in the Territory of the Former Yugoslavia since 1991, 63/255' para. 7 and United Nations General Assembly, Doc A/Res/63/254, Resolution adopted by the General Assembly on 24 December 2008, 'Financing of the International Criminal Tribunal for the Prosecution of Persons Responsible for Genocide and Other Serious Violations of International Humanitarian Law Committed in the Territory of Rwanda and Rwandan Citizens Responsible for Genocide and other Such Violations Committed in the Territory of Neighbouring States between 1 January and 31 December 1994, 63/254,' para. 3.

Financial constraints aside, it is still fair to say that, as Kenneth Roth, the Executive Director of Human Rights Watch, put it: 'Some of the ICC's problems are of its own making. The Chief Prosecutor for its first nine years ... seemed more interested in issuing arrest warrants than undertaking the tough, less glamorous work of conducting rigorous criminal investigations.'[272] Similar weaknesses in the Prosecutor's approach were identified as early as 2006 during the handling of investigations in Darfur. The Pre-Trial Chamber was not convinced by the Prosecutor's claim that he could not conduct investigations within Darfur because of the security situation. Two *amicus curiae* briefs submitted – one by Professor Antonio Cassese, the first President of the International Criminal Tribunal for the former Yugoslavia and Chair of the United Nations Commission of Inquiry, which recommended the referral of the situation in Darfur to the Court, and another by Louise Arbour, then UN Commissioner for Human Rights – pointed out several weaknesses in Moreno Ocampo's investigative performances.[273]

Professor Cassese, whose UN Commission of Inquiry team had gained access to the notorious Kobar maximum prison located on the banks of the Blue Nile River in Khartoum, Sudan, and managed to interview some detainees, had recommended that the Prosecutor should undertake 'targeted and brief interviews'.[274] For her part, Arbour recommended the Court to increase its visibility in Sudan and stated that 'it was possible to conduct investigations of human rights violations during armed conflict in general and in Darfur in particular, without putting victims at unreasonable risk'.[275]

The weaknesses in the Prosecutor's investigative strategies nearly led to the collapse of the trial of Thomas Lubanga from the Democratic Republic of the Congo due to an overreliance on reports from the United Nations Organisation Mission in the Democractic Republic of the Congo (MONUC) (including its weekly situation reports). The reports had been handed over to the Office of the Prosecutor as confidential documents and for use strictly as lead evidence

---

272 Kenneth Roth, 'Africa Attacks the International Criminal Court' *New York Review of Books* (14 January 2014).

273 *Situation in Darfur, Sudan* (ICC-02/05), Observations on Issues Concerning the Protection of Victims and the Preservation of Evidence in the Proceedings on Darfur Pending before the ICC, 25 August 2006; and *Situation in Darfur, Sudan* (ICC-02/05) Observations of the United Nations High Commissioner for Human Rights Invited in Application of Rule 103 of the Rules of Procedure and Evidence, 10 October 2006.

274 *Situation in Darfur, Sudan* (ICC-02/05), Observations on Issues Concerning the Protection of Victims and the Preservation of Evidence in the Proceedings on Darfur Pending Before the ICC, 25 August 2006, p. 5; see also Julie Flint and Alex de Waal, 'Case Closed: A Prosecutor without Borders' *World Affairs* Spring 2009 at http://www.worldaffairsjournal.org/article/case-closed-prosecutor-without-borders and Report of the International Commission of Inquiry on Darfur to the United Nations Secretary-General Pursuant to Security Council Resolution 1564 of 18 September 2004 .

275 Observations of the United Nations High Commissioner for Human Rights Invited in Application of Rule 103 of the Rules of Procedure and Evidence, 10 October 2006, para. 64.

– that is, for them to be used in carrying out further investigations. Instead, the Office of the Prosecutor relied on such reports as evidence in their case against Lubanga. However when the Court Chambers demanded that some of the evidence acquired from the UN Peacekeeping Mission be shared with Lubanga's defence team as required by the Court rules and safeguarding the commission of a fair trial, the Office of the Prosecutor could not do so without obtaining waivers for confidentiality from the UN. The process involved for the Office of the Prosecutor to obtain the waivers from the UN was complicated and laborious. It involved the Prosecutor having to renegotiate the terms of the confidentiality agreement he had with the UN.[276] As such, undue delays caused by this process almost led to the release of Lubanga because his right to a fair trial was being violated, as he was being detained for longer than what was considered necessary.

It is possible that part of the challenges faced by the Office of the Prosecutor is from the former Prosecutor's vision of the Court, which he had promised would be 'a sexy … economical court' with the goal of swift justice 'comprehensible to often-uneducated victim populations'.[277] This vision was questioned by some of the Court's faithful, such as William Pace of the Coalition for the International Criminal Court, who complained that the Prosecutor was taking on new cases without the necessary human and financial resources. Pace asked: 'How can a six- or eight-member investigation team do all of Northern Uganda, all of Democratic Republic of Congo, all of Darfur?' Then he went on to say: 'The Court is unreasonably fearful of losing support of governments who they think want everything done on the cheap.'[278] If this contributes to the poor performance by the Court, then the recent changes proposed by Bensouda as to how the Office of the Prosecutor would address preliminary investigations could be a genuine source of relief and hope for the Court's supporters.

Judge Kaul noted that while 'the Office of the Prosecutor is the engine, professional and effective investigations are the fuel of the Court'.[279] Based on his considerable experience as a judge at the Court and as a former Vice President, he fully encouraged new Bensouda to double her staff in the Investigation and Jurisdiction, Complementarity and Cooperation Division. In this regard it is reasonable to hope for an improved performance from the Office of the Prosecutor. The challenge now is to address the problems affecting the Court that are external in nature/ beyond its direct control – in other words, politics.

---

276 Heikelina Verrijn Stuart, 'The ICC in Trouble' (2000) 6 *Journal of International Criminal Justice* 409.

277 Ibid.

278 Jess Brevin, 'Justice Delayed for Global Court, Uganda, Rebels Prove Tough Test; African Politics' *Wall Street Journal* (8 June 2006).

279 Hans-Peter Kaul, 'The ICC of the Future' (6th Annual International Humanitarian Law Dialogues 2012, *Hybrid International Court: A Tenth Anniversary Retrospective on Special Court for Sierra Leone*, Chautauqua Institute Robert H. Jackson Centre, 28 August 2012).

3.3.2. POLITICS: A DOUBLE-EDGED SWORD FOR THE PROSECUTOR

In fact, although the Office of the Prosecutor has been acting seemingly oblivious of the influence of state power politics in its prosecutorial strategy, it appeared to have been aware from the onset that the independence of the Prosecutor was a very delicate compromise reached during the Rome Conference. This meant that the Prosecutor had to act carefully so as not to scare those opposed to an independent Prosecutor, and at the same time to demonstrate to those who had campaigned for an independent Prosecutor that their efforts were worth it. The fact that the majority members of the five permanent members of the UN Security Council had not ratified the Court created some potential credibility challenges. However, generally there was a spirit of goodwill towards the Court throughout the world. This extended to powerful US human rights constituencies and many states in Africa. However, Prosecutor Moreno Ocampo chose not to get carried away when he drafted his policy documents, opting instead for pragmatism.

The Prosecutor had indicated in his prosecutorial strategy documents since 2003 that he preferred that states refer situations directly to the Court under Article 14.[280] In 2006, he stated that 'while *proprio motu* power is a critical aspect of the Office's independence, the Prosecutor adopted the policy of inviting and welcoming voluntary referrals by territorial states as a first step in triggering the jurisdiction of the Court'.[281] In this he managed to eliminate any fears, primarily expressed by the more powerful states, that he was going to be reckless with his powers to initiate investigations throughout the world. At the same time, he opened his office to potential politicisation through domestic state referrals. From the outset, it seems that the Prosecutor was hesitant to use his *proprio motu* powers out of concern that he would not get the much-needed cooperation from the targeted territorial and national or victim states.

The implication was that political authorities had taken charge of the judicial process referred to the Court instead of the Office of the Prosecutor. The sentiment that had prevailed during the Rome Conference – that national governments and the UN Security Council could not be trusted to act consistently and impartially in bringing perpetrators of international crimes to justice at the Court – started to become a reality as the Office of the Prosecutor gradually succumbed to political realities and delayed commencing investigations *proprio motu*. Consequently, the majority of the situations officially investigated by the Prosecutor were referred to it by the states parties or by the UN Security Council,

---

280 Office of the Prosecutor, 'Paper on Some Policy Issues before the Office of the Prosecutor', September 2003, p. 6.

281 Schabas, 'Prosecutorial Discretion v. Judicial Activism at the International Criminal Court', note 62.

while the Prosecutor used his powers under Article 15 to open investigations into the situations in Kenya, Côte d'Ivoire and Georgia.

The Prosecutor's strategy of avoiding situations that could have led the Court into confrontation with the superpowers appeared to have worked, reassuring France, the UK and the US, all of which had tried to avoid having their nationals investigated by the Court. On 9 June 2000, France had made a declaration under Article 124 effectively rejecting the jurisdiction of the Court with respect to war crimes alleged to have been committed by its nationals or on its territory.[282] It is suggested that France was not sure how the Office of the Prosecutor would behave, hence it wanted to protect its soldiers from war crimes prosecution stemming from its presence in, and strong post-colonial ties to, Africa.[283] However, it withdrew its declaration on 13 August 2008 before the stipulated seven years had elapsed. It did not give any explanation for its withdrawal.[284] When the Prosecutor indicated and then proved that he would be taking a cautious approach with his *proprio motu* powers, France may have felt reassured. In any case, one could argue that Article 124 was not the only way that France could have avoided the Court's jurisdiction; it other permanent members of the UN Security Council could defer proceedings under Article 16. However, this process has its own consequences. Deferrals could negatively impact on the image of states, especially when they want to project an image of global uprightness with regard to the promotion of freedom, justice and the rule of law.

The UK had its own concerns and sought ways of preventing the Prosecutor from bringing up any difficult cases against its military service personnel. In fact, in 2001, during the House of Commons debates on the jurisdiction of the Court, Francis Maude, who was then the Shadow Foreign Secretary, proposed that the UK also make a declaration pursuant to Article 124 of the Rome Statute.[285] In the end, they put their trust in the ability of their domestic courts to handle cases before the Prosecutor intervened.

Concerns over possible Court action were also raised in consultations leading up to the UK's military action in Iraq. On 7 March 2003, Lord Goldsmith, the Attorney General at that time, sent an legal opinion note to Prime Minister Tony Blair in which he stated that: 'Given the controversy surrounding the legal basis of action, it is likely that the Court will scrutinise any allegations of war crimes by UK forces very closely.'[286] Senior military members of the UK such as Lord Boyce, who was the Chief of the Defence Staff in 2003, were also concerned. Boyce wanted to make sure that he was not alone. He told a journalist that the

---

282 C.N.404.2000.TREATIES-12 (Depositary Notification), signed 21 June 2000, Section III.

283 Tabak, S, 'Article 124, War Crimes, and the Development of the Rome Statute' (2009) 40 *Georgetown Journal International Law* p. 1085.

284 C.N.592.2008.TREATIES-5 (Depositary Notification), signed 20 August 2008.

285 *Official Reports*, House of Commons, 3 April 2001, vol. 366, col. 237.

286 Legal Opinion to the Prime Minister on Iraq: Resolution 1441, Lord Peter Goldsmith, 7 March 2003, para. 33.

reason he had sought legal advice was to 'make sure that we had this anchor, which has been signed by the Government law officer ... It may not stop us from being charged but by God, it would make sure other people were brought into the frame as well'.[287]

It is evident that the possibility that the Court could end up taking action against the UK created anxieties at different levels in Blair's administration. Although the expectation of close scrutiny from the Court was shared by the highest legal advisor to the Prime Minister, the Prosecutor decided that the violations committed in Iraq did not meet the Court's gravity threshold. This might well have been the case, but the fact that the Prosecutor's interpretation and application of the gravity criteria contains several loopholes raises questions. It seems there were other factors at play beyond merely legal considerations. As already discussed, WikiLeaks documents suggest that the Prosecutor wished to dispose of the Iraq issues (as opposed to investigating them).[288]

In any case, assuming that the Prosecutor's strategy was to both avoid confrontation and attract US support for the Court's activities, it succeeded. This is despite the fact that immediately after facing a 'diplomatic defeat of epic proportions'[289] during the Rome Conference, the US Senator Jesse Helms called the Court 'an international kangaroo court'. The US took several steps to oppose the Court, as already discussed, but by 2005, its opposition had waned and it allowed the UN Security Council resolution referring Sudan to the Court to be adopted. During the negotiations leading up to the adoption of the referral resolution, the US had proposed that a regional court be created and mandated by the Security Council resolution and administered by the UN in conjunction with the AU.[290] One US government official defended the proposal by suggesting that it would 'fit in with the US policy of delivering justice closer to the victims community and would avoid what US officials described as "colonial" approach of Europeans judging Africans'.[291] Sceptics viewed the proposal as a manifestation of the policy employed by the US not to legitimise the Court. However, with the benefit of hindsight, it seems the approach of the US could possibly have delivered better results, in a more reasonable timeframe, as a local hybrid could have had the political support from the UN Security Council. However, it seems that the EU's obsession with opposing the US clouded the negotiating process.

---

287 Joshua Rozenberg, 'Why Britain's Top Soldier Would Not End up in the Dock over Iraq' *Daily Telegraph* (2 May 2005).

288 Schabas, *Unimaginable Atrocities*, note 51, p. 86.

289 Bartram S Brown, 'The Statute of the ICC: From The Hague to Rome and Back Again' in Sarah B. Sewall and Carl Kaysen (eds.)(eds.), *The United States and the International Criminal Court: National Security and International Law* (Lanham: Rowman & Littlefield, 2000), p. 66.

290 See John R. Crook, 'U.S. Proposes New Regional Court to Hear Charges Involving Darfur, Others Urge ICC' (2005) 99 *American Journal of International Law* 501.

291 Cerone, 'US Attitudes Towards International Criminal Courts and Tribunals', note 220, p. 160.

Contrary to the perception that the US only warmed up to the Court after US President Barack Obama took office, the reality is that the process began before 2008. In addition to supporting the referral of the situation in Darfur, on 1 November 2005, Jendayi Frazer, the US Assistant Secretary of State, told the House of Representatives on the International Relations Committee that 'if the ICC requires assistance, the United States stands ready to assist ... we don't want to see impunity for any of these actors ... we stand ready to assist'.[292] The US further demonstrated its willingness to work with the Court when, on 29 March 2006, President George W. Bush announced that there was a process in progress to get Charles Taylor to the court in the Netherlands. This led to the transferral of Charles Taylor from Sierra Leone to the Court premises in The Hague. This move alone legitimised the Court.

Since then, several key US government officials have stressed that the Court is no longer a rogue or kangaroo court. First, under the Bush administration, State Department Legal Advisor John Bellinger acknowledged that the Court had a role to play in the overall system of international justice.[293] In August 2009, Secretary of State Hillary Clinton issued a statement that demonstrated a big shift in the US approach towards the Court while on her visit in Kenya. She said it was a source of 'great regret' that the US was not a party to the Court, but that it has supported the Court and 'continue[s] to do so'.[294] Of significant importance is what Secretary Clinton did not say – whether and when the US was going to join the Court. That said, the US has played a huge role in supporting Libya's referral to the Court and contributed troops to hunt down Joseph Kony, the leader of the Lord's Resistance Army (LRA), who is wanted by the Court for crimes committed in Northern Uganda and is suspected of being in the Central African Republic. In 2015, the US troops in the Central African Republic assisted in the transfer of Dominic Ongwen to the Court. Ongwen had been indicted by the Court and was captured by Seleka rebels in the Central African Republic before they handed him over to the US military forces. Two years earlier in 2013, the US Embassy in Kigali, Rwanda had also facilitated the transfer of another suspected wanted by the Court, Bosco Ntaganda, to The Hague. The Court had indicted Ntaganda in 2006 for allegedly committing war crimes and crimes against humanity in northeast region of the Democratic Republic of the Congo between 2002 and 2003.

It could be argued that Moreno Ocampo's strategy might have helped the Court to carefully navigate the global minefield of politics and justice. He managed to avoid confrontations with major military powers such as France, the

---

[292] Cited in ibid, p. 163.

[293] Jess Bravin, 'U.S. Warms to Hague Tribunal New Stance Reflects Desire to Use Court to Prosecute Darfur Crimes' *Wall Street Journal* (14 June 2006).

[294] Ewen MacAskill, 'Clinton: It is a "Great Regret" that the US is Not in International Criminal Court' *The Guardian* (6 August 2009).

UK, the US and Russia by not opening investigations *proprio motu* against their nationals or allies around the world. Consequently, the Court maintained its strategic position as a player in the international criminal justice. The difficulty is that politics has not been playing its part to strengthen the Court's mandate. The UN Security Council referral of Sudan and Libya was a positive move as far as extending the jurisdiction of the Court beyond the states parties; however, the UN Security Council failed to ensure that its resolutions were effectively implemented and this damaged the credibility of the Court – at least in the eyes of the victims of the atrocities.

In addition, the failure by the UN Security Council to refer the situations in Sri Lanka, Syria and the Occupied Territories of Palestine has impacted negatively on the Court. In earnest, there is not much – if anything – that the Court can do to influence which situations the UN Security Council refers to it. That said, its acceptance of the referrals of the situations in Sudan and Libya has generated the perception that the two institutions have become inseparable.

The inconsistent nature of the UN Security Council's referrals has led to the perception that there are double standards at work in the application of the Rome Statute. This has resulted in widespread dissatisfaction with both the Security Council and the Court. After the Security Council failed to pass a resolution on the deferral of Kenyan cases before the Court, Eugene-Richard Gasana, Rwandan Permanent Representative to the UN, said: 'It is unfortunate that the ICC continues to lose face and credibility in the world the more it continues to be used as a tool for the big powers against the developing nations.'[295] The role and practices of the Security Council are discussed in detail in Chapter 4.

In Sudan and Libya, the UN Security Council's level of engagement and commitment to seeing its resolutions implemented have been unreliable. This has damaged the credibility of the Court and, as Prosecutor Bensouda put it, has led to the fading of the hopes of the victims of Darfur. In her eighteenth report to the Security Council in 2013, Bensouda pointed out that she expressed her 'office's frustration and despair at the council's inaction and paralysis regarding the situation in Darfur'. She laid the responsibility of the failure to deliver international justice in Darfur squarely on the Security Council and states parties when she said: 'My Office had done its part, and it is now up to the Council and to the States parties to heed the cries of millions of victims of the crimes that continue unabated in Darfur.'[296]

Indeed, the UN Security Council's inaction concerning the Court's intervention in Darfur has been costly in terms of both the credibility of the Court and the enforcement of international justice in general. Following the impasse between

---

295 The explanation of vote by Permanent Representative, Eugene-Richard Gasana, on the UN Security Council resolution on the deferral on the Kenyan cases before the International Criminal Court, 15 November 2013.

296 UN Doc. S/PV.7080, 11 December 2013.

the AU and the UN Security Council over inaction on deferral requests, which led the AU to lose confidence in the Court, the Security Council has been silent when notified by the Pre-Trial Chamber of the Court of clear failures and/or violations by the member states of the UN to comply with the Security Council resolutions.

Since the issuance of the arrest warrant for President al-Bashir, he has managed to travel to the territory of a number of African States Parties – namely Chad, Kenya, Malawi, Djibouti Malawi,[297] Nigeria,[298] the Democratic Republic of the Congo and South Africa In 2015, he had to cut his visit to South Africa out of concern that he might have been arrested by the South African authorities – this will be discussed in further detail in Chapter 7. In summing up, Prosecutor Bensouda expressed her frustration with the Security Council's inaction by making reference to the Pre-Trial Chamber's words that:

> When the Security Council, acting under Charter VII of the United Nations Charter, refers a situation to the Court as constituting a threat to international peace and security, it is expected that the Council would respond by way of taking such measures which are considered appropriate, if there is an apparent failure on the part of the relevant state party to the Statute to cooperate in fulfilling the Court's mandate entrusted to it by the Council. Otherwise, if there is no follow-up action, on the part of the Security Council, any referral by the Council to the ICC under Chapter VII would never achieve its ultimate goal, namely to put an end to impunity. Accordingly, any such referral would become futile.[299]

3.4. *PROPRIO MOTU* POWERS IN ACTION AND THE PROSECUTOR'S FEARS CONFIRMED

The fact that the Prosecutor did not use his *proprio motu* powers to open investigations in other parts of the world reflected his self-serving pragmatism – he was determined to avoid clashing with powerful and influential states that could have damaged the nascent court. He was aware that the Court's survival was premised on state cooperation and support. Instead of initiating

---

297 See, for instance, *Bashir* (ICC-02/05-01/09) Decision Informing the United Nations Security Council and the Assembly of the States Parties to the Rome Statute about Omar Al-Bashir's Recent Visit to the Republic of Chad, 27 August 2010; *Bashir* (ICC-02/05-01/09) Decision Pursuant to Article 87(7) of the Rome Statute on the Failure by the Republic of Malawi to Comply with the Cooperation Requests Issued by the Court with Respect to the Arrest and Surrender of Omar Hassan Ahmad Al-Bashir, 12 December 2011; *Bashir* (ICC-02/05-01/09) Decision Informing the United Nations Security Council and the Assembly of the States Parties to the Rome Statute about Omar al-Bashir's Recent Visit to Djibouti, 12 May 2011.

298 President al-Bashir had to cut his trip to Nigeria amidst reports that a Nigeria human rights group had filed a case to try to compel the government to arrest him during his visit in July 2013. 'Sudan's President Bashir Leaves AU Summit in Nigeria' *BBC News* (16 July 2013).

299 UN Doc. S/PV.7080, 11 December 2013.

investigations *proprio motu* in situations such as those in Afghanistan, which featured the direct involvement of powerful states such as the US, Prosecutor Moreno Ocampo focused on Kenya and Cote d'Ivoire.

In 2010, Kenya, having opposed the idea of an independent prosecutor at the Rome Conference, became the first state subject to investigation initiated by the Prosecutor *proprio motu* after the government failed to establish a Special Tribunal to investigate and prosecute those thought to be responsible for the 2007 post-election violence.[300] The Prosecutor took action in Kenya after the Panel of Eminent African Personalities[301] handed over a sealed envelope containing the names of possible defendants and supporting evidence entrusted to it by the Commission of Inquiry into the Post-Election Violence (CIPEV), also known as the Waki Commission.

On 26 November 2009, the Prosecutor filed a request pursuant to the Pre-Trial Chamber II to authorise the commencement of an investigation into the situation in Kenya.[302] Within four months, the Pre-Trial Chamber II had authorised – by a majority – an investigation into the situation in Kenya in relation to the crimes against humanity within the jurisdiction of the Court committed between 1 June 2005 and 26 November 2009.[303] The subsequent investigation was the first to be initiated by the Prosecutor using his *proprio motu* powers. Chapter 6 provides an in-depth analysis of the events, processes and the Kenyan government's reaction to the Office of the Prosecutor and the Court's intervention.

In 2011, Côte d'Ivoire became the second African state in which the Office of the Prosecutor invoked his authority under Article 15 to initiate investigations *proprio motu*. Unlike Kenya, Côte d'Ivoire had not yet ratified the Rome Statute when, on 23 June 2011, the Office of the Prosecutor applied for authorisation to investigate the situation in Côte d'Ivoire pursuant to Article 15.[304] Côte d'Ivoire only ratified the Statute after the Court had already opened an investigation and issued warrants of arrest. As already discussed, limited financial resources impacted negatively on the Office of the Prosecutor's ability to effectively investigate and prosecutor the crimes committed by the anti-Gbagbo forces. As such, some have accused the Office of the Prosecutor of being one-sided in its investigations. This is an anomaly that the Office of the Prosecutor, with the

300 *Situation in the Republic of Kenya* (ICC-01/09-19-Corr) Pre-Trial Chamber II, Decision Pursuant to Article 15 of the Rome Statute on the Authorisation of an Investigation into the Situation in the Republic of Kenya, 31 March 2010.

301 The Panel of Eminent African Personalities consisted of the Former UN Secretary-General Kofi Annan, Benjamin Mkapa, the former President of Tanzania, and former South African First Lady Graca Machel, who were asked by the AU to assist Kenya in resolving its post-election crisis.

302 *Supra note* 295 para. 2.

303 *Supra note* 295.

304 Cote d'Ivoire ratified the Rome Statute on 15 February 2013.

assistance of the states parties, will have to address to avoid the perception that there is selective enforcement of international criminal law.

It was only in 2015 that the new Prosecutor, Bensouda, requested and was granted authorisation 'to proceed with an investigation into the Situation in Georgia covering the period from 1 July 2008 to 10 October 2008, for war crimes and crimes against humanity allegedly committed in and around South Ossetia'.[305] The Pre- Chamber I gave its authorisation for her office to conduct full-scale investigations in South Ossetia, a region that is contested between Georgia and a breakaway government supported by Russia.

The timing of both the request and the authorisation is curious in the sense that they occurred when one of the main actors in the 2008 South Ossetia conflict, Russia, was at its lowest point in terms of its relations with the Western powers following, among other things, its annexation of the Crimea, the allegations that it was behind the conflict in Ukraine, the suspected downing of a Malaysian flight by a Russian missile and also its role in the Syrian conflict. In the light of these events, one might ask why now? Was the Court's action conveniently timed to coincide with a point when international public opinion of Russia was poor or could it be that this is another case of the manipulation of the Court by the Western powers to pile pressure on Russia and its allies in the region?

There is no doubt that the Court's intervention in South Ossetia serves the interests of Georgia more than it does the Russian-backed semi-autonomous breakaway government. The fact that the Prosecutor considered South Ossetia as firmly part of the territory of Georgia, which is a state party to the Rome Statute, appears to confirm the obvious, yet it sends a clear message to Russia on behalf of Georgia that under international law, the disputed region is part of Georgia. As such, the Russian authorities were unimpressed by the decision. They accused the Court of being biased against the Ossetians and the Russians. Maria Zakharova, the Russian Foreign Ministry spokeswoman, said 'The Russian Federation is disappointed with the ICC', before adding:

> Russia has transmitted to the ICC 30 volumes of the criminal case, which confirm the crimes against Ossetian people and Russian peacekeepers committed by Mikheil Saakashvili's regime. However, the Prosecutor accuses Ossetian people and even Russian soldiers, actually works on the side of the aggressor and starts investigation against the victims. It is impossible to say that such acts do not respond to standards of justice. The Russian Federation is disappointed with the Court's action, which supported the position of Bensouda.[306]

---

305 *Situation in Georgia* (ICC-01/15-4) Request for Authorisation of an Investigation Pursuant to Article 15, 13 October 2015.

306 Rustav12, 'The Russian Federation is Disappointed with the Actions of the International Criminal Court, Maria Zakhorova' http://rustavi2.com/en/news/37700, 29 January 2016.

However, Bensouda was undeterred and said that she would go ahead with the investigations. In what appeared to be a reaction to the Prosecutor's actions in Georgia and Ukraine, the Russian Federation revoked its Rome Statute signature on the 16 November 2016.[307] Russia revoked its signature two days after the Office of the Prosecutor had published its preliminary examination, which included findings on the activities of the Russian Federation in Eastern Ukraine and Crimea. Russia had signed the Rome Statute on the 13 September 2000. It became the second State to revoke its signature from the Rome Statute, after the United States. The Russian Foreign Ministry statement indicated that Russia's main reasons for cancelling its Rome Statute signature were that the Court was ineffective and one-sided, as well as stating that it could not trust the Court's interventions in Georgia. The Court was accused of 'unprofessional conduct'. In the statement the Russian Federation aligned itself with the African Union's decision to coordinate a collective withdrawal from the Rome Statute. In what was clearly double standards on the part of superpowers with regard to international criminal justice, on the 3 November 2016, Maria Zakharova had listed a number of alleged war crimes perpetrated by the United States and NATO in Afghanistan before stating that Russia welcomed the 'International Criminal Court's initiative and believe[s] that an objective investigation into war crimes committed by foreign, including US, military personnel in Afghanistan will help prevent the further death of Afghan civilians in the course of hostilities.'[308]

On 27th of October 2016, Burundi, a state party to the Rome Statute and as already mentioned, a member of the AU Open-Ended Committee, notified the United Nations Secretary General of its intention to withdraw from the Rome Statute. This followed a Burundian parliamentary vote in favour of withdrawal on the 12 October 2016 and approval by the Senate before being signed by the Burundian President, Pierre Nkurunziza. At the time that Burundi notified the Secretary General, the Office of the Prosecutor was conducting preliminary examinations on the territory of Burundi after it had received 25 communications alleging that crimes, might have been committed or were being committed within the jurisdiction of the Court before, during and after the legislative and presidential elections in 2015. Burundi was angered by the decision of the Office of the Prosecutor to open preliminary examinations. It alleged that the Office

307 The Ministry of Foreign Affairs of the Russian Federation, 'Statement by the Russian Ministry', 16 October 2016 http://www.mid.ru/en/web/guest/foreign_policy/news/-/asset_publisher/cKNonkJE02Bw/content/id/2523566 accessed 23.12.2016.

308 See Briefing by Foreign Ministry Spokesperson Maria Zakharova, Moscow, 3 November 2016 http://www.mid.ru/en/web/guest/foreign_policy/news/-/asset_publisher/cKNonkJE02Bw/content/id/2513436#8 accessed on 23.12.2016.

of the Prosecutor was not acting independently but was merely acting at the behest of Belgium, Burundi's former colonial power, the European Union, and international organisations including the Office of the High Commissioner for Human Rights.[309] Consequently, Burundi's decision to withdraw from the Rome Statute was due to what it considered to be, 'the systematic violation of the Rome Statute and a number of actions which called into question the independence of the of the Office of the Prosecutor in relation to its actions towards Burundi'.[310]

3.5. THE AU STRIKES BACK AT THE PROSECUTOR

Africa's dissatisfaction with the Court – and in particular with the former Prosecutor and lately with Bensouda – has been expressed through various channels, including resolutions made by the AU Assembly. In 2009, the Assembly of Heads of States and Government of the AU met in Sirte, Libya, and passed a declaration expressing their concern over the conduct of the Prosecutor.[311] The Assembly went on to decide that the African States Parties to the Rome Statute should prepare guidelines and a code of conduct to govern the exercise of discretionary powers by the Prosecutor – particularly the power to initiate cases at his own discretion, as bestowed by Article 15 of the Rome Statute.

The resolution was passed in July 2009, prior to the Prosecutor ever invoking Article 15. He had only agreed to proceed with situations triggered by the UN Security Council and African States Parties: Uganda, Democratic Republic of the Congo and the Central African Republic. It is therefore unclear why the Assembly of the AU was concerned about the Prosecutor's powers under Article 15 at that stage. Perhaps it wanted him to use these powers to open situations in other parts of the world. The resolution's reference to having 'guidelines and code of conduct to govern the exercise of discretionary powers by the Prosecutor' suggests that the AU probably wanted to have some form of control over the Office of the Prosecutor.[312]

The Assembly of the AU directed pointed criticism at the Prosecutor again in 2010 when it passed another resolution raising concerns over what it claimed were 'unacceptable, rude and condescending statements' made during his

---

309 Assembly of States Parties, Statement of H.E Vestine Nahimana Ambassador of Burundi during the 15th Session of the Assembly of States Parties to the Rome, General Debate: Fifteenth Meeting of the Assembly of States Parties of the International Criminal Court, The Hague, 16–24 November 2016.

310 Ibid.

311 Decision on the Meeting of African States Parties to the Rome Statute of the International Criminal Court (ICC), 1–3 July 2009, Sirte, Libya, Doc. Assembly/African Union /13(XIII) (hereinafter Decision on African States Parties), para. 11.

312 Ibid.

handling of President al-Bashir's case.[313] Jean Ping made Africa's dissatisfaction with Moreno Ocampo clear when he told a journalist: 'Frankly speaking, we are not against [the] ICC. What we are against is Moreno Ocampo's justice.'[314] There was a perception that Prosecutor Moreno Ocampo practised double standards and perhaps a suggestion that an African prosecutor would approach issues differently. As such, the AU endorsed Bensouda for the role of Prosecutor in 2012 when Moreno Ocampo's term came to an end.[315]

Perhaps the expectation was that the appointment of an African prosecutor might improve relations between the Court and the AU. Relations could still go either way; however, early indications during Bensouda's term have not been promising. Bensouda had just taken office when the Ethiopian Prime Minister Hailemariam Desalegn, in his capacity as the Chairman of the AU, described the Court as a 'great white race hunter' hunting Africans.[316] President Uhuru Kenyatta of Kenya accused the Court of 'performing at the cue of European governments against the sovereignty of African states'[317] and President Yoweri Museveni of Uganda saw the Court as 'an incompetent institution based on self-interest'.[318] In the perceptions of other African leaders, the Court may have already been so badly tainted by the time Bensouda took the role of Prosecutor that changing it was unlikely to be an easy task for her.

The situation between the AU and the Office of the Prosecutor was not helped by the fact that Bensouda sent signals that her office would not hesitate in sustaining the active prosecutor model and would try to influence events and policy inside and outside the court room, a strategy that had been started by her predecessor. For example, on 23 September 2013, following a terrorist attack in Nairobi, South African Prosecutor Anton Steynberg and a member of the Office of the Prosecutor made a very bold suggestion during Samoei Ruto's proceedings in Trial Chamber V(a). He suggested that Ruto, who was the Deputy President

313 Decision on the Progress Report of the Commission on the Implementation of Decision Assembly/African Union /Dec.270 (XIV) on the Second Ministerial Meeting on the Rome Statute of the International Criminal Court (ICC), 25–27 July, Kampala, Uganda Doc. Assembly/African Union /10(XV), para. 9.

314 Farouk Chothia, 'African's Fatou Bensouda is New ICC Chief Prosecutor' (2011) <http://www.bbc.co.uk/news/world-africa-16029121> accessed 18.10.2016.

315 Decision on African Candidatures for Posts within the International System, 23–28 June 2011, Malabo, Equatorial Guinea, Doc. Executive Council/EX.CL/673 (XIX), para. 1(i).

316 'Ethiopian Leader Accuses International Court of Racial Bias' *Reuters* (27 May 2013).

317 Uhuru Kenyatta, 'Speech by His Excellency Hon. Uhuru Kenyatta, C.G.H., President and Commander in Chief of the Defence Forces of the Republic of Kenya' (Extraordinary Session of the Assembly of Heads of State and Government of the African Union, Addis Ababa, 12 October 2013).

318 Yoweri Kaguta Museveni, 'Statement by H.E Yoweri Kaguta Museveni President of the Republic of Uganda' (Inauguration of H.E. Uhuru Kenyatta, Kenya's President-Elect, Nairobi, 9 April 2013).

of Kenya at the time, 'take the necessary steps to put in place capable and responsible people to delegate the necessary powers to them in order to respond to the crises'.[319] President Kenyatta described the suggestion as an 'undemocratic and unconstitutional adjustments to the Kenyan Presidency' and a 'fetid insult to Kenya and Africa'.[320]

Prosecutorial activism is not unprecedented in international criminal justice. In 2010, the Chief Prosecutor of the International Criminal Tribunal for the former Yugoslavia, Serge Brammertz, insisted that Serbia should not be permitted to join the EU unless and until it secured custody over the last fugitives from the conflict: Ratko Mladic, a former Bosnian-Serb military leader, and Goran Hadzic, the former Serbian President.[321] The two suspects were subsequently arrested and surrendered to the Tribunal. Moreno Ocampo tried a similar approach in Sudan, but did not achieve the intended results. Moreno Ocampo tried to have President al-Bashir isolated both within Sudan and abroad by disclosing the amount of money that he was alleged to have in foreign bank accounts. Moreno Ocampo suggested, apparently to senior US officials, that 'if Bashir's stash of money were disclosed (he put the figure at possibly $9 billion), it would change Sudanese public opinion from him being a "crusader" to that of a thief'.[322]

Moreno Ocampo was unable to emulate what Prosecutor Serge Brammertz (who had served as Chief of Investigations under Moreno Ocampo) had achieved. Certainly, the Court operates within a different legal and political framework from the one that formed and governs the International Criminal Tribunal for the former Yugoslavia. For example, as Serbia wanted to join the EU, this desire could be and was used as leverage to coerce it into cooperating with the Yugoslav Tribunal. Such possibilities for leverage are absent in the majority of the states where the Court is controversially involved, especially in Sudan. Sudan has for a long time been treated as either a rogue state or among the states sponsoring terrorism, such that it seems to have already developed a thick diplomatic skin with regard to withstanding international pressure.

The role of international prosecutors is a complex one, ranging from that of the public face of international criminal justice to that of being principal strategists and in some cases serving political functions. The legacy of the Nuremburg Tribunals has meant that prosecutors are more likely to be remembered than judges or other members of international tribunals. The likes of Prosecutor Robert Jackson, Ben Ferencz, Richard Goldstone, Louise Arbour and Carla Del Ponte are more likely to be associated with specific episodes in the development

319 *William Samoei Ruto and Joshua Arap Sang* (ICC-01/09-01/11-T-35) Transcript, Trial Chamber V(a), 23 September 2011, p. 16.

320 Uhuru Kenyatta *supra note* 308.

321 Amann, 'Politics and Prosecutions' (eds.), note 186, (eds.), p. 30.

322 Philip Sherwell, 'Wikileaks: Sudan's President "Stashed $9 Billion"' *Daily Telegraph* (17 December 2010).

of international criminal tribunals than the names of the judges they worked for. The name Moreno Ocampo invokes mixed reactions on the streets of Khartoum and it was his portrait that was burned and trampled when the Court issued al-Bashir's arrest warrant on 4 March 2009. In Kenya, the names Moreno Ocampo and Bensouda became associated with numbers of Kenyan suspects, as if to suggest that they owned them – newspapers bore headlines containing phrases such as 'the Moreno Ocampo Six' and the 'Bensouda four', referring to the number of suspects that the two prosecutors were investigating or prosecuting.

CHAPTER 4

STATE PARTY REFERRALS, UN SECURITY COUNCIL REFERRALS AND THE SELECTION OF SITUATIONS

This chapter explores how the referrals of situations by states parties and the UN Security Council reflect their desire to ensure that international rule of law is applied in the global fight to end impunity. The chapter will highlight the referral systems used in other international human rights law machinery – namely the inter-state complaint procedure. The assumption is that the state referral mechanism in the Rome Statute was modelled on the inter-state complaint procedure. Although the state referral mechanism has not been operationalised, its analysis as applied to other human rights mechanisms could give an indication of the likelihood of it being used to refer situations to the Court. It could also be that if state referrals were to be implemented based on inter-state complaint procedures, the courts could end up opening investigations in situations occurring outside the African continent. We will then discuss the development of referral mechanisms in the *travaux préparatoires* of the Rome Statute and finally analyse the relationship between referral mechanisms and selective targeting, how the UN Security Council has referred situations to the Court and how states parties have also used the referral system.

4.1. OUTLINING THE REFERRAL SYSTEM IN INTERNATIONAL HUMAN RIGHTS

International and regional human rights treaties contain provisions outlining their implementation procedures. These procedures ensure that the treaties are respected and that, in the event of violations, appropriate action is taken to ensure that there is some form of international accountability. To that effect, one of the ways that they ensure accountability is through the inclusion of inter-state complaint procedure. For example, Article 41 of the International Covenant on Civil and Political Rights provides that a state party can file a formal complaint with the Human Rights Committee when another state party is not fulfilling its obligations.[323] The constitution of the International Labour Organization, an organisation that, in addition to being concerned with the furtherance of international industrial relations, also aims to protect fundamental human rights and provides that 'any of the Members shall have the right to file a complaint with the International Labour Office if it is not satisfied that any other member is securing the effective observance of any Convention, which both have ratified in accordance with the foregoing articles'.[324]

At a regional level, the African Charter on Human and Peoples' Rights contains provisions for inter-state complaint procedures. The procedures are provided for under the heading 'Communication from States', spanning from Articles 47–54. Article 47 provides that:

> If a state party to the present Charter has good reasons to believe that another state party to this Charter has violated the provisions of the Charter, it may draw, by written communication, the attention of that State to the matter. This communication shall also be addressed to the Secretary-General of the Organisation of African Unity and to the Chairman of the Commission.[325]

In accordance with Article 33 of the European Convention on Human Rights, any state party can refer any alleged breach of the Convention by any other state party to the European Commission of Human Rights.[326]

The raison d'etre of the inter-state complaint procedure is based on the fact that international human rights treaties set out the obligations of states parties towards their own citizens and the international community.[327] States parties to such treaties have a legal commitment to the other contracting states to afford guarantees of the rights contained in the human rights treaty in question. When a state party violates the rights of its own citizens, it is assumed that it would have also failed to honour its commitment to other states parties.[328] The concept of international law that embodies this approach, *erga omnes*, entails that states owe obligations to the international community.[329] In this regard, the behaviour of an independent state is expected to impact on the other states.

---

323 International Covenant on Civil and Political Rights (adopted 16 December 1966, entered into force 23 March 1976) 999 UNTS 171, Art. 41.

324 Constitution of the International Labour Organization (1919), Art. 26.

325 African Charter on Human and People's Rights (adopted 27 June 1981, entered into force 21 October 1986) 1520 UNTS 363), Art. 47.

326 European Convention on the Protection of Human Rights and Fundamental Freedoms (signed 4 November 1950 213 UNTS 5), Art. 24.

327 Peter Koojimans, 'Introduction to the International Systems of the Protection of Human Rights', in International Institute of Human Rights XVIIth Study Session *Collection of Lectures: Texts and Summaries* (Strasbourg, IIHR, 1986), 9–10.

328 Ibid.

329 See M. Cherif Bassioni, 'International Crimes: *Jus Cogens* and Obligatio *Erga Omnes*' (1996) 59 *Law and Contemporary Problems* 1–12.

In general, inter-state complaint procedures are under-utilised. Very few states are ready to use this procedure to address human rights violations in other states. In the few cases where inter-state complaint procedures have been invoked, the states involved would have had a hostile relationship. There would be a genuine dispute between the states concerning either the treatment accorded to the nationals or property of the complaining state.[330] Otherwise, in general, the protection of human rights in other countries is not as important to individual states as their own political or economic relations.[331]

The utilisation of inter-state complaint procedures is also limited by the fact that in most instruments, it is optional rather than mandatory. The few instruments where it is mandatory include the Constitution of the International Labour Organization, the European Convention on Human Rights and the African Charter on Human and Peoples' Rights. It could also be that some states lack the confidence to withstand any counter-complaints or 'diplomatic discomforts' if they were to take the initiative in complaining about the human rights of the other sovereign state. Inter-state complaint procedures also require considerable resources in order to conduct intensive legal research and fact-finding, and this could be too costly for some states – especially developing states.[332]

The few cases where inter-state complaint procedures have been invoked demonstrate that if applied in the enforcement of international criminal justice, they could be useful in attaining some form of geographical balance in the investigation and prosecution of international crimes. For example, on 24 February 1961, the government of Ghana wrote a letter to the ILO stating that it was not satisfied that the government of Portugal was ensuring effective observance of the Abolition of Forced Labour Convention (No. 105) in her African territories of Mozambique, Angola and Guinea – a convention both Portugal and Ghana had ratified.[333] A year earlier, Ghana's President Kwame Nkrumah had accused Portugal of practising forced labour that was akin to slavery in its colonial territory during his address to the Fifteenth Session of the UN General Assembly. The complaint made by Ghana is striking in that the complaining state did not have a direct link with the victims of the human rights violations, apart from a sense of African solidarity – which was common towards the end of colonisation of Africa.

The Rome Statute does not set any additional requirements for a state party to refer a situation to the Court. It does not require that a requesting state be the national state of the victim or the alleged perpetrator, or the territorial state.

---

330 Schabas, *An Introduction to the International Criminal Court*, note 3, p. 159.

331 Leckie, 'The Inter-state Complaint Procedure in International Human Rights Law', note 319, p. 254.

332 Ibid.

333 Report of the Commission appointed under Art. 26 of the ILO Constitution to examine the complaint filed by the Government of Ghana (Geneva, 1962), p. 1.

This means that, in theory, any state party to the Statute can refer a situation where international crimes are reported to have been committed in the territory of a state party.[334] In other words, it can be argued that what Ghana managed to do under the constitution of the International Labour Organization could be replicated under the Rome Statute.

On 8 March 2003, Léonard She Okitundu, Minister of Human Rights of the Democratic Republic of the Congo, referred Burundi, Rwanda and Uganda to the African Commission on Human and Peoples' Rights.[335] This became the first inter-state communication brought before the African Commission pursuant to Articles 47–49 of the African Charter. The Democratic Republic of the Congo filed a complaint – also referred to as a communication – accusing Burundi, Rwanda and Uganda of committing grave and massive violations of human and peoples' rights in the Congolese provinces, where there had been rebel activities since 2 August 1998. The Commission found that Burundi, Rwanda and Uganda had violated the African Charter. This landmark case demonstrated the limits of the strong bond of solidarity and general 'conspiracy of silence' pertaining to human rights violations between African states. The case demonstrates that in some situations, African states are capable of ignoring pan-Africanist relationships in pursuit of justice and accountability, especially when it involves threats to their territorial integrity.[336]

In Europe, after the 2008 armed conflict between Georgia and the Russian Federation, Georgia invoked Article 33 of the European Convention on Human Rights and instituted proceedings against the Russian Federation. It alleged that Russia had allowed, or caused, an administrative practice to develop in violation of Articles 2, 3, 5, 8 and 13 of the Convention, of Articles 1 and 2 of Protocol No. 1 and of Article 2 of Protocol No. 4. It claimed that indiscriminate and disproportionate attacks had been carried out against civilians and their property in the two autonomous regions of Georgia – Abkhazia and South Ossetia – by the Russian army and/or the separatist forces placed under their control.[337] The inter-state compliant procedures discussed here show that when a state's interests and desire for justice and accountability converge, they are prepared to sever their relations even with powerful states in their search for redress for violations of international norms – especially when they are directly affected by the actions of other states.

---

334 Antonio Cassese, *International Criminal Law* (Oxford, Oxford University Press, 2003), p. 397.

335 *Democratic Republic of Congo v. Burundi, Rwanda and Uganda*, African Commission of Human and Peoples' Rights Communication 227/99, 33rd Ordinary Session, May 2003.

336 The other two African states that resorted to the inter-complaint procedures concerning violation of human rights are Tunisia and Great Socialist Peoples Libyan Arab Jamahiriya. In 1986, Tunisia filed an application against Libya with the International Labour Organisation for violating the Protection of Wages Convention (1949) and for discriminatory employment policies.

337 *Georgia v. Russia* Application no. 38263/08 (ECtHR, 20 July 2011), para. 10.

4.2. NEGOTIATING THE TRIGGERING MECHANISMS INTO THE ROME STATUTE

The Court was designed differently from the *ad hoc* tribunals. The jurisdictions of the first-generation tribunals, Nuremburg and Tokyo, and the second-generation *ad hoc* tribunals for the former Yugoslavia and Rwanda, were pre-determined by those who established them. This made the selection of possible defendants a straightforward process for the prosecutors of such tribunals. The Court, on the other hand, was established to deal with future and unknown situations. This justified the need for a separate mechanism to activate or trigger the jurisdiction of the Court.

The concept that the new Court was not to have pre-determined and specific targets for its territorial and personal jurisdictions created a high degree of uncertainty for states, as they could not predict who the Court would select. Powerful states, especially the five permanent members of the UN Security Council, were not comfortable. In order to counter the challenge of uncertainty, powerful states such as the US, Russia and China wanted to create ways through which the Security Council could control and determine the cases that ended up being investigated and prosecuted by the Court. That is why the US wanted to enhance the role of the Security Council in the Rome Statute. Scheffer noted that some agencies within the US government were ready to trade off the requirement that the Security Council control referrals to the court on one condition – that the consent of the state nationality of the suspect be sought before they appeared before the court.[338]

4.3. THE UN SECURITY COUNCIL REFERRAL

The liberal legalist conceptualisation of law as capable of operating outside the political realm was put to the test during the drafting of the Rome Statute with regard to the relationship between the Court and the UN Security Council. The drafters had to find a formula that would not jeopardise the role of either the Court or the Security Council in addressing global impunity and the maintenance of peace and security respectively. The Draft Statute adopted by the International Law Commission in 1994 included two mechanisms for triggering the jurisdiction of the Court. These mechanisms were referral by the Security Council and by the state party.[339] The International Law Commission's proposal

338 Scheffer, *All the Missing Souls*, note 9, p. 178.

339 ILC, 'Draft Statute of the International Criminal Court in the Report of the International Law Commission on the Work of its 49th Session', UN GAOR, 49th Sess., Supp. No. 1 0, at 29–40, UN Doc. A/49/10 (1994), Art. 21.

to give the Security Council the power to trigger the jurisdiction of the Court was aimed at enabling the Security Council to make use of the Court as a tool to maintain international peace and security.[340] This is because, according to Article 24 of the UN Charter, members of the UN 'confer[ed] on the Security Council primary responsibility for the maintenance of international peace and security'.[341] The International Law Commission conceived of the Court as a judicial organ closely related to the UN (and the Security Council in particular) whose primary mission was to find ways to resolve threats to international peace and security.[342] Decisions by the Security Council to establish two *ad hoc* tribunals as measures of restoring peace and security in the former Yugoslavia and Rwanda had set a precedent that international criminal justice can contribute to the maintenance of peace and security around the globe.[343] The preamble of UN Security Council Resolution 955, adopted for the establishment of the Rwanda Tribunal, made the link clear. It sets out that the Security Council was 'convinced that in the particular circumstances of Rwanda, the prosecution of persons responsible for serious violations of international humanitarian law would enable this aim to be achieved and would contribute to the process of national reconciliation and to the restoration and maintenance of peace'.[344]

The role of the UN Security Council in international criminal justice received a further boost when the Yugoslav Tribunal confirmed that the Council was within its powers to establish international tribunals.[345] It was therefore not surprising that the permanent members pushed for the Security Council to have a key role in the Court. They wanted it to be involved in the proceedings of the Court as a means of safeguarding their interests and avoiding ambiguity and having to deal with an independent Chief Prosecutor. For the US, the Security Council's role and level of its influence over the Court's operations was a key negotiating point throughout the drafting of the Rome Statute.[346]

The African states and other Non-Aligned Movement states were opposed to the role of the UN Security Council in the proceedings of the Court. The African states' opposition to the involvement of the Security Council may have reflected doubts regarding the Council's legitimacy. As previously discussed, the African

340 Luigi Condorelli and Santiago Villalpando, 'Referral and Deferral by the Security Council' in Cassese et al. (eds.), *The Rome Statute of the International Criminal Court: A Commentary*, note 94(eds.).

341 UN Charter, Art. 24.

342 Ibid, p. 627.

343 Ibid.

344 UN Security Council Res 955 (8 November 1994) UN Doc. S/RES/1373, para. 7.

345 *Tadic* (IT-94-1-AR72), Decision on the Defence Motion for Interlocutory Appeal on Jurisdiction, 2 October 1995, paras 30–39.

346 See Schabas, *An Introduction to the International Criminal Court*, note 3, p. 25, who points out that the US wanted an international criminal court that was subordinate to the Security Council; and also Scheffer, *All the Missing Souls*, note 9, p. 179, who indicated that the US's longstanding position was for the Security Council to control of referrals to the Court.

states felt that the Security Council had often marginalised African issues – possibly because the continent had no permanent African members.

The African states' position on the relationship between the UN Security Council and the Court was articulated prior to the Rome Conference in February 1998 in the Dakar Declaration for the Establishment of the International Criminal Court. Twenty-five African governments, together with several international NGOs, adopted a declaration that envisaged an International Criminal Court that would operate independently of the actions of the Security Council.[347] The Declaration stated 'that the International Criminal Court shall operate without being prejudiced by actions of the Security Council'.[348]

At the Rome Diplomatic Conference, where the final negotiations of the Statute of the International Criminal Court took place, 49 African states were represented, some of which – Egypt, Senegal, South Africa and Lesotho – were part of the Like Minded Group. This group was committed to the establishment of a court that would be independent of the Security Council.[349] The presence of the African states at the conference and their positions reflected the global (rather than simply Western) composition of the Court.[350] The dynamism that the Africans brought to the Rome Conference is worth noting, especially in light of recent claims that the Court is founded on Western values.

African states were not the only ones to oppose the role of the UN Security Council in the role of the Court. India campaigned vigorously against the Security Council playing any role.[351] The delegate from Tanzania acknowledged the need to balance the responsibility of the Security Council under the UN Charter on the one hand and the role of the Court on the other.[352] Even so,

---

347 Dakar Declaration for the Establishment of the International Criminal Court, 6 February 1998.

348 Ibid., p. 2.

349 M. Cherif Bassiouni, 'Negotiating the Treaty of Rome on the Establishment of an International Criminal Court' (1999) 32 *Cornell International Law Journal* 443.

350 Max du Plessis, *The International Criminal Court that Africa Wants* (Pretoria, Institute of Security Studies, 2010), p. 9; see also Schabas, *An Introduction to the International Criminal Court*, note 3, p. 2, who notes the role played by South Africa and the Southern African Development Commission during the Rome Conference.

351 With regard to the role of the Security Council, the Indian delegate had the following to say: 'The Court must be entirely impartial and independent of political processes. Legally, the function of the Court was international criminal justice, not the maintenance of international peace and security. There was no legal basis on which the Security Council could either refer matters of peace and security to the Court or veto action by the Court. Any preeminent role for the Council in triggering the Court's jurisdiction constituted a violation of sovereign equality and of equality before the law because it assumed that the five veto wielding States did not by definition commit the crimes covered by the Statute of the Court or, if they did, that they were above the law and possessed de jure impunity from prosecution. The anomaly of the composition and veto power of the Council could not be reproduced in an international criminal court.' See UN Doc. A/CONF.183/SR4, para. 51.

352 UN Doc. A/CONF.183/SR3, para. 31.

there was an underlying fear that giving the Security Council any role would subject the Court to political influence. The delegate from Libya, who was probably influenced by Libya's own experiences with the Security Council in the Lockerbie case, was extremely sceptical and opposed the Security Council being given any authority over the Court. The delegate argued that the Security Council had failed to deal with many cases of flagrant aggression against Libyan territory. He added that the Security Council and its decisions were influenced by the interests and positions of certain permanent members, thus making its resolutions selective and reflective of certain double standards.[353]

Nigeria attributed its opposition to the role of the UN Security Council in the work of the Court to the past failures of the Security Council to act decisively on many issues of international concern, including the very notion of establishing an independent court.[354] Sudan, which would later become the first casualty of the Security Council's referrals to the Court, opposed the involvement of the Security Council, a political body, in the Court's judicial work. It was concerned that the UN Security Council's involvement would detract from the effectiveness of the Court.[355]

The idea of giving the UN Security Council the power to trigger the jurisdiction of the Court was a cause for concern for many states.[356] They submitted that if the Security Council were to be empowered to refer individual cases to the Court, it could end up misusing its power for political purposes and selectively targeting individuals. In the end, Article 23 specified that the Security Council could refer a 'matter' instead of a specific 'case'. The text now in the Statute provides that the Security Council can refer a 'situation' – a term that is broader than 'matter'. The task of selecting specific cases was left to the Office of the Prosecutor.

The other concern that arose during the negotiations leading up to the adoption of the 1994 Draft Statute was that, with only five permanent members of the UN Security Council having a power of veto, it would not represent the interests of the majority of the states. It was felt that conferring power onto the Security Council would introduce into the Statute a substantial inequality between the permanent members of the Security Council and other members.[357] The concern was that such inequality would negatively impact states' acceptance of and adherence to the Statute. Those who held this view wanted Article 23, which referred to the role of the Security Council, excluded from the Draft Statute altogether.

353 UN Doc. A/CONF.183//C.1/SR.6, para. 80.

354 UN Doc. A/CONF.183/C1/SR.9, para. 76.

355 Ibid, para. 68.

356 Preparatory Committee on the Establishment of an International Criminal Court – Summary of the Proceedings of the Preparatory Committee (During the Period 25 March–12 April 1996), UN Doc. A/AC 249/1, para. 147.

357 Report of the International Law Commission on the Work of its Forty-Sixth Session, UN GAOR, 49th Sess., Supp. No. 10, at 43–161, UN Doc. A/49/10 (1994), p. 41.

There was also a proposal to confer referral powers onto the UN General Assembly.[358] With Kuwait suggesting that: 'The United Nations General Assembly should also have the power to refer cases to the court, particularly where the United Nations Security Council is unable to adopt a resolution because of the use of the veto by one of its five permanent members.'[359] The proposal was rejected on the basis that, under the UN Charter, the General Assembly did not possess the same authority as the UN Security Council with regard to the maintenance of international peace and security. Under the UN Charter, the authority to decide the measures to take in order to maintain or restore international peace and security is the preserve of the Security Council.[360]

India strongly opposed the role of the UN Security Council in the Court.[361] It argued that the creation of such a role would mean that the Court was primarily a Western-dominated forum in which the majority of states did not have significant influence. For India, the reliance on the Security Council as a referral mechanism was contrary to the fundamental principle of sovereign equality.[362]

The concerns raised were not far-fetched. The UN Security Council had no consistent record of dealing with international security and peace in either a systematic way or based on a predictable criterion. During the Cold War, the permanent members of the Security Council protected some of the world's most prominent war criminals, such as Pol Pot, who led the Khmer Rouge in Cambodia, and Menguistu Haile Mariam, the most prominent officer of the communist military junta that governed Ethiopia in the 1970s, and supported proxy wars in Angola, Chad, Somalia and the former Zaire (now the Democratic Republic of the Congo). It was therefore reasonable for states to raise their concerns that the Security Council's involvement could end up threatening the legitimacy of the Court. The situation was further complicated by the fact that the three permanent members of the Security Council did not ratify the Rome Statute.

Kofi Annan, the former UN Secretary-General, wrote in his book *Interventions: A Life in War and Peace* that: 'Questions of credibility will persist so long as three of the five permanent members of the Security Council – the United States,

---

358 'Draft Statute for an International Criminal Court with commentaries in the Report of the International Law Commission on the work of its forty-sixth session', UN GAOR, 49th Sess., Supp. No. 1 0, at 43–161, UN Doc. A/49/10 (1994), p. 44; see also Christopher Keith Hall, 'The First Five Sessions of the UN Preparatory Commission for the International Criminal Court' (2000) 94 *American Journal of International Law* 773, p. 787.

359 International Law Commission Doc; A/CN.4/458 and Add. 1–8, Observations of Governments on the Report of the Working Group on a Draft Statute for an International Criminal Court, p. 54.

360 Condorelli and Villalpando, 'Referral and Deferral by the Security Council', note 331, p. 630.

361 See the statement made by Dilip Lahiri, India's Head of Delegation, Official Records Vol. II UN Doc. A/CONF.183/13 (Vol. 11), p. 86.

362 Ibid.

China, and Russia – refuse to reconsider their position and join those who have taken the courageous step to become parties to the Statute.'[363] Eventually it seems there has been a growing acceptance of the Security Council's referral role. During the AU Ministerial Preparatory meeting on the Rome Statute of the International Criminal Court held in 2009, both African States Parties and non-states parties confirmed the UN Security Council's referral role under the Rome Statute.[364]

4.4. STATE PARTY REFERRAL

The drafting history of what is now Article 14 of the Rome Statute, 'Referral of a situation by a State Party', illustrates the drafters' early recognition of the right of any state party to lodge a complaint with the Office of the Prosecutor alleging that international crime(s) had been committed. The Draft Statute, adopted by the International Law Commission in 1994, had outlined two conditions necessary for the state party to lodge a complaint with the Prosecutor. The first is that in order to lodge a complaint of genocide, the state party had to be a Contracting Party to the Convention on the Prevention and Punishment of the Crime of Genocide of 9 December 1948.[365] The second condition is that the state party must have accepted the jurisdiction of the Court over the crime in question for it to lodge a complaint to the Prosecutor.

The formulation reflects that, at the time of the adoption of the Draft Statute, the debates on whether the proposed Court was to have automatic jurisdiction or not had not been settled. As the negotiations progressed and a compromise was reached that the Court could exercise automatic jurisdiction over the crimes of genocide, crimes against humanity, war crimes and aggression, the formulation was altered. All states parties were conferred with the power to make referrals, irrespective of whether or not they were contracting parties to the Genocide Convention.

Observations submitted by more than 25 governments on the Draft Statute indicated general support for the International Law Commission's proposal for the states to trigger the jurisdiction of the Court. Austria held that conferring states parties with the power to initiate complaints 'would encourage states to become party to the statute'.[366] Tunisia wanted the right to initiate complaints before the Court extended to international organisations. For example, the same

363 Kofi Annan with Nader Mousavizadeh, *Interventions: A Life in War and Peace* (New York, Penguin, 2012), p. 153.
364 African Union, 'Report of the 2nd Ministerial Meeting on the Rome Statute of the International Criminal Court', Min/ICC/Legal/Rpt.(II), 6 November 2009, p. 4.
365 Draft Statute for an International Criminal Court (1994), Art. 25.
366 UN Doc. A/CN.4/458, 1994 Observations Made by Austria, p. 31.

concern that was raised about the UN Security Council referring individual cases to the Court was also raised with regard to the state party referral procedure. There was concern that such power could lead to a politicisation of the complaints.[367] This led to a modification of the provision that a state party refers a situation instead of a case.

There were diverging views on which states parties should have the right to trigger the jurisdiction of the Court. During the drafting process, some states felt that only interested parties should have the right to initiate complaints. Interested states were defined as custodial states, the state where the crime was committed (territorial states), the state of nationality of the suspect and the state whose nationals were victims.[368] Other states felt that since the nature of the crimes under the jurisdiction of the Court were of international concern, all states parties had an interest in seeing them prosecuted and hence should have the right to initiate complaints.[369] There still appears to be disagreement among scholars over which states parties can refer which situations to the Court. These disagreements emerged after three states (Uganda, the Democratic Republic of the Congo and the Central African Republic) referred situations in their own territories to the Court – these are now known as 'self-referrals'.

Schabas suggests that 'there is no evidence that during the drafting of the Rome Statute, either in the *travaux préparatoires* or the academic commentary, the idea that a state might refer a case against itself was never contemplated'.[370] He regards the concept of self-referral to be an invention of the Office of the Prosecutor designed to get states to refer situations to the Court.[371] Some commentators have argued that although self-referrals might not have been contemplated during the drafting history of the Rome Statute, as Cryer et al. put it, 'there is nothing in the text to prevent it'.[372] They even consider self-referrals to be practical manifestations of the states' support for international investigations; this is contrary to the general belief that such investigations are intrusive and an infringement upon state sovereignty. One could interpret the proposal to allow interested states – those where the alleged crimes were committed – to initiate complaints as somehow linked to the concept of self-referral. Whether or not the concept was contemplated during the drafting history of the Rome Statute is not significant; what is of greater relevance in this chapter is that self-referrals

---

367 UN Doc. A/AC.249/1 (1996) Summary of the Proceedings of the Preparatory Committee during the period 25 March –12 April 1996 at para. 161.

368 Ibid, para. 163.

369 Ibid.

370 Schabas, *The International Criminal Court: A Commentary on the Rome Statute*, note 61, p. 309.

371 Ibid.

372 Hakan Friman, Robert Cryer, Darrly Robinson and Elizabeth Wilmshurst, *An Introduction to International Criminal Law and Procedure* (Cambridge, Cambridge University Press, 2007), p. 134.

increase the risk of politicisation and selective enforcement. Friendly states are unlikely to use the state referral mechanism against each other, as that would be considered a hostile/humiliating action.

It has to be pointed out that selective enforcement extends beyond self-referrals. For those who view state referrals in the context of inter-state complaints mechanisms similar to those provided for in the international human rights treaties, such referrals have an equal chance of being applied in a selective manner. The potential international relations or diplomatic breakdowns that could follow a state referring another state to the Court means that the chances of such a mechanism being used between political and economic allies are very remote.[373] In international human rights treaties, inter-state complaint provisions are rarely invoked; however, when states do use them, it is usually against those with whom they have genuine disputes,[374] as was the case when the Democratic Republic of the Congo filed a communication against Burundi, Rwanda and Uganda before the African Commission on Human and Peoples' Rights.

Self-referrals are prone to abuse because it is tempting to use them against political opponents and this appeared to have been the case with the Court. They could be used to trap or manipulate the Court into being a tool used by governments to silence their own political opponents.[375] That said, the manipulation of international criminal justice to serve other ends (political or otherwise) is not a unique feature of self-referrals, but rather is inherent to the discipline of international criminal law in general.[376] If we accept that this is true, then claims by Moreno Ocampo, and many of the Court's supporters, that the Court is apolitical need to be revised, as it does not reflect reality.

4.5. THE ANALYSIS: LINKS BETWEEN REFERRAL MECHANISMS AND SELECTION OF SITUATIONS BY THE COURT – DARFUR AND LIBYA

The UN Security Council utilised the powers conferred to it in Article 13(b) to refer the situations in the Darfur region of Sudan and in Libya. The referral of the situation in Darfur originated from the recommendations made by the UN's fact-finding commission in the case of Darfur. The Commission was chaired

---

373 Schabas, *An Introduction to the International Criminal Court*, note 3, p. 159.

374 Ibid, citing the examples of inter-state complaint between Cyprus and Turkey, and Ireland and the UK.

375 Schabas, 'Prosecutorial Discretion v. Judicial Activism at the International Criminal Court', note 62, p. 731.

376 Darryl Robinson, 'The Controversy over Territorial State Referrals and Reflections on the ICL Discourse' (2011) 9 *Journal of International Criminal Justice* 355.

by Professor Antonio Cassese (Italy) and the other members were Mohammed Fayek (Egypt), Hina Jilani (Pakistan), Dumisa Ntsebesa (South Africa) and Therese Striggner Scott (Ghana). When the Commission presented its report to the Secretary-General on 25 January 2005, the report included a section on accountability mechanisms stating that:

> The Commission strongly recommends that the Security Council immediately refer the situation of Darfur to the International Criminal Court, pursuant to Article 13(b) of the ICC Statute. As repeatedly stated by the Security Council, the situation constitutes a threat to international peace and security. Moreover, as the Commission has confirmed, serious violations of international human rights law and humanitarian law by all parties are continuing. The prosecution by the ICC of persons allegedly responsible for the most serious crimes in Darfur would contribute to the restoration of peace in the region.[377]

Arbour, who was the UN High Commissioner for Human Rights at the time of the report submission, insisted that the Court was the ideal institution to investigate and prosecute those responsible for the crimes in Darfur. She stressed that:

> Designed in part for the purpose of addressing crimes that threaten international peace and security, the Court could be activated immediately. With an already existing set of well-defined rules of procedure and evidence, the Court is the institution best suited for ensuring speedy investigations leading to arrests and demonstrably fair trials.[378]

Despite her early support for the rapid intervention of the Court in Darfur, Arbour appeared to have had second thoughts in 2013. In an interview with Yves Boisvert in Montreal, she remarked that the Court's intervention in Sudan had weakened it, because it was a bad idea to refer non-states parties to the Court.[379] The credibility of the Court has been damaged by the difficulties involved in enforcing arrest warrants. It could be that the referral itself was not a bad idea, but the timing and selection of certain suspects might have been done without a sound understanding of the implications and domestic dynamics of Sudan.

On 31 March 2005, the UN Security Council, acting under Chapter VII of the UN Charter, adopted Resolution 1593 referring the situation in Darfur to the Court.[380] The voting reveals that 11 states voted in favour of the resolution,

---

377 Report of the International Commission of Inquiry on Darfur to the Secretary-General Pursuant to Security Council Resolution 1564 (2004) of 18 September 2004, UN Doc. S/2005/60, para. 572.

378 UN Security Council Verbatim Record (16 February 2005) UN Doc. S/PV/5125.

379 Yves Boisvert 'La fragile justice internationale fragilisée' *La Presse* (17 June 2013).

380 UN Security Council Resolution 1593 (31 March 2005) UN Doc. S/RES/1593.

none against and four states abstained.[381] Of the African states, Tanzania and Benin voted in favour of the resolution, while Algeria was among the states that abstained from voting. The UN Charter requires that in order for the Security Council to decide on non-procedural matters, there must be an affirmative vote of nine members, including concurring votes of the five permanent members of the UN Security Council. In relation to the referral of Sudan to the Court, it meant that even if two African states, Tanzania and Benin, had decided to show solidarity with their fellow African state by not voting in favour, the resolution would still have passed with nine votes as no permanent member of the Security Council had vetoed it. Still, it could be assumed that if Tanzania and Benin (both states parties to the Rome Statute) did not believe that the referral was the right course of action, they could at least have abstained. Their positive votes suggest that they supported the referral and the intervention of the Court in Darfur. Otherwise one would have expected them to vote against the referral and be consistent with the African principle of regional solidarity.

The Rome Statute does not explicitly state that the UN Security Council can also confer jurisdiction of the Court on non-states parties. The provision in the Rome Statute is not specific; the determination for a referral has to be when a situation threatens the peace and security of the international community. This means that such a situation could either be in a state party or a non-state party. However, when Resolution 1593 referring Sudan to the Court was adopted at the 5158th meeting of the UN Security Council held on 31 March 2005, the Sudan representative, Elfatih Mohamed Ahmed Erwa, reminded the Council that Sudan was a non-state party to the Court, alluding to the fact that the implementation of the resolution was fraught with procedural impediments.[382] Since then, Sudan has maintained that as a non-state party, it would not cooperate with the Court. As a result, there appear to be unsettled legal issues related to the immunity of heads of non-states parties in the context of Article 98, as will be discussed in Chapter 8, and in relation to the AU stance on non-cooperation with regard to the arrest and surrender of President al-Bashir.

The Sudanese representative's objection was obvious considering that the referral had extended the jurisdiction of the Court to his country, which was not a state party to the Rome Statute. The resolution suggested that his government had failed to perform its sovereign duties of protecting its own people and administering justice – a hallmark of state sovereignty – and had opened up Sudan's criminal judiciary system to the scrutiny of an external institution.

The Sudanese representative pointed out that the resolution was full of exceptions. For example, he highlighted that paragraph 6 of the resolution

381 The states that voted in *favour* were the United Republic of Tanzania, Denmark, the UK, France, Russia, Argentina, Benin, Greece, Japan, the Philippines and Romania, while those that *abstained* were Algeria, Brazil, the US and China.

382 UN Security Council Verbatim Record (31 March 2005) UN Doc. S/PV/.5158, p. 12.

provided for the selective application of the jurisdiction of the Court. Paragraph 6 shields nationals of non-states parties (other than the Sudanese) participating in the UN or AU operations in Sudan from the jurisdiction of the Court.[383] Schabas describes the paragraph, which was introduced into the resolution by John Bolton US Ambassador to the UN and a staunch critic of the Court within the George W. Bush administration, as 'legal poison'.[384] Condoleezza Rice, the former US Secretary of State, writes in her memoirs that Bolton was strongly opposed to the idea that the US supported a resolution referring a situation in Darfur to the Court. She pointed out that she had to talk President Bush into agreeing that the US would abstain from voting and thus not vetoing the resolution.[385]

In the negotiations leading up to the adoption of the referral resolution, the US government's official position had been that the Court was simply not a suitable forum for addressing the accountability issues in Darfur.[386] Perhaps they were right, although their position was a reflection of the cold attitude of the US towards the Court in 2005. As already highlighted, the US preferred the establishment of a Sudan Tribunal that would have been created by a UN Security Council resolution and administered by the UN in conjunction with the AU.[387] However, the EU and its Member States' desire for the Court to be legitimised may have led to the referral passing without a proper assessment of the implications of referring a non-state party to the Court.

The inclusion of paragraph 6 was one of the conditions laid down by the US in order for it not to veto the resolution referring Sudan. The inclusion of the paragraph was criticised by the majority of the other states in the UN Security Council. Mr Baja, the representative of the Philippines to the UN, described the inclusion of paragraph 6 as 'killing its [the International Criminal Court's] credibility – softly, perhaps, but killing it nevertheless'.[388] Although several states expressed their reservations regarding the inclusion of paragraph 6, they ultimately voted in favour of the resolution.[389]

The other criticism of the resolution raised by Sudan was that, instead of addressing the problem of accountability in Darfur, the referral had:

> [E]xposed the fact that this Criminal Court was originally intended for developing and weak states, and that it is a tool for the exercise of the culture of superiority and to

383 UN Security Council Res 1593 (31 March 2005) UN Doc. S/RES/1593.

384 Schabas, *An Introduction to the International Criminal Court*, note 3, p. 172.

385 Condoleezza Rice, *No Higher Honour: A Memoir of My Years in Washington* (New York, Simon & Schuster, 2011), p. 388.

386 Cerone, 'US Attitudes Towards International Criminal Courts and Tribunals', note 220, p. 160.

387 Ibid.

388 UN Security Council Verbatim Record (31 March 2005) UN Doc. S/PV/5158, p. 6.

389 For a detailed discussion on the legality of para. 6, see also Schabas, *An Introduction to the International Criminal Court*, note 3, pp. 173–74.

> impose cultural superiority. It is a tool for those who believe that they have a monopoly on virtues on this world, rife with injustice and tyranny.[390]

This criticism highlights the perception that the Court was established as a tool to further the values and interests of the powerful. The Sudanese representative's criticism of the Court found support elsewhere within Africa. For example, the Rwandan President also said:

> Rwanda cannot be party to ICC for one simple reason ... with ICC all the injustices of the past including colonialism, imperialism, keep coming back in different forms. They control you. As long as you are poor, weak there is always some rope to hang you. ICC is made for Africans and poor countries.[391]

The perception is that the Court was established based on selectivity rather than equality before the law. The Sudanese criticism questioned international criminal justice in its entirety, as well as its relationship with the international legal order, which seemed to be skewed in favour of powerful states such as the permanent members of the UN Security Council.

However, not every developing state agreed – there was a noticeable divergence of views among the African states. During the meeting there were three African states occupying the non-permanent seats in the UN Security Council – Algeria, Benin and the Republic of Tanzania. Benin and Tanzania voted in favour of the resolution, showing great support for the need for accountability in Darfur. The representative from Benin's remarks after the vote indicated that its position was in concordance with his country's 'respect for human dignity and the right to life that has been denied to thousands of people in Darfur, to whom the international community owes protection in view of their vulnerability'.[392] He further linked his country's position to the AU's recognition that the UN Security Council had the right to exercise its international responsibility to protect a population when the population's government either cannot or will not do so. Benin considered that rendering of justice was an element of that obligation to protect.[393] The representative from Tanzania justified his country's vote in favour of the resolution based on the fact that his country believed that the Court was the most appropriate international mechanism for dealing with the situation in Darfur, as recommended by the Commission of Inquiry.[394]

It is essential to clarify that the AU criticism of the UN Security Council was not initially about its decision to refer the situation in Sudan to the Court.

---

390 UN Security Council Verbatim Record (31 March 2005) UN Doc. S/PV/5158, p. 12.

391 D. Kezio-Musoke, 'Kagame Tells Why He is against ICC Charging Bashir' *Daily Nation* (3 August 2008).

392 UN Security Council Verbatim Record (31 March 2005) UN Doc. S/PV/5158, p. 10.

393 Ibid.

394 Ibid, p. 9.

After all, the Security Council was acting on specific recommendations made by the UN Commission of Inquiry; it was not acting in an arbitrary manner. Problems arose when the Security Council failed to deal with the AU's request to have the proceedings against President al-Bashir be deferred for at least 12 months to allow the peace to take effect.[395]

4.5.1. LIBYA AND SECURITY COUNCIL RESOLUTION 1970

During the Arab Spring in 2011, the Libyan government embarked on a ruthless crackdown on what were at the beginning largely peaceful protestors. At the beginning of the protests, the Libyan leader Muammar Gaddafi and his son Saif Islam Gaddafi made fierce and inflammatory threats against the protestors. Some of the threats were interpreted as incitement for Gaddafi supporters to commit genocide. Several senior officials in the al-Gaddafi government resigned. Some even joined the protestors.

The first UN body to come out and directly condemn the brutality of the Gaddafi regime was the UN Human Rights Council.[396] On 25 February 2011, the UN Human Rights Council unanimously adopted Resolution S-15/1, entitled 'Situation of Human Rights in the Libyan Arab Jamahiriya'. The resolution condemned the grave human rights violations that were being committed in Libya at the time. It also established an independent, impartial, credible UN-led international investigation into the human rights violations in Libya in order to ensure that there would be full accountability for those responsible for violations. During the debates that led to the adoption of the resolution, the African states spoke in support of the need for the government of Libya to use restraint and

---

395 Decision on the Application by the International Criminal Court (ICC) Prosecutor for the Indictment of the President of the Republic of the Sudan, 1–3 February, 2009, Addis Ababa, Ethiopia, Doc. Assembly/AU/221 (XII), para. 3 states that; 'the African Union urging the United Nations Security Council, in accordance with the provisions of Art. 16 of the Rome Statute of the ICC, and as requested by the PSC at its above- mentioned meeting, to defer the process initiated by the ICC'. Cf. Decision on the Meeting of African States Parties to the Rome Statute of the International Criminal Court (ICC), 1–3 July 2009 Sirte, Libya Doc. Assembly/AU/13(XIII), para. 9; 'deeply regrets that the request by the African Union to the UN Security Council to defer the proceedings initiated against President Bashir of The Sudan in accordance with Art. 16 of the Rome Statute of the ICC, has neither been heard nor acted upon, and in this regard, reiterates its request to the UN Security Council'; and para. 10 'deciding that in view of the fact that the request by the African Union has never been acted upon, the AU Member States shall not cooperate pursuant to the provisions of Art. 98 of the Rome Statute of the ICC relating to immunities, for the arrest and surrender of President Omar El Bashir of The Sudan'.

396 'UN Rights Council Recommends Suspending Libya, Orders Inquiry into Abuses', United Nations News Centre, Press Release, 25 February 2011.

to protect human security.[397] The investigating team was chaired by Professor Cherif Bassiouni (Egypt), Asma Khader (Jordanian/Palestinian) and Philippe Kirsch (Canada).

Immediately after the UN Human Rights Council's unanimous condemnation of the violations of the human rights, the UN Security Council adopted Resolution 1970. This included a paragraph that referred the situation in Libya to the Court.[398] The defecting Permanent Representative of Libya to the UN appeared to have had initiated the process when he sent a letter to the President of the Security Council calling for such a referral. The referral was part of a range of measures by the Security Council on Libya to push for the cessation of violence and the restoration of calm and stability. Perhaps this explains why the Security Council did not have to wait for the findings from a Commission of Inquiry set up by the Human Rights Council to pass the resolution, as was the case with Darfur, where it had to wait for the Cassese Report and its recommendations.

In any case, the UN Security Council acknowledged the Human Rights Council resolution, which included the establishment of a Commission of Inquiry for Libya. Perhaps the Security Council should have waited for the Commission of Inquiry's report, as this could have shown it the state of the Libyan national criminal justice system and the role it could have played in addressing the accountability for those who committed some of the atrocities. With hindsight, such an opportunity would have been helpful in light of the tug-of-war that later developed between the Court and the new Libyan government over the most appropriate forum in which to try Saif-al-Gaddafi.

A notable difference between Resolution 1970 and Resolution 1593 is that the UN Security Council unanimously adopted the former, whereas four states abstained from the latter. All the states from the African region (Gabon, Nigeria and South Africa) voted in favour of the referral of the situation in Libya. This made Resolution 1970 the first ever-unanimous UN Security Council referral. This was obviously a positive development for the supporters of international criminal justice and the Court in particular. It was perhaps an indication of either the growing acceptance of the Court by the international community or the desire to find a rapid and lasting solution to the situation in Libya. That said, the inclusion of a provision that excluded the nationals of non-states parties from the jurisdiction of the Court in Libya raised eyebrows among those supportive of equality before the law.

The UN Security Council resolutions referring the situations in Sudan and Libya to the Court specified that the Court had to prosecute international crimes committed 'in Darfur' and 'in the Libyan Arab Jamahiriya'. However, they did not

---

397 See statements made by the Representative of Nigeria on behalf of the Africa Group and the statement by the representative of Senegal, Special Session, 'The Situation of Human Rights in the Libyan Arab Jamahiriya', OHCHR, 25 February 2011.

398 UN Security Council Resolution 1970 (26 February 2011) UN Doc. S/RES/1970.

extend the Court's jurisdiction to the nationals of non-states parties that were operating in either Darfur or Libya at that time. The exclusion of the nationals of non-states parties appears to have become a standard provision of Security Council resolutions, since the US requested in 2002 that the Security Council defer the investigations and prosecutions of peacekeepers. This reflects the standing policy of the US of not allowing its nationals on official missions, such as peacekeepers, to be exposed to the Court's jurisdiction. The provision appears to sanction the selective enforcement of international criminal law. To be clear, this is not to suggest that the US prompts or prefers impunity for international crimes; it just does not permit some of its citizens, especially on those official duties, to face trial in foreign jurisdictions. In the *ad hoc* tribunals, the US did not propose the exclusion of its nationals, so both the Rwandan Tribunal and the Yugoslav Tribunal could exercise their jurisdiction over US citizens.

In the case of Libya, the immunity provision meant that NATO forces were rendered immune from prosecution. The provision on immunity, which is usually used to protect UN peacekeepers, caused media confusion in the context of Libya. Many in the press misconstrued the provision to mean that it also gave immunity to mercenaries who were alleged to have been invited to fight in Libya by Colonel Gaddafi, since they were not Libyans but foreigners. What the media missed was the fact that, unlike peacekeepers, mercenaries were not in Libya under the UN Charter. The inclusion of mercenaries in the Darfur referral was not as controversial as it was in the Libyan referral. This was because there were several foreign nationals taking part in the conflict in Libya, including alleged mercenaries, which was not the case in Darfur. It was alleged that al-Gaddafi recruited mercenaries from Ethiopia, Algeria and Tunisia to support his forces against the protestors. The media interpreted the provision as providing an escape route for the mercenaries from the jurisdiction of the Court.[399] The provision clearly set out that only foreign nationals in Libya under the authorisation of the Security Council were protected, and the mercenaries did not fall into this category.[400] In any case, the Court's priority is to focus primarily on those with greatest responsibility and not on all the perpetrators of international crimes.

One area in which UN Security Council referrals have threatened the credibility of the Court is their lack of a clear systematic criterion for referrals. This has led to claims of selective enforcement and double standards. For example, although there was credible evidence to support referrals of Darfur and Libya to the Court, there is even more compelling evidence that atrocities of the same magnitude have occurred in other parts of the world and that the Security Council appears to be treating these atrocities differently. These inconsistencies

399 Jon Swaine, 'Libya: African Mercenaries "Immune from Prosecution for War Crimes' (2011) <http://www.telegraph.co.uk/news/worldnews/africaandindianocean/libya/8350968/Libya-African-mercenaries-immune-from-prosecution-for-war-crimes.html> accessed 17.10.2016.

400 Ibid.

leave the impression that international criminal justice has not made significant strides away from general practices during the Cold War, or even the phase of *ad hoc* tribunals. This is because permanent members of the Security Council appear to protect their allies from referrals to the Court. Such double standards and selective enforcement pose a palpable threat to the legitimacy of the Court.

Some notable situations where the UN Security Council could have used its powers under Article 13(b) include those in Sri Lanka, the Occupied Territories of Palestine and Syria. These countries are non-states parties, so the Office of the Prosecutor cannot trigger the Court's jurisdiction under Article 15. The jurisdiction of the Court has to be triggered through a Security Council resolution under Chapter VII of the UN Charter. The situation in Syria reached a stage where it posed a threat to international peace and security. It generated floods of refugees into neighbouring countries, some reaching as far as Europe, and almost led into an international armed conflict involving Syria, Turkey, Israel and Russia. Despite this, the Security Council delayed taking any concrete action. This lack of action is attributed to Syria having very strong allies among the permanent members of the Security Council, who would veto any resolution that included a referral clause.

The situation in Syria deteriorated into a humanitarian catastrophe in only five years and to some extent destabilised the Middle East, including creating one of the worst refugee crisis in modern history. From the onset of the crisis in 2011, during the so-called Arab Spring, the situation was described as a threat to international peace and security. This was later confirmed with the emergence of some of the most brutal brands of terrorism ever seen – which involved state-like outfits such as so-called Islamic State, the members of which were linked to the terror attacks in Paris and Brussels in 2015 and 2016. There has been evidence that both sides in the conflict were committing international crimes. As such, there were calls for the UN Security Council to refer the situation to the Court.

The first call for Syria to be referred to the Court was made in December 2011 by Judge Navanethem Pillay, the UN High Commissioner for Human Rights, in a closed session of the Security Council.[401] Judge Pillay repeated the same calls in subsequent years – 2012, 2013 and 2014 – without any success. In her view, a referral could have played a 'significant preventative effect because it would have sent a clear message to both the government and opposition that there will be consequences for their actions'.[402] Bernard Kouchner, the former French Foreign Minister, weighed in, arguing in favour of accountability for the crimes committed in Syria. He expressed his views in an editorial (op-ed) article published in the *International Herald Tribune* in 2012: 'The urgency of the crisis

401 'Syria Should Be Referred to ICC, UN's Navi Pillay Says' *BBC News* (13 December 2011).

402 UN Human Rights Office of the Human Rights, 'Pillay Renews Calls to Refer Syria to World Court', 13 February 2013.

demands an appeal to international justice, which is the travelling companion of the right to intervene.'[403] However, he erred in suggesting that either that the UN Secretary-General or the victims could refer Syria to the Court. Still, the article underpins how the situation in Syria was a cause for concern in capitals around the world, and yet no concrete action was taken to protect the victims primarily because of a lack of consensus among the members of the UN Security Council. Russia and China in particular blocked resolutions that sought to authorise decisive measures to be taken in Syria.[404]

In 2014, Russia and China vetoed draft Resolution S/2014/348 seeking the referral of Syria to the Court.[405] The draft resolution, which had been submitted by more than 60 states, including African states,[406] sought the referral of the situation in the Syrian Arab Republic to the Court. Syrian representative described the resolution as 'political, discriminatory and interventionist par excellence'. Nigeria, Chad and Rwanda, which at the time were members of the UN Security Council on a rotational basis, voted in favour of the draft resolution. Rwanda and Chad underscored their misgivings with the Court in their remarks explaining why they had voted in favour of the referral. However, it is curious that they did not make reference to the immunity of President Bashar al-Assad of Syria as a sitting head of state – a striking point that is often floated with regard to President al-Bashir of Sudan.

For their part, China and Russia had demanded that any reference to the Court be removed from the resolution and had expressed their regrets over how Resolutions 1970 and 1973 on Libya had been implemented. They claimed that NATO, Russia's military rival, had overstepped its obligations in relation to the two resolutions by bombing Libya. It is possible that one of the reasons why al-Gaddafi failed to escape and seek refuge in another country when he was overthrown in a popular uprising in 2011 was the existence of the indictment

---

403 Bernard Kouchn2er, 'Bring Syria to Justice' *International Herald Tribune* (11 June 2012).

404 See UN Doc. S/PV.6627, 4 October 2011 – Russian Federation and China vetoed a draft resolution that had threatened, among other measures, sanctions against the Syrian authorities. France, Germany, Portugal and the UK sponsored the draft resolution, which was supported by 13 members, while Brazil, South Africa, India and Lebanon abstained; also UN Doc. S/PV.6711, 4 February 2012, China and Russian Federation vetoed the draft resolution while Azerbaijan, Colombia, France, Germany, Guatemala, India, Morocco, Pakistan, Portugal, South Africa, Togo, United Kingdom of Great Britain and Northern Ireland and United States of America voted in favour of the resolution; UN Doc. S/PV.6810, 19 July 2012, Russian Federation and China also vetoed another draft resolution on Syria; Azerbaijan, Colombia, France, Germany, Guatemala, India, Morocco, Portugal, Togo, United Kingdom of Great Britain and Northern Ireland and United States of America voted in favor and Pakistan and South Africa abstained.

405 UN Doc. S/PV.7180, 22 May 2014.

406 Botswana, the Central African Republic, Cote d'Ivoire, the Democratic Republic of the Congo, Libya, Senegal and the Seychelles.

and the international arrest warrant.[407] The indictment turned him into an unwanted guest for several states. China and Russia were therefore concerned that a strong resolution on Syria and a referral to the Court could have led to a repetition of what had happened in Libya.

The Stockholm International Peace Research Institute database, an international source on global security, also indicates that Russia is one of the two main suppliers of military hardware to Syria (the other supplier is Iran).[408] Such national interests appear to have made it politically difficult for the UN Security Council to take decisive action on Syria, let alone to refer the situation to the Court.

If Russia and China can be identified for stalling the referral of the Syria to the Court, similar claims can be made about the US in relation to the situation in the Occupied Territories of Palestine. In 2009, the UN Commission of Inquiry found out that the Israel Defence Forces had committed war crimes and crimes against humanity in the Occupied Territories during their incursion into Gaza.[409] The Commission of Inquiry recommended the involvement of the Court. It specifically stated that:

> The mission recommends that, upon receipt of the committee's report, the Security Council should consider the situation and, in the absence of good-faith investigations that are independent and in conformity with international standards having been undertaken or being under way within six months of the date of its resolution under Article 40 by the appropriate authorities of the State of Israel, again acting under Chapter VII of the Charter of the United Nations, refer the situation in Gaza to the Prosecutor of The Court pursuant to Article 13 (b) of the Rome Statute.[410]

The report, known as the Goldstone Report after its chairman, Justice Goldstone, turned out to be very divisive within the international community. States were divided mainly between the developing countries, which largely endorsed the report, and the developed states, which criticised it as being biased against Israel. The US expressed its serious concern on the recommendations of the report.

---

407 European Council on Foreign Relations (ECFR) Background Paper on International Justice and the Preventation of Atrocities Case Study 'Libya :The ICC enters During War', by Pricilla Hayner, November 2013 available at http://www.ecfr.eu/page/-/IJP_Libya.pdf accessed on 13.01.2014.

408 SIPRI, Arms Transfer Database TIV of arms export to Syria 2011-2015 http://armstrade.sipri.org/armstrade/page/values.php.

409 UN Human Rights Council, Twelfth Session, 'Report of the United Nations Fact Finding Mission on the Gaza Conflict – Conclusions and Recommendations', 15 September 2009, UN Doc. A/HRC/12/48.

410 Ibid, p. 548.

On 9 September, the US House of Congress passed resolution H.Res. 867 (111th),[411] which called for:

> [T]he President and the Secretary of State to oppose any endorsement of the Report in multilateral fora, including through leading opposition to any UN General Assembly resolution and through vetoing any UN Security Council resolution that endorses the Report's contents, seeks to act upon the Report's recommendations, or calls on any other international body to take further action regarding such Report.[412]

The resolution summarised the position of the US, making it clear that the chances for the UN Security Council to refer the situation in Gaza to the Court were non-existent. In 2010, Ileana Ros-Lehtinen, a Republican Congresswomen who sponsored Resolution 867, co-sponsored draft legislation, the American Self-Defense Protection Act of 2010, the purpose of which was: 'To safeguard the sovereignty and right to self-defence of the United States and its allies, to prohibit United States participation in the International Criminal Court, and for other purposes.'[413]

The US stalling of the entire accountability process over international crimes in Gaza confirmed that states with strong allies in the UN Security Council could be shielded from the Court's jurisdiction. This illustrates the double standards and selective triggering of international criminal justice.

In this regard, it only seems fair that the criticism of selective enforcement and double standards are better directed towards the UN Security Council instead of the Court. This is because the Security Council has the authority under Article 13(b) to refer situations, but it is selective in doing so.

The UN Security Council's lack of consistency in its approach somehow justifies the calls for its reform. This agenda for reform is overdue and has been pushed for by the developing states, including some emerging regional powers such as Brazil, South Africa, India and middle powers like Japan and Germany. However, judging from how these states have approached the issues of international human rights and international justice, it is not straightforward that their inclusion in the Security Council would make significant changes.

South Africa has struggled to demonstrate strong leadership in assisting its neighbour Zimbabwe in resolving its governance and human rights violations

---

411 See United States House of Representatives Resolution 867 – 111th Congress: Calling on the President and the Secretary of State to oppose unequivocally any endorsement or further consideration of the 'Report of the United Nations Fact Finding Mission on the Gaza Conflict' in multilateral fora. GovTrack.us (database of federal legislation). 2009. 21 November 2012 <http://www.govtrack.us/congress/bills/111/hres867>.

412 Ibid.

413 See United States House of Representative Bill. 5351 – 111th Congress: American Self-Defense Protection Act of 2010. GovTrack.us (database of federal legislation), 2010 <http://www.govtrack.us/congress/bills/111/hr5351> accessed 16.10.2016. The House Committee on Foreign Affairs is reviewing the bill and its status is that it is dead.

record. It preferred 'quiet diplomacy' to publicly condemning the alleged dictatorial tendencies of President Mugabe and his ruling Zimbabwean Africa National Union – Patriotic Front (ZANU-PF). Some commentators have attributed South Africa's failure to take a strong stance on Zimbabwe to the historical ties between the ruling elites of the two countries.

At the same time, Brazil's policies on the importance of democracy and human rights throughout Latin America, particularly in Cuba and Venezuela, have been ambiguous.[414] Similarly, although India initially promoted democracy and human rights in Myanmar, its government's position regarding the crackdown on opposition leaders in Myanmar in 2007 was more muted than expected.[415] It was only in 2012 that India appears to have abandoned its traditional ally Sri Lanka when it voted in favour of a UN Human Rights Council resolution on Sri Lanka. These few examples highlight that the reform of the Security Council might not necessarily result in the removal of selective enforcement in the triggering of the jurisdiction of the Court.

The discussion on the UN Security Council selectively triggering situations in Africa makes one ask whether African states have loyal allies within the Security Council. This is because if the allies of Sri Lanka or Syria in the Security Council could protect them from the Court, why couldn't African states be protected? This is not in any way to suggest that the Court should not intervene in Africa, but to evaluate how African states are probably viewed by their allies in particular and by the international community in general. The reality could be that the majority of African states are not as strategic as they may claim, especially in comparison to the states in other regions. African states seems to struggle when it comes to having loyal allies in the international arena. The allies they do have, for instance, in Russia and China, seem to be dependent upon how these two powerful states calculate their own relationship with the US and the UK and less to do with the strategic importance of the African states. For example, when the relations between Russia and US are warm, the former's relationship with African states weakens.

4.5.2. STATES PARTIES REFERRALS AND SELECTIVE ENFORCEMENT

As already highlighted, one of the main criticisms against self-referrals is that they are prone to politicisation and have the potential to lead to selective investigations and prosecutions. The concern is that when a state refers a

414 Jorge G. Castaneda, 'Not Ready for Prime Time: Why Including Emerging Powers at the Helm Would Hurt Global Governance' (2010) 89 *Foreign Affairs* 109, p. 115.

415 Ibid, p. 113.

situation to the Court, the chances are that it might manipulate the process by selectively drawing the attention of the Court to the crimes committed by its enemies.[416] The question of selective enforcement was raised in 2003, when the Ugandan government referred the situation surrounding the LRA in Northern and Western Uganda to the Court.[417] The Ugandan referral was based on specific personal parameters. The letter of referral made reference to the 'situation concerning the Lord's Resistance Army in northern and western Uganda'.[418] Although the inclusion of specific personal parameters in referrals is not prohibited under the Statute, the delegates at the Rome conference attempted to discourage it by favouring the use of the term 'situation' over 'case'.[419]

The Ugandan government's referral directed the attention of the Court to the LRA, which had been engaged in a protracted guerrilla conflict against President Yoweri Museveni's government for more than two decades. It tried to exclude the Ugandan government's armed forces, the Ugandan People's Defence Force, from the jurisdiction of the Court. One commentator pointed out that the Ugandan referral might also have been a bid to distract the Prosecutor from investigating the role of government forces in the Ituri region of the Democratic Republic of the Congo.[420]

While the Prosecutor initially welcomed the personal parameters defined in the Ugandan referral, he later backtracked. He stated that 'the scope of the referral encompasses all crimes committed in Northern Uganda in the context of the ongoing conflict involving the [LRA]'.[421] However, in reality, the Court only issued international arrest warrants against the LRA commanders, leading to the perception that the government's enemies were being targeted.

The perception of bias and selective enforcement arose immediately after President Yoweri Museveni and Prosecutor Moreno Ocampo appeared together during the announcement of the referral at a press conference. Their joint appearance sent the wrong signal – that the Prosecutor was perceived to be 'associating too closely with one party to the conflict, thus undermining

416 Schabas, 'Prosecutorial Discretion v. Judicial Activism at the International Criminal Court', note 62, p. 753; and also Sarah M.H. Nouwen and Wouter G. Werner, 'Doing Justice to the Political: The International Criminal Court in Uganda and Sudan' (2011) 21 *European Journal of International Law* 941.

417 Situation in Uganda (ICC-02/04-01/05), Decision to Convene a Status Conference on the Investigation in the Situation in Uganda in Relation to the Application of Article, 2 December 2005, para. 3.

418 See Schabas, *The International Criminal Court: A Commentary on the Rome Statute*, note 61, p. 307.

419 Ibid, p. 299.

420 Sarah M.H. Nouwen, *Complementarity in the Line of Fire: The Catalysing Effect of the International Criminal Court in Uganda & Sudan* (Cambridge, Cambridge University Press, 2013), p. 112.

421 Schabas, *The International Criminal Court: A Commentary on the Rome Statute*, note 61.

perception of the Court's impartiality'.[422] This joint press conference was the subject of protest by some of the senior officials in the Office of the Prosecutor.[423] The perception of bias was reinforced when not a single arrest warrant was issued for individuals serving in the Ugandan People's Defence Forces. Considerable evidence from the reports prepared by human rights NGOs and local Acholi community leaders showed that the Ugandan People Defence Forces had perpetrated international crimes against the civilians in Northern Uganda with near-immunity.[424] In response to the claims that the Court was selective, the Prosecutor argued that the gravity of the crimes committed by the LRA was greater than those committed by the Ugandan government's forces.

Naturally, the gravity of crimes within a specific situation must be taken into consideration given that, although the Court is supposed to have a global reach, it has limited human and financial resources. It has to be selective and one of the criteria it uses is the gravity of the crimes found in a given situation. This obviously is hard for the victims who have suffered from brutality on both sides of the conflict, and this is precisely why national criminal justice systems are expected to play their role in the struggle against impunity. Leaving the government forces out of investigations and prosecutions implies that Uganda's President Museveni and his government are the beneficiaries of perpetual impunity for their atrocities, although they are alleged to have been committing crimes against the Northern Ugandan population since they came to power in 1986. This is because when President Museveni assumed power after a military campaign, he barred the national truth commission from investigating any crimes committed after his rise to power.[425] This means that there has been no accountability for Museveni and his supporters.

It seems that Ugandan self-referral served President Museveni and the Ugandan government's interests in several ways. First, it reaffirmed Museveni's self-proclaimed status at the national, regional and international levels as a champion of democracy and international justice. His country was the first state party to refer a situation to the Court, giving the impression that he respects the

422 Marieke Wierda and Michael Otim, 'Justice at Juba: International Obligations and Local 21 Demands in Northern Uganda' in Nicholas Waddell and Phil Clark (ed.), *Courting Conflict? Justice, Peace and the ICC in Africa* (London, Royal African Society, 2008), p. 22.

423 See Brevin, 'Justice Delayed for Global Court', note 273, who points out that 'several ICC staff members objected to Mr Moreno Ocampo appearing publicly with Mr Museveni, citing the Ugandan government's reputed involvement in atrocities in eastern Congo, this included the then Court's ICC investigations chief Serge Brammertz'.

424 See Human Rights Watch, *Uprooted and Forgotten: Impunity and Human Rights Abuses in Northern Uganda* (New York, Human Rights Watch, 2005); and also Tim Allen, *Trial Justice: The International Criminal Court and the Lord's Resistance Army* (London, Zed Books, 2006), pp. 96–102.

425 Sverker Finnstrom, *Living with Bad Surroundings: War, History, and Evryday Moments in Northern Uganda* (Durham, NC, Duke University Press, 2008), p. 227.

international rule of law. The referral also drew international attention to the long and often forgotten conflict in Northern Uganda.

Following in the footsteps of Uganda, the Democratic Republic of the Congo referred a situation in its territory to the Court in April 2004.[426] The referral letter signed by President Joseph Kabila triggered the jurisdiction of the Court to investigate crimes 'committed anywhere on the territory of the Democratic Republic of Congo since the entry into force of the Rome Statute, on 1 July 2002'.[427] This differed from the Ugandan referral in that it did not define the personal parameters for the Court. Following the referral, the Court issued arrest warrants[428] and secured custody of the suspects, who then faced trial at The Hague. Thomas Lubanga was convicted in 2012 and sentenced to 14 years' imprisonment.[429]

The involvement of the Court in the Democratic Republic of the Congo raised several issues related to case selection and the charges pressed against some of the suspects. Professor Phil Clark, Reader in Comparative and International Politics with reference to Africa at the School of Oriental and African Studies (SOAS) in the UK, pointed out that Ituri was one of the regions in the Democratic Republic of the Congo that had a functioning judiciary system,[430] and that this judiciary system had proved its capacity by starting investigations into prosecuting some militias. The trials were probably made possible because of a massive financial investment made by the EU to rehabilitate the local judicial system.

The focus on Ituri led some observers to question the validity of the Office of the Prosecutor's strategy. Some wondered why it focused its energies somewhere where the judicial task was relatively straightforward due to the substantial local capacity instead of investigating mass atrocities committed in other regions where judicial resources were lacking.[431] The Office of the Prosecutor appears to have sought out the easiest path to execute the mandate of the Court. For example, the presence of UN peacekeeping forces in the Ituri region meant that

---

426 'Prosecutor Receives Referral of the Situation in the Democratic Republic of the Congo', ICC Office of the Prosecutor, Press Release, 19 April 2004.

427 Ibid.

428 *Lubanga* (ICC-01/04-01/06-06), Decision on the Prosecutor's Application for a Warrant of Arrest, 10 February 2006; *Ntaganda* (ICC-01/04-02/06), Warrant of Arrest, 22 August 2006; *Ngudlolo* (ICC-01/04-02/07), Decision on the Evidence and Information Provided by the Prosecution for the Issuance of a Warrant of Arrest for Mathieu Ngudjolo Chui, 6 July 2007; *Katanga* (ICC-01/04-01/07), Decision on the Evidence and Information Provided by the Prosecution for the Issuance of a Warrant of Arrest for Germain Katanga, 6 July 2007; *Mbarushimana* (ICC-01/04-01/10-2), Warrant of Arrest for Callixte Mbarushimana, 11 October 2010; *Mudacumura* (ICC-01/04-01/12), Decision on the Prosecutor's Application under Art. 58, 13 July 2012.

429 *Lubanga* (ICC-01/04-01/06), Judgment, 14 March 2012.

430 Phil Clark, 'Law, Politics and Pragmatism: The ICC and Case Selection in Uganda and the Democratic Republic of the Congo' in Waddell and Clark (eds.), *Courting Conflict?*, note 413.

431 Ibid, p. 40.

there were fewer obstacles to the Office of the Prosecutor conducting its own investigations compared to the harsher conditions in the South and North Kivu region. In the Kivu region, the military and political situation is very fluid since the outbreak of armed conflict in 2007, following the attempts and failure by the government of the Democratic Republic of the Congo to integrate rebel movements into the army. The region has several armed groups and militia allied to different powers, including the government of the Democratic Republic of the Congo, and there are suggestions that some even get support from the Rwandan government.

It is also possible that the rebel leaders in Ituri were easier targets for the Court than anywhere else because they had not participated in the peace process between the Democratic Republic of the Congo and several major rebel movements. The peace talks ended a civil war that had engulfed the Democratic Republic of the Congo, more than five regional countries and several armed groups. However, the groups in Ituri had not participated in the talks, remained armed and were considered a threat to the government in Kinshasa. This factor might have played a part in encouraging the government and the Office of the Prosecutor to focus on the Ituri region. In this case, the Prosecutor can be said to have served the government's interests in neutralising the armed groups in Ituri, which were in any case beyond the control of the government.

In addition, the vast geographical distance between Ituri and Kinshasa – it is 1,700 km from Kinshasa to Bunia – made it unlikely that the investigations would have implicated any government officials or commanders.In other provinces, such as Kivu, government forces supported some of the militia, such as the Mayi Mayi, who were also alleged to have committed atrocities, and investigations in these areas would receive less cooperation from the Congolese government.

The Prosecutor pointed out that Ituri was just the beginning of the Court's involvement in the Democratic Republic of the Congo.[432] This was probably a fair response from the Prosecutor, considering that later his office went on to open investigations and issue arrest warrants for suspects beyond the Ituri region. For example, in 2010 and 2012, the Court issued arrest warrants for Callixte Mbarushimana in connection with war crimes and crimes against humanity alleged to have been committed in the Kivu Province of the Democratic Republic of the Congo.[433] He was released from custody after the Court failed to confirm the charges against him. Nonetheless, the fact that he was selected for investigation and arrested serves to show that claims that the Court had a narrow geographical focus are not completely fair in the Congolese context.

---

432 Based on the interview held between Professor Phil Clark and Prosecutor Moreno Ocampo; see ibid.

433 *Mbarushimana* (ICC-01/04-01/10-2), Warrant of Arrest for Callixte Mbarushimana, 11 October 2010.

The same is true of Sylvestre Mudacumura, the military commander of the Democratic Forces for the Liberation of Rwanda operating in Eastern Congo, who had his arrest warrant issued in 2012. Mudacumura was, and still is, accused of being criminally responsible for war crimes and crimes against humanity committed by the Democratic Forces for the Liberation of Rwanda in the North and South Kivu Provinces.[434] The volatile nature of politics in the Democratic Republic of the Congo and its neighbouring territories often leads to rapid changes of alliances and governments. This creates opportunities for the Court in that as alliances are formed and fall apart, those on the Prosecutor's wanted list are more likely to be handed over to The Hague the moment they lose their political support from Kinshasa. While the Court might not have anticipated this, the political reality demands caution and good timing – especially for the Office of the Prosecutor.

In 2004, the government of the Central African Republic referred 'the situation of crimes within the jurisdiction of the Court committed anywhere on [its] territory'.[435] After the Office of the Prosecutor conducted preliminary investigations, it concluded that the domestic criminal justice system in the Central African Republic was unable to deal with international crimes committed on its territory. Consequently, an international warrant of arrest was issued for Jean-Pierre Bemba,[436] who had served in the Democratic Republic of the Congo as Vice President during the country's transitional period following the end of the civil war in 2003. During the civil war, he was the leader of the Mouvement de Liberation du Congo, one of the main rebel groups in the Democratic Republic of the Congo. The rebel movement was involved in the Central African Republic when President Ange-Felix Patesse's grip on power was under threat from Francois Bozize. President Patesse had approached Bemba's forces for assistance, but ultimately lost power, and subsequently Bemba's rebel movement was accused of committing war crimes and crimes against humanity. These crimes are alleged to have been committed during the period that the *Mouvement de Liberation du Congo* spent in the Central African Republic. The Court found Bemba guilty of war crimes in 2016 and sentenced him to 18 years in prison.

It could be argued that political considerations played a more significant role than legal considerations in the decision to target Bemba for the crimes committed in the Central African Republic. The charges against him could have been levelled equally at President François Bozize and some of his officials. Human Rights Watch put it blatantly when it noted that 'the majority of these

---

434 *Mudacumura* (ICC-01/04-01/12), Decision on the Prosecutor's Application under Article 58, 13 July 2012.

435 ICC Office of the Prosecutor Press Release, Prosecutor Receives Referral Concerning Central African Republic, 7 January 2005.

436 *Bemba* (ICC-01/05-01/08), Warrant of Arrest for Jean Pierre Bemba, 23 May 2008.

crimes were allegedly committed by forces affiliated with the government that voluntarily referred crimes to the ICC'.[437] The fact that Bemba had also lost an election in the Democratic Republic of the Congo, which inspired skirmishes between his armed group and that of President Kabila, made him the enemy of two sitting presidents – probably a very difficult position in which to find oneself. This created favourable conditions for his indictment by the Court as he probably did not have any form of political support. The Court essentially provided a convenient way for Bemba to be removed from the volatile political scene of the Great Lakes region.

The referral by Mali was the fourth self-referral from Africa. The Minister of Justice, Malick Coulibaly, wrote a letter, dated 13 July 2013, referring the situation. The decision by the government of Mali to refer the situation in the northern part of its territory appears to have first come out of a Malian Council of Ministers meeting on 30 May 2013. What is curious about this referral is that it came when the relationship between the AU and the Court had been poor for some time. The AU had passed several resolutions critical of the Court, in some instances threatening to encourage its member states to withdraw from the Rome Statute. It was against such a background that six members of the Economic Community of West Africa States Contact Group called upon the Court 'to initiate the necessary enquiries in order to identify the perpetrators of these war crimes and to initiate the necessary legal proceedings against them'[438] in Mali.

These moves indicate that behind the AU's highly published rhetoric against the Court, there may be some silent yet staunch supporters of the Court. It could also be an indication that foreign relations issues, such as how a state like Mali relates to an international institution, are a matter of state sovereignty and interest, and do not need to be addressed at biannual AU summits. Each state responds to its challenges and opportunities based on its national interests.

On 14 May 2013, the Turkish Elmadag law firm, acting on behalf of the Union of the Comoros, filed an application under Articles 14 and 12(2)(a) of the Rome Statute referring Israel's raid on a humanitarian aid flotilla bound for the Gaza Strip to the Court.[439] The Union of the Comoros ratified the Rome Statute on 18 August 2006. The referral requested that Prosecutor Bensouda initiate an investigation into the crimes committed during the raid. In accordance with Article 12(2)(a) of the Statute, the Court may exercise jurisdiction against a

437 *Courting History: The Landmark International Criminal Court's First Years* (New York, Human Rights Watch, 2008), p. 44.

438 ECOWAS Press Statement No. 191/2012, 'ECOWAS Calls for Government of National Unity in Mali', 9 July 2012. The coutnries involved in the ECOWAS Contact Group include Benin, Burkina Faso, Cote d'Ivoire, Liberia, Niger, Nigeria and Togo.

439 Letter from Elmadag Law Firm to the Prosecutor, 'Referral under Articles 14 and 12(2)(a) of the Rome Statute arising from the 31 May 2010, Gaza Freedom Flotilla situation', 14 May 2013.

non-state party to the Statute if 'The state on the territory of which the conduct in the questions occurred or, if the crime committed on board a vessel or aircraft, the State of registration of the vessel or aircraft' is a party to the Statute.[440] In this case, although Israel is a non-state party to the Statute, its alleged raid on a vessel flying a Union of the Comoros flag that is a state party, brings it under the jurisdiction of the Court on the territoriality principle.

When the Prosecutor requested clarification regarding the temporal and territorial scope of the referral, Elmadag confirmed that it encompassed incidents allegedly committed from 31 May 2010 to 6 June 2010 and thereafter.[441] The referral's territorial scope encompassed incidents allegedly committed on the 'other flotilla vessels bearing State party flags', which meant that Greece and Cambodia were part of the referral. The Prosecutor began to conduct preliminary examinations to determine whether there was a reasonable basis to commence an investigation, as required under Article 53 of the Rome Statute.[442]

Like the majority of the events that involve Israel and the Occupied Territories of Palestine, the referral received intense media coverage and intellectual debates. The referral is curious in that, in accordance with the precedent set by the Office of the Prosecutor and the Chambers, it falls into the category of self-referral as it is based on the crimes committed on a vessel flying the Comoros flag, while at the same time it can be considered a classic inter-state referral, since it involves the action of another state, but on the territory of the Comoros, a state party.

Of the many striking aspects of the referral, the first is that, unlike previous referrals from Uganda, the Democratic Republic of the Congo, the Central African Republic and Mali, which were filed by government officials, the Union of the Comoros' application was filed by a Turkish law firm. The same firm had also filed a communication to the Office of the Prosecutor pursuant to Article 15 as the legal representative for the Turkish NGO 'Foundation for Human Rights and Freedoms and Humanitarian Relief'.[443] Turkey is a non-state party to the Rome Statute. It is also curious that the vessel at the centre of the situation, *Mavi Marmara*, was registered in the Comoros on 22 May 2010, just over a week before the incident occurred on 31 May 2010. The ship is owned by the Foundation for Human Rights, Freedoms and Humanitarian Relief (IHH) – by 2011, the registration had already been transferred back to Turkey. This raises questions over whether there was a genuine link between the Comoros and the

440 Rome Statute, Art. 12 (2)(a).

441 Decision Assigning the Situation on Registered Vessels of the Union of the Comoros, the Hellenic Republic and the Kingdom of Cambodia to Pre-Trial Chamber 1, 5 July 2013.

442 Under Art. 53(1) of the Rome Statute, the Prosecutor is required to establish that the case is or would be admissible under Art. 17 and to take into account the gravity of the crime and whether or not the investigation would serve the interests of justice.

443 Referral under Articles 14 and 12(2)(a) of the Rome Statute arising from the 31 May 2010, Gaza Freedom Flotilla situation, Elmadag Law Firm, 14 May 2013, para. 9.

Mavi Marmara. In accordance with Article 91 of the Convention on the Law of the Sea, there 'must exist a genuine link between the State and the ship'.[444] The Prosecutor might have had to clarify her interpretation of the phrase 'genuine link' before establishing whether one existed between the Union of the Comoros and *Mavi Marmara*.

The referral attempted to address the issue of complementarity by submitting that the Comoros did not recognise the statehood of Israel, making it impractical for the Comoros to initiate investigations and prosecutions against the perpetrators of the crimes in question.[445] The applicants were aware that, according to the admissibility criteria, the Prosecutor would have to be satisfied that the Comoros was genuinely unwilling or unable to carry out the investigation or prosecution. The justification given for the Comoros' inability was not one contemplated during the drafting of the Rome Statute.

It is also worth noting that the referral was made in 2013, three years after the incident. Crimes under the jurisdiction of the Court have no statute of limitations, so in that regard there is no issue; however, the delay calls into question the gravity of the crimes, which, as already highlighted, is another criteria assessed by the Office of the Prosecutor during the preliminary examination process.

During the raid, there were nine fatalities – eight Turkish citizens and one American of Turkish origin. In addition, 34 activists were injured and hospitalised. The referral submits that the situation met the gravity criteria as defined by the *Appeals Chamber in the Prosecutor v. Thomas Lubanga Dyilo* case. It submitted that the raid was so grave that it could have resulted in armed conflict – presumably between Turkey and Israel. The applicant suggests that the reason why there was no war was the existence of the Court as 'an avenue for redress'. The legal representative also tried to raise the issue of social alarm as evidence of gravity, referring to the level of international attention that the raid received, in addition to attempting to link the situation to the broader Israel–Palestine conflict. This was unnecessary as the Court had already rejected 'social alarm' as a determinant of the gravity of crimes.

Upon completion of preliminary examinations, the Prosecutor announced that it had reached the decision not to proceed with an investigation into the situation in the Comoros, hence her office was closing the examination.[446] Specifically, she declared that the Comoros situation did not meet the gravity threshold required for the Court to intervene when she stated that 'the potential case(s) that would likely arise from the investigation into the situation would be

---

444 UN Convention on the Law of the Sea (1982) 1833 UNTS 3, 10 December 1982, Art. 91.

445 Referral under Articles 14 and 12(2)(a) of the Rome Statute arising from the 31 May 2010, Gaza Freedom Flotilla situation, Elmadag Law Firm, 14 May 2013.

446 Office of the Prosecutor, 'Situation on Registered Vessels of Comoros, Greece and Cambodia' Art. 53(1) (ICC-01/13-6-Anx.A) Report, 6 November 2014.

inadmissible by force of Article 17(1) of the Statute, i.e. insufficiently grave to warrant action by the Court'.[447]

The Prosecutor advised the authorities in the Comoros that they could challenge the decision by requesting a judicial review from the Pre-Trial Chamber I in accordance with Article 53(3)(a) of the Rome Statute. The Comoros took up this opportunity and filed an application with the Pre-Trial Chamber, in effect challenging the decision of the Office of the Prosecutor not to open an investigation. The application for judicial review was based on claims that the preliminary investigations were not thorough enough, excluded useful evidence and did not cover the entire territorial jurisdiction of the Court. The Comoros also claimed that the Office of the Prosecutor had erred in its analysis of facts, which influenced its decision on the gravity of the situation.

As already discussed, the chances of the UN Security Council referring the situation in Palestine are slim due to US support for Israel and thus its readiness to veto such a resolution. In addition, as an African state, the Comoros might have wanted to grab the opportunity to demonstrate the double standards that the Office of the Prosecutor was practising in the interpretation and application of the Rome Statute, especially the provisions on gravity. It might also simply be an indication that the Comoros actually believed in the Rome Statute justice system, as opposed to some African states, which were seeking to withdraw from the Court and were critical of its practice.

Although Article 53(3)(a) provides the legal basis for either the state party or the UN Security Council to request judicial review of the Prosecutor's decision, in the event that the Pre-Trial Chamber judges establish that the decision not to proceed by the Prosecutor was a result of an error of procedure, error of law or error of fact, 'they may request the Prosecutor to reconsider that decision'. In other words, the judges cannot overturn the Prosecutor's decision and direct her to open an investigation if the UN Security Council or the requesting states – such as the Comoros in this situation – trigger the judicial review process.[448] That said, the outcome would be different if the judges were to act on their own initiative, review the Prosecutor's decision and establish that the decision not to proceed is based on either the interests of justice or gravity. Under such circumstances, the Prosecutor would be tied to the outcome of the judges' review process.

In the case of the Comoros, the Pre-Trial Chamber I judges, Judge Joyce Aluoch (Kenya), Judge Cuno Tarfusser (Italy) and Judge Peter Kovacs (Hungary), requested that the Prosecutor reconsider the decision not to initiate an investigation into the situation referred to her by the Union of the

---

[447] Ibid, para. 24.

[448] Carsten Stahn, 'Judicial Review of Prosecutorial Discretion: Five Years on' in Carsten Stahn and Goran Sluiter (eds.), *The Emerging Practice of the International Criminal Court* (Leiden, Martinus Nijhoff, 2009).

Comoros.[449] The judges discovered that the Office of the Prosecutor had actually erred in several areas in its analysis of the available information and evidence. At one stage, the Pre-Trial Chamber rightfully pointed out that the Prosecutor's conclusions were 'unreasonable' and, in another instance, 'simplistic'. In general, the Pre-Trial Chamber I seemed not to have been impressed by the manner which the Office of the Prosecutor had conducted its preliminary investigations. It is possible that the Office of the Prosecutor tried and managed to avoid an early confrontation with Israel over a seemingly far-fetched situation. The intervention of the Prosecutor is complicated by the fact that the Court does not have direct jurisdiction over Isreal; this means the Prosecutor will have to confront the question of the genuine link between the *Mavi Marmara* and the Comoros. The hurdles seemed to have been too cumbersome to allow for the Office of the Prosecutor to investigate. It should be recalled that in around the same period, the Palestine National Authority had indicated that it wanted to join the Rome Statute, which it did in 2014. This gives the Office of the Prosecutor a clearer and straightforward jurisdiction of the Occupied Territories of Palestine. In this regard, one may sympathise with the Office of the Prosecutor for perhaps sacrificing the quest for justice by the victims of the Israeli raid in the interests of long-term strategic considerations – which is to open an investigation based on straightforward legal parameters. This is where prosecutorial discretion can be very useful.

Gabon made a referral of the situation in its territory to the Office of the Prosecutor in accordance with Article 14 of the Rome Statute in 2016.[450] The referral was made in the context of the August 2016 disputed presidential elections between the incumbent president Ali Bongo Ondimba and Jean Ping, a former Minister of Foreign Affairs and also former Chairperson of the AU Commission. The Prosecutor received the referral on 21 September 2016, requesting her office 'to open an investigation without delay' and on the 29 September she announced that her Office was opening preliminary investigations into the situation. There are a few curious points about Gabon's referral. The timing of the referral underscores the point that when it comes to international relations and respecting international treaties in particular, individual African states tend to be influenced by their domestic situations rather than the African Union's decisions. Otherwise, Gabon would not have

---

[449] *Situation on the Registered Vessels of the Union of the Comoros, The Hellenic Republic and the Kingdom of Cambodia* (ICC-01/13), Decision on the Request of the Union of the Comoros to Review the Prosecutor's Decision Not to Initiate an Investigation, 16 July 2015.

[450] République Gabonaise, Requête aux fins de renvoi d'une situation par un etat partie aupres du procureur de la Cour Panale Internationale (Article 14, Statut de Rome de la Cour Pénale Internationale, Madame Denise MekamneEdzidzie Ministre d' Etat, Ministre de la Justice et des Droits Humains, Garde des Sceaux de la République Gabonaise, le 20 Septembre 2016.

referred the situation in its territory to the Prosecutor at a time when the AU was hardening its anti-cooperation stance with the Court. In addition, the referral does not limit the territorial jurisdiction of the Court as it specifically states that the referral '*courve la totalite du territoire Gabonais...*', which means the Court has jurisdiction over the whole of Gabon. However, it seems to direct the Office of the Prosecutor to the actions and behaviour of Jean Ping, who is alleged to have incited his supporters to commit genocide and also crimes against humanity. The other curious point is how Jean Ping who, during his tenure as the Chairperson of the AU, was a very vocal critic of the Court accusing it of targeting Africa, was inviting the Court and other international human rights organisations to intervene in Gabon. On 16 December 2016, Jean Ping's team of lawyers sent a file to the Prosecutor accusing the government of President Ali Bongo of committing crimes against humanity after the presidential elections. Jean Ping's change in attitude suggests that African leadership's criticism of the Court is not based on a profound principle but a mere reflection of how they want the Court to serve their interests, especially against perceived enemies. The onus therefore lies with the different organs of the Court, the Office of the Prosecutor in particular, not to allow themselves to be used to settle domestic affairs or political struggles within States Parties. Intervening in such situations would require a broader appreciation of the socio-political dynamics on the part of the Office of the Prosecutor and if possible the Court should encourage domestic prosecutions through positive complementarity. The Court should exercise caution so that it is not dragged into each and every post-election violent episode in Africa and instead remains focused on massive atrocities, preserving its role as the court of last resort.

CHAPTER 5

ASSESSING SELECTIVE ENFORCEMENT FROM AN ADMISSIBILITY PERSPECTIVE

This chapter explores the admissibility rules within the Rome Statute, looking at how they have been applied by different organs of the Court, especially the Office of the Prosecutor and the Chambers, in order to analyse whether or not the application contributed to the claims of selective enforcement of international criminal law by the Court. The admissibility rules seek to balance the relationship between national authorities' right to prosecute and that of the Court.[451]

The establishment of the Court coincided with a period when the prevailing perception in international law was that state sovereignty was becoming less important and was thus giving way to individuals in the enforcement of international criminal law. This occurred during the period when the Appeals Chamber Judges at the Yugoslav Tribunal declared that, under international law:

> [A] state-sovereignty-oriented approach has been gradually supplanted by a human being oriented approach. Gradually the maxim of Roman *law hominum causa omene jus constitutum est* (all law is created for the benefit of human beings) has gained a firm foothold in the international community as well.[452]

Despite the perceived evolution referred to in the remarks above, it is still an undisputed legal fact that under international law, states have the right to exercise criminal jurisdiction over all acts committed in their territories and

---

451 See Bergsmo, 'The Jurisdictional Regime of the International Criminal Court', note 67, p. 358, who notes that the core of the admissibility test is whether there is a state with jurisdiction which has the willingness and ability to investigate and prosecute, and that the Court is supposed to supplement national investigations and prosecutions; El Zeidy, *The Principle of Complementarity in International Criminal Law*, note 14, who points out that 'rubric of admissibility' outlined in Art. 17 represents the most direct mechanism for allocating responsibility for a prosecution between the Court on the one hand, and one or more states that may have jurisdiction on the other hand; Schabas, *An Introduction to the International Criminal Court*, note 3, who notes that the underlying assumption behind admissibility rules in the Rome Statute is that, when domestic justice systems fail, the Court steps in as a last resort.

452 *Tadic* (IT-94-1-AR72), Decision on the Defence Motion for Interlocutory Appeal on Jurisdiction, 2 October 1995, para. 85.

elsewhere by their citizens.[453] Sovereign absolutism insists on the primacy of sovereign states in the management of global affairs.

The state-oriented international system often makes states sceptical of the prospect of letting super-international institutions such as the Court (or even the UN) take over their sovereign duties. Part of that scepticism is a result of uncertainty that may result in surrendering some sovereign rights to international forums, as that would mean losing a measure of their control and self-determination. As a result, states tend to ensure that the principle of state sovereignty is highly respected whenever possible, even in areas where they are willing to cede some of their sovereign powers. Therefore, when entering into multilateral treaties such as the Rome Statute, sovereign absolutists tend to lean towards the preservation of traditional sovereign rights.

Still, it is important to underscore the fact that states have different perceptions of both their sovereign rights and their capabilities in exercising them, including criminal jurisdiction over their population. It is also argued that states' views and perceptions of the Court's threat to their sovereignty are often shaped by the likelihood of their citizens committing crimes under the jurisdiction of the Court. Joe Martin Stigen, Professor of Public and International Law at the University of Oslo, noted that the Court many not be regarded as a huge threat by Scandinavian states in the same way as it is by states like the US, France, and China, which have military commitments throughout the world.[454]

The admissibility regime of the Court creates space that allows two legal systems to co-exist, operating parallel to each other with clear rules determining the system that proceeds first.[455] The regime is premised on the recognition that it is the primary duty of every sovereign state to exercise its criminal jurisdiction over those responsible for international crimes[456] and that the Court is complementary to national criminal jurisdictions. In this way, the Rome Statute accommodated the concerns of the states that were content that their own administration of justice could adequately address cases of international crimes without the Court's intervention.[457] It is also argued that the statutory nature of admissibility became a crucial matter after the US realised that it had effectively lost its battle to give the UN Security Council control over the Prosecutor. An independent prosecutor made the US – and potentially other permanent members of the Security Council – uncertain as to how and who the

453 Brownlie, *The Principles of Public International Law*, note 69.

454 Stigen, *The Relationship between the International Criminal Court and National Jurisdiction*, note 64, p. 16.

455 Schabas, *An Introduction to the International Criminal Court*, note 3, p. 187.

456 Paragraph 6 of the Preamble to the Rome Statute states that 'it is the duty of every State to exercise its criminal jurisdiction over those responsible for international crimes'.

457 Robert Cryer et al., *An Introduction to International Criminal Law and Procedure* (Cambridge, Cambridge University Press, 2007), p. 127.

Court would target for prosecutions. To that end, it wanted to ensure that at least national jurisdictions were given priority.[458]

In addition to the largely political considerations already explored, one cannot rule out that practical factors also played their part in the decision to give primacy to domestic criminal jurisdictions in addressing international crimes. The general assumption is that domestic jurisdictions have advantages over international jurisdictions when it comes to efficiency and effectiveness.[459]

This chapter will attempt to explore how the Office of the Prosecutor and the Court Chambers applied the admissibility rules in order to establish how cases from African states ended up being the only ones that passed the admissibility criteria for the Court to go ahead with the official opening investigations and prosecutions. We will also examine the rules that legally allow states to challenge admissibility and how Kenya and Libya have tried to apply them.

5.1. THE LEGAL BASIS FOR ADMISSIBILITY IN THE ROME STATUTE

The legal basis for determining which legal system would proceed with the investigation and prosecution of international crimes is outlined in the Statute.[460] Article 17 fleshes out what 'complementary' implies in practical terms. Together, the provisions under Article 17 make it clear that national legal systems have primacy over the Court. The Court can only assert its jurisdiction over the accused if it is satisfied that the national legal system is unable or unwilling to undertake genuine investigations or prosecutions. Taken this way, initially the burden of proof lies with the Prosecutor to demonstrate that the state in question is not carrying out its responsibility of investigating and prosecuting those suspected of committing international crimes.[461] Based on these provisions, it can be argued that the Rome Statute creates a treaty obligation that states parties prosecute international crimes – and an expectation that a failure to do so

---

458 See Scheffer, *All the Missing Souls*, note 9, p. 12.

459 Report of the Ad Hoc Committee on the Establishment of an International Criminal Court, UN GAOR, 50th Sess., Supp. No. 22, UN Doc. A/50/22 (1995), paras 48–49; see also Cassese, 'The Rationale for International Criminal Justice', note 70, p. 213.

460 Paragraph 10 of the Preamble to the Rome Statute emphasises that the Court shall be complementary to national criminal jurisdictions; Art. 1 provides that the Court shall 'exercise its jurisdiction over persons for the most serious crimes of international concern, as referred to in this Statute, and shall be complementary to national criminal jurisdictions.'

461 Morten Bergsmo, 'The Jurisdictional Regime of the International Criminal Court (Part II, Articles 11–19)' (1998) 6 *European Journal of Crime, Criminal Law and Criminal Justice 345*, p. 359.

attracts the intervention of the Court.[462] In other words, in order to avoid having the Court interfere in their domestic affairs, states would have to investigate or prosecute international crimes themselves. As such, instead of those states complaining of being targeted by the Court, they could actually demonstrate that they can deal with suspects of international crimes within their domestic systems so as to preserve their sovereignty.

That said, it is still unclear whether alternative forms of accountability such as truth and reconciliation commissions are considered in deciding the admissibility of cases before the Court.[463] The UN International Commission of Inquiry on Darfur noted that:

> [A] Truth and Reconciliation Commission could play an important role in ensuring justice and accountability. Criminal courts, by themselves, may not be suited to reveal the broadest spectrum of crimes that took place during a period of repression, in part because they may convict only on proof beyond a reasonable doubt.[464]

The UN Security Council also made reference to a possible role for a truth and reconciliation commission in Darfur when it referred the situation in Darfur to the Court. Resolution 1593 states that the Security Council:

> [E]mphasises the need to promote healing and reconciliation and encourages in this respect the creation of institutions, involving all sectors of Sudanese society, such as truth and/or reconciliation commissions, in order to complement judicial processes and thereby reinforce the efforts to restore long-lasting peace, with AU and international support as necessary.[465]

In Sudan, however, the Court has not been called on to determine admissibility based on the existence of alternative or parallel mechanisms in the form of truth and reconciliation, so it is hard to see how the Court could reconcile the need to prosecute with alternative accountability mechanisms. The only situation where it has almost been called to do so was in Uganda, where traditional mechanisms such as *mato oput* were introduced as an alternative form of justice.[466] Traditional justice mechanisms were included in the Annex to Agenda 3 in the Agreement

---

462 On the need to punish international crimes, see Diane Orentlicher, 'Setting Accounts: The Duty to Prosecute Human Rights Violations of a Prior Regime' (1991) 100 *Yale Law Journal* 2537; and Ken Obura, 'Duty to Prosecute International Crimes under International Law' in Chacha Murungu and Japhet Biegon (eds.)(eds.), *Prosecuting International Crimes in Africa* (Pretoria, Pretoria University Law Press, 2011), p. 19.

463 See Schabas, *An Introduction to the International Criminal Court*, note 3, p. 198.

464 'Report of the International Commission of Inquiry on Darfur to the Secretary-General Pursuant to Security Council Resolution 1564 (2004) of 18 September 2004', UN Doc. S/2005/60, para. 617.

465 UN Doc.S/RES/1593 (2005), para. 7.

466 Allen, *Trial Justice*, note 415, pp. 128–68.

on Accountability and Reconciliation between the Government of Uganda and the LRA/Movement, signed on 19 February 2009 in Juba, South Sudan.[467] The delegates representing the two sides of the conflict had agreed that once the peace deal was concluded, the Ugandan government would challenge the admissibility of the case against the LRA/Movement leaders.[468] However, the peace deal was not concluded because Joseph Kony failed to appear to sign the agreement. It is fair to conclude that perhaps it is not a question of one (truth and reconciliation) or the other (prosecution) – the two could actually be applied in a concurrent manner, as was the case with Sierra Leone. In Sierra Leone, there was a Truth Commission and a Special Court for Sierra Leone functioning almost side-by-side.

5.2. THREE STAGES OF ADMISSIBILITY ASSESSMENT UNDER THE ROME STATUTE

The Rome Statute set out an admissibility assessment with three distinct stages.[469] The first assessment occurs during the preliminary examination in accordance with Article 53. The second, which basically entails a review process of the Prosecutor's preliminary examination by the Pre-Trial Chamber, is in accordance with Article 18. The third occurs when a specific case has been identified, in accordance with Article 19 of the Statute.

The 2013 Office of the Prosecutor policy document provides that, in order for the first stage of the admissibility assessment to be initiated, a situation where crimes under the jurisdiction of the Court has to be triggered by any of the three triggering mechanisms as discussed in Chapters 3 and 4. The mechanisms are as follows: (a) communications to the Office of the Prosecutor under Article 15 – this could be from individuals or groups, states, intergovernmental organisations, NGOs or other reliable sources; (b) referrals from states parties or the UN Security Council; or (c) referrals by a non-state party that has accepted the exercise of jurisdiction by the Court pursuant to Article 12(3). This procedure is also affirmed by Regulation 25 of the Regulations of the Office of the Prosecutor.[470]

At the preliminary examination stage, Article 53(1) provides that the Prosecutor shall, having evaluated the information made available to him or her,

---

467 Annex to the Agreement on Accountability and Reconciliation between the Lord's Resistance Army/Movement and the Government of Uganda Juba, South Sudan, 19 February 2008.

468 Otim and Wierda, 'Justice at Juba', note 413, p. 24.

469 Mohamed M. El Zeidy, 'Admissibility in International Criminal Law' in William A. Schabas and Nadia Bernaz (eds.), *Routledge Handbook of International Criminal Law* (Abingdon, Routledge, 2011), p. 217.

470 Regulations of the Office of the Prosecutor ICC-BD/05-01-09, 23 April 2009, reg. 25.

initiate an investigation unless he or she determines that there is no reasonable basis to proceed – this task is conducted by the Jurisdiction, Complementarity and Cooperation Division.[471] At this stage, the Office of the Prosecutor has the discretion to decide whether or not to start the pre-investigation of a situation. In other words, the Office of the Prosecutor has the power to make autonomous choices as to whom to incriminate, on which charges, on the basis of which evidence and at which moment in time.[472] Giving this discretion to the Office of the Prosecutor recognises that some form of selective enforcement of criminal law is inevitable and that this is not inherently wrong.[473] Prosecutorial discretion is expected to empower the Prosecutor to withstand pressure and temper political interference by various extraneous actors in the investigation and prosecution of international crimes.[474]

The inherent challenge is how to balance such discretion with accountability, considering that the chances are that the Prosecutor's discretion could lead to inaction in certain situations, such as Afghanistan, which could lead to a sharp decline in the trust shown towards the Court. Carsten Stahn, Professor of International Criminal Law and Global Justice at Leiden Law School, pointed out that the drafters of the Rome Statute privileged discretion over accountability; as such, judicial review of prosecutorial inaction was widely ignored.[475] Article 15(6) provides that the Prosecutor 'shall inform those who provided the information' if he or she concludes that there is no reasonable basis for interventions following preliminary examination. It seems that the lack of strong internal accountability mechanisms for the Office of the Prosecutor has exposed it to criticisms of bias against Africa; the initial decision not to open official investigations in Iraq is frequently cited as an example of the Prosecutor's bias.

The second stage of the admissibility assessment lies with the Pre-Trial Chambers of the Court. This is a follow-up stage carrying forward from the outcome of the preliminary examination by the Prosecutor. Once the Chief Prosecutor has determined that there are reasonable grounds upon which to open an investigation, he or she is required to notify all states parties and those states that would normally exercise jurisdiction over the crimes concerned. In return, if there is a state that is investigating (or has investigated) its nationals or

---

471 The Jurisdiction, Complementarity and Cooperation Division is one of the three functional divisions of the Office of the Prosecutor. The others are the Investigations Divisions and the Prosecution Division. See Ignaz Stegmiller, *The Pre-investigation Stage of the ICC: Criteria for Situation Selection* (Berlin, Duncker & Humblot, 2011), p. 457.

472 Salvatore Zappala, 'Prosecutorial Discretion' in Cassese (ed.), *The Oxford Companion to International Criminal Justice*, note 70, p. 471.

473 Ibid, p. 472; and Cryer, *Prosecuting International Crimes*, note 46, p. 192.

474 Stahn, 'Judicial Review of Prosecutorial Discretion', note 439, (eds.), p. 253.

475 Ibid, p. 255.

others within its jurisdiction in respect of criminal acts under the jurisdiction of the Court, that state is required to inform the Court of its intention to commence investigations within one month of receiving the notification from the Prosecutor.[476] The state can even request that the Prosecutor defer his or her investigations to the national domestic justice system.

However, if the Prosecutor decides to go ahead with the investigation, he or she will have to get authorisation from the Pre-Trial Chamber to proceed.[477] At the second stage, the admissibility determination is no longer limited to the evidence and information presented and held by the Office of the Prosecutor alone – it also extends to that held by states. At this stage, states can present their own efforts to investigate and prosecute international crimes. The US introduced Article 18 during the late stages in the Preparatory Committee and then at the Rome Conference in order to provide a procedure that would, at the onset of a referral, recognise the ability of national judicial systems to investigate and prosecute the crimes concerned.[478] The application of the provision at an early stage of the Prosecutor's investigations was aimed at ensuring that states are given every opportunity to investigate cases before the intervention of the Court.[479] The Prosecutor and the Court only intervene after establishing that the state authorities have failed to genuinely investigate and prosecute.

During the Rome Conference, the African delegates received the US proposal with mixed reactions, just like the majority of the delegations.[480] Some delegations viewed it as an additional hurdle for the Court,[481] while others welcomed it as another layer protecting state sovereignty – a crucial concept in many African states.

The usefulness of Article 18 has yet to be tested. This is because the majority of the situations in which the Prosecutor has decided to open investigations have been 'self-referrals', which has technically meant that the states involved waived their ability to request a deferral of proceedings. This applies to Uganda, the Democratic Republic of the Congo, the Central African Republic and Mali, all of which referred their situations to the Court. Their referrals led to simple,

---

476 Rome Statute, Art. 18(2).

477 Rule 55(2) of the Rules of Procedure and Evidence provides that 'the Pre-Trial Chamber shall examine the Prosecutor's application and any observations submitted by a state that requested a deferral in accordance with article 18, paragraph 2, and shall consider the factors in article 17 in deciding whether to authorise an investigation.'

478 See Summary Records of the Meetings of the Committee of the Whole, UN Doc. A/CONF.183/C.1/SR.11, para. 25.

479 Bruce Broomhall, *International Justice and the International Criminal Court: Between Sovereignty and the Rule of Law* (Oxford, Oxford University Press, 2003), p. 87.

480 Schabas, *The International Criminal Court: A Commentary on the Rome Statute*, note 61, p. 355.

481 UN Doc. A/CONF.183/C.1/SR.12, 13 (Malawi), 59 (Sierra Leone).

affirmative findings of admissibility due to their failure to conduct the relevant domestic proceedings.[482]

At the third stage, admissibility assessment, the Prosecutor has to come up with a concrete case. At this stage, the Chambers of the Court, the accused and the state can challenge the admissibility of a case.[483] Both the state and the accused are allowed to challenge admissibility once, prior to or at the commencement of the trial.[484] States that wish to challenge the admissibility of a case are required to do so 'at the earliest opportunity'.[485] This provision was probably to ensure that the Court does not invest time and effort in cases that end up being taken over by the domestic criminal jurisdictions.[486]

5.3. STATUTORY FACTORS THAT REGULATE THE COURT'S DECISION TO INTERVENE IN A GIVEN SITUATION

The legal framework applied throughout the admissibility assessments is outlined in Article 53(1)(a)–(c) of the Rome Statute. Under this provision, the Prosecutor's decision to initiate an investigation is based on whether the communication or referral covers crimes within the jurisdiction of the court, that those crimes are admissible and that action would serve the interests of justice.

Article 53(1)(a) requires the Prosecutor to consider whether the information available provides a reasonable basis upon which to believe that the crime within the jurisdiction of the Court has been or is being committed.[487] This requirement also applies to the Pre-Trial Chamber. According to Article 15(4), the Pre-Trial Chamber is required to consider whether 'the case appears to fall within the jurisdiction of the Court'. Although not explicitly stated in Article 53(1)(a), the jurisdictional requirements that the Prosecutor has to satisfy extend beyond subject-matter jurisdiction to include temporal jurisdiction, territorial and personal jurisdiction.[488]

The temporal jurisdiction of the Court is determined by three factors. The first determinant is the date of entry into force of the Rome Statute: 1 July 2002. This means that all international crimes committed prior to this date are outside the

482 El Zeidy, 'Admissibility in International Criminal Law'(eds.), note 459, p. 218.
483 Rome Statute Art. 19(2)(a) and Art. 19(2)(b).
484 Rome Statute Art. 19(4).
485 Rome Statute Art. 19(5).
486 Burke-White and Scott Kaplan, 'Shaping the Countours of Domestic Justice', note 68, p. 263.
487 Rome Statute, Art. 53(1)(a).
488 Schabas, *The International Criminal Court: A Commentary on the Rome Statute*, note 61, p. 660; see also Policy Paper on Preliminary Examinations 2013, p. 9.

jurisdiction of the Court. For example, international crimes that might have been committed during the Congo War – which started in August 1998 and involved several African states, ending in the Lusaka Peace Agreement on 31 August 1999 – would not be covered by the Court.[489] There are still suggestions from African states that the jurisdiction should have at least been applied retrospectively to include crimes committed during the colonial and apartheid periods. In 2002, during the South African parliamentary debate on the Implementation of the Rome Statute of the International Criminal Court Bill, the Honourable M.A. Mzizi, a member of the Inkhatha Freedom Party, speaking in support of the Bill, added that:

> From our point of view it is somewhat unfortunate that the powers of the International Criminal Court will not apply retrospectively to crimes committed by individuals in the recent past. The scars left by these crimes will therefore probably not be addressed, as we experienced in our TRC.[490]

In Kenya some were even planning to take historical land injustices to the Court.[491] These sentiments underscore the psychological impact on historical injustices on Africa and how it affects perception on issues of justice and accountability for human rights abuses. It would be naïve for one to ignore such social facts about Africa in the context of the contemporary implementation of international criminal law on the continent. The lingering question is always how should Africa's historical injustices be addressed. The historical injustices which are still part of African memory include transatlantic slave trade, pre-colonial human rights abuses in Congo Free State – now the Democratic Republic of the Congo – the Hereros in the former South-West Africa and alleged abuses of the Libyans by the Italians. It is obvious that the Court is not a panacea for all the world's historical injustices, but it should be sensitive to such historical realities and find amicable means of engaging with them if it confronts them. Assuming that the Court is operating in a historical vacuum and is immune to the historical past would be nothing short of the proverbial ostrich burying its head in the sand.

The second determinant of the temporal jurisdiction of the Court is the date of entry into force of the Rome Statute for the state party concerned. Normally this is the date that the state ratified the Statute. It could also be the day specified in the referral document to the Court from the state party. The third determinant is the date specified in the UN Security Council referral or the date indicated in a declaration lodged pursuant to Article 12(3).

---

489 Gerard Prunier, *From Genocide to Continental War: The Congolese Conflict and the Crisis of Contemporary Africa* (London, Hurst Publishers, 2009).

490 *South Africa National Assembly, Proceedings of the National Assembly*, 11 June 2002, p. 174.

491 *Kenya Senate Hansard Report (Electronic Version)*, 24 September 2015, p. 33.

Article 5 limits the subject-matter jurisdiction of the Court to crimes against humanity (as defined in Article 7), war crimes (as defined in Article 8), genocide (as defined in Article 6) and the crime of aggression. The drafters of the Rome Statute adopted a highly positivistic approach in the definition of crimes in order to rein in the discretion of the judges. This approach differed from the one used by the drafters of the statutes for the *ad hoc* tribunals, where judges had some form of leeway to define crimes and take the initiative vis-à-vis judge-made law.[492] Although some commentators view judge-made law as having made a contribution to the development of international criminal law in the *ad hoc* tribunals, it seems that the drafters of the Rome Statute wanted to be sure what they were signing up for. They developed detailed definitions of the crimes to prevent judges from defining the scope of international crimes along the way.[493] In general, the Court operates within a very rigid jurisdictional framework as far as subject-matter jurisdiction is concerned. It does not enjoy a similar degree of latitude to the *ad hoc* tribunals.

Still, some delegates during the Rome Conference would have preferred the Court to have a broader subject-matter jurisdiction. The present subject-matter jurisdiction is biased towards the Nuremburg Charter, so it can be said to be primarily a reflection of what the victorious powers were prepared to criminalise. There is no doubt that the criminal acts under each crime have increased significantly.

However, one must keep in mind that it was in 1989, when a coalition of 16 Caribbean and Latin American states represented by Arthur N. Robinson, the Prime Minister of Trinidad and Tobago, proposed that the UN General Assembly should establish an international criminal court as a measure to combat drug trafficking.[494] Commenting on the proposal by Trinidad and Tobago, Robert Cryer, Professor of International and Criminal Law at Birmingham Law School, observes that:

> This [the possibility of an international criminal court] was suggested as a means for countries whose judicial systems were unable to cope with the power and influence of rich drug barons, and to ensure that prosecution occurred in an independent forum, less subject to the pressures that could be brought to bear on national politicians, judges and prosecutors.[495]

---

492 Schabas, *An Introduction to the International Criminal Court*, note 3, p. 125.

493 See Cryer, 'The Philosophy of International Criminal Law', note 94, p. 254. For a critic of such a limiting approach, see Schabas, *An Introduction to the International Criminal Court*, note 3, p. 125, who argues that the detailed definition may also serve to narrow the scope of war crimes in some cases. In the future, judges will have greater difficulty undertaking the kind of judicial law making that Yugoslav Tribunal performed in the *Tadić* case, and this will make it harder for justice to keep up with the imagination and inventiveness of war crimes.

494 See UNGA Res 44/89 (1989); and Schabas, *The International Criminal Court: A Commentary on the Rome Statute*, note 61, p. 11.

495 Cryer, *Prosecuting International Crimes*, note 46, p. 57.

The irony is that although it was the wish of the coalition of Caribbean and Latin American states to combat drug trafficking that somehow rejuvenated the otherwise stagnant process of establishing an international criminal court, when the Rome Statute was adopted in 1998, its subject-matter jurisdiction did not include drug crimes.[496] The effort by some of the principal sponsors to have drug crimes included in the Rome Statute failed . In the end the their proposal was given some nominal reference in Article 5 of the Rome Statute similar to the crimes of aggression.[497] This meant drug crimes were left for consideration by a Review Conference, which was scheduled for a period of seven years from the entry into force of the Rome Statute. However, when the Review Conference was held in 2010 in Kampala, Uganda, the crime of drug trafficking was still left out of the jurisdiction of the Court.

Throughout the history of the drafting of the Rome Statute, drug-related crimes were considered not to meet the required gravity to be considered part of the crimes under the jurisdiction of the Court. However, those who promoted their inclusion argued that the crimes threatened the sovereignty of smaller states that had no capacity to deal with powerful drug dealers.[498] One could also argue that the seriousness of drug crimes was evident through the fact the more than 20 treaties had been adopted to address the drug problem, albeit without much success. Patrick Robinson, the former President of the International Criminal Tribunal for the former Yugoslavia, noted that such a number of treaties reflected the level of international concern at the rise of drug abuse.[499]

At the Rome Conference, a delegate from Thailand pointed out that the previous multilateral mechanisms had failed and hence there was a need for a new institution – the Court – to address the problem: 'The court could be a credible alternative mechanism in the suppression of crimes relating to narcotic drugs, since cooperation through bilateral agreements or Interpol was ineffective.'[500] However, despite such a level of advocacy and several attempts by the group of Caribbean states to put forward proposals that would increase the gravity of drug-related crimes in order to meet the required standard by the drafters, such crimes were excluded from the jurisdiction of the Rome Statute. When the Review Conference was held in 2010, the promoters of the inclusion of drug-related crimes in the Rome Statute dropped their proposals.[501]

---

496 See Art. 5 of the Rome Statute of the International Criminal Court, United Nations Diplomatic Conference of Plenipotentiaries on the Establishment of an International Criminal Court, July 17 1998, UN Doc. A/CONF.183/9.

497 Some of the principal sponsors of the proposal include Barbados, Dominica, India, Jamaica, Sri Lanka and Trinidad and Tobago; for the proposal, see A/CONF.183/C.1/L.71.

498 See Patrick Robinson, 'The Missing Crime' in Cassese et al. (eds.), *The Rome Statute of the International Criminal Court: A Commentary*, note 94.

499 Ibid.

500 A/CONF 183/SR.7, para. 18.

501 Schabas, *An Introduction to the International Criminal Court*, note 3, p. 96.

In addition to the technical reasoning for the exclusion of the drug crimes from the jurisdictional regime of the Court, national political interests played a leading role. For example, the US had made a decision as early as 1994 against the inclusion of drug crimes within the jurisdiction of the Court. Its position was primarily influenced by the lawyers in the Justice Department's Criminal Division and the National Security Council, who had no interest in sharing the classified intelligence and undercover investigations involved in fighting drug-related crimes.[502]

African states, the Comoros and Madagascar proposed the inclusion of mercenarism – the state of being a mercenary – as one of the categories of crimes under the jurisdiction of the Court.[503] The proposal was modelled around the 1989 UN International Convention against the Recruitment, Use, Financing and Training of Mercenaries. However, mercenarism was not even considered for inclusion in the International Law Commission list of treaty crimes because the 1989 UN Convention never entered into force.[504] At the Rome Conference, the Comoros representative Chaharizade Assoumany pointed out that her country was keen that 'acts committed by mercenaries should be included as crimes under the Statute because they constituted a serious threat to the stability and constitutional order of States'.[505]

It is not surprising that the proposal did not gain overwhelming support, as it is a reflection of a regional historical problem experienced in Africa. Still the proposal did not garner enough regional support. It was only Angola and Nigeria who at least openly promoted it. One can observe that by trying to have mercenarism included as part of the subject-matter jurisdiction of the Court, it is possible that the promoters viewed it as a way that they could solve the problem of mercenarism – one of the main threats to regional peace and security in Africa, as reflected in several regional treaties. There is general agreement, at least among African leaders, that one of the main causes of African instability is interference by foreign and Western actors, especially through the use of mercenaries. This view is based on the role played by mercenaries during proxy wars in Angola, the Democratic Republic of the Congo, Sudan and Libya. There is, however, a lingering debate as to whether governments can also be accused of using mercenaries to support themselves to stay in power – for example, when the Angolan government relied on the Cubans during the civil war in the 1970s, reports that the President of Equatorial Guinea relied on Moroccans to strengthen his grip on power, or more recently that President Gaddafi employed mercenaries during the unrest in Libya in 2011. Perhaps the lack of consensus in

---

502 Scheffer, *All the Missing Souls*, note 9, p. 170.

503 A/CONF.183/C.1/L.46 and Corr.1.

504 Robinson, 'The Missing Crime', note 488, p. 521.

505 A/CONF.183/C.1/SR.27, para. 61. The proposal to include mercenarism in the Rome Statute was also supported by Angola and Nigeria: A/CONF.183/C.1/SR.28, paras 41 and 97.

this regard might have also contributed to the lack of solid African support for the Comoros and Madagascar proposal.

As regards the territorial and personal jurisdiction of the Court, the Prosecutor is guided by Articles 12(2) (the communication or referral has to concern a crime that occurred in the territory of a state party or was committed by a national of a state party), Article 12(3) (the crime has to have occurred in a state that has lodged a declaration accepting the jurisdiction of the Court) and Article 13(b) is when the Security Council refers a situation, acting under Chapter VII of the UN Charter.

The second factor that the Prosecutor and the Court have to be satisfied with in order to decide whether or not there are reasonable grounds to intervene in a situation is that of admissibility. In determining admissibility, the two pertinent factors are complementarity and gravity. That said, some scholars suggest that admissibility is a criteria used to implement the complementarity principle.[506]

Mohamed M. El Zeidy, Legal Officer for Pre-Trial Chamber II at the Court, conducted an in-depth analysis of the principle of complementary and pointed out that it had existed in different forms since the end of the First World War as a way to manage the relationship between two forums enforcing international criminal justice.[507] He referred to the complementarity regime included in the Rome Statute as the Rome Statute Complementarity Model to reflect its unique features.[508] The regime has attained an axiomatic status in the language and debates concerning the Court, yet the term is neither present nor defined anywhere in the Rome Statute.[509] The closest that the Rome Statute comes to

506 See El Zeidy, *The Principle of Complementarity in International Criminal Law*, note 14, p. 159, who states that in order to implement the complementarity principle, the Prosecutor and the Chambers of the Court should respect and adhere to the Statute's admissibility criteria; and also Stigen, *The Relationship between the International Criminal Court and National Jurisdiction*, note 64, p. 2, who suggests that admissibility and prosecutorial discretion are aspects of complementarily. For a different interpretation, see Schabas, *An Introduction to the International Criminal Court*, note 3, p. 189, who notes that there are three components to admissibility determination – complementarity, gravity and *non bis in idem*; and Mark A. Drumbl, *Atrocity, Punishment and International Law* (Cambridge, Cambridge University Press, 2000), p. 141, who states that Art. 17 of the Rome Statute governs the admissibility of cases.

507 See El Zeidy, *The Principle of Complementarity in International Criminal Law*, note 14, p. 56, who suggests that the provisions found in the peace treaties that were concluded after the First World War reflected the real origins of the notion of complementarity in the modern era.

508 Ibid, p. 157.

509 Schabas, *An Introduction to the International Criminal Court*, note 3, p. 190; and Stigen, *The Relationship between the International Criminal Court and National Jurisdiction*, note 64, p. 157.

referring to the principle is in paragraph 10 of the Preamble and Article 1.[510] *Black's Law Dictionary* describes complementarity:

> As a doctrine, that a country with control of a person accused of committing international crimes has jurisdiction to charge and try a person; because the jurisdiction of the Court is complementary to the criminal jurisdiction of countries, that tribunal can assert jurisdiction over the accused, only if the country is unable or unwilling to undertake a genuine investigations and prosecution.[511]

The complementarity principle is regarded as the cornerstone of the central philosophy of the Court. Judge Kaul describes it as 'the decisive basis for the entire ICC system. It is also the key principle to determine the relationship of the ICC to national jurisdictions'.[512] It was even doubted that the states would have adopted the Statute in 1998 had the principle of complementarity not been included.[513] This was reflected in the remarks made by the French negotiator Marc de Brichambaut to his American counterpart, David Scheffer, when towards the end of the Rome Conference he said the following:

> I'm going to sign the treaty tomorrow because we know that no French national will ever appear before the International Criminal Court. We will ensure that our courts take the case first and dispose of it nationally. We will amend what we have to, even our constitution, to guarantee that no French citizen ever ends up in The Hague.[514]

Still, the safety net offered by the complementarity principle did not manage to persuade some states – the US in particular – to join the Rome Statute. It seems that the notion of a Court having the authority to assess the admissibility of cases, and more specifically the willingness and ability of national prosecutorial systems, was a bridge too far for the US to cross. It was not comfortable trusting an institution that was not accountable to any democratically elected executive

---

510 Paragraph 10 of the Rome Statute states that 'the International Criminal Court established under this Statute shall be complementary to national criminal jurisdictions' and Art. 1 states that 'An International Criminal Court … is hereby established. It shall be a permanent institution and shall have the power to exercise its jurisdiction over persons for the most serious crimes of international concern, as referred to in this Statute, and shall be complementary to national criminal jurisdictions. The jurisdiction and functioning of the Court shall be governed by the provisions of this Statute'.

511 *Black's Law Dictionary*, Standard Ninth Edition, (West Publishing Co, 2009).

512 Hans-Peter Kaul, 'The International Criminal Court – Its Relationship to Domestic Jurisdictions' in Stahn and Sluiter (eds.), *The Emerging Practice of the International Criminal Court*, note 439, p. 33.

513 Schabas, *The International Criminal Court: A Commentary on the Rome Statute*, note 61, p. 336.

514 Scheffer, *All the Missing Souls*, note 9, p. 221.

to make judgments on its national policies and decisions. As one commentator put it:

> In ICC cases in which a state's national is prosecuted for an official act that the state maintains was lawful or that the state maintains did not occur, the lawfulness or the occurrence of that official state … would form the very subject matter of the dispute.[515]

The suspicious attitude shown by the US towards the Court was also galvanised by the fact that it has many of its citizens stationed around the world on military duty, so it felt more vulnerable to the Court than most other states. Initially, this concern was also shared by France and the UK. However, they changed their position during the negotiations.

The complementarity regime obliges the Court to decline jurisdiction over a case unless the Prosecutor can show that the state involved is unwilling or unable to carry out the investigation or prosecution.[516] Once the Prosecutor can demonstrate that the relevant national justice systems are operational and acting in good faith, then the matter is inadmissible before the Court. This makes the interpretation of unwillingness and inability crucial to the effectiveness of the complementarity regime in separating the matters that deserve the Court's attention from those that do not. As already pointed out, this could be a demanding and controversial endeavour.[517] This is because 'a number of thorny questions arise [with regard to the interpretation of complementarity] what exactly does unwilling or unable genuinely to carry out the investigation or prosecution mean for the purposes of Article 17?'[518] Without being overly ambitious in attempting to analyse the two terms, the following section briefly highlights some of the aspects of these terms that are relevant to how the Court intervenes in certain situations and not in others.

5.3.1. UNWILLINGNESS

Article 17(2) of the Rome Statute outlines two interlinked elements that can assist the Court in making a determination of a state's willingness to investigate or prosecute international crimes. The first element can be found in Article 17(2), which makes reference to 'the principles of due process recognised by international law'.[519] The second defines three scenarios that refer to unwillingness. The dictionary definition of the noun 'unwillingness' is 'not wanting to do something

---

515 Madeline Morris, 'High Crimes and Misconceptions: The ICC and Non-party States' (2001) 64 *Law and Contempory Problems* 13, p. 21.

516 Bergsmo, 'The Jurisdictional Regime of the International Criminal Court', note 67, p. 359.

517 Ibid.

518 Drumbl, *Atrocity, Punishment and International Law*, note 496, p. 141.

519 Rome Statute, Art. 17(2).

and refusing to do it'.[520] In the context of the Rome Statute, 'unwillingness' is defined in terms of three scenarios that could occur during national proceedings against a suspect of international crimes. The scenarios involve proceedings that: (a) shield the person concerned from criminal responsibility; (b) are delayed in a manner inconsistent with the intent to bring the persons concerned to justice; and (c) are not independent or impartial.[521]

Some commentators suggest that the first element was initially intended to add objectivity to the Court's assessment of whether proceedings are independent or impartial; however, in the end, it was included to be applied to all three scenarios.[522] There seems to be no single universal interpretation of the formula of 'principles of due process recognised by international law'. Some link it to the need for the state to respect the human rights of the accused, while others link it to the victims' right to have a perpetrators punished under international law,[523] and still others attribute its inclusion to an attempt to limit the matters admissible before the Court – some delegations were concerned that, without it, too much discretion would be vested in the Court.[524]

Instead of limiting the discretionary powers of the Court, the requirement appears to actually give the Court a broader degree of latitude when determining the admissibility of cases. It opens up the possibility for the Court to make determinations on sovereign states' decisions not to prosecute based – for instance – on their own national prosecutor's discretion.[525] It is suggested that due to its lack of clarity, the reference to 'the principles of due process recognised by international law' should be removed from the Rome Statute because:

> [I]t provides the ICC with a legal loophole to overrule national judgments when the Court disagrees with the outcome in the national proceedings. Vesting the ICC with such discretion is both inconsistent and incompatible with the principle of complementarity.[526]

---

520 *Oxford Advanced Learners' Dictionary*, 9th edn. (Oxford, Oxford University Press, 2011).

521 Bergsmo, 'The Jurisdictional Regime of the International Criminal Court', note 67, p. 359; and El Zeidy, *The Principle of Complementarity in International Criminal Law*, note 14, p. 167.

522 Benzing, 'The Complementarity Regime of the International Criminal Court', note 65, p. 606; and El Zeidy, *The Principle of Complementarity in International Criminal Law*, note 14, p. 170.

523 Benzing, 'The Complementarity Regime of the International Criminal Court', note 65, p. 607.

524 James Sloan, 'The ICC and Domestic Enforcement in Canada and the UK' in Christopher P.M Waters (ed.), *British and Canadian Perspectives on International Law* (Leiden, Martinus Nijhoff, 2006), p. 64.

525 Jimmy Guruk, 'United States Opposition to the 1998 Rome Statute Establishing an International Criminal Court: Is the Court's Jurisdiction Truly Complementary to National Criminal Jurisdictions?' (2002) 35 *Cornell International Law Journal* 592, who suggests that a lack of clarity in the formula 'principles of due process recognised by international law' could result in the Court determining the US's national proceedings to have been not conducted, independently or impartially 'because the United States' interpretation of relevant legal authority was inconsistent with 'principles of due process recognized by international law'.

526 Ibid.

The reference to due process being recognised by international law as part of the test to determine unwillingness invites criticism of the complementarity principle on the basis that it also encourages mimicry.[527] National legal processes have to approximate those of the Court, including their specific trials and sanctioning modalities.[528] In addition, the Third World Approaches to International Law scholarship, part of which seeks to advance the interests of Third World peoples by making international law more inclusive and participatory, would view complementarity as yet another way in which domestic mechanisms are being shaped according to a Western-oriented international legal system, marginalising local mechanisms at the expense of promoting originality and mechanisms that are grounded in and shaped by the common history values and realities of the states parties. Basically it encourages standardisation at the expense of innovation in international criminal justice.

The reference to principles of due process recognised by international law also raises additional questions. It precludes any other transitional justice mechanisms that states may adopt to respond to atrocities or informal justice mechanisms as criteria for the Court to exclude its jurisdiction in a situation. During the Rome Conference, South Africa pushed for the recognition of non-criminal justice methods of addressing impunity. The aim was to ensure that its truth and reconciliation programme was not viewed as unwillingness to address crimes committed during the apartheid era.[529] Still, there are a wide range of other informal justice mechanisms that were not formally recognised in the Rome Statute and could potentially impact on the Court's determination of unwillingness and inability. These mechanisms include traditional justice ceremonies such as the *mato oput* 'reconciliation'[530] in Northern Uganda and the *Dia* 'blood money' in North Darfur.[531]

In many African states, informal justice mechanisms and a belief in the role of supernatural agencies are recognised and exist in parallel to Western-based common and civil law systems. The traits of such African justice systems include an overreliance on principles of social obligation, a spirituality sanctioned moral order and cases being settled through political negotiation and spiritual atonement.[532] This makes it difficult for the Court, which is predominately shaped around the Western concept of law, to objectively make a judgment on the unwillingness and inability of African states relying on informal justice systems

527 Drumbl, *Atrocity, Punishment and International Law*, note 496, p. 144.

528 Ibid, p. 143.

529 Schabas, *An Introduction to the International Criminal Court*, note 3, p. 43.

530 Allen, *Trial Justice*, note 415.

531 See reference to the *Dia* system See AUPD.(2009) Darfur: The Quest for Peace, Justice and Reconciliation .Report of the African High-Level Panel on Darfur (AUPD), African Union para. 212.

532 D.H. Johnson, 'Judicial Regulation and Administrative Control: Customary Law and the Nuer 1898–1954' (1986) 27 *Journal of African History* 59, pp. 59–60.

without being accused of ethnocentrism. In the end, the objective application of complementarity tests is complicated and likely to favour the Court's intervention, thereby discarding local justice knowledge and practice systems. Similar observations can be made about states that have legal frameworks based on Islamic law.

Islamic law has a different philosophical approach compared to criminal justice and some of its sentencing practices and evidence-gathering procedures could arguably be viewed as a violation of human rights standards. For example, under Islamic law, flogging, banishment, amputation (*qat*) of the right hand and retaliation for injuries incurred are acceptable as part of sentencing.[533] This partly explains why the majority of Arab and Islamic states have not ratified the Rome Statute.

Jomo Kenyatta, in his anthropological book on the Gikuyu people of Kenya, *Facing Mt. Kenya*, describes the aim of Gikuyu criminal procedure as getting 'compensation for the individual or group against whom the crime was committed'.[534] The *kiama*, which is the council of elders and which presided over the criminal justice system, including those involving murder and manslaughter, 'was not chiefly concerned with the motive of the crime of the way in which the crime was committed, but with the fact that one man had taken another man's life'.[535] Since there was no system of imprisonment, the common forms of punishment included compensation and the offender being permanently ostracised from society. Kenyatta argues that the stigma attached to the ostracism was far greater and very much worse than that attached to the European form of imprisonment, and that 'many Kikuyu would prefer to go to jail rather than to be ostracised'.[536] The role and position of such informal traditional justice mechanisms in the determination of inability is yet to be explored and could be a source of controversy between the affected communities and the Court.

The Saif Gaddafi and Senussi admissibility cases highlight how the application of complementarity tests can trigger clashes over the different philosophies on punishment that exist in different societies, fuelling the debate over restorative and retributive justice, and Western and non-Western justice.[537] In these cases, the existence of capital punishment in the Libyan Criminal Code was raised and became a source of contention. During one of the hearings, the Libyan

---

533 Rudolph Peters, *Crime and Punishment in Islamic Law: Theory and Practice from the Sixteenth to the Twenty-First Century* (Cambridge, Cambridge University Press, 2005).

534 Kenyatta Jomo, *Facing Mt. Kenya: The Tribal life of the Gikuyu* (New York, Vintage Books, 1965).

535 Ibid, p. 217.

536 Ibid, p. 220.

537 *Saif Al-Islam Gaddafi and Abdullah Al- Senussi* (ICC-01/11-01/11), Decision on the Admissibility of the Case against Saif al-Islam Gaddafi, 31 May 2013; and *Saif al-Islam Gaddafi and Abdullah al-Senussi* (ICC-01/11-01/11), Decision on the Admissibility of the Case against Abdullah Al Senussi, 11 October 2013.

representative reminded the Court that when the issue of sentencing was negotiated during the Rome Conference, the Court was not given the authority to determine on the sentencing practices of independent states.[538]

As regards the second element of determining admissibility based on the three scenarios of shielding, unjustified delay and a lack of independent or impartial proceedings, the general interpretation is that the Court is asked to test the good faith of national authorities in relation to how they conduct their investigations or the prosecution of international crimes.[539] Commentators have diverging views on whether the three scenarios are exhaustive or merely illustrative.[540] It seems plausible to consider the list to be exhaustive, given that the vision of the complementarity principle is that the Court is the last resort and is subordinate to the national justice systems. Liberal interpretation, or leaving the judges with the freedom to add and craft additional factors, would have scared the delegations who had linked their support to the Court to the inclusion of the complementarity principle. If the positivist approach that was adopted in drafting and defining the crimes under the jurisdiction of the Court us any indication, then it is fair to say that the drafters might have preferred an exclusive list to an illustrative one.

The unwillingness criterion is applied to determine the intentions of the state vis-à-vis its actions in addressing impunity. In this regard, the obligation to investigate rests on the state and some commentators argue that such an obligation cannot be substituted by either non-state actors – organised armed groups party to non-international armed conflicts – or international entities.[541] This is inexplicable, considering that the legal framework applicable to non-international armed conflicts and the Rome Statute recognises that commanders and superiors of organised armed groups have certain responsibilities to suppress international crimes committed by their subordinates or to submit such matters

538 *Saif al-Islam al-Gaddafi and Abdullah al-Senussi* (ICC-01/11-01/11), Decision on the Admissibility of the Case against Saif al-Islam al-Gaddafi, 31 May 2013, para. 169.

539 Bergsmo, 'The Jurisdictional Regime of the International Criminal Court', note 67, p. 359.

540 The commentators who see the list as exhaustive include El Zeidy, *The Principle of Complementarity in International Criminal Law*, note 14, p. 168; Benzing, 'The Complementarity Regime of the International Criminal Court, note 65, p. 606; Stigen, *The Relationship between the International Criminal Court and National Jurisdiction*, note 64, p. 258; and Kai Ambos, *The Colombian Peace Process and the Principle of Complementarity of the International Criminal Court: An Inductive, Situation-Based Approach* (Dordrecht, Springer, 2010), p. 66. The commentators that have a liberal interpretation of Art. 17(2) and view the list as illustrative include Darrly Robinson, 'Serving the Interest of Justice: Amnesties: Truth Commissions and the International Criminal Court' (2003) 14 *European Journal of International Law* 481, 500; and Christopher Keith Hall, *Suggestions Concerning International Criminal Court Prosecutorial Policy and Strategy and External Relations* (Expert consultation process on general issues relevant to the ICC Office of the Prosecutor, ICC Prosecutorial Policy and Strategy and External Relations, 2003), p. 15.

541 Ambos, *The Colombian Peace Process*, note 530, p. 66.

to the competent authorities for investigation and prosecution.[542] On 15 June 2009, in a decision on the conformation of charges in the Bemba case, the Pre-Trial Chamber II indicated that Bemba had an obligation to punish his troops for the international crimes they committed. It interpreted the duty to repress as follows:

> The duty to 'repress' encompasses two separate duties arising at two different stages of the commission of crimes. First, the duty to repress includes a duty to stop ongoing crimes from continuing to be committed. It is the obligation to 'interrupt a possible chain effect, which may lead to other similar events'. Second, the duty to repress encompasses an obligation to punish forces after the commission of crimes.[543]

Suggesting that the duty to prosecute is limited only to the state would imply that even if the commanders of organised armed groups, such as the LRA in Northern Uganda or the Justice Equality Movement (JEM)in Sudan, prosecuted their own soldiers for international crimes, their cases would still be considered admissible by the Court. In addition, the fact that Article 17(1) specifies that the case is inadmissible where it is being investigated or prosecuted by a state raises questions regarding whether any action by regional courts (such as the *ad hoc* Hybrid Court that was proposed by the AU's Peace and Security Council for Darfur) would be discounted. Although the Court appears to have adopted a statist approach, as witnessed in its handling of the Article 12(3) declaration by the Palestinian National Authority, it would be counterproductive for it to completely ignore regional efforts to combat impunity on the bases of a narrow interpretation of the obligations in the Rome Statute. Kenya proposed an amendment to the Rome Statute to allow the recognition of regional judicial mechanisms under the complementarity regime of the Court.[544] The proposal is reflective of how the AU wants to apply two parallel approaches in dealing with the ICC. That is on the one hand it is seeking to push back on the Court, and on the other promoting alternative regional mechanisms. The success of the latter depends on the readiness of African leaders to embrace accountability and also

542 Article 28(a) of the Rome Statute provides that: 'A military commander or person effectively acting as a military commander shall be criminally responsible for crimes within the jurisdiction of the Court committed by forces under his or her effective command and control, or effective authority and control as the case may be, as a result of his or her failure to exercise control properly over such forces, where … (ii) That military commander or person failed to take all necessary and reasonable measures within his or her power to prevent or repress their commission or to submit the matter to the competent authorities for investigation and prosecution.'

543 *Bemba* (ICC-01/05-01/08), Decision Pursuant to Article 61(7)(a) and (b) of the Rome Statute on the Charges of the Prosecutor against Jean-Pierre Bemba Gombo, 15 June 2009, para. 439.

544 Assembly of States Parties Doc. ICC-ASP/13/31, Report of the Working Group on Amendments, 7 December 2014, p. 17.

to provide political and financial support to the regional court, such that it can operate independently.

5.3.2. INABILITY

In accordance with Article 17(3), the inability of a state to investigate or prosecute international crimes is determined based on whether 'due to a total or substantial collapse or unavailability of its national judicial system, the state is unable to obtain the accused or the necessary evidence and testimony or otherwise unable to carry out its own proceedings'.[545] Unlike 'unwillingness', this criterion for determining admissibility is generally taken to be objective and fact-driven.[546] It seeks to encompass three conditions that can arise and make cases admissible before the Court.

The first condition is that of a total collapse of the state national judicial system, such as the one witnessed following the genocide in Rwanda in 1994. The second condition, that of 'substantial collapse', refers to a situation where a state judicial system exists but has limited capacity – the system does not cover the entire territory, for instance, due to some parts being under the control of rebel movements. The third condition refers to 'unavailability', which has been interpreted by international criminal law scholars as referring to a scenario where, although a national judicial system exists, it is not suitable to investigate or prosecute the case due to either legal or factual obstacles.[547] The legal obstacles could include immunity laws, especially in situations involving states that are non-states parties to the Rome Statute. Such states would not have waived the immunity of their state officials as provided for under Article 27 of the Rome Statute.[548] In the Comoros referral, the lawyers representing the Comoros introduced another determinant of inability in highlighting their lack of recognition of Israel's statehood. Under complementarity they submitted that 'to date Comoros does not recognise the statehood of Israel and therefore it is impractical for Comoros to initiate investigations and prosecutions against the perpetrators of the crimes in question'.[549]

---

545 Rome Statute, Art. 17(3).

546 John T. Holmes, 'Complementarity: National Courts versus the ICC' in Cassese et al. (eds.), *The Rome Statute of the International Criminal Court: A Commentary*, note 94, vol. 1, p. 677.

547 Jakob Pichon, 'The Principle of Complementarity in the Cases of the Sudanese National Ahmad Harun and Ali Kushayb before the International Criminal Court' (2008) 8 *International Criminal Law Review* 185, p. 197.

548 Schabas, *An Introduction to the International Criminal Court*, note 3, p. 80.

549 Referral under Articles 14 and 12(2)(a) of the Rome Statute arising from the 31 May 2010, Gaza Freedom Flotilla situation, 14 May 2013, para. 23.

There is controversy over whether unavailability also applies in a situation where international crimes are punished as ordinary crimes by a domestic judicial system.[550] Those in support of this interpretation of unavailability expect the Court to declare cases that are punished as ordinary crimes in domestic courts admissible under the Rome Statute. The preamble of the Statute emphasises that the determination to punish and prevent international crimes is linked to the fact that such crimes threaten international peace, security and wellbeing. Hence, in order to illustrate the gravity of such crimes, it is argued that they should not be prosecuted as such in domestic courts.

At the same time, there is a view that such an interpretation undermines the purpose of the complementarity principle, which is to preserve the principle of sovereignty that protects a state's right to determine its own laws.[551] Scheffer supports such a position and supports his argument using purely pragmatic reasons. He argues that a national prosecutor might choose to charge suspects with ordinary crimes, such as murder, instead of 'harder-to-prove' international crimes, such as crimes against humanity, for the purposes of securing a conviction under domestic law.[552]

However, in the context of the underlying rationale for international tribunals, it seems clear that the distinction between ordinary crimes and international crimes is necessary to ensure that there is some consistency in the fight against global impunity. In this regard, the position adopted by the Yugoslav Tribunal in its landmark Interlocutory Appeal on Jurisdiction Decision in *Tadić v. Prosecutor* is worth mentioning. It pointed out that international tribunals were established to represent the international community of nations and were empowered to deal with 'transboundary matters which though domestic in nature may affect international peace and security'.[553]

This approach highlights one of the distinctions between international criminal law and domestic criminal law. In the former, the prosecutor acts on behalf of the international community against the defendant, whereas in the latter, the prosecutor acts on behalf of the national community. That said, when international criminal law is decentralised and enforced by national prosecutors, they are acting on behalf of the international community and are expected to apply laws accordingly.

550 Pichon, 'The Principle of Complementarity', note 537.
551 Ibid, p. 197.
552 Scheffer, *All the Missing Souls*, note 9, p. 122.
553 *Tadić* (IT-94-1-A) Decision on the Defence Motion for Interlocutory Appeals on Jurisdiction, 2 October 1995, para. 58.

5.4. ADMISSIBILITY PUT INTO PRACTICE BY THE OFFICE OF THE PROSECUTOR AND THE CHAMBERS

When Prosecutor Moreno Ocampo was sworn in as the first Chief Prosecutor, he said:

> As a consequence of complementarity, the number of cases that reach the Court should not be a measure [of] its efficiency. On the contrary, the absence of trials before this Court, as a consequence of the regular functioning of national institutions, would be a major success.[554]

It seems that the key assumption made by the Prosecutor in this statement was that states would play their complementarity role by showing a willingness and ability to investigate and prosecute international crimes. He obviously did not envisage a situation where states would voluntarily decline to exercise their jurisdiction in favour of the prosecution before the Court.

The Solicitor General of Uganda stated that the Court was 'the most appropriate and effective forum for the investigation and prosecution of those bearing the greatest responsibility for the crimes within a referred situation'.[555] In some sense, the Prosecutor's approach reflected a rather idealistic understanding of the role of the Court. This is because the establishment of the Court was a response to enforcement problem at a domestic level that was leading to chronic impunity for international crimes.

Subsequently, by the time the first Prosecutor's term had ended, his office had been called upon to make admissibility determinations in at least 19 situations. The majority of the situations in which the Court ended up opening either investigations or prosecutions were self-referrals. As already discussed in Chapter 4, the UN Security Council also referred two situations, Sudan and Libya, and the Prosecutor used his *proprio motu* powers to initiate investigations in Kenya and Côte d'Ivoire. All in all, the Prosecutor decided to proceed in eight situations, all of which involved Africa. It was only in 2016 that the Office of the Prosecutor took on its first case outside Africa when it investigated the situation in Georgia.

The following discussion focuses on analysing how the Court organs (both the Prosecutor and the Chambers) interpreted Article 53(1) when deciding whether or not to initiate investigations or prosecutions in the situations that

554 Statement made by Mr Luis Moreno Ocampo, Ceremony for the Solemn Undertaking of the Chief Prosecutor of the International Criminal Court, Peace Palace, The Hague, 16 June 2003.

555 *Kony et al.* (ICC-02/04-01/05), Decision on the Admissibility of the Case under Article 19(1) of the Statute, 10 March 2009, para. 37.

the Court handled between 2003 and 2015. The discussion is divided into three parts to correspond with the three elements that are evaluated when establishing a reasonable basis to proceed. These elements are that the crimes within the jurisdiction of the Court were committed, that the potential cases would be admissible under Article 17 and that an investigation would serve the interests of justice. However, since the interests of justice criterion has not been applied as a justification thus far, the discussion will focus primarily on jurisdiction and admissibility, which encompass both complementarity and gravity.

5.5. CRIMES WITHIN THE JURISDICTION OF THE COURT

As highlighted in the previous section, the first factor the Prosecutor has to consider is whether or not the information presented to the Office of the Prosecutor 'provides a reasonable basis to believe that a crime within the jurisdiction of the Court has been or is being committed'.[556] As such, the information or communications that the Office of the Prosecutor receives is not equivalent to complaints used in continental legal systems, where the Prosecutor is obliged to take appropriate action once a complaint has reached his or her desk. Communications do not always lead the Prosecutor to conduct preliminary examinations. Usually, civil society organisations or lawyers and NGOs submit communications. According to the 2015 report on the preliminary examination activities of the Office of the Prosecutor, it had received 11,568 communications as of October 2015.

The huge volume of communications to the Office of the Prosecutor suggests that there is a constituency – perhaps local populations – that believes that the Court can play a role in its pursuit for justice. That said, a high percentage of these communications, some of which generate a media frenzy of global proportions, pertained to crimes outside of the Court's jurisdiction. This suggests that the Court may need to strengthen its outreach efforts and raise awareness of its functions. These outlying crimes do not fall within the temporal (that is, acts committed before 1 July 2002), subject matter or personal/territorial jurisdiction of the Court. For example, in the Court's report to the UN in 2013, it is stated that: 'From 1 August 2012 until 30 June 2013, the Office of the Prosecutor received 572 communications relating to Article 15 of the Rome Statute, of which 477 were manifestly outside the Court's jurisdiction.'[557]

[556] Rome Statute, Art. 53(1)(a).

[557] Report of the International Criminal Court to the General Assembly, UN Doc.A/68/314, 13 August 2013, para. 86.

One high-profile communication that generated international media interest was made in 2011 by the victims of the Roman Catholic Church, who asked the Office of the Prosecutor to investigate Pope Benedict XVI for crimes against humanity.[558] The Vatican participated at the Rome Conference and contributed actively during the debates around forced pregnancies and abortion as acts under crimes against humanity. However, it did not ratify the Rome Statute, hence the Court's jurisdiction does not extend to the Vatican.

As regards subject-matter jurisdiction, the Office of the Prosecutor indicated that it received communications on topics such as immigration, asylum, medical negligence, social security and pensions, environmental damage, drug trafficking, money laundering and judicial corruption.[559] Some of the communications pertained to the crime of aggression, especially in the context of Iraq.[560] The crime of aggression was included in the Rome Statute, but the Court was not authorised to investigate or prosecute it until an agreement was reached on the definition of aggression and the conditions under which the Court could act.

The situation in Iraq has been frequently referenced to substantiate claims that the Court is selective in its approach. Many strong supporters of the Court, including South Africa's Archbishop Desmond Tutu, are baffled at how the US and the UK invaded Iraq in 2003 in an act that destabilised the entire state and region and violated customary international law, and yet none of the leaders of these two states has been held criminally responsible. It is therefore not surprising that the Office of the Prosecutor received more than 200 communications concerning the situation in Iraq, most of which made reference to the illegality of the war in Iraq and allegations of war crimes, crimes against humanity and wilful killing or inhuman treatment of civilians.[561]

The Office of the Prosecutor received and analysed 12 communications concerning the situation in Venezuela, a state party to the Rome Statute.[562] He found that there was no reasonable basis on which to proceed with investigations or prosecution on the basis of a lack of subject-matter jurisdiction. As regards the allegations of crimes against humanity, which featured in the communications, the Office of the Prosecutor explained that:

> In order to constitute a crime against humanity, Article 7(1) of the Rome Statute provides that particular acts must have been committed as part of a widespread or systematic attack directed against any civilian population. This test creates a stringent

558 Karen McVeigh, 'People Accused of Crimes against Humanity by Victims of Sex Abuse' *The Guardian* (13 September 2011).

559 See 'Communications Received by the Office of the Prosecutor of the ICC', Press Release, 16 July 2003; and 'Update on Communications Received by the Office of the Prosecutor of the ICC', Office of the Prosecutor, 2006.

560 See also the discussion in Chapter 3 of this book.

561 See Letter of the Prosecutor dated 9 February 2006 (Iraq).

562 Venezuela deposited its instrument of ratification of the Rome Statute on 7 June 2000.

> threshold. Even on a generous evaluation of the information provided, the available information did not provide a reasonable basis to believe that the requirement of a widespread or systematic attack against any civilian population had been satisfied.[563]

When the UN Security Council adopted Resolution 1593 referring the situation in Darfur to the Court, it ordered the Prosecutor to address the Council within three months and every six months thereafter regarding actions taken pursuant to the resolution.[564] The resolution prompted the Chief Prosecutor to gather information and analyse the situation in Darfur in accordance with the statutory requirements set out in Article 53(1).

On 1 June 2005, after an initial investigation of approximately three months, the Office of the Prosecutor concluded that there was sufficient evidence that there were cases within the Court's jurisdiction in Darfur. In a letter to Judge Claude Jorda, the Prosecutor concluded that there was 'a reasonable basis' upon which to initiate an investigation into the situation in Darfur.[565] He also stressed that he had discretion over whether or not to proceed with an investigation, even with situations referred to the Court by the UN Security Council.[566] This suggests that the Court does not operate as a permanent version of the *ad hoc* international criminal tribunal that takes orders from the Security Council. One commentator argues that it is not for the Court's prosecutor to determine whether or not to proceed under Article 53(1) when the Security Council invokes its Chapter VII authority in making a referral. This is because the referrals under Chapter VII are mandatory, binding expressions of international law.[567] Still, Chapter VII creates obligations to the UN member states and not to the Court, which is an independent entity altogether. In this regard, it makes sense and is within the rules of international law for the Office of the Prosecutor to push back at the referrals from the Security Council.

What we can establish for certain is that the Prosecutor can limit active investigations in a situation. In 2014, Prosecutor Bensouda told the UN Security Council that she was to 'hibernate investigative activities in Darfur'.[568] She based her decision on two factors: first, what she called lack of Security Council foresight in what should happen in Darfur; and, second, the need to shift her Office's limited resources to other urgent cases, especially those in which a trial

563 Letter of the Prosecutor dated 9 February 2006 (Venezuela).

564 UN Doc. S/Res/1593 (2005), para. 8.

565 Report of the Prosecutor of the International Criminal Court, Louis Moreno Ocampo, to the Security Council, Pursuant to UNSCR 1593 (2005), p. 4; see also Luis Moreno Ocampo 'Letter to Judge Claude Jorda', 1 June 2005.

566 Schabas, *An Introduction to the International Criminal Court*, note 3, p. 189.

567 Jens David Ohlin, 'Peace, Security, and Prosecutorial Discretion' in Stahn and Sluiter (eds.), *The Emerging Practice of the International Criminal Court*, note 439, (eds.), p. 189.

568 The Office of the Prosecutor, 'Statement to the United Nations Security Council on the Situation in Darfur, pursuant to UNSCR' (2005), para. 4.

was approaching.[569] Her decision reflects some sentiments of frustration with the Security Council's failure to act decisively in the situation in Darfur, especially regarding the lacking political support to ensure the predictable cooperation of Sudan and other State Parties. The Security Council permanent members are divided on how Darfur should be handled, with one side, including the US, France and the UK, favouring accountability, while the other side, including the Russian Federation and China, preferring to follow a more nuanced approach to Sudan.

In the case of Darfur, the Prosecutor's role in determining whether crimes within the jurisdiction of the Court had been committed in Darfur was facilitated by the fact that a UN Commission of Inquiry had already established in its report that it was likely that crimes against humanity and war crimes had been committed. The Commission of Inquiry had found out that 'some of these violations [in Darfur] are very likely to amount to war crimes, and given the systematic and widespread pattern of many of the violations, they would also amount to crimes against humanity'.[570]

On the question of whether or not acts of genocide had occurred in Darfur, the Commission concluded that the Sudanese government had not pursued a policy of genocide. It argued that 'the crucial element of genocidal intent appears to be missing, at least as far as the central Government authorities are concerned'.[571] This differed from the position taken by the US, which was that the events in Darfur constituted genocide.[572] Despite the nature of the Commission's findings, the Prosecutor asked the Pre-Trial Chamber to issue an arrest warrant for President al-Bashir for war crimes, crimes against humanity and genocide.[573] The Pre-Trial Chamber elected not to include genocide in its first arrest warrant

---

569 Ibid.

570 Report of the International Commission of Inquiry on Darfur to the United Nations Secretary-General, Pursuant to Security Council Resolution 1564 of 18 September 2004, Geneva, 25 January 2005, para. 630.

571 Ibid., para. 640.

572 See Schabas, *Unimaginable Atrocities*, note 51, p. 102; Rice, *No Higher Honour*, note 376, p. 387, who points out that once a group appointed by Colin Powell returned from Darfur with the finding of genocide, the situation in Darfur took on new urgency in the Bush administration. The finding shifted from implementation of the Comprehensive Peace Agreement to include trying to save the people of Darfur; Gerard Prunier, *Darfur The Ambiguous Genocide* (London, Hurst & Company, 2010), p. 140, who states that he was assured that Colin Powell had practically been ordered to use the term 'genocide' during his high-profile 9 September 2004 testimony to the Senate Committee on Foreign Relations; and Mamdani, *Saviors and Survivors*, note 130, p. 279, who highlights the double standards shown by the US in branding Sudan's handling of the civil war in Darfur to be as acts of genocide when it has also carried out violence which had similar consequences, if not worse, in Iraq.

573 *Situation in Darfur* (ICC-02/05-157-AnxA), 'Public Redacted Vision of the Prosecutor's Application under Article 58', 14 July 2008; and Andrew T. Cayley, 'The Prosecutor's Strategy in Seeking the Arrest of Sudanese President Al Bashir on Charges of Genocide' (2008) 6 *Journal of International Criminal Justice* 829.

decision, which was issued on 4 March 2009.[574] The Office of the Prosecutor appealed this decision. On 3 February 2010, the Appeals Chamber called the decision 'an error of law' because the judges had sought more explicit proof than that required under Article 58 to issue an arrest warrant.[575] Subsequently, the Pre-Trial Chamber issued a second arrest warrant that included genocide charges.

Looking at the situation in Kenya, when the Pre-Trial Chamber II decided on 31 March 2010[576] to authorise the Prosecutor's application pursuant to Article 15 of the Rome Statute to open an investigation into the post-election violence in Kenya, Judge Hans-Peter Kaul wrote a dissenting opinion expressing his disagreement with the majority of the judges' interpretation of the contextual elements of crimes against humanity.[577] In his opinion, the Court lacked subject-matter jurisdiction in the situation in Kenya on the basis that the crimes committed fell short of the required threshold under Article 7(2) of crimes against humanity. He argued that as there was neither a state-like organisation nor an organisational policy involved, the crimes committed were common crimes that could be dealt with by the Kenyan judicial system. He highlighted the importance of distinguishing between international crimes and domestic common crimes when he wrote:

> [T]here are in law and in the existing systems of criminal justice in this world, essentially two different categories of crimes which are crucial in the present case. There are, on the one side, international crimes of concern to the international community as a whole, in particular genocide, crimes against humanity, and war crimes pursuant to articles 6, 7 and 8 of the Statute. There are, on the other side, common crimes, albeit of serious nature, prosecuted by national crimes justice systems such as that of the Republic of Kenya.[578]

Kaul's dissenting opinion indicated that the supporting material from the Prosecutor failed to indicate that the crimes against humanity were committed by a state-like organisation in pursuit of an organisational policy – contextual elements that are required for crimes against humanity. He disagreed with

574 *Bashir* (ICC-02/05-01/09) Decision on the Prosecution's Application for a Warrant of Arrest against Omar al-Bashir, 4 March 2009, para. 206.

575 *Bashir* (ICC-02/05–01/09-73), Judgment on the Appeal of the Prosecutor against the Decision on the Prosecution's Application for a Warrant of Arrest against Omar Hassan Ahmad al-Bashir, 3 February 2010, p. 39.

576 *Situation in Kenya* (ICC-01/09), Decision Pursuant to Article 15 of the Rome Statute on the Authorisation of an Investigation into the Situation in the Republic of Kenya, 31 March 2010.

577 The judges included Judge Ekaterina Trendafilova, Presiding Judge (Bulgaria), and Judge Cuno Tarfusser (Italy).

578 *Situation in Kenya* (ICC-01/09–19-Corr), Dissenting Opinion of Judge Hans-Peter Kaul to the 'Decision Pursuant to Article 15 of the Rome Statute on the Authorisation of an Investigation into the Situation in the Republic of Kenya', 31 March 2010, para. 10.

the notion that any non-state actor can be qualified as an organisation within Article 7(2)(a) of the Rome Statute, stating that such an approach 'may expand the concept of crimes against humanity to [include] any infringement of human rights'.[579]

Kaul pointed out that stretching the interpretation of crimes against humanity to common crimes:

> [M]ight infringe on State sovereignty and the action of national courts for crimes which should not be within the ambit of the Statute. It would broaden the scope of possible ICC intervention almost indefinitely. This might turn the ICC, which is fully dependent on State cooperation, in a hopelessly overstretched, inefficient international court, with related risks for its standing and credibility.[580]

This dissenting opinion addresses two issues – a legal issue and a policy issue. Legally, it appeared to have wanted to ensure that the Court's interpretation of crimes against humanity had progressed from the interpretation used in *ad hoc* tribunals, where state policy or organisational policy was not a requirement. The Rome Statute had addressed this by including this requirement in its definition of crimes as contained in Article 7(2)(a).

The Yugoslav Tribunal in *Prosecutor v. Kuranac* claimed that the element of state policy never existed in the definition of crimes against humanity.[581] Cherif Bassiouni, a leading expect on international criminal law and one of the drafters of the Rome Statute, criticised this claim for misapplying the law with respect to the requirement of a state policy in crimes against humanity.[582] He claims that such an interpretation transforms crimes against humanity into domestic crimes that only become international crimes when committed on a widespread

579 Ibid, para. 53.

580 Ibid, para. 10.

581 *Kunarac el al.* (IT-96-23 and IT-96-23/1-A) Judgment, 12 June 2002, para. 98 stating that 'Contrary to the Appellants' submissions, neither the attack nor the acts of the accused needs to be supported by any form of 'policy'or 'plan'. There was nothing in the Statute or customary international law at the time of the alleged acts 'which required proof of the existence of a plan or policy to commit these crimes.' As indicated above, proof that the attack was directed against a civilian population and that it was widespread or systematic are legal elements of the crime. But in order to prove these elements, it is not necessary to show that they were the result of the existence of a policy or plan. It may be useful in establishing that the attack was directed against a civilian population and that it was widespread or systematic (especially the latter) in order to show that there was in fact a policy or plan, but it may be possible to prove these things by reference to other matters. Thus, the existence of a policy or plan may be evidentially relevant, but it is not a legal element of the crime).

582 M. Cherif Bassiouni, 'Revisiting the Architecture of Crimes against Humanity: Almost a Century in Making, with Gaps and Ambiguities Remaining: The Need for a Specialised Convention' in Leila Nadya Sadat (ed.), *Forging a Convention for Crimes Against Humanity* (Cambridge, Cambridge University Press, 2011), p. 54; see also William A. Schabas, 'State Policy as an Element of International Crimes' (2008) 98 *Journal of Criminal Law and Criminology* 953.

or systematic basis.[583] Such an approach would mean that all human rights violations would qualify as international crimes. The policy issue that Judge Kaul also seems to be addressing is that an open-ended definition of crimes against humanity would stop states accepting the Court out of fear that it would jump on any human rights infringement in their sovereign territories.

In August 2012, during an address at the 6th annual international humanitarian law dialogues under the title 'Hybrid International Courts: A Tenth Anniversary Respective on the Special Court for Sierra Leone', at Chautauqua Institution, Robert H Jackson Centre, Judge Kaul revisited the Court's jurisprudence on crimes against humanity. In his address on 'The ICC of the Future', he expressed his hope that:

> The current majority jurisprudence [regarding crimes against humanity pursuant to Article 7 of the Statute] established in the Kenya cases will have become obsolete and overturned by future ICC decisions … A vague formula that any kind of non-state actor may qualify as an 'organisation' within the meaning of article 7(2)(a) of the Statute, that 'has the capability to perform acts which infringe on basic human values' remains totally unconvincing to me.[584]

Perhaps if the Court had adopted Judge Kaul's approach, it might have reached the conclusion that it had no subject-matter jurisdiction in Kenya and that the cases were inadmissible. This would not have implied that there were no crimes committed in the post-election violence in Kenya, but rather that Kenya's judicial system was capable of dealing with the proceedings. This would have of course saved the Court much of the criticism it received for intervening in yet another African country: Kenya.

The difficulty with insisting that the cases could have been handled by Kenya's criminal justice system is that the Kenyan authorities were given time to set up a mechanism that could have delivered justice and they failed to do so. Be that as it may, the contextual elements of the crimes against humanity were questionable, which could have rendered the case inadmissible before the Court. The Court could have taken a positive complementarity approach and encouraged and supported the Kenyan authorities to conduct their own investigations and prosecutions.

5.6. ADMISSIBILITY IN THE CONTEXT OF SELF-REFERRAL

Several self-referrals made the Office of the Prosecutor's role in assessing admissibility easy. Theoretically this meant that there was no need to determine

583 Bassiouni, 'Revisiting the Architecture of Crimes against Humanity', note 572, p. 55.
584 Kaul, 'The ICC of the Future', note 274, p. 10.

inability or unwillingness. The Prosecutor decided to officially open investigations in Uganda, the Democratic Republic of the Congo, the Central African Republic and Mali, all of which had referred their own situations. In relation to Uganda, which made its referral on 16 December 2003,[585] the Attorney General explained the decision to refer the LRA situation to the Court, saying:

> Uganda has referred this situation to the ICC primarily because, without international cooperation and assistance, it cannot succeed in arresting those members of the LRA leadership and others most responsible for the above crimes. Furthermore, Uganda is of the view that they are matters of concern to the international community as a whole. It is thus befitting both from a practical and moral viewpoint to entrust the investigation and prosecution of these crimes to the Prosecutor of the ICC.[586]

When the Pre-Trial Chamber II authorised the issuance of warrants of arrest against the LRA leadership, it took note of the statements in the 'Letter of Jurisdiction' from the Ugandan government, dated 28 May 2004. In the letter, the Ugandan government put out a statement saying that it had been unable to arrest individuals who may bear the greatest responsibility for the crimes referred and that the Court was the most appropriate and effective forum for the investigation and prosecution of those deemed responsible. The Ugandan government had not conducted and did not intend to conduct national proceedings.[587] As a result, the Pre-Trial Chamber II concluded that the case against Kony 'appears to be admissible'.[588]

In the context of the Juba peace talks between the Ugandan government and the LRA/Movement in 2008 and the subsequent agreement that called for the Ugandan government to establish an accountability mechanism for the atrocities committed in Northern Uganda, the Pre-Trial Chamber II exercised its *proprio motu* power to determine the admissibility of the case against the leadership of the LRA.[589] It wanted to establish if the Ugandan government was still unwilling

585 'Referral of the Situation Concerning the Lord's Resistance Army', Submitted by the Republic of Uganda, Attorney General F.J Ayume SC, MP, Republic of Uganda, 16 December 2003. For a detailed analysis of the Ugandan conflict, see Mohamed M. El Zeidy, 'The Ugandan Government Triggers the First Test of the Complementarity Principle: An Assessment of the First State's Party Referral to the ICC' (2005) 5 *International Criminal Law Review* 83; and Nouwen and Werner, 'Doing Justice to the Political', note 407.

586 'Referral of the Situation Concerning the Lord's Resistance Army', Submitted by the Republic of Uganda, Attorney General F.J Ayume SC, MP Republic of Uganda, 16 December 2003, para. 25.

587 *Kony* (ICC-02/04-53), Warrant of Arrest for Joseph Kony Issued on 8 July 2005, as Amended on 27 September 2005, para. 37.

588 Ibid.

589 *Kony et al.* (ICC-02/04-01/05), Decision Initiating Proceedings under Article 19, Requesting Observations and Appointing Counsel for the Defence, 21 October 2008, p. 8; see also Burke-White and Scott Kaplan, 'Shaping the Countours of Domestic Justice', note 68.

or unable to carry out the investigation and prosecution under its own authority. This move was also triggered by the conflicting messages that the Ugandan government had started sending through the media about the referral and the Court's involvement. For instance, the Pre-Trial Chamber had become aware of media reports stating that the Ugandan government wanted to withdraw its referral to the Court. During a visit to the Commonwealth Secretariat in March 2008, President Museveni had told reporters that: 'When the LRA people come back then they will be under our jurisdiction ... What we have said in the agreement is that instead of using this formal, western type of justice [the ICC] we will use traditional justice.'[590]

The Pre-Trial Chamber II concluded that the case was still admissible under Article 17.[591] It held that it was still unclear whether the accused could be prosecuted in Uganda because the peace agreement and the Annex that were supposed to form the basis for the trial had not been signed.[592] This meant that the conditions that had led the Ugandan government to refer the situation had not changed and there had been no further moves to punish the LRA. The Pre-Trial Chamber II ruling served two purposes as far as admissibility was concerned: first, it established that the case was still admissible before the Court; and, second, it reminded the Ugandan government that it was the Court – and not any other institution – that determined admissibility once its jurisdiction had been triggered.[593] This would have limited Uganda's options in the event that a peace deal was eventually concluded. In any case, when one of the suspects, Dominic Ongwen, was surrendered to the US Special Forces in the Central African Republic, the Ugandan government transferred him to the Court, which shows that it was ready to comply with the Court's decision.

Barely four months had elapsed following Uganda's self-referral when the Democratic Republic of the Congo followed suit and referred a situation in its territory to the Court. On 3 March 2004, the Congolese government sent a letter to the Prosecutor stating, 'les autorites compétentes ne sont malheureusement pas en mesure de mener des enquetes sur les crimes mentionnes ci-dessus ni d'engager les poursuites necessaires sans la participation de la Cour Penale Internaionale' ('The competent authorities are unfortunately not able to conduct investigations into the crimes mentioned above nor to commence the necessary proceedings without the participation of the International Criminal Court').

Schabas pointed out that although both the referrals waived admissibility, they differ, in that the Congolese referral did not indicate that it was unwilling

590 Tom Burgis, 'Uganda Disputes ICC Charges against Kony' *Financial Times* (11 March 2008).

591 *Kony et al.* (ICC-02/04-01/05), Decision on the Admissibility of the Case under Article 19(1) of the Statute, 10 March 2009, p. 27.

592 Ibid, para. 49. See also Antonio Cassese et al. (eds.), *International Criminal Law: Cases & Commentary* (Oxford, Oxford University Press, 2011), p. 530.

593 El Zeidy, 'Admissibility in International Criminal Law', note 459, (eds.), p. 219.

or unable to proceed.[594] The referral made the preliminary examination easier for the Prosecutor and there were no issues of jurisdiction or admissibility in the application for an arrest warrant for Thomas Lubanga.[595] However, before the Pre-Trial Chamber I issued Lubanga's arrest warrant, it argued that it was necessary to determine whether his case fell within the jurisdiction of the Court and was admissible.[596]

Consequently, in its decision to issue an arrest warrants, the Court introduced another element into the assessment of admissibility – the concept of inactivity. This is not mentioned in Article 17(1).[597] In finding the Lubanga case admissible, the Pre-Trial Chamber first reiterated its own definition of 'case' before stressing that it is a *conditio sine qua non*, in that for a case arising from the investigation of a situation to be inadmissible, national proceedings must encompass both the person and the conduct which is the subject of the case before the Court.[598]

In assessing the national proceedings in the Democratic Republic of the Congo, the Pre-Trial Chamber I gave its own interpretation of the self-referral made by President Joseph Kabila. It considered the 2003 self-referral to be an indication that the Democratic Republic of the Congo was unable to undertake the necessary investigations and the necessary prosecutions. However, it also acknowledged that the situation had changed in 2006 in the region of Ituri, where a Tribunal de Grande Instance had reopened in Bunia. The reopening of the Tribunal de Grande Instance was part of the outcome of the *Programme de restauration de la justice à l'est du Congo* (REJUSCO).[599] This was a joint programme run by the EU and the Belgian, British and Dutch governments. It was aimed at supporting legal systems in Ituri, North Kivu and South Kivu. In June 2006, the European Commissioner reported that he had approved €7.9 million in funding for the programme.

However, when the Chamber analysed the Congolese authorities' warrants of arrest used against Lubanga, they established that they did not encompass the alleged practice and policy of enlisting conscripting and using children under the age of 15 to participate in hostilities between July 2002 and December 2003. The Chamber held that the case was admissible because no state with jurisdiction over the case was acting, or had acted, to address it. It concluded

---

594 Schabas, *An Introduction to the International Criminal Court*, note 3, p. 44.

595 *Lubanga* (ICC-01/04-01/06) Decision on the Prosecutor's Application for a Warrant of Arrest, Art. 58, 10 February 2006, para. 19.

596 Ibid, para. 18.

597 El Zeidy, 'Admissibility in International Criminal Law', note 459, (eds.), p. 219.

598 *Lubanga* (ICC-01/04-01/06) Decision on the Prosecutor's Application for a Warrant of Arrest, Art. 58, 10 February 2006, para. 31.

599 See Human Rights Watch, *Making Justice Work: Restoration of the Legal System in Ituri, DRC: A Human Rights Watch Briefing Paper* (New York, Human Rights Watch, 2004); and European Commission, 'The European Commission Contributes to the Testoration of Justice in the East of the Democractic Republic of Congo' (26 June 2006).

that 'in the absence of any acting State, the Chamber need not make analysis of unwillingness or inability'. One wonders whether it would have been easier to assist the Congolese government to add the missing charges and prosecute Lubanga than having to start a complete new process at The Hague – which ended up being so protracted and resource-intensive.

It is worth noting that the Prosecutor's selection of the suspect and charges in the case of Lubanga was criticised by academic commentators and the victims in Eastern Congo. The Prosecutor had always professed to target the individuals bearing the greatest responsibility for the crimes committed, yet the selection of Lubanga was not reflective of such an approach. Pascal Kambale, a Congolese human rights lawyer, argued that 'for most Congolese, Thomas Lubanga did not fit into the category of persons bearing the greatest responsibility for the crimes committed during the second phase of the Congolese war'.[600]

During the period when the largest percentage of international crimes were committed in 2002 (the referral letter covered crimes committed from 1 July 2002) in Ituri, Lubanga is reported to have been a mid-level actor as an aide to Mbusa Nyamwisa, who was the leader of the armed group Rassemblement Congolais pour la Democratie-Mouvement de Liberation (this is alleged to have had strong links with and support from the Ugandan army). Even after 2003, when Lubanga had formed his own-armed group, the Union des Patriotes Congolais (UPC), he is reported to have been supported by the Ugandan army. Gérard Prunier, a French academic and historian specialising in the Horn of Africa, described Lubanga as Uganda's main proxy in the Ituri region.[601] If these claims were verifiable, the Office of the Prosecutor should at least have also targeted either Mbusa Nyamwisa or some Ugandan military generals.

There was also some dissatisfaction with the Prosecutor's choice of charges against Lubanga. When Lubanga was in Congolese custody, he was facing charges of genocide and crimes against humanity from the Congolese authorities.[602] Commentators concluded that the decision of the Court to seek the transfer to and prosecution of Lubanga in The Hague did not encourage the national justice systems to assume their duties under international law. The decision virtually made the concept of the Court as a last resort in the struggle against global impunity null and void. As regards the nature of the charges, it is reported that many in the Democratic Republic of the Congo found it deeply disturbing that after two years of investigation, the conscription of child soldiers was the worst crime the Prosecutor could come up with.[603]

---

600 Pascal Kambale, 'The ICC and Lubanga: Missed Opportunities' *African Futures* (20 May 2013).

601 Prunier, *From Genocide to Continental War*, note 479, p. 293. During the *Lubanga* Trial, Prunier was the Expert Witness for the Prosecution.

602 *Lubanga* (ICC-01/04-01/06) Decision on the Prosecutor's Application for Warrant of Arrest, Art. 58, 24 February 2006, para. 34.

603 Kambale, 'The ICC and Lubanga', note 590, p. 6.

The Congolese National Non-governmental Organisation Coalition for the Court, which claims membership of more than 100 leading human rights organisations, joined a group of international human rights NGOs in sending a letter to the Prosecutor in which they expressed their disappointment 'that two years of investigation by the office in the DRC have not yielded a broader range of charges against Mr Lubanga'. They cited examples of how Lubanga's militia was involved in the commission of far more serious crimes, including the killing of 350 individuals in the course of a military operation that also resulted in the 'complete destruction' of more than 20 villages in February and March 2003. They concluded the letter by saying that 'the failure to include additional charges for the most serious crimes in the case against Thomas Lubanga could undermine the credibility of the ICC in the DRC'.[604]

On 21 December 2004, the Central African Republic was the third African state to make a self-referral to the Court. The referral was directly linked to *Central African Republic v. Ange Felix Patasse and others*, a case that the national justice system had failed to handle. The origins of the referral can be traced back to the decision made by the presiding investigating judge at the Bangui Regional Court on 16 September 2004 to refer that case and others to the Criminal Court of the Central African Republic. On the same date, the Bangui Court of Appeals overruled this decision, holding that the crimes in question fell under the jurisdiction of the Court. The decision to refer the situation in the Central African Republic appears to have followed on from that decision.

On 11 April 2006, the Cour de Cassation, the highest criminal court of the Central African Republic, confirmed the decision. In its judgment, it stated that:

> [T]he incapability of the judicial services of the Central African Republic genuinely to carry out an effective investigation or prosecution concerning them is clear ... furthermore, the fact that the presiding investigating judge referred to the Criminal Court of the Central African Republic persons who are all outside the national territory shows that incapacity and establishes their impunity ... recourse to international cooperation remains the only means to prevent that impunity in this case ... the Central African Republic has ratified the Rome treaty establishing the International Criminal Court which offers the possibility to search [for] and punish the perpetrators of the most serious crimes which affect the international community as a whole, in the place of States which are unable genuinely to carry out an effective investigation or prosecution ... the presiding investigating judge was wrong not to decide to make use of that possibility.[605]

A spokesperson of the Central African Republic Ministry of Justice pointed out that the Court was the appropriate forum for prosecuting some of the

604 Ibid.

605 Central African Republic, Court of Cassation, *Central African Republic v Ange Felix Patasse and others*, Case Judgement, 11 April 2006.

suspects: 'Bemba cannot be judged by our national courts; only the ICC with its reputation and resources can do that.'[606]

It took the Office of the Prosecutor close to three years following the referral in December 2004 to make a public announcement that he was opening an investigation in the Central African Republic, finally doing so in May 2007. The delay prompted the Central African Republic to challenge the Office of the Prosecutor before the Pre-Trial Chamber,[607] confirming the early appetite for the Court on the continent. In response, the Pre-Trial Chamber said that the preliminary examination of the situation must be completed within a reasonable time from the reception of a referral by a state party and requested that the Office of the Prosecutor submit a report on the status of the preliminary examination – including an estimate of when it would be concluded.[608] This created tension between the Office of the Prosecutor and the Pre-Trial Chamber over functional independence and the interpretation of the provisions of Article 53(3).[609]

The Prosecutor pointed out that nowhere in the Statute or Rules of Procedure and Evidence was there a provision establishing a definitive time period for a preliminary examination.[610] In deciding to open an investigation in the Central African Republic, he claimed the decision made by the Cour de Cassation was important 'because under the Rome Statute, the ICC is a Court of last resort and intervenes in situations only when national judicial authorities are unable or unwilling to conduct genuine proceedings'.[611] This suggests that the decision of the Cour de Cassation might have contributed to the delay of opening the investigation.[612] It could be that the prosecutor wanted to ensure that he respected the sovereign rights of the Central African Republic in accordance with the admissibility rules.

---

606 Statement by David Gamou, a spokesman for the Ministry of Justice for Central African Republic, in Bangui, as quoted by IRIN New Agency 'CAR-DRC: ICC reviewing suit against ex-president, official says', 26 April 2006.

607 *Situation in the Central African Republic* (ICC-01/05-1), Decision Requesting Information on the Status of the Preliminary Examination of the Situation in the Central African Republic, 30 November 2006.

608 Ibid.

609 Schabas, *The International Criminal Court: A Commentary on the Rome Statute*, note 61, pp. 667–68.

610 Situation in the Central African Republic (ICC-01/05), Prosecutor's Report Pursuant to the Pre-Trial Chamber III's 30 November 2006 Decision Requesting Information on the Status of the Preliminary Examination of the Situation in the CAR, 15 December 2006.

611 'Prosecutor Opens Investigation in the Central African Republic', ICC-OPT-20070522-220, 22 May 2008.

612 On 26 April 2006, the Prosecutor said that 'there was a case pending before the [Central African Republic] national highest court of appeal [the court of cassation], and the final decision came a few weeks ago; now we are busy with the admissibility analysis'. See 'CAR-DRC: ICC Reviewing Suit against Ex-president, Official Says' *IRIN* (26 April 2006).

In Mali, the Prosecutor conducted a preliminary examination to determine whether there was a reasonable basis on which to proceed with an investigation. This was completed in January 2013, a year on from the referral. In a detailed 53-page report on the preliminary examination in Mali and pertaining to admissibility, the Office of Prosecutor concluded that 'the potential cases that would likely arise from an investigation into the situation would be admissible. The Office of the Prosecutor may revisit this assessment following any information received by States pursuant to the Article 18 notification procedure'.[613]

The conclusion was reached after the Office of the Prosecutor found that following the withdrawal of the judicial services from the northern cities, the Malian authorities were unable to prosecute crimes allegedly committed by armed groups in Mali. During the preliminary examination, the Prosecutor also found that the Malian authorities had established a special administrative commission of inquiry and had confirmed that no other juridical proceedings had been instituted.[614] It is worth noting that, in the conclusion, the Prosecutor left room for states with jurisdiction and/or states also investigating or prosecuting crimes in Mali to challenge the admissibility of cases under Article 18. This is a curious addition to the conclusion – it could have been designed to pre-empt any possible admissibility challenges from other states involved in the non-international armed conflict continuing in the territory of Mali, including the French military and the ECOWAS peacekeepers. The fact that the Malian government had indicated that it was conducting its own investigations in certain areas allowed for the possibility of an admissibility challenge even after the self-referral.

The Appeals Chamber confirmed that 'inaction on the part of a state having jurisdiction renders a case admissible before the Court'.[615] According to the Appeals Chamber, Article 17(1)(a) requires the Court to conduct a two-step test when considering an admissibility assessment or challenge. The two-step test is guided by two questions. The first requires the Court to establish whether at the time of the admissibility challenge, the state with jurisdiction had started an ongoing investigation into or prosecution of the case. The Court must try to establish whether the state is unwilling or unable to genuinely carry out such an investigation or prosecution.[616] Both the Pre-Trial Chamber and the Appeals Chamber have concluded that examining the question of unwillingness and inability where there were no national proceedings would be to 'put the

613 'Situation in Mali Article 53(1) Report', Office of the Prosecutor, 16 January 2013, para. 141.

614 Ibid, para. 138.

615 *Germain Katanga and Mathieu Ngudjolo Chui* (ICC-01/04-01/07-1497) Judgement on the Appeal of Mr Germain Katanga against the Oral Decision of Trial Chamber II of 12 June 2009 on the Admissibility of the Case, 25 September 2009, para. 78.

616 Ibid.

cart before the horse'.[617] The Appeals Chamber noted that this interpretation is widely shared among commentators on the complementarity principle.[618]

The 2013 Policy Paper of Preliminary Examinations adopted this formula as part of its policy for assessing the admissibility of cases. It states that:

> As confirmed by the Appeals Chamber, the first question in assessing complementarity is an empirical question: whether there are or have been any relevant national investigations or prosecutions. This is expressly stated in articles 17(1)(a) ('being investigated or prosecuted'), 17(1)(b) ('has been investigated') and 17(1)(c) ('tried'). The absence of national proceedings, i.e. domestic inactivity, is sufficient to make the case admissible. The question of unwillingness or inability does not arise and the Office does not need to consider the other factors set out in article 17.[619]

The concept of inactivity referred to by the Pre-Trial Chamber II appears to have become a default criteria, despite it not having been explicitly included in the Rome Statute. It has become part of the Court's vocabulary to the extent that it has rendered the inability criterion relatively insignificant.[620] This broad criterion appears to have been adopted to accommodate self-referrals, but its inclusion in determining admissibility is likely to make it very easy for the Court to find that national judicial systems are falling short.

States have also played a role in this through the concept of 'uncontested admissibility', which is linked to the concept of self-referrals. This refers to states not contesting the admissibility of cases.[621] When Uganda, the Democratic

617 *Katanga* (ICC-01/04-01/07) Appeals Chamber, Judgment on the Appeal of Mr Germain Katanga against the Oral Decision of the Trial Chamber II of 12 June 2009 on the Admissibility of the Case, para. 78. See also *Situation in the Republic of Kenya* (ICC-01/09-19), Pre-Trial Chamber II Decision Pursuant to Article 15 of the Rome Statute on the Authorization of an Investigation into the Situation in the Republic of Kenya, para. 54.

618 For the commentators with a similar interpretation of Art. 17, see Benzing, 'The Complementarity Regime of the International Criminal Court', note 65, who states that: 'the First requirement provided by article 17(1)(a) is that a state – both a State party or a non-State Party either is investigating or prosecuting the same case at hand, or has investigated it and refrained from prosecuting the person concerned. Mere inaction of a State in the face of crimes having been or being committed thus leads to the admissibility of situations and cases before the ICC'. According to El Zeidy, 'Admissibility in International Criminal Law', note 459, p. (eds.)261: 'The admissibility assessment under Art. 17(1) (a)–(c) is twofold ... Firstly there is a requirement to check ... whether the State has taken action in relation to a certain situation or case that satisfies Art. 17(1)(a)–(c) ... A negative answer will render the situation or case admissible under the plain meaning of article 17.'

619 Policy Paper on Preliminary Examinations, November 2013, para. 47.

620 Schabas, *The International Criminal Court: A Commentary on the Rome Statute*, note 61, p. 344.

621 Informal Expert Paper, 'The Principle of Complementarity in Practice', Office of the Prosecutor; and William A. Schabas, 'Prosecutorial Discretion and Gravity' in Stahn and Sluiter (eds.), *The Emerging Practice of the International Criminal Court*, note 439, (eds.) p. 238.

Republic of the Congo, the Central African Republic and Mali triggered the jurisdiction of the Court in their territories, they effectively declined to exercise their jurisdiction in favour of prosecution before the Court.

5.7. THE ADMISSIBILITY OF SITUATIONS REFERRED BY THE UN SECURITY COUNCIL

As should be expected when international justice is forced upon a state, the likelihood of resistance is high and this is expressed in various ways, including challenging the admissibility of cases. When on 31 March 2005 the UN Security Council adopted Resolution 1593 referring the situation in Darfur to the Court, it prompted the Office of the Prosecutor to begin gathering information and analysing the situation in Darfur in accordance with the statutory requirements set out in Article 53(1).

When presenting his first report to the UN Security Council, the Prosecutor stated that as part of the preliminary examinations, he had studied the Sudanese institutions, laws and procedures encompassing the Sudanese justice system, the administration of criminal justice in various parts of Darfur, traditional systems for alternative dispute resolution and *ad hoc* mechanisms that were created by the Sudanese authorities in the context of the conflict in Darfur. Some of the institutions whose work was analysed included the Special Courts created under the Special Courts Act in 2004 and the Specialised Courts that replaced them, pursuant to a decree issued by the Chief Justice in 2005.[622]

On 1 June 2005, the Prosecutor concluded that there was sufficient information to infer that there were admissible cases in relation to Darfur.[623] He then issued a press release stating that he was officially initiating an investigation on 6 June 2005.[624] A day later, on 7 June, Jalal el-Din Mohammed Osman, the President of the Supreme Court and Chief Justice of Sudan, issued a decree establishing the Special Criminal Court on the Events in Darfur.[625]

In his report to the UN Security Council, the Prosecutor stressed that the admissibility assessment was an ongoing exercise related to the specific cases to be prosecuted by the Court. This left the door open for the Sudanese authorities

---

622 Report of the Prosecutor of the International Criminal Court, Louis Moreno Ocampo, to the Security Council, Pursuant to UNSCR 1593 (2005).

623 Ibid., p. 4.

624 See Fifth Diplomatic Briefing of the International Criminal Court, The Hague, 26 October 2005, p. 5.

625 See letter dated 18 June 2005 from the Charge d'affairs a.i. of the Permanent Mission of the Sudan to the United Nations Security Council President stating that 'Sudan had established a Special Courts with the mandate to rule on any complaint submitted to it involving violations of honour, killing, bloodshed and the plundering or destruction of property'. S/2005/403, 22 June 2005.

to conduct their own investigations and prosecutions of those suspected of committing international crimes in Darfur. The Rome Statute provides that states with jurisdiction over a case can challenge admissibility 'prior to or at the commencement of the trial'.[626] The challenge has to be made at the earliest opportunity, which suggests that if there were to be subsequent developments in Darfur in terms of the investigation and prosecution of those with greatest responsibility for the crimes committed since 2002, the Sudanese government could always inform the Court of these and perhaps start the process of challenging admissibility.

In the Prosecutor's third report to the UN Security Council, issued in June 2006, he stated that 'it does not appear that the national authorities have investigated or prosecuted, or are investigating and prosecuting, cases that are or will be the focus of OTP attention such as to render those cases inadmissible before the Court'.[627] In the same report, the Prosecutor pointed out that the Special Courts established in Darfur were 'relatively inaccessible' and suffered from limited resources, a lack of expertise and security issues.

Juan Mendez, acting as the Special Adviser of the UN Secretary-General on the Prevention of Genocide, visited Darfur in 2005 and expressed his own disappointment at the failure by the Special Criminal Courts for Events in Darfur to prosecute international crimes:

> [M]y impression is very discouraging, quite frankly. For months nothing was done about the literally hundreds of cases of destructions of villages ... They have dealt with some cases that seem to be marginal to the serious events that happened in 2003 and 2004.[628]

It is worth noting that during the preliminary examination and early investigation stages, the Sudanese government demonstrated high levels of cooperation. The government facilitated five fact-finding visits for the Court officials from The Hague to Khartoum and allowed it to have access to records on national proceedings and meetings with government ministers and the police. In his fifth report to the UN Security Council, the Prosecutor explained that:

> From 27 January to 7 February 2007, the Office carried out a mission in Khartoum to gather information on such developments. The Prosecution met with the Minister of Justice, the Under-Secretary for the Ministry of Justice, the Chief Justice of West Darfur and the President of the Special Court for West Darfur. The Prosecution interviewed

626 Rome Statute, Art. 19(4).

627 Third Report of the Prosecutor of the International Criminal Court to the UN Security Council Pursuant to UNSCR 1593 (2005), p. 7.

628 'Sudan's Special Court on Darfur Crimes Not Satisfactory, UN Genocide Expert Says' *UN News Centre* (16 December 2005).

> the three special advisers of the Judicial Investigations Committee (JIC). Following that mission, the Prosecution received a letter on 15 February 2007 (dated 31 January 2007) from the Minister of State for Foreign Affairs, Ali Ahmed Karti, addressing the issue of complementarity and referring again to the investigations being carried out in respect of Shattaya and Deleig.[629]

According to the Prosecutor, this cooperation came to a grinding halt when the Office of the Prosecutor filed its evidence on the crimes committed in Darfur and identified two possible suspects, Ali Muhammad Ali Abd-Al-Rahman (Ali Kushayb) and Ahmad Muhammad Harun (Ahmad Harun).[630] In early 2007, Ali Ahmed Karti, the Sudanese Minister for Foreign Affairs, sent a letter making reference to the vision behind the principle of complementarity. He stated that as Sudan was investigating the crimes committed in Darfur, it could not allow another investigation to take place in its territory, reasoning that any such investigations would violate the rights of the accused. The Prosecutor considered this to be an indication that Sudan would use its right to challenge the issue of admissibility at a later date.

In the *Ali Kushayb* case, the Prosecutor completely circumvented the challenge of providing his interpretation of 'unwillingness' by arguing that the investigations that were carried out by the Sudanese authorities did not encompass the same conduct that was the subject of the Court's investigation.[631] This is commonly referred to as the same person/same conduct test of complementarity. However, one would have assumed that since Kushyab was investigated by the Sudanese government before it decided to release him, the assessment of the principle of complementarity could have easily been conducted within the legal framework of Article 17(1)(b), which states that that a case is admissible where:

> [It] has been investigated by a state which has jurisdiction over it and the state has decided not to prosecute the persons concerned, unless the decision resulted from the unwillingness or inability of the state genuinely to prosecute.[632]

Instead of addressing the question of whether the Sudanese authorities decided not to prosecute because of unwillingness or inability, the Prosecutor took the inactivity route. He argued that his investigations were related to events that had occurred in December 2003 and involved the murder of 26 people, including multiple rapes and notorious examples of inhuman treatment.

---

629 Fifth Report of the Prosecutor of the International Criminal Court to the UN Security Council Pursuant to the UN Security Council 1593 (2005).

630 Ibid.

631 Fifth Report of the Prosecutor of the International Criminal Court to the UN Security Council Pursuant to UNSCR 1593 (2005), p. 8.

632 Rome Statute, Art. 17(1)(b).

The Sudanese authorities, on the other hand, investigated an incident that occurred on a different date, which involved the murder of an unspecified number of civilians. In addition, the Sudanese authorities' investigations did not include rape or other forms of inhumane treatment.[633] There is no doubt that the Prosecutor's investigation better captured the seriousness of crimes that Kushayb was suspected of having committed, so one can understand the decision to declare the case admissible. What is not clear, though, is whether the same conclusion could not have been reached based on unwillingness and not inactivity, since the former appears to be the appropriate legal basis for determining the principle of complementarity.[634] However, since Sudan has refused to either cooperate with or recognise the Court's jurisdiction and has not challenged the admissibility of the case, it might take time to have this clarified by the Court.

As we have already discussed, on 26 February 2011, Libya – a non-state party to the Rome Statute – was unanimously referred by the UN Security Council to the Court.[635] Following on from the precedent set in the Darfur referral, the Security Council invited the Prosecutor to address the Security Council within two months of the adoption of the resolution and every six months thereafter on actions taken pursuant to Resolution UNSCR 1970.

Since referrals do not automatically trigger the opening of investigations in a situation, the Prosecutor's first step in Libya was to conduct a preliminary examination to establish whether or not the statutory requirements provided in Article 53 were satisfied. By 3 March 2011, less than 10 days after the referral by the Security Council, the Prosecutor had already determined that the statutory criteria for the opening of an investigation into the situation in Libya had been met.[636] He explained that his office had not found evidence of any genuine national investigations into the cases it would investigate. In his remarks to the 20th Diplomatic Briefing on 8 April 2011, he pointed out that, unlike the situation in Sudan, where the government had started some national proceedings (albeit for less significant crimes and perpetrators), he had found no indication of any national proceedings in Libya. He moved fast and his Office opened its investigations on 3 March 2011.[637]

The Prosecutor's preliminary examination of the situation in Libya took probably the shortest time in the short history of the Court – it was concluded

---

633 *Kushayb* (ICC-02-05-56) Prosecutor's Application under Art. 58 (7) of the Statute, 27 February 2007, para. 265.

634 See Schabas, *The International Criminal Court: A Commentary on the Rome Statute*, note 61, p. 344; and also Pichon, 'The Principle of Complementarity', note 537, p. 225.

635 UN Doc. S/RES/1970 (2011).

636 Office of the Prosecutor, 'Report on Preliminary Examination Activities', 13 December 2011, para. 118; and First Report of the Prosecutor of the International Criminal Court to the UN Security Council Pursuant to the UNSCR 1970 (2011), 4 May 2011, p. 4.

637 Luis Moreno Ocampo Remarks to the 20th Diplomatic Briefing The Hague, 8 April 2011.

over the course of a few days. As we have seen, this is completely different from the case of the Central African Republic, which had referred its situation to the Court in January 2005 only to have the Prosecutor wait to open investigations until May 2007. The pace of the preliminary examination activities in the situation in Libya drew attention to the capability and expertise of the Office of the Prosecutor to conduct examinations and investigations of international crimes in ongoing conflicts and urban settings.

It is a challenging task to determine the international humanitarian law principles of proportionality and distinction in armed conflicts occurring in urban settings, as occurred in Misrata and Benghazi during the Arab Spring.[638] This is because when an armed conflict occurs in an urban setting, there is an intermingling of military assets with civilians and civilians' objects.[639] Given that such complex questions had to be addressed and the fact that the Office of the Prosecutor had not engaged with Libya in order to gain some in-depth understanding of the context prior to the referral, one wonders whether the short time that was taken during preliminary examinations activities was adequate to inform the decision of the Prosecutor or whether it was a rather cursory procedure.

The concern that the Office of the Prosecutor was conducting 'hit-and-run investigations' had been raised over Darfur and the Democratic Republic of the Congo. In Darfur, some critics of the Office of the Prosecutor have attributed the Pre-Trial Chamber's initial rejection of the three genocide charges in the indictment of President al-Bashir to the lack of evidence. They pointed out that:

> There [was] much speculation, inside and outside the ICC, at how Moreno Ocampo arrives at his figures for death rates in Darfur. Unpublished UN monitoring figures for 2008 range from 60 to 350 violent fatalities a month, for an average of about 130. The activist group Genocide Intervention Network has a similar number, of around 150 a month. Moreno Ocampo has a very different figure. Speaking at a conference at Yale University on February 6, this year [2009], the Prosecutor claimed that 'as of today, 5,000 people are dying each month in Darfur', including through 'slow death' by hunger and disease. The OPT itself possesses no specialist epidemiologists or demographers who might generate such figures, and no one working in Darfur proposes figures even remotely close to these.[640]

The limited investigative capacity of the Office of the Prosecutor was usually attributed to its structure, which – if compared to the prosecutors for the

---

[638] Mark Lerace, 'Complexities in Prosecuting International Crime: The ICC Libyan Warrants' in Gideon Boss, William A. Schabas and Michael P. Scharf (eds.)(eds.), *International Criminal Justice: Legimacy and Coherence* (Cheltenham, Edward Elgar, 2012), p. 111.

[639] Ibid.

[640] Julie Flint Julie and Alex de Waal, 'Case Closed: A Prosecutor without Borders' *World Affairs* (Spring 2009), p. 9.

Yugoslav and Rwanda Tribunals – was small. For instance, the Yugoslav Tribunal had analysis teams that were later transformed into Leadership Research Teams or Military Analysis Teams.[641] It is understandable that the Court could hardly have adequate capacity for investigations and research in all situations within its broad jurisdiction, but the Prosecutor's preference for economical investigation teams did not encourage thorough investigations. A commentator at the Coalition for the Court had asked 'how can a six-or eight-member investigation team do all of northern Uganda, all of [the Democratic Republic of the Congo], all of Darfur?'[642]

After the completion of the official investigations in Libya, the Prosecutor filed an application requesting the issuance of warrants of arrest for Muammar Gaddafi, his son Saif and Abdullah al-Senussi on 16 May 2011. He alleged that they were criminally responsible for the commission of crimes against humanity, of murder and the persecution of civilians from 15 February 2011 onwards. On 27 June 2011, the Pre-Trial Chamber I authorised the issuance of warrants of arrest for President Gaddafi, Saif Islam Gaddafi and Senussi for murders as a crime against humanity under Article 7(1)(a) and persecution as a crime against humanity under article 7(1)(h).[643] The case against President Gaddafi was terminated on 22 November 2011 after he was killed.

The new government in Libya filed an application challenging the admissibility of these cases. As a new government, the Libyan authorities saw the prosecuting of figures from a previous regime as an opportunity to assert their sovereignty and legitimacy. The first application was filed on 1 May 2012 in the Saif Gaddafi case and the second application was filed on 2 April 2013 in the Senussi case. Saif Gaddafi was arrested in Libya on 19 November 2011 and Senussi was arrested in Mauritania on 17 March 2012. Both Gaddafi and Senussi were in custody in Libya when the admissibility challenges were made.

On 31 May 2013, the judges of the Pre-Trial Chamber I ruled that the case of al-Gaddafi was admissible before the Court[644] and approximately five months later, on 11 October 2013, it ruled that al-Senussi's case was inadmissible before the Court.[645] The major factual difference between the two was that Senussi

---

641 Gregory Townsend, 'Structure and Management' in Luc Reydams, Jan Wouters and Cedric Ryngaert (eds.)(eds.), *International Prosecutors* (Oxford, Oxford University Press, 2012), p. 231.

642 See Brevin, 'Justice Delayed for Global Court', note 273, p. 5.

643 *Situation in Libya* (ICC-01/11–01/11-1), Decision on the 'Prosecutor's Application Pursuant to Art. 58 as to Muammar Mohammed Abu Minyar Gaddafi, Saif al-Islam Gaddafi and Abdullah al-Senussi', 27 June 2011; see also Anna Bishop, 'Failure of Complementarity: The Future of the International Criminal Court Following the Libyan Admissibility Challenge' (2013) 22 *Minnesota Journal of International Law* 388.

644 *Gaddafi et al.* (ICC-01/11-01/11-344-Red), Decision on the Admissibility of the Case against Saif Al-Islam Gaddafi, 31 May 2013.

645 *Gaddafi et al.* (ICC-01/11-01/11-466-Red) Decision on the Admissibility of the Case against Abdullah al-Senussi.

was in the custody of the new Libyan government, which probably meant that the new government in Libya could prosecute him. However, the situation was different with Gaddafi, who appeared to have been in the custody of a militia group.

The Pre-Trial Chamber's diametrically opposed decisions in what at first sight appeared to be two similar cases caught the eye of the UN Security Council. The Russian representative asked for a detailed explanation from the Prosecutor during a Security Council meeting,[646] claiming that it was unclear why the Libyan authorities were unable to guarantee due judicial process in Gaddafi's case and later ruled that Libya wished to, and was able to, conduct that judicial investigation in the case of Senussi.[647] The Prosecutor's response was well supported by the Office of the Prosecutor's own policies and the Court's jurisprudence on admissibility assessments – that the Court's decisions were not 'a judgement or reflection on the national justice system as a whole', but a case-by-case analysis.

The ruling on Gaddafi's case provides some insight into the Court's interpretation of the phrase 'principles of due process' recognised by international law in Article 17(2). The fact that the Libyan authorities had confirmed that some of the charges that al-Gaddafi faced attracted the death penalty,[648] combined with the significant practical impediments for securing his legal representation in view of the security situation in Libya and the security risks faced by lawyers who were willing to act for associates of the former Gaddafi regime, could have played a role in influencing the Court's decision to find al-Gaddafi's case admissible.

The Pre-Trial Chamber I confirmed that in addition to being willing to intervene in a situation because of inaction, it was also ready to intervene when the rights of the accused were likely to be in danger. Such an approach is likely to lower the threshold for the Court in terms of declaring the admissibility of cases. This is because the majority of developing countries struggle to comply with set international human rights standards, let alone with due process rights during trials for international crimes, which are complex and require expert human resources and considerable financial backing.

However, the Pre-Trial Chamber's ruling in the al-Senussi case restores some confidence in the Court's approach to assessing admissibility – or at the very least reflects the fact that the Court is a dynamic and a learning institution. The submissions by the Libyan government appear to have helped the quality of the Court's assessment. For example, its request to the Pre-Trial Chamber was for the case against al-Senussi to be declared inadmissible before the Court, or for

646 See UN Doc. S/PV.7059, p. 5.

647 See ibid.

648 See International Criminal Court, Summary of the Decision on the Admissibility of the Case against Mr Gaddafi, 31 May 2013.

the Court 'to consider implementing a positive approach to complementarity by declaring the case inadmissible subject to the fulfilment of express conditions or other on-going obligations'.[649]

The evidence that Libya submitted to support its challenge provided the relevant indicators of the state's willingness and ability to carry out proceedings against Senussi. Prosecutor Bensouda acknowledged this point when she presented her sixth report to the UN Security Council. She commended Libya's active involvement in the admissibility proceedings for 'setting an example of how States can invoke complementarity to protect their sovereign right to investigate and prosecute their nationals'.[650] However, the fact that Libya has not transferred al-Gaddafi to the Court reflects the contradictions and complexity involved in enforcing international criminal justice.

5.8. THE ADMISSIBILITY OF SITUATIONS OPENED BY THE PROSECUTOR UNDER ARTICLE 15 POWERS

Turning back to the situation in Kenya, the Office of the Prosecutor opened preliminary examinations when violence erupted following the national elections on 27 December 2007. The Prosecutor reported that he received 30 communications from individuals and groups concerning the violence. On 16 July 2009, the AU Panel of Eminent African Personalities chaired by Kofi Annan handed the Prosecutor a sealed envelope and six boxes containing documents and supporting material compiled by the Commission of Inquiry into the Post-Election Violence (CIPEV), also known as the Waki Commission.[651] The sealed envelope was handed over after the Kenyan Parliament failed to adopt the Constitution of Kenya (Amendment) Bill 2009 to pave the way for the establishment of a Special Tribunal to seek accountability of the persons bearing the greatest responsibility for crimes (particularly crimes against humanity) related to the 2007 post-election violence.

By the time the Office of the Prosecutor filed an application requesting authorisation with the Pre-Trial Chamber, it had concluded from the pre-preliminary examination that there were no national investigations or pending

---

649 *Gaddafi et al.* (ICC-01/11-01/11-466-Red) Decision on the Admissibility of the Case against Abdullah al-Senussi, para. 23.

650 UN Doc. S/PV.7059, p. 2.

651 The Waki Commission, composed of both international and national investigators (Mr Justice Philip Waki, a judge of Kenya's Court of Appeal, Mr Gavin McFadyen from New Zealand, Mr Pascal Kambale from the Democratic Republic of the Congo, and David Majanja and George Kegoro, both from Kenya) was mandated 'to investigate the facts and circumstances surrounding the violence, the conduct of state security agencies in their handling of it, and to make recommendations concerning these and other matters'. See the Government of Kenya, 'Report of the Commission of Inquiry into the Post-Election Violence'. 16 October 2008.

proceedings against those bearing the greatest responsibility for the crimes against humanity allegedly committed in Kenya and the Prosecutor was confident that the cases that were to arise from its investigation of the situation would be admissible.

Kenya became the first state to challenge the Court's assertion of jurisdiction over its nationals. It filed an application challenging the admissibility of the cases against Francis Kirimi Muthura, Uhuru Muigai Kenyatta, Mohammed Hussein Ali, William Samoei Ruto, Henry Kiprono Kosgey and Joshua Arap Sang, who had been summoned appear before the Court.[652] The application, which included annexes amounting to 900 pages, argued that the Pre-Trial Chamber must make its determination that the cases were inadmissible 'with a full understanding of the fundamental and far-reaching constitutional and judicial reforms both recently enacted and anticipated as well as the investigative process that the currently underway'.[653]

On 30 May 2011, the Pre-Trial Chamber II's Presiding Judge Ekaterina Trendafilova, Judge Hans-Peter Kaul and Judge Cuno Tarfusser unanimously denied Kenya's admissibility challenge.[654] In its decision, it referred to the Appeals Chamber judgment in the Katanga admissibility case, where it was ruled that the admissibility of the case must be determined 'on the basis of the facts as they exist at the time of the proceedings concerning the admissibility challenge'.[655] Since Kenya had provided no proof that there were ongoing investigations against the six suspects summoned by the Court, the Pre-Trial Chamber found that there was a situation of inactivity and consequently had to determine the case admissible.

According to the Kenyan government, the reforms that it had undertaken were to enable it to continue with the process of investigating crimes related to the 2007–08 post-election violence. As the Office of the Prosecutor noted in its submissions to the Pre-Trial Chamber, the Kenyan government made a lot of promises in lieu of proving that it was indeed investigating the cases that the Court was interested in.

The Kenyan government unsuccessfully filed an appeal on 6 June 2009. The main focus of its appeal was the interpretation of Article 17(1)(a). It reiterated the position that it had taken during the Pre-Trial Chamber II that, in assessing national proceedings, the phrase 'the case is being investigated' should be interpreted to 'cover the same conduct in respect of persons at the same level

---

652 *Situation in the Republic of Kenya* (ICC-01/09-01/11-101), Decision on the Application by the Government of Kenya Challenging the Admissibility of the Case Pursuant to Art. 19(2)(b) of the Statute (30 May 2011).

653 Ibid, para. 13.

654 Ibid.

655 *Katanga et al.* (ICC-01/04-01/07 OA 8), Judgement on the Appeal of Mr Germain Katanga the Oral Decision of Trial by Chamber II of 12 June 2009 on the Admissibility of the Case, 25 September 2009, para. 57.

in the hierarchy being investigated by the ICC'.[656] Professor Charles C. Jallow, who had written extensively on international criminal law and the AU, pointed out that the Kenyan government's approach to complementarity was to argue for some 'some degree of flexibility for states to exercise their discretion in deciding who to prosecute'.[657] The argument is that 'there simply must be a leeway in the exercise of discretion in the application of the principle of complementarity' because there is a presumption in favour of national jurisdictions.[658] This approach reflects a trend among pragmatists or political realists to seek to preserve the right of the state to choose the best option when seeking to balance peace and justice.[659] The problem, however, is that the establishment of the Court became a necessity after it was established that the state authorities tended to avoid prosecuting their officials for international crimes. Letting state authorities decide who to and who not to prosecute would seem to be going back to the original status quo, where government officials would be likely to enjoy immunity.

The Appeals Chamber judges dismissed the appeal, adopting the view that the Court was the appropriate forum for prosecuting the atrocities. The Appeals Chamber judges, Presiding Judge Daniel David Ntanda Nsereko (Uganda), Judge Sang-Hyun Song (Republic of Korea), Judge Akua Kuenyehia (Ghana) and Judge Erkki Kourula (Finland), first clarified the phrase '[the] case is being investigated' by emphasising that the meaning changes in accordance with the stage of the proceedings in which it is being applied.It noted that in the context of Article 19, the determination of admissibility is case-specific, which requires an examination of whether the national proceedings encompass the same individuals for the same conduct as that which forms the basis of the proceedings before the Court.[660]

The Appeals Chamber went on to assert that as Kenya was challenging the admissibility of a case, it bore the burden of proof and must provide specific evidence with sufficient probative value that it was indeed investigating the six suspects the Court was interested in.[661] The majority judges found that

---

656 The Government of Kenya had argued that the definition of a 'case' had not been settled by the Court, hence it preferred the interpretation taken by the Pre-Trial Chamber in the Art. 15 decision.

657 Charles C. Jalloh, 'Situation in the Republic of Kenya. No ICC-01/09-02/11-274. Judgement on Kenya's Appeal of Decision Denying Admissibility' (2012) 106 *American Journal of International Law* 118, p. 119.

658 *Uhuru et al.* (ICC-01/09-02/11-274) Judgment on the Appeal of Republic of Kenta against the Decision of the Pre-Trial Chamber II of 30 May 2011 entitled 'Decision on the Application by the Government of Kenya Challenging the Admissibility of the Case Pursuant to Art. 19(2)(b) of the Statute', 30 August 2011, para. 29.

659 Henry A. Kissinger, 'The Pitfalls of Universal Jurisdcation: Risking Judiciary Tyranny' (2001) 80 *Foreign Affairs* 95.

660 *Uhuru et al. supra note* 648 at para. 46.

661 Ibid, para. 61; and Jalloh, 'Situation in the Republic of Kenya', note 647, p. 121.

Kenya had simply failed to convince the Court that it was investigating the same suspects that the Court was interested in, thereby confirming the Pre-Trial Chamber's decision.[662] Judge Anita Ušacka (Latvia) issued a dissent to the judgment where she indicated that the Appeals Chamber could have taken a more liberal view of complementarity to ensure that national justice jurisdiction received some preferential treatment. She wanted the assessment to be adapted to fit the Kenyan situation.

Charles Chernor Jalloh noted that the rather static approach adopted by the majority of the Appeals Chamber judges stifled the growth of effective national jurisdictions willing and able to prosecute crimes in Africa.[663] He argues that Kenya has a relatively functional criminal justice system and the Appeals Chamber could have done more to support its fledgling efforts to undertake criminal justice reforms and establish a dialogue with the Court.

However, the issue addressed by the Appeals Chamber was not the unwillingness or inability of the Kenyan government or the genuineness of its proceedings, but whether there were investigative steps being taken in relation to the suspects identified by the Court.[664] The Appeals Chamber found that Kenya had failed to demonstrate that it had taken any such steps, despite having a functional criminal justice system. The issue appears to be more about the failure of the Kenyan government to investigate certain individuals linked to the political hierarchy in favour of focusing on low-level or marginal perpetrators. This is an example of the impunity gap that the Court was essentially established to end.

Côte d'Ivoire, which was not a state party to the Rome Statute until 2013, submitted a declaration in accordance to Article 12(3) on 1 October 2003 accepting the jurisdiction of the Court for international crimes committed on its territory as of 19 September 2002.[665] On 14 December 2010, the newly elected President Allasane Quattara sent a letter to the Prosecutor, the President and the Registrar of the Court confirming the validity of the 2003 declaration and his commitment to cooperating with the Court.[666] Around the same time, the Office of the Prosecutor received communications from several sources regarding the post-election violence in Côte d'Ivoire, including documents from the Cabinet

662 *Ibid Uhuru et al.* para. 61.

663 Jalloh, 'Situation in the Republic of Kenya', note 647, p. 122.

664 *Uhuru et al.* (ICC-01/09-02/11-274) Judgment on the Appeal of Republic of Kenta against the Decision of the Pre-Trial Chamber II of 30 May 2011, Decision on the Application by the Government of Kenya Challenging the Admissibility of the Case Pursuant to Art. 19(2)(b) of the Statute, 30 August 2011, para. 40.

665 Declaration de reconnaissance de la Competence de la Cour Pénale Internationale, Republique de Côte d'Ivoire, 18 Avril 2003.

666 *Situation in the Republic of Côte d'Ivoire* (ICC-02/11-3), Request for Authorisation of an Investigation Pursuant to Article 15, 23 June 2011, para. 17.

of former President Laurent Gbagbo on alleged crimes against humanity committed there.[667]

Based on communications received from various sources, the Office of the Prosecutor conducted preliminary examinations of the situation in Côte d'Ivoire and concluded that the statutory criteria established by the Rome Statute for the opening of an investigation was met. The Prosecutor then filed an application with the Pre-Trial Chamber III for authorisation to open an investigation as required under Article 15. In the application, the Prosecutor submitted that:

> Because no national investigations or proceedings are pending in Côte d'Ivoire against those bearing the greatest responsibility for the most serious crimes falling within the jurisdiction of the Court allegedly committed in Côte d'Ivoire since 28 November 2010, the Prosecution submits that the potential cases that would arise from its investigation of the situation would be currently admissible.[668]

The Pre-Trial Chamber III Majority Judges Elizabeth Odio Benito (Costa Rica) and Adrian Fulfold (UK) authorised the commencement of the investigations by the Office of the Prosecutor, with Judge Silvia Fernandez de Gurmendi (Argentina) issuing a separate and dissenting opinion.

5.9. GRAVITY

Another component of admissibility that the Prosecutor has to consider when deciding whether or not to initiate an investigation is gravity.[669] Article 17(1)(d) requires that the Court should determine that a case is inadmissible where it is not of sufficient gravity to justify further action by the Court. That said, the criterion of gravity is neither defined in the Rome Statute nor in the Rules of Procedure and Evidence. In plain English, the noun 'gravity' refers to something of extreme importance – a cause for worry – and in this context it is synonymous with seriousness.

The Office of the Prosecutor incorporated this requirement in its Policy Paper Preliminary Examinations, published in 2013, which stated that when assessing gravity, it would include both quantitative and qualitative considerations.[670] In the paper, the Office of the Prosecutor identifies and defines the factors that guide its assessment of gravity. This list of factors is illustrative rather than exclusive and includes scale, manner of commission of the crimes and their impact.[671]

667 Ibid, para. 21.
668 Ibid, para. 52.
669 Rome Statute, Art. 53(1)(c) and Art. 17(1)(d).
670 Policy Paper on Preliminary Examinations, November 2013, para. 61.
671 Ibid, para. 62.

In the Rome Statute, the concept of gravity serves two purposes.[672] The first is to delimit the subject-matter jurisdiction of the Court to the core crimes of genocide, crimes against humanity, war crimes and aggression. These were the crimes considered to be the 'most serious crimes of concern to the international community as a whole'.[673] Second, it serves as an admissibility criterion applied by the Prosecutor to determine whether or not to proceed with an investigations in a given situation or case. In this context, gravity is equivalent to the concept of triage in the medical world – the process of sorting injured people into groups based on their need for, or likely benefit from, immediate medical treatment. Unlike the other prerequisites for admissibility, gravity does not presuppose the existence of national proceedings.[674]

The inclusion of the gravity criterion in the Rome Statute acknowledges that even when dealing with the most serious crimes listed under Article 5, some form of prioritisation was needed, given the Court's limited financial and human resources. As Schabas noted, international justice, and especially the Court, can only aspire to deal with a handful of the crimes that are committed.[675] From this perspective, the Court's exclusive focus on Africa would be attributable to the gravity of the crimes committed in the region being judged to be more than those of the crimes committed in Afghanistan, the Occupied Territories of Palestine or Iraq, for example.

This is the picture that the Prosecutor tried to give in his statements with regard to the crimes in Northern Uganda and the Democratic Republic of the Congo. While addressing the Diplomatic Corps in 2004, Prosecutor Moreno Ocampo said that 'the situation involves allegations of large-scale crimes against civilians, including summary executions, torture and mutilation, child sexual abuse, rape, forcible displacement, and looting and destruction of civilian property'.[676] As regards the situation in the Democratic Republic of the Congo, he remarked:

> Ituri remains a priority for my office. Two weeks ago, more than one hundred people were reportedly killed in Gobu. The crimes are on-going. We cannot allow the situation to continue unchecked. According to information received, there are many groups committing crimes. We cannot deal with all of them at once. However, as we are a permanent Court, we can work on the situation as long as needed. Decisions on investigation and prosecution will be guided by the factors in the Statute (Article 53). This includes the interests of victims and the interests of justice.[677]

672 Margaret M. de Guzman, 'Gravity and the Legitimacy of the International Criminal Court' (2009) 32 *Fordham International Law Journal* 1400.

673 Rome Statute, Art. 5.

674 Stigen, *The Relationship between the International Criminal Court and National Jurisdiction*, note 64, p. 186.

675 Schabas, *Unimaginable Atrocities*, note 51, p. 83.

676 'Statement of the Prosecutor Luis Moreno Ocampo to Diplomatic Corps, The Hague, The Netherlands', 12 February 2004.

677 Ibid, p. 4.

The Prosecutor's views on the gravity of the situations in Uganda and the Democratic Republic of the Congo became more pronounced when his selection of target cases was made public in 2005 and 2006. In 2005, faced with criticism over his decision to proceed with investigations against the LRA and not the Uganda People's Defence Force, the Prosecutor invoked the concept of gravity and stated that LRA had killed many more people that the soldiers of the Uganda People's Defence Force.[678] In 2006, he compared the crimes committed in Iraq by British troops to the crimes committed in the Democratic Republic of the Congo when explaining his decision not to proceed with investigations into the war crimes committed by the British serviceman during and after the invasion of Iraq. He suggested that the number of victims in Iraq were far less in comparison to other situations in long-running conflicts in Northern Uganda and the Democratic Republic of the Congo.[679]

It is very difficult to say for sure which of these two wars resulted in the highest number of deaths for, as already discussed, the quantitative formula applied by the Prosecutor was criticised, as it assumes that the number of reported victims per conflict is reliable. Such an assumption is not accurate considering that the figures on victims in many conflicts are likely to be contested for various reasons and by various parties to the conflict. Schabas is critical that the Prosecutor did not compare the total number of deaths in Iraq with the total in the Democratic Republic of the Congo or Uganda, nor did he compare the total number of deaths resulting from the crimes attributed to specific perpetrators with those blamed on British troops in Iraq. Schabas suggests that the Prosecutor should pay more attention to factors that are germane to the gravity of a situation:

> Even if it is admitted that wilful killing attributable to British forces only concerns 15 or 20 victims, surely the fact that this results from an aggressive war that has brought the deaths of hundreds of thousands of Iraqi civilians is germane to the gravity determination.[680]

Kai Ambos, Professor of Criminal Law, Criminal Procedure, Comparative Law and International Criminal Law at the Georg-August Universität Göttingen in Germany, acknowledges that the Office of the Prosecutor might not have had much room for manoeuvre with regard to Iraq, considering that it only had jurisdiction over British troops by way of the active personality nationality[681] and this could be the reason why the Prosecutor tried to find excuses. This would

678 Office of the Prosecutor of the ICC 'Statement by the Chief Prosecutor on the Uganda Arrest Warrants' The Hague 14 October 2005.

679 Letter of Prosecutor dated 9 February 2006 (Iraq).

680 Schabas, 'Prosecutorial Discretion v. Judicial Activism at the International Criminal Court', note 62, p. 748.

681 Ambos, *The Colombian Peace Process*, note 530.

have complicated the effectiveness of any investigations, as the Prosecutor would have had to deal with both the Iraqi and British authorities. However, Professor Ambos held that the Office of the Prosecutor should have at least taken a more systematic and consistent approach to assessing gravity in the first place.[682]

It can be argued that the development of a Policy Paper on preliminary examination would eventually address this pattern of inconsistency. As already pointed out in this section, the Policy Paper indicated that the Office of the Prosecutor will address both the quantitative and qualitative factors. It is, however, reasonable to suggest that although gravity is not supposed to be controversial as it pertains to selecting situations for intervention, it has to be applied in a consistent and transparent manner to avoid claims that it masks other ulterior motives. The decisions not to open investigations against the Uganda People's Defence Force or in Iraq appear to reflect the role of politics and not the legal basis in the implementation of international justice.

The Prosecutor appeared to have been motivated by a desire to avoid confrontation with the UK and the Ugandan government – hence the explanations based on gravity.[683] In fact, in Ituri, in the situation that the Prosecutor said was a priority because more than 100 people have been killed in Gobu, he only ended up targeting one junior perpetrator (Thomas Lubanga), whom he charged with conscripting children and using them as child soldiers.

In the *Lubanga* case, the Pre-Trial Chamber attempted to import teleological reasoning into the interpretation of the gravity criterion by introducing the concept of social alarm.[684] The Chamber stated that in addition to conduct being either systematic or large scale, due consideration should be given to the social alarm caused to the international community.[685] Since social alarm does not appear in the Statute, the Appeal Chamber made sure it stamped on these attempts by the Pre-Trial Chamber to allow subjective, moralistic judgments to impact the determination of admissibility.

Robert Cryer notes that the Appeals Chamber wanted to reassure and demonstrate to states that they would get what they asked and signed for at the Rome Conference. This approach is attributed to its President, Judge Philippe Kirsch, who, during the drafting of the Rome Statute, was the Chairman of the Committee of the Whole at the Rome Conference and was considered to be a supporter of referring to the legislative history of the Rome Statute and regarded

---

682 Ibid, p. 44.

683 Schabas, *Unimaginable Atrocities*, note 51, p. 85.

684 *Lubanga* (ICC-01/04-01/06-8), Decision on the Prosecutor's Application for a Warrant of Arrest, 10 February 2006, paras 42–64; see also Cryer, 'The Philosophy of International Criminal Law', note 94, p. 257.

685 *Lubanga* (ICC-01/04-01/06-8), Decision on the Prosecutor's Application for a Warrant of Arrest, 10 February 2006, paras 42–64.

to have a keen sense of what states wanted to see.[686] The role played by the Appeals Chamber fits very well with the intentions of the drafters of the Rome Statute – to check that the relevant organs are bound by the Rome Statute and that they at the very least apply the admissibility assessments in a consistent and predictable manner.

686 Robert Cryer 'International Criminal Law Philosophy' in Orakhelashvili (ed.), *Research Handbook on the Theory and History of International Law*, note 94, p. 257.

CHAPTER 6

THE AU AND AFRICAN STATES' SHIFT FROM COOPERATION TO NON-COOPERATION WITH THE COURT

The AU and the Court have had a dynamic relationship.[687] They were both inaugurated in 2002 and share the fundamental goal of fighting impunity for the perpetrators of war crimes, genocide and crimes against humanity.[688] Despite these shared goals, the two institutions have a complex relationship. We have seen that members of the AU were initially among the key enthusiasts for the establishment of the Court. Their support extended beyond the establishment of the Court to its ratification and, as we will discuss later, some of the African states even resisted pressure from the US to sign bilateral agreements that would prevent them from extraditing US citizens to The Hague.[689]

The AU's predecessor, the OAU, was actively involved in the negotiations leading up to the Rome Conference. It is reported that on 10 June 1998, during the 34th Assembly of Heads of State and Government of the OAU, meeting in Ouagadougou, Burkina Faso, adopted the Dakar Declaration on the International Criminal Court.[690] This affirmed the commitment of the African states and

---

687 Jalloh, 'Regionalizing International Criminal Law?', note 141; du Plessis, *The International Criminal Court that Africa Wants*, note 341; Kamari Maxine Clarke, *Fictions of Justice: The International Criminal Court and the Challange of Legal Pluralism in Sub-Saharan Africa* (Cambridge, Cambridge University Press, 2009); Eberechi Ifeonu, *From Consent to Suspicion: Understanding the African Unions Emerging Resistance to the Enforcement of International Criminal Justice in the African Region* (VDM Verlag Dr Muller Aktiengesellschaft & Co.Kg, Saarbrucken, 2009); Mamdani, *Saviors and Survivors*, note 130; and Murungu and Biegon (eds.), *Prosecuting International Crimes in Africa*, note 452.

688 Constitutive Act of the African Union (2000), Art. 4(o), which states that, 'the Union shall function in accordance with the following principles:"Respect for the sanctity of human life, condemnation and rejection of impunity and political assassination, acts of terrorism and subversive acts", and Rome Statute of the International Criminal Court (adopted 17 July 1998, entered into force 1 July 2002),2187 UNTS 3 (Rome Statute), preamble para. 5,stating that "the States Parties to the Statute" Determined to put an end to end impunity for the perpetrators of these crimes and thus to contribute to the prevention of such crimes'

689 See du Plessis, *The International Criminal Court that Africa Wants*, note 341; and Jalloh, 'Regionalizing International Criminal Law?', note 141.

690 See Resolution on the Ratification of the Treaty on the International Criminal Court, 22–31 October 1998, ACHPR 24th Ordinary Session, Banjul, Gambia, 31 October 1998. However,

NGOs to the establishment of the Court and underlined the importance of the establishment of the Court for Africa and the global community as a whole.[691] Around 43 African states participated in the Rome Conference, with a few states such as Gambia, Somalia, Equatorial Guinea and Sao Tome absenting themselves.

The relationship between the AU and the Court appeared to have been cordial until the Prosecutor indicated that he was going to file an application for the arrest of the Sudanese President Omar al-Bashir in 2008. The relationship then deteriorated to such an extent that the negotiations for the signing of a cooperation agreement between the AU and the Court stalled, and the AU Assembly passed a resolution suspending any possibility of the Court opening a Liaison Office at the AU headquarters in Addis Ababa, Ethiopia.[692] According to the Prosecutor's report to the UN Security Council, the Office of the Prosecutor had started negotiations for signing a relationship agreement with the AU in 2004 and continued after the referral of al-Bashir.[693] The turning point in the relationship came when the AU Assembly adopted a resolution of non-cooperation with the Court with regard to the arrest and surrender of first al-Bashir[694] and then President Gaddafi.[695]

On 14 January 1999, the Senegalese National Assembly authorised President Abdou Diouf (1981–2000) to ratify the Rome Statute.[696] Consequently, on 2 February 1999, Senegal became the first state to ratify the Rome Statute. It was through the ratification by states such as the Democratic Republic of the Congo and other states on 11 April 2002 that the threshold of 60ratifications was achieved to facilitate the Statute's entry into force.[697] As of March 2016, 123 states had ratified the Statute, while at the same time Jamaica, El Salvador, Malaysia, Togo, Mozambique and Morocco had indicated that they were preparing to

---

the 43rd Assembly of Heads of State and Government of the OAU document on decisions and resolutions does not make specific reference to the Dakar Declaration.

691 'Dakar Declaration for the Establishment of the International Court', Dakar, Senegal, 6 February 1998.

692 See Decision on the Progress Report of the Commission on the Implementation, 27 July 2010.

693 First Report of the Prosecutor of the International Criminal Court, Mr Luis Moreno Ocampo, to the Security Council Pursuant to UN Security Council 1593 (2005), of 29 June 2005, p. 6.

694 Decision on the Meeting of African States Parties, 3 July 2009: 'deciding that in view of the fact that the request by the Africa Union has never been acted upon, the AU Member States shall not cooperate pursuant to the provision of Art. 98 of the Rome Statute of the ICC relating to immunities, for the arrest and surrender of President Omar El Bashir of The Sudan'.

695 AU, Decision on the Implementation of the Assembly Decisions on the International Criminal Court, Assembly /AU/Dec/366 (XVII), Malabo, Equatorial Guinea 30 June–1 July 2011, para. 6.

696 See International Commission of Jurists, 'Senegal is the First State to Ratify the International Criminal Court's Statute', Press Release, 26 January 1999.

697 The Democratic of Congo and Ireland ratified the Rome Statute on 11 April 2002.

become states parties.[698] Out of the 123 states parties, 34 were African states.[699] This made Africa the region with the highest representation in the Assembly of States Parties.[700] Asia-Pacific and Eastern Europe had 18 each, and Latin America and Caribbean States had 27, with 25 states from Western Europe and other areas making up the remainder.

There are geographical variations in the number of African states that are states parties to the Rome Statute. It is noteworthy that within Africa, there are sub-regions, commonly known as Regional Economic Communities, and usually states in such regions possess different approaches in relation to how the AU should lead the continent. However, it should be noted that some states have overlapping memberships – it is possible for a state to be a member of more than three Regional Economic Communities. That aside, 14 out of the 15 members of ECOWAS are states parties to the Statute. Togo is the only member that has not ratified the Rome Statute. In Southern Africa, a total of 12 out of 15 members are also states parties to the Statute – the exceptions being Angola, Mozambique and Zimbabwe. The other states parties are Uganda, Burundi and Kenya (from the East African Community). Rwanda is the only member of the community that is a non-state party, having distinguished itself as sceptical and critical of international criminal justice mechanisms – from the International Criminal Tribunal for Rwanda[701] to the exercise of universal jurisdiction[702] and the

[698] Based on a presentation made by Matias Hellman, the External Relations Adviser at the International Criminal Court, to a group of visiting Transitional Justice Fellows with The Hague Institute of Global Justice, The Hague, 26 June 2014.

[699] The following list gives the African States Parties and the year they ratified or acceded to the Rome Statute: Senegal (1999); Ghana (1999); Mali (2000); Lesotho (2000); Botswana (2000); Sierra Leone (2000); Gabon, (2000); South Africa (2000); Nigeria (2001); the Central African Republic (2001); Benin, (2002); Mauritius (2002); the Democratic Republic of the Congo (2002); Niger (2002) Uganda (2002); Namibia (2002); Gambia (2002); the United Republic of Tanzania (2002); Malawi (2002); Djibouti (2002); Zambia (2002); Guinea (2003); Burkina Faso (2004); Congo (2004); Burundi (2004); Liberia,(2004); Kenya (2005); Comoros (2006); Chad (2007); Madagascar (2008); the Seychelles (2010); Tunisia (2011); Cape Verde (2011); Côte d'Ivoire (2013)

[700] The Assembly of States Parties is the primary administrative body for the Court and is made up of all member states. It meets annually and each state has one vote. See William A. Schabas, *An Introduction to the International Criminal Court* (Cambridge University Press, Cambridge, 2011) p. 23; and Rome Statute, Art. 112.

[701] See the remarks of the Rwandan Representative to the UN Security Council explaining his government's vote against the adoption of Resolution UN Doc. S/RES/955 1994, which states, among other things, the Rwandan government's bottom line on the inclusion of death penalty in the sentencing policy and also its disagreements with the proposed temporal jurisdiction: UN Doc. S/PV.3453, pp. 13–16. See also Letter dated 26 July 2002 from the Permanent Representative of Rwanda to the United Nations addressed to the President of the Security Council UN Doc. S/2002, 26 July 2002 pointing out what the Rwandan government considered to be the shortcomings of the Tribunal, which included inefficiency, corruption, nepotism, lack of protection of witnesses, harassment of witnesses, employment of *génocidaires* as members of the defence teams and the slow pace of trials.

[702] See a speech by Paul Kagame at the 63rd United Nations General Assembly, 23 September 2008, pointing out that universal jurisdiction risked being abused by powerful nations

Court.[703] That said, and as already discussed, on 22 May 2014, Rwanda voted in favour of a UN Security Council draft resolution referring Syria to the Court. However, the draft resolution was not adopted after Russia and China exercised their power of veto to block it.[704]

Tunisia is the only state party to the Rome Statute from the Union du Maghreb Arabe, which includes Algeria, Morocco, and Libya. Gabon and Central African Republic belong to the Economic Community of Central African States. Djibouti and the Comoros are also states parties, although they appear not to belong to an identifiable sub-region outside of the generic AU. These variations are useful to avoid unnecessary sweeping generalisations regarding levels of support or otherwise for the Court in Africa. If basic numbers are anything to go by, it would appear that the Court has been better received in West and Southern Africa than in Central and North Africa. It should therefore not be a surprise that many of the criticisms of the Court as being biased against Africa come from states within this region (Rwanda, Kenya, Uganda, Sudan and earlier Libya).

One trait that stands out in both the politics of the establishment and the existence of the Court has been its resilience – that is, its ability to withstand external shocks and adversity. However, it has lost part of its identity due to the external shocks it encountered immediately following its establishment – the opposition of the US and the subsequent rise of the EU as its source of financial and political support had the largest impacts.[705] As discussed in Chapter 3, the US under the administration of George W. Bush undertook several initiatives to prevent the Rome Statute's entry into force. The basis of the opposition of the US to the Court can be confusing.[706] The US had supported a version of the Statute that would have allowed the UN Security Council to refer situations involving non-states parties to the Court, but would not have allowed either states or the Prosecutor to refer cases; it seems the failure of the Rome Conference to accommodate this version of the Court was genuinely central to

extending their jurisdiction over weaker countries. For a detailed discussion, see Jalloh, 'Universal Jurisdiction, Universal Prescription?', note 19.

703 See 'The Explanation of Vote by Permanent Representative, Eugene Richard Gasana, on the UN Security Council Resolution on the Deferral on the Kenyan Cases before the International Criminal Court', *Permanent Mission of Rwanda to the United Nations*, 15 November 2013, which points out that 'it is unfortunate that the ICC continues to lose face and credibility in the world the more it continues to be used as a tool for the big powers against the developing nations'.

704 UN Doc. S/PV.7180, 22 May 2014.

705 For the role of the EU in supporting the Court, see Salla Garsky, 'Strong, Independent, and Effective: The European Union's Promotion of the International Criminal Court' in Astrid Boening, Jan-Frederik Kremer and Aukje van Loon (eds.), *Global Power Europe, Vol. 2 Policies, Actions and Influence of the EU's External Relations* (New York, Springer, 2013); and Groenleer and Van Schaik, 'United We Stand?', note 148. For the opposition of the US, see William A. Schabas *An Introduction to the International Criminal Court* (Cambridge University Press, Cambridge, 2011) at pp. 25–34; and Scheffer, *All the Missing Souls*, note 9.

706 Schabas, *An Introduction to International Criminal Court*, note 3, p. 25.

the US opposition.[707] The US wanted the Security Council to play a prominent role in the operations of the Court – a position that was not supported by the majority of delegations at the Rome Conference.[708] In the end, and as observed by Broomhall and Scheffer, it seems that the manner in which Article 12 of the Rome Statute was drafted, giving the Court jurisdiction over nationals of non-states parties if they commit atrocities in the territory of a state party, combined with a prosecutor empowered with *proprio motu* powers, determined the US opposition to the Court.[709]

Scheffer also notes that although US President Bill Clinton had warmed to and endorsed the idea of a permanent international criminal court following his visit to Rwanda, some of the top US officials – such as Senator Jesse Helms, who at that time was Chairman of the Senate Foreign Relations Committee – were opposed to the establishment of such a court.[710] Senator Helms had even vowed that such a tribunal would be 'dead on arrival' in the Senate before the Rome Conference was even convened.[711] The US signed the Rome Statute on 31 December 2000, making it the 138th signatory,[712] but President Clinton did not submit it to the Senate. He also recommended that his successor not submit the Statute to the Senate for advice and consent until the fundamental concerns of the US were addressed.[713]

When President George W. Bush took office, he abandoned the Rome Statute. This legally allowed his administration to initiate the signing of bilateral immunity agreements also known as 'Article 98 agreements' with the allies of the US throughout the globe. This included states parties to the Rome Statute. The agreement meant that those that were party to it could not surrender each other's nationals to the Court unless both parties had agreed on this course of action in advance. Scheffer disagrees with the Bush administration's interpretation of Article 98(2). He argues that the agreements are based on an erroneous interpretation and application of Article 98(2) of the Rome Statute.[714]

---

707 For example, Hillary Clinton, in a meeting that included David Scheffer at the White House during negotiating period of the Rome Statute, is reported to have asked how the negotiations had gotten so convoluted with such complexities over jurisdiction and wondered why the drafters were not having a global war crimes tribunal modelled on the Yugoslav Tribunal, which was created by the Security Council. See Scheffer, *All the Missing Souls*, note 9, p. 196.

708 Schabas, *An Introduction to International Criminal Court*, note 3, p. 27.

709 See Bruce Broomhall, 'Toward US Acceptance of the International Criminal Court' (2001) 64 *Law and Contemporary Problems* 141; and Scheffer, 'The United States and the International Criminal Court', note 204.

710 Scheffer, *All the Missing Souls*, note 9, p. 186.

711 Barbara Crossette, 'Helms Vows to Make War on UN Court' *New York Times* (27 March 1998).

712 Scheffer, *All the Missing Souls*, note 9, p. 242.

713 American Service-Members'Protection Act of 2002, approved August 2002 and amended through P.L.110-181, enacted 28 January 2008, para. 6.

714 See David Scheffer, 'Art. 98(2) of the Rome Statute: America's Original Intent' (2005) 3 *Journal of International Criminal Justice* 333; and Schabas, *The International Criminal Court: A Commentary on the Rome Statute*, note 61, pp. 1036–46.

Article 98(2) was designed to avoid conflict between states' obligations under the Rome Statute and other existing international law obligations that could arise from either customary international law or treaty law and not new legislation such as the 98 Articles agreements.[715] The AU has since asked its states parties to explore the possibility of signing similar agreements.

To pressure states into signing bilateral agreements, the US included a provision in its controversial American Service-Members' Protection Act (ASPA) that prohibited the US from providing military assistance to states that had ratified the Rome Statute but had not signed the Article 98 agreements.[716] This was the complete opposite of the EU's stance. As discussed earlier, the EU made either signing or taking concrete steps towards signing and ratifying the Rome Statute a condition for a state to receive financial support. The ASPA was introduced by Senator Jesse Helms to protect US military personnel and other elected and appointed officials of the US government from criminal prosecution by the Court. On August 2002, President Bush signed the Bill into law.

The controversial Act was criticised by the EU and some of the allies of the US, especially the Netherlands, because of sections like Section 2008(a), which authorises the US President to use all means deemed necessary and appropriate to bring about the release an American national in the custody of any state on behalf or at the request of the Court.[717] This was later referred to as the Hague Invasion Act.

The Bilateral Immunity Agreements tested the resolve of Africa states in support of the Court. In Africa more than 40 states (including several states parties to the Rome Statute) signed Bilateral Immunity Agreements with the US. Among these were states like Uganda, Botswana, Djibouti, the Central African Republic and the Democratic Republic of the Congo, some of which rely on the US for military assistance. It is possible that this made it easier for President Barak Obama's administration to send US troops into the volatile central African region to hunt down Joseph Kony as it did not have to worry that its citizens might end up at The Hague.

However, other African states parties (Kenya, Mali, Namibia, Niger, South Africa and Tanzania) refused to bow down to US pressure and did not sign Article 98 agreements,[718] leading to funding cuts by the US government. This quickly resulted in the US scoring an own goal because the decision subsequently affected its efforts against terrorism. By 2006, these agreements were acknowledged to be actually interfering with US foreign policy, especially

715 Scheffer, 'Art. 98(2) of the Rome Statute', note 704, p. 336.

716 Sean D. Murphy, 'American Servicemembers' Protection Act' (2002) 96 *American Journal of International Law* 975, p. 976.

717 American Service-Members' Protection Act of 2002, *supra note* 703.

718 Beth Elise Whitaker, 'Soft Balancing among Weak States in Africa' (2010) 86 *International Affairs* 1109, p. 1113.

the war against terrorism.[719] John P. Cerone, Professor of International Law at Tufts University, reports that in March 2006, Condoleezza Rice referred to the agreements as 'statutory requirements concerning the ICC ... were sort of the same as shooting ourselves in the foot'.[720] In response, Section 2007 of the ASPA was repealed in 2008, thereby restoring all military aid to the strategic allies in the war against terror, including those that had not signed the Article 98 agreements.

The Obama administration continued warming to the Court, adopting a more positive approach and in some cases providing support. During Hillary Clinton's confirmation hearing as Secretary of State before the Senate Foreign Relations Committee, she said: 'Whether we work toward joining or not we will end hostility toward the ICC and look for opportunities to encourage effective ICC action in ways that promote US interests by bringing war criminals to justice'.[721] Since then, the US has participated in the Assembly of States Parties as an observer. Notably, it participated in the Kampala Review Conference (also as an observer) and, as mentioned earlier, deployed 100 combat troops in 2011 to help in the search for Joseph Kony, for whom the Court had issued an arrest warrant, and in 2013 facilitated the transfer of Bosco Ntanganda to the Court after he surrendered to the US Embassy in Rwanda.[722]

It is worth stating that in addition to the US, the other permanent members of the UN Security Council that had not ratified the Rome Statute by 2016 were Russia and China. However, unlike the US, they did not try to undermine the establishment of the Court. For Russia, all was well until the Office of the Prosecutor was authorised to open investigations in Georgia, including in the region of Ossetia, which is under the control of an armed group under the heavy influence of and support from Russia. China seems to be indifferent. However, Judge Kaul recalls being told together with Philippe Kirsch by the Legal Adviser of the Chinese Foreign Ministry that:

> China, even as a non-state party, wants to be regarded as friend of the ICC. We will follow a wait-and see policy for some time and observe whether the Court will behave as a purely judicial institution or whether it engages in politically motivated prosecutions. If the latter is not the case, the time for Chinese membership may come.[723]

China's status as a permanent member of the UN Security Council and its growing global influence – especially its increased presence in Africa – would

---

719 Cerone, 'US Attitudes Towards International Criminal Courts and Tribunals', note 220, p. 163.

720 Ibid.

721 Walter Pincus, 'Clinton's Goals Detailed' *Washington Post* (6 August 2009).

722 Jeffrey Gettleman, 'Rebel Leader in Congo is Flown to The Hague' *New York Times* (22 March 2013).

723 Kaul, 'The ICC of the Future', note 274, p. 2.

definitely make its ratification of the Rome Statute a very positive development for the Court. Among other things, it would be likely to increase support for the UN Security Council's referrals of non-states parties to the Court. To be fair, so far China's voting patterns on referral resolutions in the Security Council suggests that it addresses each resolution on a case-by-case basis while maintaining its strict policy of non-interference in the political affairs of sovereign states.

In 2005, China abstained in relation to UN Security Council Resolution 1593 referring Sudan to the Court,[724] and in 2011, it voted in favour of Security Council 1970 referring Libya to the Court.[725] However, China, together with Russia, systematically used its veto power to block the referral of the situation in Syria to the Court.[726]

6.1. AN UNEASY ENCOUNTER BETWEEN THE AU AND THE COURT IN DARFUR

As the US was warming up to the Court, a new cold front began to rise from within Africa. This should be a cause for concern considering that Africa had previously embraced the Court and that its frequent internal conflicts made it fertile ground for demonstrating the fruits of international criminal justice. The fact that the Court has mostly only officially opened investigations and prosecutions in Africa has led to conflict between some African states, the AU and the Court. This controversy is based on the claims that the Court is selectively targeting Africa in its enforcement of international criminal justice while ignoring atrocities that are committed in other regions.[727] The Court is accused of rendering justice according to double standards. These sentiments were expressed by one of the African leaders in 2011 during the 66th Session of the UN General Assembly when he said:

> We in Africa are also duly concerned about the activities of the International Criminal Court which seems to exist only for alleged offenders of the developing world, the majority of them Africans. The leaders of the powerful Western States guilty of international crimes, like Bush and Blair, are routinely given the blind eye. Such selective justice has eroded the credibility of the ICC on the Africa continent.[728]

724 See UN Doc. S/PV.5158, 31 March 2005.

725 See UN Doc. S/PV.6491, 26 February 2011.

726 See UN Doc. S/PV.7180, 22 May 2014.

727 Richard Lough, 'African Union Accuses ICC Prosecutor of Bias' *Reuters* (30 January 2011).

728 Robert Mugabe, 'Statement by His Excellency the President of the Republic of Zimbabwe Comrade Robert Gabriel Mugabe, During the General Debate of the 66th Session of the United Nations General Assembly New York,' 22 September 2011.

Even supporters of the Court have expressed concern, with Tutu expressing concern about various inconsistencies in applying similar standards for the prosecution of international crimes. In 2012, he refused to share a platform with former British Prime Minister Tony Blair and withdrew from speaking at a conference because of the former Prime Minister's involvement in the war in Iraq.[729] He later wrote to *The Observer* newspaper in the UK explaining his decision to shun Blair. He stated that he could not sit with someone who justified the invasion of Iraq with a lie: 'in a consistent world, those responsible for this suffering and loss of life should be treading the same path as some of their African and Asian peers, who have been made to answer for their actions in The Hague'.[730]

In his address to the Extraordinary Session of AU Heads of States and Governments given on 12 October 2013, the former Nigerian President Goodluck Jonathan raised the issue of selective justice: 'The ICC, despite its universal jurisdiction, seems to be devoting unusual energy and enthusiasm to the prosecution of cases from Africa, compared to cases from other parts of the world.'[731] The two statements by Presidents Mugabe and Jonathan do not categorically deny that atrocities occur in Africa or that there is a need for them to be addressed by the Court, but the concern seems to be that the Court is focusing on Africa, suggesting that they would be satisfied if the Court was to exercise its jurisdiction beyond – as well as within – Africa's borders. It is possible that even if the Court is to open investigations in Syria and Afghanistan, Africa will continue to be the Court's main focus simply because the rate at which conflicts arise where international crimes are likely to be committed is very high in this continent.[732]

The question then is: what does it matter if the Court is focusing where the demand for its intervention is high? It matters first as an issue of perception that is developing among African states that the Court has strayed from its noble ideals of international justice, which in turn could have a negative impact on the level of the support that it receives from African states. Second, the Court was established with a broad jurisdiction – although it is not quite universal, as suggested by the Nigerian president in the statement above, its jurisdiction is broader than that of the *ad hoc* tribunals.

---

729 Christopher Hope, 'Archbishop Desmond Tutu Pulls out of Event with Tony Blair Because of Iraq War' *Daily Telegraph* (28 August 2012).

730 Desmond Tutu, 'Why I Had No Choice But to Spurn Tony Blair' *The Observer* (2 September 2012).

731 Goodluck Jonathan, 'Statement by President Goodluck Jonathan at the Extraordinary Session of African Union Heads of State and Government in Addis Ababa, 12 October 2013'.

732 Charles Chernor Jalloh, 'Universal Jurisdiction, Universal Prescription? A Preliminary Assessment of the African Union perspective on Universal Jurisdication' (2010) 21 *Criminal Law Forum* p, (note 45) ,6.

Kofi Annan described the Court as 'a gift of hope to future generations, and a giant step forward in the march towards universal human rights and the rule of law'.[733] Legal systems – including the Rome Statute system – are not only expected to possess rule of law, but are also judged based on it.[734] Almiro Rodrigues, a former judge at the International Criminal Tribunal for the former Yugoslavia, stated that tribunals 'can only function legitimately if they are seen to abide by the rule of law in their dispensation of justice'.[735] At the same time, there are some objections to the notion of applying rule of law standards developed primarily for national legal systems in the appraisals of an international legal system.[736] Cryer pointed out that international criminal law deals with the criminal prosecution of individuals in a similar manner to that which occurs at the domestic level, so it should not be problematic to apply the same standards of the rule of law at an international level.[737]

Therefore, if the allegations by some African political leaders and scholars that the Court is selectively focusing on Africa were proven, it might mean that the Court would have failed to uphold the principle of the international rule of law, which is the bedrock of the liberal legalism[738] upon which the international criminal justice system is based . This alleged selective focus on Africa complicates the relationship between the Court and Africa. The perception has reawakened historical sensitivities and has led to negative attitudes towards the Court in some African states. Instead of viewing the Court as a universal tool that can be used to end impunity, it began to be viewed by some African leaders as a tool of neo-colonialism used by powerful states against their adversaries.[739]

---

733 'Secretary-General Says Establishment of International Criminal Court is Major Step in March Towards Universal Human Rights, Rule of Law', UN Doc. Press Release L/2890, 20 July 1998.

734 Joseph Raz, *The Authority of Law: Essay on Law and Morality* (Oxford, Oxford University Press 1983), p. 211.

735 See Almiro Rodrigues, 'Undue Delay and the ICTY's Experience of Status Conferences: A Judge's Personal Annotations' in José Doria, Hans-Peter Gasser and M. Cherif Bassiouni (eds.)(eds.), *The Legal Regime of the International Criminal Court Essays in Honour of Professor Igor Blishchenko* (Leiden, Martinus Nijhoff, 2009), p. 209.

736 For a detailed discussion on this, see Bruce Broomhall, *International Justice and the International Criminal Court: Between Sovereignty and the Rule of Law* (Oxford, Oxford University Press, 2003), pp 53–55, who points out that the applicability of the doctrine of the rule of law to international law has not been rigorously analysed as such.

737 Cryer, *Prosecuting International Crimes*, note 46, p. 197.

738 The philosophy behind liberal legalism is that the world order must be based on the foundation of core values which are promoted by the observance of rule of law. See D. Armstrong T. Farrell and H. Lambert, *International Law and International Relations* (Cambridge, Cambridge University Press, 2007), p. 197.

739 Mamdani, *Saviors and Survivors*, note 130, p. 286, who theorises the international community's intervention in Darfur, suggesting that the Court is primarily being used against the adversaries of the US; Paul Kagame, the President of Rwanda, told a journalist in an interview that the Court marks the return of past injustices such as colonialism and imperialism: 'Rwanda's Kagame Says ICC Targeting Poor, African Countries' *Associated Foreign Press* (31 July 2008).

This view has a historical basis in that the majority of African leaders interpret the Western European colonisation of Africa to be a demonstration of Europe's strong and long-term interest in Africa's resources. African states' sentiments towards the Court were expressed in more than 10 decisions of the AU Assembly of Heads of States and Government adopted between 2009 and 2016.[740]

The sharp tension between the AU and the Court first arose in 2008. Prior to the Prosecutor's request for the issuance of a warrant of arrest for President al-Bashir, the Peace and Security Council (an AU decision-making organ for the prevention, management and resolution of conflicts) had expressed concern over the misuse of indictments under universal jurisdiction principle against African leaders to the then Deputy Prosecutor, Fatou Bensouda, during its 141st meeting, held on 11 July 2008.[741] This was in response to concerns first raised by the AU Assembly, which was critical of the application of universal jurisdiction

740 See, first, Decision on the Application by the International Criminal Court (ICC) Prosecutor for the Indictment of the President of the Republic of the Sudan, 1–3 February, 2009, Addis Ababa, Ethiopia, Doc. Assembly/AFRICAN UNION/221 (XII) (hereinafter Decision on the Application); second, Decision on the Meeting of African States Parties to the Rome Statute of the International Criminal Court (ICC), 1–3 July, Sirte, Libya, Doc. Assembly/AFRICAN UNION/13 (XIII) (hereinafter Decision on the Meeting of African States Parties); third, Decision on the Report of the Second Meeting of States Parties to the Rome Statute on the International Criminal Court (ICC), 31 January–2 February 2010, Addis Ababa, Ethiopia, Doc. Assembly/AFRICAN UNION/8 (XIV) (hereinafter Decision on the Report of the Second Meeting of States Parties); fourth, Decision on the Progress Report on the Commission on the Implementation of Decision Assembly/AFRICAN UNION/DEC.270 (XIV) on the Second Ministerial Meeting on the Rome Statute of the International Criminal Court (ICC), 25–27 July 2010, Kampala, Doc. Assembly/AFRICAN UNION/10 (XV) (hereinafter Decision on the Progress Report of the Commission on the Implementation); fifth, Decision on the Implementation of the Decisions on the International Criminal Court, 30–31 January 2011, Addis Ababa, Ethiopia, Doc EX.CL/639 (XVIII) (hereinafter Decision on the Implementation); sixth, Decision on the Implementation of the Assembly Decisions on the International Criminal Court, 30 June–1 July 2011, Malabo, Equatorial Guinea, Doc. EX.CL/670 (XIX) (hereinafter Decision on the Implementation of the Assembly Decisions); seventh, Decision on the Progress Report of the Commission on the Implementation of the Assembly Decisions on the International Criminal Court (ICC), 29–30 January 2012, Addis Ababa, Ethiopia, Doc.EX.CL/710 (XX) (hereinafter Decision on the Progress Report of the Commission on the Implementation); eighth, Decision on the Implementation of the Decisions on the International Criminal Court (ICC), 15–16 July 2012, Addis Ababa, Ethiopia, Doc.EX.CL/731 (XXI) (hereinafter Decision on the Implementation of the Decisions on the International Criminal Court); ninth, Decision on International Jurisdiction, Justice and the International Criminal Court (ICC), 26–27 May 2013, Addis Ababa, Ethiopia, Doc. Assembly/AFRICAN UNION/13 (XXI) (hereinafter Decision on International Jurisdiction); tenth, Decision on Africa's Relationship with the International Criminal Court (ICC), 12 October 2013, Addis Ababa, Ethiopia, Ext/Assembly/AFRICAN UNION/Dec.1 (hereinafter Decision on Africa's Relationship).

741 Peace and Security Council, Press Statement, PSC/PR/BR(CXLI), 11 July 2008. The members of the Peace and Security Council at that time were Gabon, Ethiopia, Algeria, Angola, Nigeria, Burundi, Chad, Uganda, Rwanda, Tunisia, Swaziland, Zambia, Benin, Burkina Faso and Mali.

by some European judges against African leaders.[742] The Peace and Security Council expressed 'its strong conviction that the search for justice should be pursued in a way that does not impede or jeopardise efforts aimed at promoting lasting peace'.[743]

The Peace and Security Council's reference to the AU's decision, adopted in July 2008 in the press statement issued after its meeting with Bensouda reflected the fact that the concerns that Africa was being selectively targeted already existed prior to the application of the arrest warrant for President al-Bashir, but in the context of the application of universal jurisdiction. It is possible that during the meeting with the Deputy Prosecutor, the Peace and Security Council was forewarned about the pending request for the indictment of al-Bashir.

Regarding the application of universal jurisdiction, the tipping point was linked to the activities of French investigative magistrate Jean-Louis Bruguiere and Spanish judge Fernando Andreu, who together issued arrest warrants against an estimated 40 civil and military leaders from within the Rwandan government in 2006 and 2008, respectively. Although arrest warrants were also issued against citizens of countries including Tunisia, Djibouti, Cote d'Ivoire and Libya by other European judges, it was the Rwandan President Paul Kagame who took the lead in campaigning against what he called an abuse of universal jurisdiction by European judges. When he addressed the AU Assembly in Sitre, where the declaration against the abuse of universal jurisdiction was issued, he criticised the arrest warrants and accused some of the Western judges of being hypocrites. He stated that the same people responsible for bringing the slave trade, colonialism and apartheid to Africa were attempting to 'turn themselves into policemen of the world by issuing arrest warrants against African leaders'.[744]

Despite the Peace and Security Council's reservations on the Office of the Prosecutor's expressed intention to file an application for the issuance of an arrest warrant for President Bashir, the Office of the Prosecutor went ahead. It filed an application under Article 58 requesting that Pre-Trial Chamber I to issue an arrest warrant for Bashir for his alleged criminal responsibility in the commission of genocide, crimes against humanity and war crimes in the Darfur region of Sudan. The Peace and Security Council issued a communiqué in response to this development after its 142nd meeting on 21 July 2008,[745] reiterating the concerns that were raised earlier during its 141st meeting with

742 Decision on the Report of the Commission on the Abuse of the Principle of Universal Jurisdiction, 30 June–1 July 2008, Sharm El-Sheikh, Egypt, Doc. Assembly/African Union / Dec.199 (XI); see also the AU-EU Technical Ad Hoc Expert Group Report on the Principle of Universal Jurisdiction, 16 April 2009; Jalloh, 'Universal Jurisdiction, Universal Prescription?', note 45.

743 Peace and Security Council, Press Statement, PSC/PR/BR(CXLI), 11 July 2008.

744 'African Union Refuses Arrest against Rwandans' *Rwanda Focus* (7 July 2008).

745 Peace and Security Council, Communiqué of the 142nd Meeting of the Peace and Security Council, PSC/MIN/Comm (CXLII) Rev.1, 21 July 2008.

Bensouda. It is important to point out that at this stage, the Court had already issued warrants of arrest for two Sudanese, Ahmad Harun and Ali Kushayb, for crimes committed in Darfur and the AU did not get involved.

In August 2008, the Sudanese government considered launching a campaign during the UN General Assembly's 63rd session for the Assembly to request an Advisory Opinion from the International Court of Justice regarding the authority of the UN Security Council to refer cases to the Court.[746]Advisory Opinions from the International Court of Justice are not binding, but do carry enough legal weight and moral authority to influence international public opinion on specific issues. The rationale behind Sudan's desire to campaign for the General Assembly to request an Advisory Opinion is that individual sovereign states cannot legally approach the International Court of Justice with such requests. In accordance with Article 96 of the UN Charter and Article 65 of the Statute of International Court of Justice, the right to request an Advisory Opinion is limited to UN organs such as the General Assembly or the Security Council.[747]

In the case of Sudan, the potential backlash in the event of the International Court of Justice's Advisory Opinion confirming that the UN Security Council's action was in compliance with both the UN Charter and its role under the Rome Statute might have dissuaded the Sudanese government. According to Hadi Shalluf, who was *ad hoc* counsel for the defence in the situation regarding Darfur, such an Advisory Opinion would have morally obliged Sudan to comply with Resolution 1593.[748]

The Office of the Prosecutor's application for the arrest warrant attracted enormous attention and triggered a series of events that started to strain the relationship between some members of the AU and the Court. The Peace and Security Council asked the UN Security Council to invoke Article 16 and defer the process initiated by the Court, and at the same time the AU Commission tried to find ways of encouraging the Sudanese government to take concrete steps towards investigating human rights violations in Darfur and bringing the perpetrators to justice.[749]

Sudan's initial response was positive. The statement from the Sudanese Ministry of Foreign Affairs welcomed the AU's request for the UN Security Council to defer the application of the Prosecutor. It stressed that 'such a deferral [will] give room for the political process to reach the desired end and reinforce the efforts

---

746 'Sudan to Request ICJ Opinion on UN Security Council Authority to Refer Case to ICC' *Sudan Tribune* (29 July 2008); and also 'Sudan Takes ICC Battle to the UN General Assembly' *Sudan Tribune* (15 August 2008).

747 See UN Charter, Art. 96; and Statute of the International Court of Justice, Art. 65.

748 'Sudan Takes ICC Battle to the UN General Assembly' *Sudan Tribune* (15 August 2008).

749 Peace and Security Council, Report of the Implementation of Communique of 142nd Meeting of the Peace and Security Council Held on 21 July 2008 on the Sudan, PSC/MIN/3 (CLI), 22 September 2008.

of the UN/UN Chief Mediator'.[750] The statement also welcomed the 'affirmation by the [Peace and Security Council] of the principle of complementarity'.[751] For the Sudanese, the request for deferral was positive as it would have given the Sudanese judiciary the opportunity to bring the perpetrators of human rights violation in Darfur to justice. At this stage, the Sudanese government appeared ready to allow the involvement of lawyers designated by the AU and the Arab League in the judicial proceedings to increase credibility.[752] However, this position had changed by the time the AU High-Level Panel on Darfur proposed the establishment of a hybrid court, which is discussed in detail below. This was perhaps due to the UN Security Council's indecisiveness regarding the deferral request.

The UN Security Council attempted to address the AU's request when discussing the renewal of the mandate of the AU–UN Hybrid Operation in Darfur during its 5,947th meeting on 31 July 2008.[753] This was still before the issuance of the arrest warrant. On that day, the Security Council adopted Resolution 1828 with 14 votes in favour to none against, with one abstention.[754] The Security Council was divided on the issue of deferring the process in Sudan. The US, Belgium and Italy were clearly opposed to the deferral proposal. The US abstained, with Alejandro Daniel Wolff, the Deputy Permanent US Representative to the UN, explaining that 'the language added to the resolution would send the wrong signal to President al-Bashir and undermine efforts to bring him and others to justice'.[755] Information available through WikiLeaks suggests that the US had not taken an official position as regards the deferral request, although it remained resolute that accountability was necessary for crimes committed in Darfur.[756]

The US, Belgium and Italy wanted justice to take its course in Darfur. Their argument was that the judicial process had started with the referral of the situation to the Court three years earlier and the Court had already issued arrest warrants for two leading government officials.[757] They viewed a request to defer a process initiated by the Court three years after the process had begun as being inconsistent with the purpose of Article 16. In other words, if African states were serious about their concern that the Court should not intervene in Darfur, they should have raised the issue in March 2005 when the referral was made. This was not the case and, as already discussed, two African states had voted in favour of the referral.

---

750 Ibid, para. 3.
751 Ibid.
752 Ibid, para. 6.
753 UN Doc. S/PV.5947, 31 July 2008.
754 Ibid, p. 2.
755 Ibid, p. 8.
756 '63rd UN General Assembly: United States Goals and Priorities' *WikiLeaks* (17 September 2008).
757 UN Doc. S/RES/1593.

The Libyan representative raised concerns that, despite attempts to amend the draft resolution to include the language requesting the UN Security Council to defer the proceedings on the basis of the provisions of Article 16, he had not received the hoped-for response from certain members. As we shall see later, Rwanda made the same complaint when it sponsored the failed deferral request for Kenya in November 2013. Although the Libyan representative did not give names, it was largely the US, Belgium and Italy that wanted the course of justice to be respected and felt discussions regarding the work of the Court were out of place during a meeting on peacekeeping. In the end, Libya expressed hope that its issue with Article 16 would be reconsidered at a later date.[758] The representative from Burkina Faso also insisted that the issue be returned to at some point in the future.[759]

Although Africa was represented by three states (Burkina Faso, Libya and South Africa) serving their rotational tenure as non-permanent members of the UN Security Council, it was the Russian Federation that issued a direct criticism of the UN Security Council's handling of the AU's deferral request. Vitaly Ivanovich Churkin, the Russian Federation's representative, seemed to have favoured the deferrals of proceedings and pointed out that concerns regarding the deferral were shared by several organisations that represented 'quite simply the views of two thirds of the international community'.[760] He went on to assert 'unfortunately, that concern was not fully reflected in the resolution as a result of resistance by a number of UN Security Council members'.[761] The Chinese delegate shared these sentiments.[762]

The UK, acting as the informal coordinator and sponsor of the resolution, was open to a discussion of a deferral by the UN Security Council. Sir John Sawers, its permanent representative to the UN, said:

> We will not stand in the way of a Security Council discussion of whether there is a case for invoking Article 16 of the Rome Statute in relation to President Al-Bashir, but that discussion will raise profound questions about the relationship between peace and justice.[763]

Although this statement was deliberately flexible, it clearly encouraged a cautious approach.

Having said that, Article 16 does not specify when it can or cannot be triggered, providing only that 'no investigation or prosecution may be commenced or proceeded with'. The term 'proceeded with' suggests that the process can still

758 UN Doc. S/PV.5947, 31 July 2008, p. 7.
759 Ibid, p. 8.
760 Ibid.
761 Ibid.
762 Ibid, p. 6.
763 Ibid.

be deferred once in motion. However, the *travaux préparatoires* of Article 16 indicate that this was a compromise introduced to accommodate the proposal made by the US that the UN Security Council should have a bigger role in court.[764] This was intended to curb the referral role of the states parties and the independent prosecutor. Scheffer noted that 'the original intent underpinning article 16 was to grant the Security Council power to suspend investigations or prosecution of situations if priorities of peace and security compelled a delay of international justice'.[765] It was included so that the Security Council could check on the state party or the Prosecutor's *proprio motu* investigations; thus, it would have been odd to argue for the inclusion of Article 16 as a check on Security Council referrals.[766]

At the same time, events are dynamic and at times require a pragmatic approach. Perhaps when the UN Security Council referred the situation in Sudan to the Court in 2005, a judicial process was the best option, but by 2008, the dynamics in Sudan had changed, encouraging those involved to give peace a chance. At least the Security Council should have been in a position to reconsider some of its decisions to reflect the reality on the ground. This could be the rationale behind the AU's request. The AU clearly stated that the situation in Darfur was delicate in nature and the Pre-Trial Chamber's approval of the Prosecutor's application would seriously undermine ongoing efforts aimed at facilitating the early resolution of the conflict.

The manner in which the UN Security Council treated the AU's deferral request was a complete departure from its treatment of the request for deferral made by the US, which eventually led to the controversial Resolution 1422. The US request was addressed immediately and with urgency, possibly because the US is a permanent member of the Security Council and could have vetoed the resolution blocking the renewal of the peacekeeping mission in Bosnia and Herzegovina. The African states' proposal was treated with indifference, possibly underscoring the fact that African issues were not taken seriously due to the lack of political and military strength of the African states. It could also be that the passing of Resolution 1422 had created such bad feeling regarding the role of the UN Security Council in the work of the Court that deferrals became unpopular within the international community.

In response to its continuous snubbing by the UN Security Council, the AU did not relent. It sought both legal and political solutions to address the situation. During the 7th Session of the International Criminal Court's Assembly of States Parties, the African Group (the African states parties) emphasised its own understanding of the purpose of Article 16, reconciling the interests of peace

---

764 David Scheffer, 'The Security Council's Struggle over Darfur and International Justice' *Jurist Legal News and Research* http://www.jurist.org/forum/2008/08/security-councils-struggle-over-darfur.php (accessed 15 November 2016).

765 Ibid.

766 Ibid.

and justice. As already discussed, this was not the understanding shared with the permanent members of the UN Security Council members, who regarded it as a controlling mechanism for any unpredictable actions by either the Office of the Prosecutor or the states parties. In any case, it is also the Security Council's responsibility, and not the AU's, to determine when and where international and peace and security were being threatened. In a statement made on behalf of the African Group, the delegation of Tanzania stated:

> The African Group is highly respectful of the mechanism derived for reconciling the interests of peace and justice. The International Criminal Court in its work is not to take into consideration political implications. That responsibility lies with the Security Council, in terms of Article 16 of the Statute. With regard to the indictment of President Omar al-Bashir, the AU found that there were, under the current circumstances, and given the peace process in Sudan, a basis [*sic*] for the Security Council to avail itself of the powers granted to it under Article 16 of the Rome Statute, to request a deferral of the situation. This is no way contrary to the fight against impunity.[767]

It is striking that this was the only paragraph where the African Group made reference to the deferral of the process initiated by the Prosecutor. This is striking because the impression created by the AU Assembly decisions and the Peace and Security Council reports is that the entire continent was concerned and desperately wanted the UN Security Council to act. In fact, the statement from Sierra Leone (a state party which at that time was also facing the challenge of addressing atrocities committed on its territory) suggested that it did not necessarily agree with the general view that the Court was selectively targeting Africa. The representative stated that:

> We have heard a lot about so-called (African justice), in the newspapers, on the radios and television and in many arenas. My delegation would like to underscore the fact that the ICC is a product of the work of all countries in the world and that for Sierra Leone, the ICC is African justice just as much as it is European, Latin-American, or indeed any other kind of justice. It is a justice that needs support from other accountability mechanisms to achieve universal justice, but we would like to state clearly that it is needed also in Africa.[768]

The lack of focused attention on the calls for deferrals by the African Group in the Assembly of States Parties may suggest that the most vocal opponents of the Court were primarily non-states parties, such as Rwanda and Libya.

---

767 Assembly of States Parties, Statement by the Delegate of the United Republic of Tanzania on Behalf of the African Group, General Debate of the Seventh Session of the Assembly of States Parties to the Rome Statute of the International Criminal Court, The Hague, 15 November 2008, p. 2.

768 Assembly of States Parties, Statement by the Delegation of the Republic of Sierra Leone to the Seventh Session of the ICC Assembly of States Parties, The Hague, 15 November 2008.

6.2. THE JILTED LOVER'S RESPONSE: AFRICA'S DETERIORATING RELATIONSHIP WITH THE COURT – THE AFTERMATH OF 4 MARCH 2009

On 4 March 2009, the Pre-Trial Chamber issued an arrest warrant for President al-Bashir based on his alleged responsibility for crimes against humanity and war crimes.[769] The Prosecutor's application for the arrest warrant included genocide charges against al-Bashir. However, the Pre-Trial Chamber rejected the charge by a 2:1 majority. Reactions to the decision to issue the warrant varied. The day before the announcement of the arrest warrant, al-Bashir had dismissed it, telling the Court to 'eat' the warrant.[770] The official presidential response was that the warrant was not worth the ink with which it was written.[771] In Khartoum, the Sudanese government mobilised thousands of supporters to show their backing for the President, while denouncing the Court and Prosecutor Moreno Ocampo. It also decided to suspend the operations of more than 10 international humanitarian agencies, resulting in a reduction in the number of humanitarian providers in Darfur. This marked a gradual reduction in the humanitarian space as the government tried to crack down on the presence of international humanitarian actors in Darfur and in Sudan in general out of suspicion that the actors were working in collusion with the Court in gathering information and evidence. The international organisations vehemently rejected such allegations.

The then Senegalese President Abdoulaye Wade accused the Court of targeting Africa in the following statement:

> The problem is that today many Africans have the impression that this tribunal is only there to judge Africans and this wasn't my intention when I signed for it. Wherever in the world the people committing genocide are, we should judge them, but not only judge the Africans.[772]

The AU Assembly's response to the decision included the adoption of Resolution Assembly/AU/Dec.245 (XIII) in Sitre, Libya during the summit held on 1–3 July 2009. The resolution formed the foundation of the AU's official position regarding the Court, which is of non-cooperation in relation to the arrest and surrender of al-Bashir. Although it was primarily adopted with specific focus on

---

769 *Hassan Ahmad al-Bashir* (ICC-02/05–01/09) Decision on the Prosecution's Application for a Warrant of Arrest against Omar Hassan Ahmad al-Bashir, 4 March 2009, p. 92.

770 Xan Rice, 'Sudanese President Tells International Criminal Court to "Eat" Arrest Warrant' *The Guardian* (3 March 2009).

771 Moorcraft, *Omar al-Bashir and Africa's Longest War*, note 30, p. 169.

772 See Statement made by Abdoulaye Wade, the President of Senegal, on the day that the arrest warrant for President al-Bashir was announced on 4 March 2009: 'World Reaction: Bashir Warrant' *BBC News* (4 March 2009).

Sudan and al-Bashir, the resolution turned out to have set the general tone of the AU's position regarding the Court. The then AU Chairperson, al-Gaddafi, is said to have been the sole architect of the resolution. The resolution referred to the AU's deep regret that the UN Security Council had not acted upon its deferral request:

> In view of the fact that the request by the AU has never been acted upon, the AU Member States shall not cooperate pursuant to the provisions of Article 98 of the Rome Statute of the ICC relating to immunities for the arrest and surrender of President Omar El Bashir of the Sudan.[773]

The resolution was deliberately specific regarding the arrest and surrender of President al-Bashir, meaning that AU member states could still cooperate with the Court in the arrest and surrender of other Sudanese government and/or rebel officials. This reflects some form of selectivity in the way in which Africa was responding to the Court – in principle, it was not for impunity, but rather was against the targeting of a head of state. In addition, the AU did not deny the fact that perhaps Bashir should be tried and should prove his innocence before the Court; they just wanted the proceedings to be suspended for a specific period. It is worth noting that throughout the debates about President Bashir and his indictment he has not indicated his position on the charges leveled against him. Instead the focus has been on the legitimancy of the Court's actions towards him. After his indictment, he told Professor Paul Moorcraft that he considered the indictment 'a political issue and double standards because there are obvious crimes, like Palestine, Iraq and Afghanistan, but they do not find their way to the ICC'.[774]

The Sirte non-cooperation resolution is also interesting in the sense that although the grievances it sought to address were with the UN Security Council, it targeted the Court. Perhaps the Court was considered an easy target by the AU, as there might be very limited action that the AU could take against the Security Council. One way in which the AU could register its disapproval of the Security Council's treatment of African issue was by boycotting the three seats reserved for Africa within the Security Council. If this happens, the Security Council would have to function with only 12 members, which violates the UN Charter. However, the success of such a move would require unwavering collective action from the African states, which could be difficult to achieve given that a seat at the Security Council is highly coveted. In 2013, Saudi Arabia rejected its seat at the Security Council in protest at how it was handling the situation in Syria

773 Decision on the Meeting of African States Parties to the Rome Statute of the International Criminal Court (ICC), Assembly/AFRICAN UNION/Dec.245 (XIII) in Sirte, Libya during the summit held on 1–3 July 2009, paras 9–10.

774 Moorcraft, *Omar al-Bashir and Africa's Longest War*, note 30, p. 169.

and also the warming of relations with Iran, Saudi Arabia's regional enemy. The rejection was not effective because there were other states from the region that were willing to fill the gap – Jordan stepped in and occupied the seat as a representative from the Middle East region.

During the Fifteenth Ordinary Session of the AU Assembly, which was held in Kampala, Uganda just a few months before the 1st Review Conference of the Court, the AU Assembly adopted a resolution that contained sharp language in its criticism of the Court and the UN Security Council's handling of the situation in Sudan. Whereas in the previous resolution terms such as 'urges' and 'deeply regrets' were used in reference to the Security Council's inaction, during this session, the Assembly used the stronger diplomatic term 'disappointment'. The relevant paragraph expresses 'disappointment that the UN Security Council has not acted upon the request made by the AU to defer the proceedings initiated against President Hassan al-Bashir'.[775] During the session, the AU reiterated its calls for AU states not to cooperate with the Court in the arrest of President al-Bashir.[776]

As discussed earlier, the AU Assembly temporarily denied the Court's request to open a Liaison Office in Addis Ababa, Ethiopia at the AU headquarters.[777] The decision to deny the Court's request contradicted the position taken by the African States Parties (the African Group). During the seventh session of the Assembly of States Parties in 2008, the African Group had voiced its support for the creation of a Liaison Office at the headquarters of the AU in Addis Ababa in order to facilitate the efficient interface between all members of the regional body.[778] It even claimed to have been looking forward to the AU concluding a relationship agreement with the Court in order to enable better cooperation between the two bodies.[779]

Assuming that the African Group was part of the resolution adopted later in Kampala, such a sudden change of approach and sentiments towards the Court is remarkable. It suggests that during AU Assembly Sessions, states parties seem to have been put under substantial pressure to subscribe to the collective regional anti-Court rhetoric. However, the same states appear to adopt a different approach when they are at the Assembly of States Parties, where they appear to adopt a more nuanced approach towards the Court. It is tempting to say that the states that are states parties to the Rome Statute probably do not have the same

775 Decision on the Progress Report of the Commission on the Implementation of Decision Assembly/AFRICAN UNION /Dec (XIV) on the second Ministerial Meeting on the Rome Statute of the International Criminal Court (ICC), para. 4.

776 Ibid.

777 Ibid.

778 Statement by the Delegation of the United Republic of Tanzania on Behalf of the African Group, General Debate of the Seventh Session of the Assembly of States Parties to the Rome Statute of the International Criminal Court, The Hague, 15 November 2008.

779 Ibid.

influence in the AU Assembly as those states that are not states parties to the Statute. This applies to Libya under al-Gaddafi, Rwanda, Algeria and Zimbabwe, which are (or were) vocal critics of the Court, yet they are non-states parties. At the same time, it is hard to imagine that the views of states parties such as Nigeria and South Africa, which are considered to be the economic giants of Africa and also contribute significantly to the AU's budget, are pushed aside by non-states parties in the AU when it comes to issues pertaining to the Court. The change of approach could simply show how fast the relationship has deteriorated between the two institutions.

Elsewhere in Africa, the relationship between the Court and the Ugandan government became shaky, despite early signs of cordial and mutual understanding, which started in 2004 when President Yoweri Museveni appeared at a press conference with the Prosecutor at the Hotel Intercontinental Hyde Park, London to officially announce that Uganda had referred the situation in Northern Uganda to the Court. The press release issued by the Court noted:

> President Museveni has indicated to the Prosecutor his intention to amend this amnesty so as to exclude the leadership of the LRA, ensuring that those bearing the greatest responsibility for the crimes against humanity committed in Northern Uganda are brought to justice.[780]

As the title of the press release suggests, it was clear at the time of the referral that the focus of the investigations was the LRA, although there were allegations that the Uganda People's Defence Force had also committed international crimes in Northern Uganda. The press release points out that the key issue for the Court was locating and arresting the LRA's leadership.[781]

Commentators have tried to identify the motivation behind Uganda's self-referral.[782] A common thread in the suggested motivations is a reluctance by some of the commentators to believe that a genuine quest for justice was the driving force behind the move. They consider President Museveni to have been driven by his political interests. First, he wanted to and managed to draw the attention of the international community to what Jan Egeland, the then UN Under-Secretary-General for Humanitarian Affairs, has described as the 'most

---

780 International Criminal Court Press Release ICC-20040129-44, President of Uganda Refers Situation Concerning the Lord's Resistance Army (LRA) to the ICC, 29 January 2004.

781 Ibid.

782 See Nouwen and Werner, 'Doing Justice to the Political', note 407, which suggests that the self-referrals were part of the Ugandan government's strategy to defeat the LRA, which it had battled for more than ten decades. For a different view, see Schabas, *An Introduction to the International Criminal Court*, note 3, p. 165, who points out that the idea of the self-referrals came from The Hague not Kampala, meaning that the Prosecutor had a role in the self-referral.

forgotten and neglected crisis in the world'.[783] Second, he managed to get the AU and the US and other neighbouring states to join his war against the LRA. Northern Uganda became relatively peaceful as the weakened LRA went into neighbouring states – the Democratic Republic of the Congo, South Sudan and the Central African Republic – where they continued to terrorise civilians. He practically managed to export terror from Uganda to the neighbouring states.

When the Court agreed to officially open investigations, it faced the risk of being abused by one party in the conflict, which in this case was the Ugandan government.[784] In order to reassure critics that he would not stray from the founding principles of the Rome Statute and the independence of the Court, the Prosecutor noted:

> My Office has informed the Uganda authorities that we must interpret the scope of the referral consistently with the principles of the Rome Statute, and hence we are analysing crimes within the situation of northern Uganda by whomever committed.[785]

In general terms, the majority of the perceived goals of President Museveni's referral appear to have been met. However, as time passed and the context evolved, President Museveni's appetite for the Court waned. He started to threaten the Court with withdrawals once he realised that he could not compel the Court to comply with his demands, for instance regarding the withdrawal of the arrest warrants against the LRA for them to face trial in Uganda. President Museveni told journalists that: 'What we have agreed with our people is that they should face traditional justice, which is more compensatory than retributive systems'.[786]

The change of attitude was linked to the fact that on 29 June 2007 and during the Juba peace talks, the Ugandan government and the LRA had signed an Agreement on Accountability and Reconciliation, and on 19 February 2008, an annex to the Agreement on Accountability and Reconciliation was also signed. Together the two documents provided a legal and institutional framework for the establishment of a special division of the High Court of Uganda to try individuals who were alleged to have committed serious crimes during the conflict.[787] The agreements also recognised the role that Ugandan traditional justice mechanisms could play in ensuring accountability.

Although the final peace agreement was not signed following Joseph Kony's failure to show up for signing both in Ri-Kwangba on 10 April 2008 and to

---

783 Cited in Nouwen and Werner, 'Doing Justice to the Political', note 407, 948.

784 Mamdani, *Saviors and Survivors*, note 130, p. 284.

785 'Letter to President Kirsch from the Chief Prosecutor Louis Moreno Ocampo dated 17, June 2004', annexed to Decision Assigning the Situation in Uganda to Pre-Trial Chamber II, *Situation in Uganda* (ICC-02/04), 5 July 2004.

786 'Museveni Reject Hague LRA Trial' *BBC News* (12 March 2008).

787 Annexure to the Agreement on Accountability between the Government of the Republic of Uganda and the Lord's Resistance Army/Movement Juba, Sudan, 19 February 2008.

attend the signing ceremony in Juba, the Ugandan government started the implementation of the Agreement on Accountability and Reconciliation. In 2008, it set up the War Crimes Division, which was later formalised through Legal Notice 10/2011 issued by the Chief Justice and was changed into the International Crimes Division of the High Court.

Legal Notice 10/2011 outlines the International Crimes Division's subject-matter jurisdiction as follows:

> Any Offences relating to genocide, crimes against humanity, war crimes, terrorism, human trafficking, piracy and any other international crime as many have been provided under the Penal Code Act, Cap 120, the Geneva Conventions Act Cap 363 and the International Criminal Court Act of 2010 or under any other penal enactment.

It was probably a combination of these developments that followed the Juba peace talks, together with Kony's leveraging participation and signing of the peace agreement on the withdrawal of the Court arrest warrants that compelled President Museveni to contemplate a withdrawal from the Rome Statute justice system. Ugandan traditional and religious leaders from Northern Uganda had also pressed for the withdrawal of the proceedings at the Court. The established International Crimes Division was therefore seen as an easy way out from the Court. It not only demonstrates Uganda's concrete action towards the implementation of the Juba Agreement on Accountability and Reconciliation, but it also created the basis upon which Uganda could challenge the admissibility of the cases at the Court.

As discussed in the previous chapter regarding admissibility, the Pre-Trial Chamber pre-emptively exercised its *proprio motu* power to consider whether the cases against Kony and the others accused were still admissible. One commentator noted that the Pre-Trial Chamber's action was intended to send a clear message to states, including Uganda, that it is the Court that has the upper hand in making determinations on admissibility once its jurisdiction has been triggered.[788] The Pre-Trial Chamber pointed out that the statements made by the government:

> once the jurisdiction of the Court is triggered, it is for the latter and not for any national judicial authorities to interpret and apply the provisions governing the complementarity regime and to make a binding determination on the admissibility of a given case.[789]

The approach adopted by the Pre-Trial Chamber in this regard frustrated President Museveni since he might have believed that as a head of a sovereign

[788] El Zeidy, 'Admissibility in International Criminal Law', note 459, (eds.), p. 219.

[789] *Kony et al.* (ICC-02/04-01/05), Decision on the Admissibility of the Case under Article 19(1) of the Statute, 10 March 2009, para. 45.

state, it was his prerogative to decide how and where his citizens were to be prosecuted. Perhaps he thought that the same method that he used to invite the Court to his territory could be easily used to uninvite it. This might have led to the change in the Ugandan government's attitude towards the Court's intervention in Africa.

During the 68th UN General Assembly, President Museveni was categorical in his criticism of the Court. He described its actions as representing a shallow, biased mishandling of complex African issues, before calling on it to stop its proceedings in Kenya.[790] This is surprising considering that he had stood next to the Prosecutor, Moreno Ocampo, during a press conference announcing the referral of the situation in Northern Uganda to the same Court, a few years earlier. It seemed that he had overestimated the amount of influence he could exercise over the Court. It is probably that sense of losing control, autonomy and self-determination that triggered his negativity towards the Court.

It was evident that President Museveni was being pragmatic in his approach to the Court's intervention in his country and East Africa, a region he appeared to treat as his own backyard. In this situation he was only comfortable with the Court insofar as it served his strategic interests and he could control it. It was therefore up to the Court to allow itself to be manipulated in that way or not. In this regard, the Court was not willing to go as far as entertaining Museveni's own preferences.

To be fair, Uganda's approach is not unique. It appears to be a common trait of states – including liberal democracies – whose support for international criminal justice could be self-serving.[791] They tend to resist the prosecution of their own nationals and those of their allies, although they are ready to support the prosecution of others. For example, France offered its military aircraft to transfer Thomas Lubanga from the Democratic Republic of the Congo to The Hague to face trial for war crimes at a time when France itself had invoked an Article 124 declaration, which denied the Court jurisdiction over French nationals for war crimes.[792] The UK – which is one of the main supporters of the Court – is sensitive in relation to having its nationals prosecuted by the Court. In any case, the fact that Uganda was ready to surrender Dominic Ongwen to the Court demonstrate that, despite its president's rhetoric against the Court, there is some recognition and acceptance of the Court's role with regard to the LRA. However, it sends the wrong signals to other African states as it weakens their stance in terms of portraying the Court as undermining Africa.

790 Statement by H.E. Yoweri Kaguta, Museveni President of the Republic of Uganda, at the 68th United Nations General Assembly, New York, 24 September 2013, p. 10.

791 See Gary Jonathan Bass, *Stay the Hand of Vengeance: The Politics of War Crimes Tribunals* (Princeton, Princeton University Press, 2000).

792 Schabas, *An Introduction to the International Criminal Court*, note 3, p. 47. However, by 2010, France had withdrawn its declaration under Art. 124 and during the Review Conference held in Kampala, Uganda, the provision was removed from the Rome Statute altogether.

Kenya's aggressive criticism of the Court occurred after 15 December 2010 – the date on which the Prosecutor named prominent Kenyan politicians as the suspects in the 2007 post-election violence. The list of the suspects included Uhuru Muigai Kenyatta (Deputy Prime Minister and Minister of Finance), Francis Kirimi Muthaura (Head of the Public Service and Secretary to the Cabinet), Mohammed Hussein Ali (Chief Executive and Head of the National Postal Corporation and former Chief of Police), William Samoei Ruto (Minister of Higher Education, Science and Technology), Henry Kiprono Kosgey (Member of Parliament) and Joshua Arap Sang (Head of Operations of a private radio station, Kass FM).[793] In April 2016, the charges against all the suspects were dropped.

The Kenyan situation has generated considerable controversy, raised questions on the integrity of the Court and heightened the scrutiny of the Office of the Prosecutor's investigative strategies and also witness protection. The Kenyan government, including President Uhuru Kenyatta, has been at the forefront of campaigning for either the withdrawal of the African States Parties from the Court or reforming the Court. In 2015, at the Fourteenth Session of the Assembly of States Parties, Kenya brought along an unprecedented record of delegates – 90. Among their objectives was to push the Court into withdrawing the case against their Deputy President, Samoei Ruto.[794] A few months later in January 2016 and during the AU Assembly, President Kenyatta made a proposal for a roadmap for the withdrawal of the African States Parties from the Court.

In the midst of all these developments, what seems to be easily forgotten about Kenya is that it was through the failure of its own series of internal processes that attracted the Court to its territory. The process started with the establishment of the Commission of Inquiry into Post-Election Violence (CIPEV), which was chaired by Philip Waki and hence was also known as the Waki Commission. Unlike the International Commission of Inquiry on Darfur, chaired by Antonio Cassese, which was established by the UN Secretary-General following Security Council Resolution 1564, the Waki Commission was established by the Kenyan authorities through Gazette Notice No 4473 of 23 May 2008. The Waki Commission's findings, which were all adopted by the Kenyan Parliament, include the establishment of:

> A special tribunal, to be known as the Special Tribunal for Kenya … that will sit within the territorial boundaries of the Republic of Kenya and seek accountability against

793 See *Situation in the Republic of Kenya* (ICC-01/09-01/11), Decision on the Prosecutor's Application for Summons to Appear for William Samoei Ruto, Henry Kiprono Kosgey and Joshua Arap Sang, 8 March 2011; and *Situation in the Republic of Kenya* (ICC-01/09-02/11), Decision on the Prosecutor's Application for Summons to Appear for Francis Kirimi Muthaura, Uhuru Muigai Kenyatta and Mohammed Hussein Ali, 8 March 2011.

794 International Criminal Court, Assembly of States Parties, 'Delegations to the Fourteenth Session of the Assembly of States Parties to the Rome Statute of the International Criminal Court', The Hague, 18–26 November 2015.

> persons bearing the greatest responsibility for crimes, particularly crimes against humanity, relating to the 2007 General Elections in Kenya.[795]

The Commission recommended that the Special Tribunal should apply the Kenyan law and the International Crimes Bills, which at that time had not yet been enacted. In addition, the Special Tribunal was also comprised of Kenyan and international judges and staff.

The report from the Commission also recommended a fallback plan in the event that no effective Special Tribunal was established. The plan was that:

> If either an agreement for the establishment of the Special Tribunal is not signed, or the Statute for the Special Tribunal fails to be enacted, or the Special Tribunal fails to commence functioning as contemplated above, or having commenced operating its purposes are subverted, a list containing names of and relevant information on those suspected to bear the greatest responsibility for crimes falling within the jurisdiction of the proposed Special Tribunal shall be forwarded to the Special Prosecutor of the International Criminal Court. The Special Prosecutor shall be asked to analyse the seriousness of the information received with a view to proceeding with an investigation and prosecuting such suspected persons.[796]

The Commission's reasoning in terms of how Kenya was supposed to proceed with addressing the accountability needs of the victims of the post-election violence of 2007 reflected a clear understanding of the complementarity principle as envisaged in the Rome Statute system. Domestic remedies were given primary responsibility and the Court was recognised as a court of last resort. Its jurisdiction was only to be triggered in the event that the domestic systems were unwilling, unable or incapable of addressing the accountability needs.

Regrettably, the 10th Kenyan Parliament could not pass the Constitution Amendment Bill that could have paved the way for it to enact a statute to establish a Special Tribunal, as had been recommended by the Waki Commission.[797] A total of 101 Members of Parliament voted in favour and 93 voted against. Still, the number of votes in favour fell short of the fixed majority of 65 per cent hence the motion to amend the Constitution was rejected.[798] What is notable is that the then Kenyan President, Mwai Kibaki, his Prime Minister, Raila Odinga, and Uhuru Kenyatta voted in favour of amending the Constitution, whereas Samoei Ruto voted against the motion. Those in favour of the motion demonstrated their appreciation that the Court was a court of last resort and that it was the

---

795 Government of Kenya, Kenyan Commission of Inquiry into Post-Election Violence, 16 October 2008, p. 472.

796 Ibid.

797 *National Assembly Official Report (Hansard)*, 11 February 2009.

798 Ibid, p. 34.

duty of the Kenyan authorities to intervene. The legislator Abdikadir Hussein Mohamed, who was also the Chairman of the Departmental Committee on Administration of Justice and Legal Affairs, rightly pointed out that:

> Essentially, the ICC will possibly not go ahead and carry out prosecution, if we can do this well and better. The whole idea of setting up the ICC was to deal with crimes against humanity or genocide when nations that have the first jurisdiction are unable, unwilling or incapable of handling those matters.[799]

Rachel Wambui Shebesh, an Orange Democratic Movement MP, weighed in to support the motion. She made reference to her meeting with the then Prosecutor, Moreno Ocampo, at the sidelines of a Pan-African Parliament Committee on International Relations meeting, where he warned Kenya against not taking their situation to The Hague. He is reported to have told her: 'Do not even for one minute, if you have any other route, want to go the route of The Hague.'[800] This statement indicates that contrary to the view that the Prosecutor wanted to intervene in Kenya from the outset, which affected the ability of the domestic mechanisms to play a role, he actually wanted Kenya to assume its responsibility as a sovereign state.

Those who opposed the motion focused on highlighting that even if a Special Tribunal were to be established, the Kenyan judiciary had in the past struggled to pass the necessary integrity test. Reference was made to how the Special Tribunal was likely to succumb to political influence. The Honourable Cyrus Jirongo, a Member of Parliament from the Kenya African Democratic Development Union (KADDU) Party, representing the constituency of Lugari, expressed his concern that the Tribunal was unlikely to have the capacity to prosecute either the President or the Vice President. From his perspective, the tribunal that was being proposed was for the small people: 'This country has a history of punishing the small people when the big ones have committed the crimes.'

In addition, there was concern about the protection of witnesses who would come to testify at the tribunal. Peter Mungai Mwathi, Member of Parliament from a political party called FORD-P (Forum for Restoration of Democracy-People) representing the constituency of Limuru, raised this issue, as Kenya has a history of witnesses being murdered in the 1990s, when a commission of inquiry was established when one of the ministers in the government was killed. As such, those who opposed the motion rallied behind the slogan: 'Don't be vague, let's go to The Hague.' The Hague was seen as the only viable and credible way of achieving accountability against those responsible for the post-election violence in 2007.

---

[799] *Kenya National Assembly Official Record (Hansard)*, 3 February 2009, p. 50.

[800] Ibid, p. 50.

Some Members of Parliament preferred the trials to be held in The Hague instead of Kenya because they had miscalculated the speed with which the Court was expected to conduct the trial. For example, William Samoei Ruto, who later became one of the defendants at the Court, said: 'The ICC will begin hearing the Kenyan case in 2090. Who amongst us will be alive then?'[801] This remark suggests that those responsible for the post-election violence were likely to escape criminal accountability if the trial were to be held at the Court instead of as a domestic trial.

However, when it became clear that the Court was ready to proceed with the trial at a more rapid speed than had perhaps been anticipated by the defendants, the Kenyan government's first reaction was to turn to the UN Security Council for a deferral under Article 16.[802] On 31 January 2011, the AU's Assembly of Head of States and Government supported and endorsed Kenya's request for the Security Council to defer proceedings in Kenya.[803] This prompted the Security Council to engage in an informal interactive dialogue to discuss Kenya's proposal on 18 March 2011. Informal interactive dialogues are private meetings convened in order to hold an off-the record discussion with one or more non-Council members and are held in the Conference Room and not in the Security Council Chamber. The permanent representative of Kenya to the UN attended the informal interactive dialogue and argued that a deferral would have given his country time to establish alternative domestic adjudicative mechanisms.[804]

The Orange Democratic Movement, a Kenyan political party that was part of the coalition government in Kenya, had an ambiguous position regarding the deferral request. Its official position was not to support the deferral request. The general position adopted by the majority of the members in the UN Security Council was that the situation in Kenya did not amount to a threat to international peace and security, which is a prerequisite for the Security Council to act under Article VII.[805] As discussed in Chapter 5, Kenya also unsuccessfully challenged the admissibility of the cases against its nationals pursuant to Article 19.[806]

---

801 'Kid Gloves are off' *News Africa* (20 May 2011).

802 See UNSC Doc/S 2011/201 'Letter dated 23 March 2011 from the Permanent Representative of Kenya to the United Nations addressed to the President of the Security Council' 29 March 2011.

803 Decision on the Implementation, 30–31 January 2011, Addis Ababa, Ethiopia, Doc EX.CL/639 (XVIII), para. 6, which states that the AU 'Supports and Endorses Kenya's request for a deferral of the ICC Investigations and prosecutions in relation to the 2008 post-election violence under Art. 16 of the Rome Statute to allow for a National Mechanism to Investigate and prosecute the cases under a reformed judiciary provided for in the new constitutional dispensation…'

804 Security Council Report, Report Update Kenya and the ICC, 6 April 2011 No. 1, p. 2.

805 Ibid, p. 2.

806 *Situation in the Republic of Kenya* (ICC-01/09-09/11-101) Decision on the Application by the Government of Kenya Challenging the Admissibility of Case Pursuant to Article 19(2)(b) of the Statute, 30 May 2011.

The Court's intervention in Kenya was also discussed at the East African Community level. The East African Community is a regional integration organisation comprised of Kenya, Uganda, Tanzania, Rwanda and Burundi. On 26 April 2012, the East African Legislative Assembly passed a resolution seeking the East African Community Council of Ministers to 'implore the International Criminal Court' to transfer the case of the accused four Kenyans (this was after the Pre-Trial Chamber II had decided not to confirm charges against two suspects) facing trial in respect of the aftermath of the 2007 Kenya general elections to the East African Court of Justice and to reinforce the treaty provisions'.[807]

The resolution was proposed by Ugandan lawyer and Member of Parliament Dan Wandara Ogalo, who equated the Court with the British Privy Council, which functioned as an appeals court against the decisions of final courts in the British colonies.[808] He also raised the concern that five years had passed since the alleged international crimes were committed in Kenya and the Court was still in the preliminary stages of its investigations suggesting that justice delayed is justice denied. In addition, he was concerned about the externalisation of justice, pointing out that Kenyans were to be excluded from the process as the majority of them could not travel and witness the trial in the Netherlands.

Although the majority supported the motion, some Members of Parliament were concerned that the East African Community was not well equipped to address the needs of justice in relation to the four suspects and the victims of the post-election violence. Augustus Chemonges Lotodo of Kenya pointed out that decisions within the East African Community take a long time and this could also end up delaying and thus denying justice for the victims.[809] His concern related to a motion that was presented at a time when the East African Community Court of Justice had no jurisdiction to deal with human rights issues, let alone international crimes.

After the resolution was adopted, the East African Community started drafting proposals to extend the jurisdiction of the East African Community Court of Justice to deal with genocide, crimes against humanity, terrorism and war crimes.[810] Generally the tone of the debates within the East African Legislative Assembly on this issue reflected an acknowledgement of the need for justice

---

807 The Official Report of the Proceedings of the East African Legislative Assembly 140th Sitting Second Assembly: Fifth Meeting-Fourth Session, East African Legislative Assembly, 26 April 2012

808 Ibid, p. 29; for a detailed analysis of the role of the Privy Council, see also Ivor Richardson, 'The Privy Council as the Final Court for the British Empire' (2012) 43 *Victoria University of Wellington Law Review* 103.

809 The Official Report of the Proceedings of the East African Legislative Assembly 140th Sitting Second Assembly: Fifth Meeting-Fourth Session, East African Legislative Assembly, 26 April 2012, p. 48.

810 'Secretariat Wants EAC Court to Handle War Crimes' *The East African* (13 April 2013).

and to end impunity for atrocities, while at the same time emphasising African independence as a justification for the trials to be transferred to the jurisdiction of the East African Community.

When two of the defendants – William Samoei Ruto and Uhuru Kenyatta – won general elections in 2013, the intensity of Kenya's attempt to stop the proceedings at the Court increased. Barely a month after Kenyatta was sworn as President, Kenya's permanent representative at the UN sent a note to the President of the UN Security Council requesting the termination of the proceedings before the Court.[811] This was a bizarre request considering that the Court is – at least in theory – an institution independent of the Security Council. The Rome Statute provides that the Security Council can only either refer or defer situations to the Court and it does not have the legal authority to terminate the proceedings, since the Court is an independent judicial institution. The Security Council could not respond positively to the Kenyan request and some members said that they had wished that Kenya had limited its request to an Article 16 deferral instead of asking that the proceedings be terminated altogether.

Kenya continued its diplomatic offensive against the Court's intervention in its territory. In May 2013, it managed to get the issue put on to the AU Assembly's agenda, which led to the adoption of a resolution supporting and endorsing the East African Community's request for a referral of the Court's investigation and prosecutions in relation to the 2007 post-election violence in Kenya, in line with the principles of complementarity.[812] The Republic of Botswana expressed reservations regarding this decision. It is not even clear to which body the AU Assembly wanted to refer the Court's investigations. There is no provision in the Rome Statute for investigations to be referred to another institution. Perhaps this was leading to a request for the UN Security Council to defer the situation. Still, a deferral would not transfer the proceedings from the Court to another jurisdiction, but rather would temporarily suspend investigations.

In addition, and without elaboration, the decision stressed 'the need for international justice to be conducted in a transparent and fair manner, in order to avoid any perception of double standards, in conformity with the principle of international law'.[813] This can only be understood in the context of the allegations that the Court was selectively focusing on Africa. However, it fails to acknowledge that there are other international criminal justice mechanisms established in other parts of the world, such as the Special Tribunal for Lebanon, Cambodia and the former Yugoslavia.

---

811 'Kenya Asks UN to Halt ICC Charges against Kenyatta' *BBC World News* (9 May 2013).

812 Decision on International Jurisdiction, Justice and the International Criminal Court (ICC), 26–27 May 2013, Addis Ababa, Ethiopia, Doc. Assembly/AFRICAN UNION/13 (XII), para. 7.

813 Ibid, para. 5.

After the AU Assembly summit in 2013, the Ethiopian Prime Minister put it crudely when he claimed that the Court's process was flawed and had 'degenerated to some kind of race hunting', equating its intervention with a form of safari hunting, which is a lucrative tourism business that some African states are known for. The supporters of justice for the victims of atrocities might actually see the Prime Minister's remarks as reflecting a turn of events – the hunters, brutal political, militia leaders and the mandarins of impunity were becoming the hunted by the Court, the aim of which was to make them accountable for how they treat the ordinary citizens within their borders.

In 2013, the AU convened an Extraordinary Session to discuss the relationship between it and the Court. Kenya is reported to have been behind the mobilisation for the Session in order to push the African states to take a stronger position on the subject of the Court. During the Extraordinary Session, held on 12 October 2013, President Kenyatta referred to the Court as 'a painfully farcical pantomime, a travesty that adds insults to the injury of victims. It stopped being the home of justice the day it became the toy of declining imperial powers'.[814]

At the same session, it was decided, among other things, that: AU head of states of governments should not be investigated or prosecuted before any international court or tribunal; the Court should suspend proceedings against President Uhuru Kenyatta and Deputy William Samoei Ruto until they completed their terms of office; a deferral would be requested for the Kenyan and Sudan cases; the process of expanding the mandate of the African Court on Human and Peoples' Rights to try international crimes would be fast-tracked; the African States Parties would propose relevant amendments to the Rome Statute in accordance with Article 121 and would raise the issue of indicting African sitting heads of state and governments by the Court at the Assembly of States Parties.[815]

The Extraordinary Session was held against a background of international media reports that it was to adjudicate on the *en masse* withdrawal of African States Parties from the Court.[816] These reports prompted supporters of international justice like Desmond Tutu and Kofi Annan to express their dismay to the AU leaders and to throw their support behind the Court. However, the outcome of the Extraordinary Session was not an *en masse* withdrawal, but rather a litany of decisions expressing the AU's policy orientation of non-cooperation with the Court that had been first introduced in Sirte, Libya in 2009.

---

[814] 'President Uhuru Hits out at the West over ICC' *Kenya Daily Nation* (12 October 2013).

[815] Decision on Africa's Relationship with the International Criminal Court, Extraordinary Session of the Assembly of the African Union, 12 October 2013, Addis Ababa, Ethiopia, Ext/Assembly/African Union/Dec/Dec.1, para. 10.

[816] Bill Corcoran, Desmond Tutu, David Smith and Kofi Annan: 'African Justice is Weak' *The Guardian* (10 October 2013).

The call for immunity for sitting heads of state and government is a curious development in a continent that had fully supported the establishment of an international criminal court. The decision pushes back the vision of an international criminal justice that is capable of fully applying rule of law. It reduces the Court to a mechanism used only against those no longer in power. In legal terms, it seems that the AU was attempting to influence the Court's mission by telling it who and who not to investigate or prosecute. In any case, the Court does not depend on the AU's decisions, although it is possible that such decisions might complicate the level of cooperation between African States Parties and the Court.

The renewed calls for the UN Security Council to defer the proceedings against President Kenyatta and his deputy were based on the role that Kenya was playing in the fight against terrorism in the East African region and also the terrorist attack in Westgate, Nairobi. These factors were considered by the AU to be sufficient to meet the preconditions necessary for the Security Council to act under Chapter VII. On 15 November 2013, the Security Council failed to adopt a draft resolution to defer criminal proceedings against the President and Deputy President of Kenya at the Court.[817] The draft resolution was sponsored by Rwanda, Togo and Morocco, was endorsed in a letter signed by around 40 AU heads of state and governments and was sent to the Security Council.[818] The letter stated that:

> In light of the peace and security situation in Kenya and the Region, the AU Member States would like to submit a formal request for a deferral of the proceedings initiated by the ICC against the President and Deputy President of the Republic of Kenya in order to provide them with the time required for the enhancement of the effort aimed at combatting terrorism and other forms of insecurity in the country and the region.[819]

The failure by the UN Security Council to address the express concern of around 40 African states aggravated the already complicated relationship between the AU, the Court and the Security Council. The level of tension was captured in the remarks by the Rwandan representative to the UN, Ambassador Eugene Gasana, when he said: 'The failure to adopt this draft resolution, endorsed by the whole

[817] UN Doc. SC/7060, 15 November 2013. The Security Council members that voted in favour of the draft resolution were Azerbaijan, China, Morocco, Pakistan, the Russian Federation, Rwanda and Togo, while those that abstained were Argentina, Australia, France, Guatemala, Luxembourg, the Republic of Korea, the UK and the US.

[818] See Annex to the letter dated 16 October 2013 written by the African Union Commission Chairperson Nkosazana Dlamini Zuma addressed to the United Nations Security Council President, Doc. BC/U/1814.10.13, Addis Ababa, 16 October 2013. The African states that had not signed the letter include: Cameroon, Cape Verde, Burkina Faso, Cote d'Ivoire, Equatorial Guinea, Gabon, Gambia, Liberia and Tunisia.

[819] Ibid, p. 3.

African continent, is a shame, yes indeed, it's a shame. Let it be written today in history that the Security Council failed Kenya and Africa on this issue.'[820]

The rejected draft resolution had tried to link terrorism in the Horn and East Africa and the role that Kenya was playing in fighting Al-Shabab in Somalia as the basis for the deferral. The draft proposal considered the investigation and prosecution of President Uhuru and Deputy President Ruto to be a distraction to the fulfilment of their duties, including in the fight against terrorism in the sub-region – a view not shared by the some members of the Security Council. Those who voted against the resolution stated that they could not see the direct link between the prosecution of Uhuru and his deputy and threats to international peace and security. While it was acknowledged that the issues between Kenya and the Court needed to be addressed, it was suggested that this take place at the Assembly of States Parties of the Court rather than at the Security Council.

The question then is whether the deferral request at the UN Security Council was justified in the first place. This is arguably a question of perception. The inconsistencies in the outworkings of the Security Council's adoption of Chapter VII resolutions indicate a lack of a standard definition of what exactly constitutes a Chapter VII resolution. The Security Council has adopted several resolutions in which it explicitly acted under Chapter VII, without first having determined the existence of a threat to the peace.[821] For instance, when the Security Council unanimously and controversially passed Resolution 1422 in 2002, issuing immunity to UN peacekeepers from the Court's jurisdiction, it did not expressly link its decision to act under Chapter VII to the existence of international peace and security.[822]

The UN Security Council has generally adopted a very broad interpretation of the notion of threats to the peace, but the establishment of immunities on the basis of Article 39 of the UN Charter marked a new development in the practice of the Council.[823] It can therefore be argued that if there is an elastic approach to the interpretation of when Chapter VII can be invoked, then there were genuine grounds for the African states' request for a deferral. In fact, with the US having benefited from the same arrangement and interpretation of the UN Charter, it seems odd that the proposal from African states was rejected even when the situation in Kenya was at a critical stage.

---

820 UN Doc. SC/7060th Meeting, 'The Explanation of Vote by Permanent Representative, Eugene-Richard Gasana, on the UN Security Council Resolution on the Deferral on the Kenyan Cases before the International Criminal Court', 15 November 2013.

821 See Patrik Johansson, 'The Humdrum Use of Ultimate Authority: Defining and Analysing Chapter VII Resolutions' (2009) 78 *Nordic Journal of International Law* 309.

822 See UN Doc. S/RES/1422, 12 July 2002; and UN Doc. S/RES/1487, 12 June 2003.

823 Carsten Stahn, 'The Ambiguities of Security Council Resolution 1422' (2002) 14 *European Journal of International Law* 85, p. 86.

CHAPTER 7

AFRICAN STATES' REACTION TO THE AU'S CALL FOR NON-COOPERATION WITH THE COURT

When the decision not to cooperate with the Court was passed in Sirte in 2009, President al-Gaddafi was the AU Chairperson and his handling of the situation was problematic for the other African states. The representatives from Botswana and Chad – both of which are states parties to the Rome Statute – were opposed to the way in which he failed to allow other delegates at the meeting to present their opinions on the issue.[824] Chad went on to declare its reservations and refusal to abide by the AU's decision.[825] Botswana was categorical in its disagreement with the decision and stated that:

> [I]t does not agree with this decision and wishes to reaffirm its position that as a State party to the Rome Statute of the International Criminal Court, it has treaty obligations to fully cooperate with the Court in the arrest and transfer of the President of the Sudan to the International Criminal Court.[826]

Chad, which at the time of the AU's decision was in a state of diplomatic and armed conflict with Sudan, indicated that it was not ready to abide by the decision.[827] In 2005, the Court had concluded a general framework for cooperation with the government of Chad and subsequently managed to open an administrative and logistical support field office in Chad to facilitate investigations across the border in Darfur.[828] However, Chad's position changed along the way, especially after

---

824 Wene Owino, 'Botswana Faults Gaddafi over "Hasty" AU Decisions' *Kenya Daily Nation* (7 July 2009); for further commentary on the Sirte Decision, see also 'African Union Dismisses Criticisms on ICC Resolution' *Sudan Tribune* (20 July 2009).

825 See Reservation entered by Chad on African Union Assembly Decision on the Meeting of African States Parties to the Rome Statute (ICC), Assembly/African Union/Dec.245 (XIII), Rev.1, 3 July 2009.

826 See Letter dated 8 July 2009 from the Permanent Representative of Botswana to the United Nations addressed to the Secretary-General, UNGA, Doc A/63/926, 13 July 2009.

827 African Union Assembly Decision on the Meeting of African States Parties to the Rome Statute (ICC), Assembly/African Union/Dec.245 (XIII), Rev.1, 3 July 2009.

828 Report of the International Criminal Court, UN Doc. A/61/217, 3 August 2006, paras 17, 24.

its relations with Sudan improved. As a result, it allowed President al-Bashir to visit its territory to attend the Community of Sahel-Saharan States (CEN-SAD) in 2010, 2014 and 2016 without arresting and surrendering him to the Court in accordance with the Rome Statute.

Human Rights Watch warned Chad that by not honouring its obligations under the Rome Statute, 'it was risking the shameful distinction of being the first state party to harbour a suspected war criminal'.[829] On 27 August 2010, the Pre-Trial Chamber I informed the UN Security Council and the Assembly of States Parties of Chad's lack of cooperation in arresting and surrendering al-Bashir.[830] The Chadian Interior Minister defended his government's decision by citing the AU non-cooperation decision.[831] This was rather curious considering that Chad had made a reservation on the AU's resolution asking member states not to cooperate with the Court. The Minister went on to make reference to the possibility that President al-Bashir might be protected by immunity and that Chad, as a sovereign state, had the right to chart its own foreign policy: 'What country has ever arrested a sitting head of state? Bashir won't be arrested in Chad. Chad is a sovereign and independent state ... we are not dependent on the injunctions of international organisations.'[832]

Al-Bashir has visited Chad on several occasions since his 2010 visit, and it is clear from Chad's changing position that its foreign policy and positive relations with Sudan have taken precedence over compliance with international obligations under the Rome Statute. In other words, it can be said that for Chad, the advantages of violating the Rome Statute outweighed the costs of observing it.

As can be seen from the examples of Botswana and Chad, it is crucial to note that despite the AU's attempts to give the impression that its decisions are always adopted by consensus, this does not always seem to be the case.[833] The AU is not made up of ideologically and politically monolithic states and there were internal disagreements over how to react to the indictment of President al-Bashir within Africa as a whole. Although some African States wanted to abide by the AU's decision, the vigilant civil society played a critical role in ensuring that

---

829 Moumine Ngarmbassa, 'Sudan's al -Bashir Defies ICC with Chad Visit' *Mail and Guardian* (22 July 2010).

830 *Situation in Darfur, Sudan* (ICC-02/05-01/09), 'Decision Informing the United Nations Security Council and the Assembly of the States Parties to the Rome Statute about Omar al-Bashir's Recent Visit to the Republic of Chad', 27 August 2010.

831 'Chad Rolls Red Carpet for Sudanese President, Says Bashir is Safe from Arrest' *Sudan Tribune* (22 July 2010).

832 Ibid.

833 Article 7(1) of the Constitutive Act (2000) of the African Union states that the decisions of the Assembly have to be taken by consensus or a two-thirds majority of the Member States of the AU.

they could not easily discard their obligations under the Rome Statute, as was discussed in brief earlier in this book.

7.1. KENYA CAUGHT BETWEEN ITS ROME STATUTE OBLIGATIONS AND THE AU'S NON-COOPERATION RESOLUTION

On 27 August 2010, President al-Bashir was invited by President Kibaki to attend the promulgation of Kenya's new constitution. During the visit, the Kenyan authorities did not arrest and surrender him to the Court. As a result, Kenya was confronted for inviting al-Bashir and for not complying with its obligations under the Rome Statute. Moses Masika Wetangula, the Kenyan Minister of Foreign Affairs from 2008 to 2012, delivered a ministerial statement to the Kenyan National Assembly laying out Kenya's justification for having taken this course of action.

Wetangula explained to the Kenyan parliamentarians that Sudan was Kenya's neighbour (this was before the separation of South Sudan from Sudan), hence the invitation was made in the principle of good relations with one's neighbours. In addition, he mentioned that Kenya was the guarantor of the Sudanese Comprehensive Peace Agreement and that it wanted to ensure progress towards the conclusion of the implementation of the Sudanese peace process.[834] The justification indicated that for Kenya, geopolitics and not international law influenced its foreign policy and whether or not it was to abide by the Rome Statute. This has to be expected for a state that wants to project itself as a regional power in East Africa, particularly with its role in the Sudanese peace process and through its military intervention in Somalia against Al-Shabab.

Kenya aligned its justification with the AU Assembly decisions of non-cooperation with the Court in the arrest and surrender of President al-Bashir. At this point, one of the parliamentarians sought clarification on how the AU resolutions were adopted. Rachel Shebesh, a Member of Parliament for the Orange Democratic Movement party, said:

> I would like him [the Minister of Foreign Affairs] to clarify that an AU decision, especially this that came in regard to President Al-Bashir was not a decision that was agreed upon by all nations but it was a decision that all nations were told to uphold.[835]

---

834 Ministerial Statement on Presence of Sudanese President Omar Al-Bashir During Promulgation of New Constitution of Kenya, *Kenya National Assembly Office Reports (Hansard)*, 31 August 2010.

835 *Kenya National Assembly Official Records (Hansard)*, 31 August 2010, p. 40.

This statement by Shebesh, who was also a member of the Pan-African Parliament, confirms Botswana and Chad's claims that President Gaddafi, who was the Chairperson of the AU Assembly, did not allow any meaningful discussion on the issue in Sirte and appears to have imposed the decision onto other states. Such an approach would have violated both the Constitutive Act of the AU's procedures on the decision-making process by the Assembly, but also went against the fundamental trait that lay at the heart of African philosophy, which is consensus building – the *indaba* spirit. It also exposed double standards by some Africa state leaders who berate the UN Security Council's five permanent members for imposing its decisions on small and medium-sized states, yet exhibit the same hegemonic habits within Africa.

European governments also condemned Kenya for failing to abide by its obligations under the Rome Statute. Equally, Kenya also had sympathisers. The Commonwealth Secretary-General, Kamalesh Sharma, an Indian diplomat, expressed sympathy with the Kenyan predicament when he remarked that: 'Every member state signatory to the Rome statute [establishing the Court] has to weigh its obligations according to the commitments it has made to other organisations as well.'[836] In response, Christian Wenaweser, the then President of the Court's Assembly of State Parties – disagreed with Sharma's comments, adding: 'What was alarming to me was that [Sharma's] comments seemed to indicate he agreed with the view expressed by the Kenyan officials that the obligation to the AU overrides the obligations to fully cooperate with the ICC.'[837]

From an analytical standpoint, one could argue that since there is no hierarchical structure governing the interplay between the Rome Statute and the Constitutive Act of the AU, clashes of this type are inevitable. This sits in contrast to the UN Charter, wherein Article 103 establishes a hierarchy for the obligations of members to the UN and to any other international agreement. President Wenaweser's remarks assume that such a hierarchy exists between the Rome Statute and the Constitutive Act. Since the AU's decision not to cooperate with the Court was predicated on Article 98 of the Rome Statute, it can be argued that the decision has a solid legal foundation.

Article 98 states that the Court may not request the surrender of a person in a manner that would require a state to act inconsistently with its obligations under international law in respect of the immunity of that person.[838] The reasoning behind this provision is also reflected in the preamble to the Rome Statute, where the states parties reaffirmed the purposes and principles of the UN Charter.[839] It

836 Julian Borger, 'Commonwealth Chief Admonished by ICC over "War Crimes" Remarks' *The Guardian* (27 October 2010).

837 Ibid.

838 Rome Statute, Art. 98.

839 Ibid, preamble, para. 6.

is a recognition that a new international criminal law system was emerging and was embedded upon an existing international legal system, which could still be used as a reference point when there is no clarity, as in the case of the immunity of President al-Bashir.

Elsewhere, the European Court of Justice in the *Kadi* case annulled the regulation adopted pursuant to the UN Security Council that required states to freeze the financial assets that are suspected to have been used or accessed by al-Qaeda.[840] Although the annulment did not establish a new hierarchical structure to govern international law and European law, it did provide some insight into the impasse that can result when states are caught between obligations to two separate international treaties. Advocate General Maduro stated: 'The relationship between international law and the community legal order is governed by the community legal order itself and the international law can permeate that legal order only under the conditions set by the constitutional principles of the community.'[841]

With this in mind, there is arguably nothing alarming about Kenya's choice to abide by the AU obligations instead of the Rome Statute. In 2014, the Nigerian Coalition for the International Criminal Court (NCICC) sought an Advisory Opinion from the African Court on Human and Peoples' Rights on the matter of competing obligations between Nigeria's obligations under the Rome Statute and under the Constitutive Act.[842] This underscores the fact that the scenarios of states being caught between two competing legal obligations is still an unsettled area in international law.

In any case, the Kenyan High Court issued a provisional arrest warrant for al-Bashir following an application by Kenyan Section of the International Commission of Jurists.[843] The application, which was filed on 18 November 2010 requesting the High Court to issue a provisional warrant of arrest against President al-Bashir and also to order the relevant ministry to effect the warrant of arrest if and when al-Bashir entered the territory of Kenya. The High Court Judge Nicholas Ombija, also known as a 'no-nonsense judge' in Kenyan media circles for his controversial judgments, did not just grant the application of

---

840 Joined Cases C-402/5 P and C-415/05 P, *Kadi & Al Barakaat v. Council* (2008) 3 CMLR 41.

841 Ibid, Opinion of Advocate General Maduro, para. 24; and Albert Posch, 'The Kadi Case: Rethinking the Relationship between EU Law and International Law' (2009) 15 *Columbia Journal of European Law Online* 1.

842 Chino Edmund Obiagwu, 'Enforcing International Justice through Domestic Courts: Nigeria's Experience' in Oby Nwankwo and Benson Olugbuo (eds.)(eds.), *Domestic Implementation of the Rome Statute of the International Criminal Court (ICC) in Nigeria and the Fight against Impunity in Africa* (Nigerian Coalition for the International Criminal Court, Lagos, 2015), pp. 215–22.

843 *Kenya Section of the International Commission of Jurists v. Attorney General and Another* [2011] eKLR Judgments – High Court at Nairobi – Miscellaneous Criminal Application 685 of 2010.

warrant of arrest. He went further and tried to address the potential problem that might arise in the event that the Minister of Internal Security fails, neglects or refuses to execute the same:

> In the event, however, the Applicant [ICJ-Kenya Chapter] has no capacity, it will be at liberty, should it deem fit, to bring an application for the prerogative order of mandamus, for an order directed at the Minister in-charge of Internal Security to arrest President Omar Ahmad Hassan al-Bashir should he set foot in Kenya in future. The fate of the mandamus application shall be decided at another forum – Judicial Review.[844]

It is evident that the High Court avoided leaving any loopholes that would result in leaving al-Bashir able to visit and leave Kenya without being arrested. Following the judgment, al-Bashir could not travel to Kenya and the venue of the –Intergovernmental Authority on Development (IGAD) conference was moved from Kenya to Addis Ababa. In practice, this means that al-Bashir cannot visit Kenya without being arrested. The landmark judgment where a sitting head of state was issued with an arrest warrant by another country demonstrated what could be achieved in terms of ending impunity if the judiciary is free to act independently.

Regrettably, the High Court did not go into great detail in terms of how it viewed the status of sitting head of states and governments whose immunity is not waived either by their own states through the ratification of a treaty such as the Rome Statute or explicitly by a UN Security Council resolution. The judge referred to the principle of universal jurisdiction and how it was applied in the case of Chile's General Augusto Pinochet to underscore that accountability for certain international crimes is not excusable under international law. The difference between Pinochet and al-Bashir is that the latter is a sitting head of a state, unlike Pinochet, who had already left power in Chile when he was arrested.

Naturally, the High Court judgment put the executive arm of the Kenyan government in the spotlight. First, the executive had to find a solution as to how to handle President al-Bashir during his future visits, including the IGAD summit that was pending. Second, Kenya had to reassure Sudan, which had threatened to launch several retaliatory measures against Kenya in response to the High Court decision authorising the arrest of President Bashir if he were to visit Kenya. The measures included an economic embargo on the importation of tea from Kenya – in 2010, Kenya had exported tea worth US$250 million, imposing an air embargo on all flights that use Sudanese airspace to and from Kenya. About 70 per cent of the flights to Kenya use Sudanese air space. In addition, the Sudanese government threated to remove Kenyan peacekeepers serving with the United Nations African Union Mission in Darfur (UNAMID)

---

844 Ibid.

in Darfur. The risks were too high for the Kenyan authorities not to take action; as such, President Kibaki responded by sending his Foreign Minister to deliver a Diplomatic Note to al-Bashir. The Diplomatic Note stated that the 'courts in Kenya are not under the control of the Executive and that when a decision such as that is made, the appropriate avenue for redress is appeal and that [the] Government had instructed the Attorney-General to file an appeal'.[845]

The content of the Diplomatic Note accentuates some level of separation of powers between the executive and the judiciary in Kenya, as well as the fact that the President's hands were tied. It was issued as a direct response to the Sudanese government, which had requested the executive to reverse the High Court's decision. This was obviously a difficult request for the Kenyan government to deal with, which at that time had a very vigilant and dynamic civil society. When the issue was discussed within the Kenyan Parliament, the house was divided, with some parliamentarians raising concern that the judgment displayed some form of insensitivity to Kenya's national regional interests, while others insisted that the national interests of Kenya should be balanced against the need for justice and the accountability for 300,000 Darfurians suspected of having been killed during the conflict. The judgment exposes some of the nuances that are often missed in terms of how Africa is united against the Court. It seems that there is not a commonly shared view in favour or against the Court within different arms of the same government and between different African governments – instead, the picture is ambiguous.

7.2. MALAWI: KEEPING UP WITH ITS ROME STATUTE OBLIGATIONS UNDER CHANGING LEADERSHIP

The Malawian government's stance on whether to or not to comply with the Court or the AU's decisions changed between the presidency of the late President Bingu Wa Mutharika and his successor, Joyce Banda. Malawi is a state party to the Rome Statute. When President Mutharika was the Chairperson of the AU Assembly, he had made his hostility towards the Court well known. He viewed the intervention of the Court in Sudan as detrimental to the AU's efforts to solve its own problems. He stated that African leaders were concerned that the indictment of al-Bashir polarised the different positions of the stakeholders in the peace process.[846] This claim is difficult to comprehend considering that since

845 Ministerial Statement Court Ruling against President of Sudan, *Kenya National Assembly Official Records (Hansard)*, 6 December 2011.

846 'Africa of the New Beginning', Statement by His Excellency Professor Bingu Wa Mutharika, President of the Republic of Malawi and Chairman of the African Union, at the Sixty-Fifth Session of the United Nations General Assembly, New York, 23 September 2011.

al-Bashir's indictment, there has been a series of peace talks in Doha resulting in the signing of the Doha Document for Peace in Darfur in 2011.

In 2011, al-Bashir visited Malawi to attend a Common Market for Eastern and Southern Africa (COMESA) meeting and was not arrested. The Court requested that the Malawian government explain its failure to arrest and surrender al-Bashir.[847] In response, the Malawian authorities argued that their decision rested on two legal bases. First, as the head of state of a non-state party to the Rome Statute, al-Bashir was immune from arrest under customary international law. Article 27 of the Rome Statute, which waives the immunity of heads of state and governments of states parties, was not applicable to Sudan since it had not ratified the Rome Statute. In this regard, Malawi had accorded the Sudanese president privileges and immunities 'in line with the established principle of public international law and in accordance with the immunities and privileges of the Act of Malawi'.[848]

In other words, Malawi's approach was consistent with state practice as far as the domestication of the Rome Statute was concerned. Dapo Akande, Professor of Public International Law at Oxford University, observes that:

> Many of these States have national legislation, implementing the ICC Statute, in which they draw a distinction between the immunity of States parties to the Statute and the immunities of those States not party recognising the former have waived their immunities via Art 27 but that the latter have not.[849]

Second, just like Kenya, Malawi had decided to align itself with the AU's decision for African states not to cooperate with the Court. This decision was premised on Article 98 of the Rome Statute.[850]

In response to questions of relating to President al-Bashir's immunity, the Pre-Trial Chamber I held that:

> [C]ustomary international law creates an exception to Head of State immunity when international courts seek a head of state's arrest for the commission of international crimes. There is no conflict between Malawi's obligations towards the Court and its obligations under customary international law; therefore, Article 98(1) of the Statute does not apply.[851]

---

847 *Bashir* (ICC-02/05-01/09), Decision Pursuant to Article 87(7) of the Rome Statute on the Failure by the Republic of Malawi to Comply with the Cooperation Requests Issued by the Court with Respect to the Arrest and Surrender of Omar Hassan Ahmad Al Bashir, 12 December 2011, para. 7.

848 Ibid; see also the Malawi Immunities and Privileges Act 1984.

849 Dapo Akande, 'ICC Issues Detailed Decision on Bashir's Immunity (... at Long Last ...) But Gets the Law Wrong' *EJIL: Talk!* (15 December 2011) <http://www.ejiltalk.org/icc-issues-detailed-decision-on-bashir%E2%80%99s-immunity-at-long-last-but-gets-the-law-wrong> (accessed 19 October 2016).

850 *Supra* note 837 para. 8.

851 Ibid, para. 43.

Thus, Malawi was found to have failed to meet its obligation to arrest and surrender President al-Bashir. This decision was communicated to the UN Security Council and the Assembly of States Parties. The Court's findings have been criticised for not adequately interpreting the implications of Article 98, which seems to be the main issue and the basis upon which the AU and its member states justify their position of non-cooperation with the Court. Instead of addressing Article 98 issues, the Court focused on Article 27, a provision that primarily concerns personal immunity.[852]

The AU appeared to have picked up on this attempt by the Pre-Trial Chamber to deem Article 98 irrelevant. This prompted the AU to reaffirm its own understanding and the applicability of Article 98 in the context of President al-Bashir. During its twentieth session, the AU Assembly reaffirmed:

> [I]ts understanding that Article 98(1) as included in the Rome Statute establishing the ICC out of the recognition that the Statute is not capable of removing an immunity which international law grants to officials of States that are not parties to the Rome Statute, and by referring the situation in Darfur to the ICC, the UN Security Council, intended that the Rome Statute would be applicable including Article 98.[853]

In short, the AU appeared to acknowledge that the UN Security Council's referral of the situation in Darfur to the Court extended the obligations under the Rome Statute to Sudan, which is a non-state party. This meant that it acknowledged the applicability of both Article 27 and Article 98, which states that;

> The Court may not proceed with a request for surrender or assistance which would require the requested State to act inconsistently with its obligations under international law with respect to the State or diplomatic immunity of a person or property of a third State, unless the Court can first obtain the cooperation of that third State for the waiver of the immunity.[854]

In this case, the states wanting to cooperate with the Court in the arrest and surrender of President al-Bashir would first have to obtain consent from Sudan as the third state, since the UN Security Council did not specifically remove the immunity of al-Bashir in Resolution 1593, which obliges Sudan to cooperate with the Court. The resolution is silent on how other states relate to the Court and Sudan.[855]

---

852 Schabas, *An Introduction to the International Criminal Court*, note 3, p. 80.

853 African Union, 'Decision on the Progress Report of the Commission on the Implementation of the Decision Assembly /AU/Dec.270 on the Second Ministerial Meeting on the Rome Statute of the International Criminal Court, ICC Doc. Assembly /AU/10 (XV)' para. 6.

854 Rome Statute, Art. 98.

855 Dapo Akande, 'The Legal Nature of Security Council Referrals to the ICC and its Impact on al-Bashir's Immunities' (2009) 7 *Journal of International Criminal Justice* 333.

Malawi's position changed following the sudden death of President Mutharika in April 2012. His successor, Joyce Banda, declined to host President al- Bashir, who was expected to visit Malawi in order to attend an AU summit in Lilongwe. The summit was subsequently moved to Addis Ababa. According to the President of the International Criminal Court's Report of the Bureau on Non-cooperation, the Court and Malawi had been making progress with regard to honouring obligations under the Rome Statute before the death of President Mutharika.[856] Still, it is hard to imagine that Mutharika, who had publicly shown that he was a staunch critic of the Court's indictment of al-Bashir during his term of office as the Chairperson of the AU, would have refused to host the prestigious AU biennial summit due to obligations imposed by the Court.

The complexity of the AU's relationship with the Court lies in the fact that: (i) the AU does not have obligations under the Rome Statute as it is not – and cannot be – a state party; and (ii) the membership of these two multilateral institutions overlaps, creating the possibility of conflicting legal obligations. The African States Parties to the Court are obliged to comply with their legal duties according to the Rome Statute and to cooperate with the Court. Their membership of the AU, on the other hand, requires them to comply with certain legal duties under the Constitutive Act (2002). The complex conflicts created by this matrix of legal obligations became evident when Chad and Kenya failed to cooperate with the Court in the arrest and surrender of al-Bashir.

This complexity also manifested itself in October 2014, when President Uhuru Kenyatta decided to travel to The Hague to attend a status conference on Kenya's level of cooperation with the Court in the investigations and trials related to the post-2007 election violence. Kenyatta's decision to attend this was inconsistent with the decision of the AU Extraordinary Summit, which stated:

> That President Uhuru Kenyatta will not appear before the ICC until such time as the concerns raised by the AU and its Member States have been adequately addressed by the UN Security Council and the ICC.[857]

There was a possibility that the Office of the Prosecutor could have issued an arrest warrant had President Kenyatta not made the personal appearance at The Hague, which could have complicated his role as the President of Kenya.

It is clear that although it might be easy for a regional body to come up with hardline positions on non-cooperation, it is individual states that would normally have to live with the consequences of their actions within the international governance system. In the case of Kenya, it is possible that apart

---

856 International Criminal Court-Assembly of States (ICC, ASP/11/29), 'Report of the Bureau on non-Cooperation', 1 November 2012 para 5.

857 Extraordinary Session of the Assembly of the African Union, 12 October 2013, Addis Ababa, Ethiopia, Ext/Assembly/AU/Dec.12, para. XI.

from pressure that came from civil societies for President Kenyatta to attend the status conference, other domestic policy issues played a crucial role. Kenya is a regional hub hosting several UN headquarters and its geographical location is strategic for air travel across Africa. The consequences of having the president of such a state have an arrest warrant issued against him had he not attended the status conference could have had a devastating effect on the stability of the economy and the entire region. Kenyatta would simply have been marginalised and considered to be an international justice fugitive. Sudan is in a similar situation, and President al-Bashir is now forced to plan his foreign trips with great caution. The warrant for his arrest has actually put the UN mission in Sudan in a curious diplomatic position with the government. In this regard, Kenyatta acted with great wisdom to make such a personal appearance at The Hague.

7.3. NIGERIA AND CLOSING THE IMPUNITY GAP

Nigeria ratified the Rome Statute in September 2001. At the time of writing, it was still in the process of assimilating the Rome Statute into domestic law in accordance with its Constitution. The Bill for the domestication of the Rome Statute has been a victim of political transitions in Nigeria. President Olusegan Obasanjo left office before he signed the Bill into law. He had his reservations, which under close examination demonstrates his lack of understanding that the Court operates under the complementarity principle.[858] Still, Nigeria continues to be one of the active African States Parties. In 2011, five of its nationals were part of the Court staff, including a sitting judge, Judge Unile Eboe Esuju. By 2015, Nigeria had contributed US$1,227,274 through the assessed contributions to the Court's budget. However, it had arrears amounting to US$278,426 and its last payment was made in 2013.

Al-Bashir visited Nigeria in July 2013 to attend an AU summit on HIV/AIDS, tuberculosis and malaria. Prior to this visit, there had been reports that in 2009, he was also invited to attend the AU's Peace and Security Council session by the former Nigerian President Umaru Yar'Adua. The purpose of this was to discuss the report of the African Penal on Darfur, which was led by the former President of South Africa, Thabo Mbeki. In the end, al-Bashir stayed away from the session following a campaign by Nigerian-based and international human rights organisations for Nigeria to arrest and surrender him if he set foot on Nigerian territory. In the end, the then Vice President of Sudan, Ali Osman Taha, led the Sudanese delegation to the session. In 2013, al-Bashir had to leave Nigeria less

---

858 Chinedum Odenyi, 'The Domestic Implementation of International Treaties in Nigeria: Understanding the Role of the National Assembly' in Nwankwo and Olugbuo (eds.), *Domestic Implementation of the Rome Statute*, note 832, pp. 82–88.

than 24 hours after his arrival. He arrived on Sunday 14 July and left on 15 July 2013 immediately after the opening ceremony of the conference.

The reasons behind al-Bashir's hurried departure from Nigeria differ depending on who is asked. The spokesman at the Sudanese Embassy in Nigeria explained it in terms of other engagements that were lined up for al-Bashir.[859] Some attributed it to his fear of being arrested and surrendered to the Court. This is likely to be the case, considering that when his visit and presence in Nigeria was known, the Nigerian authorities came under immerse pressure to respect their obligations under the Rome Statute and cooperate in his arrest and surrender. The Pre-Trial Chamber II issued a decision 'requesting the Federal Republic of Nigeria to immediately arrest Omar al-Bashir and surrender him to the Court'.[860]

The NCICC filed an application in the High Court seeking an order compelling the Nigerian President to arrest President al-Bashir as soon as he arrived in Nigerian territory and to surrender him to The Hague.[861] The application was filed on 15 July 2013 and preparations were being made for the hearing to be held the following day. However, al-Bashir left on the same day that the application was made, hence the subsequent hearing was stopped. .

Nigeria received a great deal of criticism across the board for both hosting President al-Bashir and disregarding its obligations under the Rome Statute to cooperate with the Court in arresting him and surrendering him to The Hague. Members of the NCICC organised a demonstration at the conference venue waving placards with messages such as 'Nigeria is not a safe haven for war criminals' and 'Omar al-Bashir is a war crimes fugitive'. The EU High Representative raised the EU's concern over al-Bashir's visit to Nigeria.[862]

The Nigerian government responded first by reaffirming its commitment to cooperate with the Court and to end impunity.[863] This was crucial considering that the Office of the Prosecutor was conducting preliminary examinations in Nigeria. Second, it justified the presence of al-Bashir on its territory based on the AU procedures where 'Member States of the African Union do not require an invitation of the host governments [in this case Nigeria] to attend such summits'.[864] This has become a standard justification given by African States Parties in explaining the presence of al-Bashir in their territories and their

---

859 'Sudan's Bashir Rushes Home from Nigeria after Calls for His Arrest' *Sudan Tribune* (16 July 2013).

860 *Bashir* (ICC-02/05-01/09), Decision Regarding Omar Al-Bashir's Visit to the Federal Republic of Nigeria, 15 July 2013.

861 Obiagwu, 'Enforcing International Justice through Domestic Courts', note 832, (eds.), p. 212.

862 European Union Delegation to the United Nations, 'EU HR Ashton Concerned by Visit of Sudanese President Al Bashir to Nigeria', 16 July 2013.

863 *Bashir* (ICC-02/05-01/09) Pre-Trial Chamber II Decision on the Cooperation of the Federal Republic of Nigeria Regarding al-Bashir's Arrest and Surrender to the Court, 5 September 2013, para. 11.

864 Ibid.

failure to arrest and surrender him. In 2014 and 2015, the Democratic Republic of the Congo and South Africa pointed to COMESA and the AU respectively to justify al-Bashir's presence.[865] The explanation is grounded on the general state practise where an intergovernmental organisation such as the UN, the EU and, in this case, the AU invites member states to attend a conference or a summit and the hosting state's role would be to facilitate visas, security and the logistics needs of delegates.

The second justification offered by Nigeria for disregarding its obligation was that President al-Bashir hurriedly left the summit. It argued that such a sudden departure 'occurred at the time that officials of relevant bodies and agencies of … Nigeria were considering the necessary the steps to be taken in respect of his visit in line with Nigeria's obligation's.[866] The Pre-Trial Chamber judges, Ekaterina Trendafilova (sitting as the Presiding Judge), Judge Kaul and Judge Cuno Tarfussser, were convinced by Nigeria's justifications and decided not to refer its failure to abide by its obligations to the Assembly of States Parties or the UN Security Council as required by the Rome Statute. The Chamber concluded its decision by requesting that Nigeria immediately arrest al-Bashir and surrender him to the Court if he ever sets foot on Nigerian territory. The NCICC filed an application with the High Court with a view to ensuring that the domestic courts issued a provisional arrest warrant against al-Bashir

It is curious that the Nigerian authorities through the Attorney General only raised the issue of the AU's non-cooperation position as its defence after the NCICC had filed its application. One would have thought that such a position would be used as the first line of defence. In addition, and following the similar line of argument raised by the Kenyan authorities in *Kenya Section of the International Commission of Jurists v. Attorney General and Another*, the Nigerian Attorney General questioned the *locus standi* of the NCICC. The judgment issued in 2016 questioned the locus standing of the Plaintiffs and according to Chino Edmuch Obiagwu a criminal law and human rights expert and the Chairman of NCICC, they are planning to appeal against the judgment.[867] According to Chino Edmund Obiagwu, NCICC, the case has potential of setting a:

> [V]eritable precedent for judicial orders on the implementation of treaty obligations of the country under the Rome Statute, irrespective of the fact that the Statute is not yet incorporated in the domestic laws.[868]

---

865 See *Bashir* (ICC-02/05-01/09) Pre-Trial Chamber II, Decision on the Cooperation of the Democratic Republic of the Congo Regarding Omar Al Bashir's Arrest and Surrender to the Court, 9 April 2014, para. 12.

866 *Bashir* (ICC-02/05-01/09) Pre-Trial Chamber II Decision on the Cooperation of the Federal Republic of Nigeria Regarding Omar Al Bashir's Arrest and Surrender to the Court, 5 September 2013, para. 12.

867 Email Correspondence with Chino Edmund Obiagwu the Chair of the NCICC 1 November 2016 (copy with the author)

868 Obiagwu, 'Enforcing International Justice through Domestic Courts', note 832, p. (eds.)215.

This is because Nigeria – unlike Kenya and South Africa – has not yet incorporated the Rome Statute into its domestic law. The Nigerian Constitution prefers a dualist theory, hence international treaties have to be enacted into domestic law by the National Assembly before they have force of law.[869] Regardless of the fact that Nigeria is yet to incorporate the Rome Statute, this could not be treated as an impediment to the High Court issuing a provisional arrest warrant, considering that it is generally legally accepted that the recognition and observance of certain fundamental human rights treaties create obligations even in the absence of national laws. As such, Nigeria cannot justify its non-compliance with international obligations – in this case the Rome Statute – by citing its inability to enact the relevant internal laws. This is due to the fact that when Nigeria (or any other state for that matter) ratifies an international treaty, it is the state, which constitutes three organs – the executive, the legislature and the judiciary – that collectively assumes the obligation.

The failure of one arm of the state to comply or give effect to the Rome Statute, as was the case with President Obasanjo, does not let Nigeria off the hook in relation to its international obligations to cooperate with the Court. The European Court of Justice case law has confirmed this principle when Member States have failed to fulfil their obligations due to a lack of national implementing measures.

As was highlighted earlier regarding the question of the hierarchy of state obligations between the Rome Statute and the Constitutive Act, the NCICC filed an application with the African Court on Human and Peoples' Rights requesting an Advisory Opinion. The request was still pending at the time of writing. The African Court on Human and Peoples' Rights is authorised to deliver Advisory Opinions under Article 4(1).[870] The wording in Article 4(1), 'or any other relevant human rights instruments', gives the Court wider subject-matter jurisdiction of what it can deliver Advisory Opinions on, compared to, for example, the African Commission on Human and Peoples' Rights, whose interpretative powers of which are limited to the African Charter[871] and not any other treaty or human rights instruments. The UN Office of the High Commission on Human Rights provides a non-exhaustive list of what it considered to be universal human rights instruments. The list is an assortment of conventions, declarations and resolutions, and it includes the Rome Statute. In this regard, subject-matter jurisdiction may not be the legal impediment for the African Court on Human

869 Constitution of the Federal Republic of Nigeria (1999), Section 12(1).

870 Protocol on the Establishment of an African Court on Human and Peoples' Rights (1998). Art. 4 (1) provides that: 'At the request of a Member State of the OAU, the OAU, any of its organs, or any African organization recognized by the OAU, the Court may provide an opinion on any legal matter relating to the Charter or any other relevant human rights instruments, provided that the subject matter of the opinion is not related to a matter being examined by the Commission.'

871 African Charter on Human and Peoples' Rights (1981), Art. 45(3).

and Peoples' Rights not to deliver an Advisory Opinion involving the Rome Statute as requested.

Moreover, the role of the African Court on Human and Peoples' Rights in issuing Advisory Opinions is not limited to a specific territory. This is in contrast to the American Convention on Human Rights, which limits the territorial reach of the Inter-American Court to the protection of human rights in the territories of American states. With respect to who may request an Advisory Opinion from the Court, there is a provision in the Protocol that empowers 'any African organisation recognised by the OAU'.[872] This has been interpreted to include those African civil society organisations that have formal status with the then OAU (now the AU), for instance, either those with observer status with the African Commission or that have the accreditation with the Economic, Social and Cultural Council (ECOSOCC) of the AU. In the request, NCICC indicated that it has observer status with the African Commission on Human and Peoples' Rights, which should qualify it to request Advisory Opinions from the African Court.

Still, the African Court will have to determine all these factors and provide its own interpretation of the Protocol, and one can only hope that it will use this opportunity to stamp its own mark on the small yet growing international criminal law jurisprudence on the continent. The issue of superiority of obligations is likely to remain nebulous and to harm the relationship between the AU and the Court. The request for an Advisory Opinion on this subject allows the African Court to make its own contribution towards the interpretation of the Rome Statute.

7.4. SOUTH AFRICA: CAUGHT BETWEEN THE DESIRE TO SHOW ITS TRUE PAN-AFRICANISM CREDENTIALS AND ITS POSITION AS AN UPHOLDER OF INTERNATIONAL LAW OBLIGATIONS

The AU's non-cooperation position in relation to the Court has made the relationship between South Africa and the Court ambiguous. Just like Nigeria, South Africa is both a state party to the Rome Statute and one of the prominent members of the AU. Since the end of apartheid and after the first democratic elections in 1994, South Africa considered the promotion of the African agenda to be the cornerstone of its foreign policy. It is among Africa's five wealthiest states and contributes more than 15 per cent of the AU's annual budget. It hosts

872 Supra note 860, Art. 4(1).

the Pan-African Parliament, the New Partnership for Africa's Development (NEPAD) and African Peer Review Mechanisms Secretariats. It also contributes armed forces for peacekeeping missions in Africa. It first deployed peacekeepers to Darfur in 2004 through the African Mission in Sudan (AMIS). South African peacekeepers have been deployed in other parts of Africa, including Burundi, the Democratic Republic of the Congo, and at the border between Ethiopia and Eritrea until 2008. These factors are likely to play a role in shaping South Africa's own approach to the Court both as a sovereign state and also as a member of the AU. The balancing act is obviously a tricky one, essentially because the demands for respecting its international obligations under the Rome Statute appear to be conflicting with its own national interest as a driver of the African agenda and as a potential true African representative at the UN Security Council.

South Africa's role in the establishment of the Court and its early support for the new institution is well documented. It was one of the first states to ratify the Rome Statute and within Africa was among the first to enact the enabling domestic law, the Implementation of the Rome Statute of the International Criminal Court Act, in 2002. The South African Judge Pillay Navanethem was elected by the Africa states to be a judge at the Court and served there between 2003 and 2008. Up to 2016, South Africa had made contributions assessed at US$5,882,020 to the budget of the Court. This makes it Africa's highest contributor to the Court, followed by Nigeria.

President Al-Bashir is reported to have previously cancelled a couple of visits to South Africa due to the threat of being arrested. Almost a month after the arrest warrant was issued, the South African presidency confirmed that they had invited al-Bashir together with other African presidents to attend President Jacob Zuma's inauguration ceremony,[873] although they had hoped that he was not going to show up for the event, as that could have put South Africa in a difficult position of having to arrest him. The South African International Affairs Director, General Ayanda Nstaluba, confirmed these fears to the media when he acknowledged that al-Bashir's indictment could present a problem: 'We hope that in the interest of the relations between South Africa and Sudan we will not have an unfortunate event.'[874] South Africa was saved from possible diplomatic embarrassment as al-Bashir did not attend the inauguration ceremony. It is possible that South Africa called and informed him that it was better for him not to turn up for the inauguration. At this stage, the AU had not adopted its non-cooperation resolution in relation to the Court.

However, this was not the case by the time that South Africa hosted the FIFA World Cup in 2010 and there was the possibility of al-Bashir attending the official opening ceremony. This prompted a Democratic Alliance MP, Kenneth Sililo

[873] Wilsom Johwa, 'Sudan Dilemma for Zuma's Inauguration' *Business Day* (6 May 2009).
[874] Ibid.

Mudu, to ask President Zuma in the National Assembly whether al-Bashir, who had been invited to attend the opening ceremony, would be arrested. Zuma's response was rather nuanced: 'South Africa respects international law and we certainly are signatories, and we abide by the law.'[875] He further elaborated that the AU had not said: 'We must not arrest al-Bashir.'

At first glance, President Zuma's response could be interpreted as an outright affirmation that South Africa was going to arrest President al-Bashir the moment he stepped onto South African soil. However, the wording is not conclusive. Zuma did not to specifically give an affirmative answer, but restricted himself to a general statement that South Africa respects international law, which of course includes customary international law.

International law is very broad and, of course, South Africa is expected to respect its international obligations. However, as it turned out in 2015 (and as will be discussed later on), the international law to which President Zuma referred also encompassed customary international law, which includes the immunity of sitting heads of state. Al-Bashir did not attend the World Cup official opening ceremony, which perhaps confirms that he was concerned that there was a real threat of him being arrested.

Having said that, on 13 June 2015, President al-Bashir went to South Africa and briefly attended an AU summit before leaving and returning to Sudan under unclear conditions. Unlike his previous attempts to travel to South Africa, it seems this time, al-Bashir had received some assurance either from the AU or the South African government that he was not going to be arrested if he attended an AU summit. It turned out that South Africa had done its homework before al-Bashir's trip.

On 12 June 2015, a day before President al-Bashir's visit, the South African Embassy in the Netherlands met with Judge Cuno Tarfussser, the Presiding Judge of the Pre-Trial Chamber II, representatives of the Register and the Office of the Prosecutor for consultations, as permitted under Article 97 of the Rome Statute. Article 97 provides for states parties to approach the Court as soon as they identify challenges that may impede or prevent the execution of the Court's request to arrest and surrender a suspect. The list of possible problems, which is not exhaustive, includes when the information provided by the Court is insufficient, when the person is not located and when the execution of the request would lead the requested state to 'breach a pre-existing treaty obligation undertaken with respect to another State'.[876]

During the meeting – which was convened outside normal working hours at 5 pm, perhaps to underscore the urgency of the matter – the South African

[875] South African Parliament, Proceedings of the National Assembly Record, 27 May 2010, pp. 37 and 38.

[876] Rome Statute, Art. 97.

Ambassador raised the point that 'there was lack of clarity in the law and the Republic of South African was subject to competing obligations'.[877] The competing obligations to which South Africa was referring are not stated in the document that was made available to the public. Still, one can only infer that the obligations referred to here could have been those under the Rome Statute and the AU's decision. This could be deduced from Judge Tarfussser's response. South Africa was told that: 'There is no ambiguity in the law and that [the] Republic of South Africa is under the obligation to arrest and surrender to the Court Omar al-Bashir.'[878]

Judge Tarfussser relied heavily on the Pre-Trial Chamber II's decision on the cooperation of the Democratic Republic of the Congo to emphasise the need for states to cooperate fully with the Court in the arrest and surrender of President al-Bashir.[879] In addition, he referred to the Pre-Trial Chamber II's own interpretation of Resolution 1593 (2005), which referred the situation in Darfur to the Court. The interpretation, which is based on the restrictive theory of immunity, argues that the resolution had implicitly waived the immunities granted to al-Bashir under international law.

Despite the outcome of the Article 97 consultative meeting and the Pre-Trial Chamber II's clarification of South Africa's obligations, President al-Bashir visited South Africa and was not arrested. However, he had to cut the length of his stay and left the country under very questionable circumstances. His visit turned out to be very costly for the South African government's image, as its High Court ruled that by not complying with the order to arrest al-Bashir, it violated the national Constitution.[880] The High Court further ordered the South African government to 'take all reasonable steps to prepare and arrest President Bashir'.[881] At the time of writing, the South African Supreme Court of Appeal was still seized with the case after the Minister of Justice and Constitutional Development and others had appealed the whole High Court judgment dated 24 June 2015.[882] The visit almost led to the impeachment of President Zuma by the South African Parliament.

Internationally, there were media reports that when President al-Bashir was still in South Africa and was facing the threat of possible detention, the South

---

877 *Bashir* (ICC-02/05-01/09), Decision Following the Prosecutor's Request for an Order Further Clarifying that the Republic of South Africa is under the Obligation to Immediately Arrest and Surrender Omar Al-Bashir, 13 June 2015, para. 4.

878 Ibid, para. 5.

879 *Bashir* (ICC-02/05-01/09), Decision on the Cooperation of the Democratic Republic of the Congo Regarding Omar al-Bashir's Arrest and Surrender to the Court, 9 April 2014, paras 28–31.

880 *The South African Litigation Centre v. Minister of Justice and Constitutional Development and Others*, High Court of South Africa, Case Number: 27740/2015, Judgment.

881 Ibid.

882 *Minister of Justice and Constitutional Development and Others v South African Litigation Centre*, Supreme Court of South Africa, HC Case 27740/2015, Notice of Motion.

African peacekeepers based in al-Fasher (the state capital of North Darfur) as part of UNAMID were threatened with violence. In The Hague, there was some form of misunderstanding between the Office of the Prosecutor and the South African Embassy as to whether the meeting held on 12 June was conclusive or rather was a preliminary consultation. The misunderstanding escalated to the level that the Prosecutor felt compelled to make a request to the Pre-Trial Chamber II for a reclassification of confidential filings on the meetings relating to al-Bashir's travel to South Africa. She argued that her request was in the interests of transparency as she had issues with how South Africa had suggested that the Article 97 consultations had not actually taken place.[883] The South African Embassy rejected the Prosecutor's views, citing the fact that it was the first state party to apply Article 97 and had first-hand experience of the challenges created in resorting to such consultations without clear implementing procedures. South Africa has already made proposals to develop procedures for the implementation of Article 97.[884] In other words, for South Africa, there was nothing unusual about considering the meeting held on 12 June 2015 to be simply a preparatory meeting instead of a conclusive consultation under Article 97.

Inside South Africa, the visit triggered a series of legal battles between the South African Litigation Centre and the Minister of Justice and Constitutional Development and other relevant institutions of the South African law and order machinery. The battle started on 14 June 2015 when the South Africa Litigation Centre confirmed that President al-Bashir had arrived in South Africa and filed an application with the High Court of South Africa. The application requested the High Court to rule that the failure of the South African authorities to take the necessary steps to arrest and/or detain al-Bashir was inconsistent with the Constitution of the Republic of South Africa, to compel the South Africa authorities to prepare and arrest al-Bashir and to detain him pending a formal request for his surrender to the Court.

Alternatively, the High Court was requested to compel the South African authorities to take reasonable steps to provisionally arrest al-Bashir in terms of the implementation of the Rome Statute and compelling the respondents to prevent al-Bashir from leaving the country. On the same day, Justice Hans-Joachim Fabricius issued an interim order for al-Bashir to be prohibited from leaving South Africa until a final order was made on the South African Litigation Centre's application.[885]

---

883 *Bashir* (ICC-02/05-01/09) Prosecution Request for it to Be Heard Should the Domestic Legal Proceedings in the Republic of South Africa Not Be Finalised by 31 December 2015, and for Confirmation of South Africa's Continuing Obligations to Arrest and Surrender Omar al-Bashir and for Reclassification of Filings, 26 October 2015, para. 9.

884 ICC-ASP/14/L.1.

885 *Southern Africa Litigation Centre and the Minister of Justice and Constitutional Development and Others*, Case Number 27740/15, 14 June 2015, Interim Order.

Despite the interim order, President al-Bashir managed to leave South Africa on 15 June 2015. He left before the end of the AU summit. In any case, the High Court issued its judgment which the Government of South Africa immediately appealed to the Supreme Court. In particular, the judgment held that South Africa had the duty to arrest al-Bashir even though he was a sitting head of state; as such, it had acted in a manner that was inconsistent with the Constitution.

The High Court's reaction to the non-compliance with its interim order alluded to how democracy and the rule of law were being risked in South Africa because the government ignored its constitutional obligations and failed to abide by court orders:

> A Court is the guardian of justice, the cornerstone of a democratic system based on the rule of law. If the State an organ of State or State official does not abide by Court orders, the democratic edifice will crumble stone-by stone until it collapses and chaos ensues.[886]

In their defence, the respondents (the government ministries and their departments) suggested that as a hosting country for the AU summit, South Africa was obliged to uphold and protect President al-Bashir's inviolability in accordance with the AU terms and conditions. The relevant terms and conditions outlined in Article VII of the host agreement are that South Africa shall accord the 'Members of the Commission and Staff Members, the delegates and other representatives of Inter-Governmental Organisations attending the Meeting, the privileges and immunities'. Following a Cabinet meeting, where the issue of al-Bashir's invitation and attendance of the AU summit was discussed, the Minister of International Relations and Cooperation formally recognised the host agreement, including granting immunities and privileges to the relevant participants as required by the agreement. The Minister's argument was that she acted in accordance with the South African Immunities Act.[887] In this regard, al-Bashir was considered to have been covered by the immunities and privileges under the terms and conditions of the host agreement. This did not impress the High Court, which argued that the OAU Convention on Privileges and Immunities, which formed the basis for privileges and immunities incorporated into the host agreement, was not part of South African national law. The Convention had not been incorporated into domestic law in accordance with the South African Constitution.

What is surprisingly missing in the South African defence is any reference to the AU's non-cooperation position. This is rather curious for two reasons. The first is the fact that some African States Parties – Chad, Malawi, the Democratic

886 Ibid, Judgment, para. 37.2.

887 Diplomatic Immunities and Privileges Act 37 of 2001, as amended by Diplomatic Immunities and Privileges Amendment Act 35 of 2008, Art. 5(1).

Republic of the Congo and Nigeria (although belatedly) – have used this position as their primary line of defence against any criticism of their discarding of their obligations under the Rome Statute. The second is that South Africa presents itself as the driver of the African agenda, of which non-cooperation is one of the current features. It perhaps confirms that South Africa was not convinced that the AU resolution would have an impact on its international obligations. This was suggested by Nomfanelo Koto, the spokeswoman of the Department of International Relations and Cooperation, when she said that 'the AU resolution was not indicative of SA's attitude to the ICC'.[888] The other possibility is that during the 12 June 2015 consultative meeting with the Court, South Africa clearly understood that there was no uncertainty between its obligations under the Rome Statute and the Constitutive Act of the AU, so using the non-cooperation argument was probably a non-starter.

The African National Congress (ANC), which is the ruling party in South Africa, reacted to the issue of President Bashir's visit and the subsequent falling out with the Court at its National General Council (NGC).[889] The National General Council, an annual event that is also considered a political school for the entire party, took place in October 2015 approximately four months after the South African government had been criticised for not arresting and surrendering President Bashir. At the Council, the ANC recommended that the Government of South Africa 'begin the process of withdrawal of its membership of the ICC, preceded by the discussions that are taking place among the member states of the ICC and those taking place within the African Union on the ICC matter'.[890] The national parliament of South Africa was asked to start the process of 'amending the Act implementing the Rome Statute to align with the Diplomatic Immunities and Privileges Act of 2008'.[891]

A year had passed when, on 19 October 2016, the South African Minister of International Relations and Cooperation, Ms Maite Nkoena Mashabane, submitted South Africa's instrument of withdrawal to the United Nations' Secretary General. South Africa justified its withdrawal on what it considered to be incompatibility between its obligations with respect to a peaceful resolution of conflicts in Africa, with how its obligations under the Rome Statute are interpreted by the Court.[892] At the Fifteenth Meeting of the Assembly of State

---

888 Hopewell Radebe, 'Botswana Shows up SA on AU "Reprieve" for Bashir' *Business Day* (8 July 2009).

889 African National Congress, 'Report of the 4th National General Council held at the Gallagher Estate, Midrand, Gauteng' 08–11 October 2015.

890 Ibid at p.64.

891 Ibid at p.64.

892 South Africa, 'Instrument of Withdrawal signed by the Minister of International Relations and Cooperation of the Republic of South Africa' 19 October 2016; see also 'Declaratory statement by the Republic of South Africa on the decision to withdraw from the Rome Statute of the International Criminal Court', United Nations, Reference: C.N.786.2016.TREATIES-XVIII.10 (Depositary Notification).

Parties of the International Criminal Court, the South African Minister of Justice and Correctional Services, Mr T.M. Masutha, elaborated on his country's decision to withdraw by alluding to three main issues. First, the incompatibility between South Africa's obligations under the Rome Statute with those on diplomatic immunity of Heads of State under customary international law, second the justice and peace debate; third was the unequal and unfair treatment of States by the Court.[893]

If one looks at the political changes and developments that have occurred in Africa over the past five years, it is easy to put South Africa's decision to withdraw into perspective. To begin with, at least one of the African Union's biannual summits used to be held either in Sirte, Libya or Sharm El Sheikh, Egypt, which were both non-party states to the Rome Statute. This meant they did not have any obligations under the Rome Statute to arrest and surrender indicted presidents such as President Bashir. With both Libya and Egypt not available to host AU summits due to the ongoing political instability (Libya) and transitions (Egypt) there are very few states that can host AU Summits without having to violate their Rome Statute obligations. To date, Rwanda and Equatorial Guinea (both non-party states) have been ready to step in, yet the problem for the AU is that there are very few candidates as more than half its membership has obligations under the Rome Statute. The question is why is it so important for the AU to accommodate the Sudanese President at its Summits or any regional gatherings? One answer is that Sudan's geographical location makes it an indispensible member of the AU. Until 2011 it had nine neighbouring states (now seven), the majority of which are currently experiencing conflicts that have direct or indirect connections with Sudan, be it through the flow of refugees or claims and counter claims of harbouring rebel movements. In addition, Sudan is a crucial member of the Nile Basin Initiative, established into order that countries which share the Nile Basin can achieve equitable utilisation of the Nile water resources. In other words, it is difficult to try and resolve some of the challenges facing the Middle East and North Africa region and East Africa or Central Africa regions without involving the Sudanese leadership. South Africa, which is a founding member of the AU and has been involved in mediating peace on the continent including in Darfur and South Sudan, might have felt that its obligations under the Rome Statute had become a bottleneck, limiting its effectiveness as a regional power. Following its withdrawal, however, South Africa would be able to host as many AU Summits as possible and also to invite President Bashir without any concern about criticism from the Court.

---

893 Assembly of States Parties, Opening Statement by Mr T. M.Masutha, MP, Minister of Justice and Correctional Services, Republic of South Africa, General Debate: Fifteenth Meeting of the Assembly of States Parties of the International Criminal Court, The Hague, 16–24 November 2016.

7.5. AN ATTEMPT TO AMEND ARTICLE 16: THE PUSH FOR A POWER SHIFT FROM THE UN SECURITY COUNCIL TO THE UN GENERAL ASSEMBLY

In Sirte in 2009, the AU Assembly requested that the African Commission convene a preparatory meeting of African States Parties at expert and ministerial levels (Foreign Affairs and Justice) to prepare for the International Criminal Court Review Conference that was due to be held in Kampala, Uganda in May and June 2010. The suggested agenda for the preparatory meeting had seven points, which included discussions on role of the UN Security Council in referring situations to the Court, Article 16 of the Rome Statute, which authorises the Security Council to defer proceedings for one year, the procedures of the Court and clarification on the immunities of officials whose states are not states parties to the Rome Statute.

A total of 26 out of a possible 30 African States Parties attended the meeting to address the issues raised in Sirte, which was held in Addis Ababa on 3–6 November 2009. There were also several non-states parties in attendance, taking the total number of participating states to more than 40. The African States Parties agreed to maintain Article 13 unchanged, which granted the Security Council the authority to refer situations to the Court. However, they proposed an amendment to Article 16. The text of the amendment, which was supposed to be sponsored and submitted to the Assembly of States Parties by four African States Parties (South Africa, Nigeria, Burundi and Tanzania), had two components. First, it identifies how the deferral was to be triggered. It gives the state with jurisdiction over the situation before the Court the power to request for a deferral. Second, it provides an alternative to the UN Security Council's failure to act within six months on a referral request. The alternative is that a state party could also make the same request to the 'UN General Assembly to assume the Security Council's responsibility under para 1 consistent with Resolution 377(v) of the UN General Assembly'.

UN General Assembly Resolution 377(v), also known as the Uniting for Peace Resolution, was adopted at the peak of the Cold War in 1950 to side-step the UN Security Council's primary responsibility for taking collective security measures on issues pertaining to peace and security. It was sponsored by the US and other Western powers, and their aim was to ensure that there was an alternative to the power of veto trumping majority rule in the UN Security Council. It was during this period that the Union of Soviet Socialist Republics (USSR) used its veto power to impede resolutions.

The core of the resolution can be split into three parts: the first is that the UN General Assembly can act in the event of inaction by the UN Security Council due to a lack of unanimity among the permanent members; second, the General Assembly only intervenes if there is a threat to the peace, a breach of peace or an act of aggression; third, the General Assembly may meet in emergency special sessions within 24 hours. At the time of its adoption, USSR was critical of the resolution, arguing that it was illegal and undermined the object of veto in the Security Council, and that if the permanent members of the Security Council's right to veto was now objected to, then an amendment to the UN Charter was necessary. Those in support of the resolution argued that although the Security Council had the primary responsibility of maintaining peace and security, this right was not an exclusive one.

It is therefore no surprise that the African States Parties and the other African states that attended the preparatory meeting opted to use Resolution 377(v) as their basis for amending Article 16. As has already been discussed throughout this book, African states seem to be disillusioned by the UN Security Council and would prefer to have very little to do with it. Still, the presentation and support for the proposals to amend Article 16 was marred by discord among the African States Parties. First, the African States Parties failed to come up with a common strategy to use in order to lobby other regional groups to support their proposals. Second, although South Africa, Nigeria, Burundi and Tanzania had been identified as sponsors of the amendments, eventually it was South Africa alone that introduced the proposals, as representatives from other states developed cold feet during the 8th Session of the Assembly of States Parties. Some even suggested that they had not received further communications from their respective capitals regarding the proposal. There was actually no consensus in terms of support for the proposals, so that when South Africa introduced them, only two African States Parties – Namibia and Senegal – spoke in support of them, compared to 13 non-African States Parties that took to the floor and spoke against them.

As already highlighted, the decision to add Article 16 to the Rome Statute was not a popular one. States were against the idea of any political entity being given a role in the core functions of the Court. As such, the view expressed during the Assembly of States Parties was that 'an expansion of that provision would not serve the interest of the Court and could not, therefore, be supported by States Parties'.[894]

Furthermore, the Court is an independent institution with its own legal identity and is not part of the UN (and vice versa). This means that amendments to the Rome Statute would not have any direct legal impact on the structure of the relationship between the UN Security Council and the UN General Assembly, as provided for in the UN Charter.[895]

---

894 Report on the Ministerial Meeting of the Rome Statute of the International Criminal Court, African Union Executive Council, Sixteenth Ordinary Session, 25–29 January 2010, Addis Ababa, Ethiopia EX.CL/568 (XVI), Annex 2.

895 Ibid.

When the AU Assembly sensed that there was disunity among the African States Parties towards supporting the amendment proposals, it encouraged:

> [A]ll Member States to speak with one voice to ensure that the proposed amendment to Article 16 of the Rome Statute which would allow the UN General Assembly to take over the power of the UNSC to defer cases for one (1) year in cases where the UNSC has failed to take a decision within a specified timeframe.[896]

Although the proposed amendment is still under consideration, according to the Court's Working Group on Amendments, one practical challenge for any proposed amendment to Article 16 would be guaranteeing either a consensus or a two-thirds majority,[897] particularly given that the proposal received a less than enthusiastic response – even from the African states – when it was presented by South Africa.

Perhaps the AU could focus on identifying the required conditions or benchmarks that will need to be met before Article 16 is triggered. Such a framework of benchmarks could be useful in deciding whether or not in a given situation there is a serious commitment to end impunity, yet there are also other demanding priorities that require immediate attention. The benchmarks could include effective cooperation between the state in question and the Court during the deferral period.

7.6. THE AU'S PROPOSED ALTERNATIVE JURIDICAL MECHANISMS TO CURB THE COURT'S INTERVENTION: THE PROPOSAL FOR A HYBRID COURT FOR DARFUR

In 2009, the AU High-Level Panel on Darfur (hereinafter the High-Level Panel) recommended the establishment of a Hybrid Court to address the problem of impunity in the region of Darfur.[898] The Hybrid Court was expected to handle the most serious crimes and was to be run by both Sudanese and non-Sudanese judges and senior legal support staff. The recommendation was made after the High-Level Panel established that the victims of atrocities in Darfur did not trust the Sudanese judiciary. Some proponents for the Hybrid Court saw it as a measure that could be used to persuade the UN Security Council to invoke

---

896 Adopted by the Fifteenth Ordinary Session of the Assembly of the Union on 27 July 2010, Kampala, Uganda, para. 7.

897 See Charles C. Jalloh, Dapo Akande and Max du Plessis, 'Assessing the African Union Concerns about Article 16 of the Rome Statute of the International Criminal Court' (2011) 4 *African Journal of Legal Studies* 5.

898 Africa Union Report, Darfur The Quest for Peace, Justice and Reconciliation Report of the African Union High -Level Panel on Darfur, para. 320.

Article 16 and defer the proceedings against President al-Bashir.[899] Others argued that adjudication by a hybrid court would potentially provide a basis upon which Sudan could challenge the admissibility of its cases, pursuant to the principle of complementarity.[900]

Regardless, the Sudanese authorities rejected the recommendation. The rationale for this was that such courts would undermine both the Constitution of Sudan and the independence of its judiciary.[901] This reasoning was weak, given that having foreign judges serving in states' national justice systems was and is still common in Africa and began immediately after independence. Ali Al'amin Mazrui, an academic professor and political writer on African and Islamic studies, noted that immediately after achieving independence, it was not at all unusual for African countries to seek out high-ranking judges from other parts of the world.[902] The top judges in Tanzania were at one time from the West Indies and, in Uganda, a Nigerian judge, Sir Udo Udoma, was the Chief Justice in the critical years following its independence.[903] British citizens served as judges under Idi Amin in Uganda and one had to flee the country after giving a ruling against the regime.[904] Herbert Chitepo, the first black lawyer what was then Southern Rhodesia (now Zimbabwe), was Director of Public Prosecutions in Tanzania in the mid-1960s.

Perhaps Sudan's rejection of the proposal to establish hybrid courts was linked to the fact that post-independence it did not have Commonwealth judges or foreign judges as was the case with other post-colonial African states. Although the legal system in colonial Sudan was based on the British legal system – common law – successive military coups had transformed the legal system from common law into civil law and subsequently to Sharia law for personal law matters, including marriage, divorce and inheritance. This change was linked to the presence of legal professionals returning from training in neighbouring Egypt[905] and Sudan's drift towards being an Islamic state.

At the same time, the fact that Sudan failed to consider a recommendation made by the AU raises questions about the level to which AU member states readily comply with AU recommendations when national interests are at stake. On its part, the AU's failure to impose any punitive measures on Sudan for its refusal to comply with its recommendations exposes its limitations as an effective regional organisation. One can argue that what the AU High-Level

---

899 Ibid, para. 249.
900 Ibid.
901 'Sudan Reiterates Rejection of Darfur Hybrid Courts' *Sudan Tribune* (31 October 2009).
902 A. Ali and Alamin M. Mazrui, *The Power of Babel: Language and Governance in the African Experience* (Woodbridge, James Currey, 1998), p. 112.
903 Ibid.
904 Ibid, p. 113.
905 Mohamed El Amin El Bushra, *Criminal Justice and Crime Problem in Sudan: A Comparative Study* (Khartoum, Khartoum University Press, 1998).

Panel came up with were simply recommendations that did not have the force of law, so there was no need for the imposition of any punitive sanctions on Sudan. However, if the purpose of the Panel was to find mechanisms to address impunity and accountability in Darfur, then the lack of an implementation plan demonstrates that the AU initiative was not successful.

7.7. CONFERRING INTERNATIONAL CRIMINAL JURISDICTION ONTO THE AFRICAN COURT ON HUMAN AND PEOPLES' RIGHTS

As soon as it became apparent that the UN Security Council was not ready to engage effectively with the AU's deferral request, a small number of vocal African leaders became opposed to the very idea of African citizens being tried at The Hague. For this reason, the AU reiterated the need to operationalise the decision it made during the Twelfth Ordinary Session of the AU Assembly held in Addis Ababa in 2009 to examine the implications of giving the African Court on Human and Peoples' Rights jurisdiction to prosecute international crimes committed in Africa.[906] To this end, a protocol was drafted to amend the protocol on the Statute of the African Court of Justice and Human and Peoples' Rights.[907]

There is some controversy regarding exactly what triggered the AU's decision to confer international criminal jurisdiction onto its Human Rights Court. The general view is that the initiative was a direct result of an acrimonious relationship that developed between some of the AU member states and the Court after the indictment of President al-Bashir. On the other hand, commentators such as Don Deya, the Chief Executive Officer of the Pan African Lawyers Union (PALU), attribute the initiative to events beyond the scope of that relationship. He suggests three possible explanations. The first is the dialogue between the AU and the EU in the context of the controversial exercise of universal jurisdiction by some European judges against African government officials.[908] The second was the growing frustration among African governments with the delays in the prosecution of Hissène Habré of Chad. The third is the requirement in Article 25(5) of the African Charter on Democracy, Elections and Governance that the perpetrators of unconstitutional changes in government must be tried before a competent court of the AU.[909]

906 Decision on the Implementation of the Assembly on the Abuse of the Principle of Universal Jurisdiction, Assembly/AFRICAN UNION/Dec.213(XII), 1–3 February 2009, para. 9.

907 Decision on the Protocol on Amendments to the Protocol on the Statute of the African Court on Human and Peoples' Rights, Assembly of the African Union, 19th Ordinary Session, Assembly/AU/Dec. 427 (XIX) (2012).

908 See AU -EU Technical Ad Hoc Expert Group on the Principle of Universal Jurisdiction, 16 April 2009.

909 African Charter on Elections, Democracy and Governance, 30 January 2007, entered into force on 4 July 2012.

The first and third factors identified above fail to fully explain the source of the initiative. In a nutshell, the AU-EU report made references to the AU's decision in 2009, which means that it could not have triggered the process alone. Moreover, the African Charter on Democracy, Elections and Governance only entered into force in 2012, which makes it difficult to imagine that the AU governments were already preoccupied with the need to establish a court for a charter that had not been universally ratified by the African states. One could argue that the drafters of the Charter were already thinking about the future court in the same manner that the drafters of the Genocide Convention included a clause on prosecution by a court that might be established in the future. As a result, it was arguably the Court's intervention in Africa that generated the fresh impetus for the establishment of a regional court.

As soon as the AU Assembly made its decision to explore the possibility of conferring international criminal jurisdiction onto an African court, several draft protocols were prepared and reviewed by the AU's legal experts. In 2012, several Ministers of Justice and/or Attorney Generals adopted the drafted protocol, although many had reservations regarding the provision related to the crime of 'unconstitutional change of government'.[910] During the January 2013 Twentieth Ordinary Session of the AU, the Assembly decided that it needed to study the matter further. It wanted to discuss the term 'popular uprising' and the financial and structural implications of extending the Court's jurisdiction to international crimes.[911]

Certainly there is no legal impediment within the Rome Statute that would stop either the AU or the East African Community from establishing criminal courts to prosecute their citizens. However, it is not clear in the Rome Statute whether investigations or prosecutions by international intergovernmental organisations qualify as a basis on which to challenge admissibility. This is to be put to the test when the Assembly of States Parties start deliberations on the Kenyan proposal for regional organisations to be recognised under the admissibility regime of the Court, as already highlighted. So far, the Rome Statute is based on a positivistic approach where the state is the only key actor with regard to admissibility issues.[912]

Nevertheless, such mechanisms would contribute to the global campaign to end impunity. However, it seems that the AU initiative was driven more by a desire to protest against Africa's marginalisation by the UN Security Council and the selective focus of the Court than by a long-term commitment towards ending impunity. Ademola Abbass, International Law Professor at the United

---

910 Ademola Abass, 'The Proposed International Criminal Jurisdiction for the African Court: Some Problematical Aspects' [2013] *Netherlands International Law Review* 27, p. 29.

911 Ibid.

912 Rome Statute, Art. 17.

Nations University, describes the proposed Draft Protocol on Amendments to the Protocol on the Statute of the African Court of Justice and Human and Peoples' Rights as a protest treaty, fuelled more by momentary passions than a genuine desire for legislation.[913] Its drafting process appears to have been fast-tracked, without adequate consultation with primary stakeholders.

Max du Plessis, Associate Professor of Law at the University of KwaZulu-Natal in South Africa, noted that during the round table consultations organised by the Institute of Security Studies in South Africa in April 2012, legal advisors and senior representatives from several Southern African countries confirmed that the extraordinarily complex process had been rushed.[914] In the end, the subject-matter jurisdiction of the proposed Court appears tangential to the international understanding of what constitutes international crimes. It actually confirms the perception that the international crimes codified in the Rome Statute falls short of addressing some of the crimes affecting African states. As already discussed during the Rome Conference, some African delegates unsuccessfully proposed the inclusion of the crimes of mercenaries and terrorism under the jurisdiction of the Court. In the end, the protocol accommodated crimes specific to Africa that were not addressed by the Rome Statute.

This was arguably a positive development for the continent. The Court was never established to be a panacea capable of ending all impunity – this is why other mechanisms (such as the Special Court for Sierra Leone established in 2002, the Special Tribunal for Lebanon established in 2007 and the Extraordinary African Chambers established in Senegal in 2013) were created to fill the jurisdictional gaps that could not be addressed by the Court. The assumption is that the African regional court would serve the purpose of filling jurisdictional gaps such as the temporal jurisdiction for the crimes committed in Burundi and the Democratic Republic of the Congo prior to 2002. Its purpose should not be to compete with the Court. It is obvious that tension between the AU and the Court has contributed to the increased intensity of Africa's call for the establishment of a regional court. This has generated some suspicion that perhaps the AU's initiative was driven by the desire to shield its leaders from the Court.

Such suspicion only increased when the Special Technical Committee on Justice and Legal Affairs of the AU introduced a provision granting immunity from prosecution to sitting African heads of state and senior government officials to the Protocol for the African Court of Justice and Human and Peoples' Rights.[915]

---

913 Abass, 'The Proposed International Criminal Jurisdiction for the African Court', note 895.

914 See Max du Plessis, 'Implications of the AU Decision to Give the African Court Jurisdiction over International Crimes' institute for Security Studies, June 2012, No. 235.

915 'Opening Statement by Prof. Vincent O. Nmehielle Legal Counsel & Direction for Legal Affairs of the African Union Commission' at the 1st Session of the Specialized Technical Committee on Justice and Legal Affairs (Government Legal Expert), 6–14 May 2014, Addis Ababa, Ethiopia.

Professor Vincent O. Nmehielle, the Legal Counsel and Director for Legal Affairs of the AU, suggested that the consideration of immunity and its inclusion in the Protocol was linked to 'various decisions adopted by the Assembly of the Union on the proceedings initiated by ICC against African sitting Heads of State and Government'.[916] On 16 May 2014, the Draft Protocol was submitted and adopted by Ministers of Justice/Attorneys General and ministers responsible for issues of human rights, constitutionalism and the rule of law. The provision on immunity states that:

> No charges shall be commenced or continued before the Court against any serving African Union Head of State of Government, or anybody acting or acting or entitled to act in such capacity, or other senior state official based on their functions, during their tenure of office.[917]

The African leaders meeting during the 23rd Ordinary Session of the AU in Equatorial Guinea adopted the Protocol to establish the African Court of Justice and Human and Peoples' Rights, including the provision granting them and other senior state officials immunity from prosecution. The Protocol has still to be ratified before it enters into force. The step of including an immunity provision, which has been widely criticised by human rights international and African-based human rights organisations, is not only a setback in the global struggle against impunity for international crimes, but also raises significant questions about the African leaders' readiness to be held accountable for their actions, even by their own domestic and regional mechanisms. In a way, the decision vindicates the rationale and existence of the Court, which when operating effectively would be able to close in on such suspects that are immune from prosecution at the domestic and regional levels.

---

916 Ibid.

917 Draft Protocol on Amendments to the Protocol on the Statute of the African Court of Justice and Human Rights, *First Meeting of the Specialized Technical Committee on Justice and Legal Affairs 15–16 May 2014, Addis Ababa, Ethiopia*, STC/Legal/Min/7(I) Rev. 1, Art. 46A *bis*..

CHAPTER 8

AFRICA AND THE INTERNATIONAL CRIMINAL COURT: THE LESSONS AND PROSPECTS

To take part in the African revolution it is not enough to write a revolutionary song; you must fashion the revolution with the people. And if you fashion it with the people, the songs will come by themselves and of themselves. In order to achieve real action, you must yourself be a living part of Africa and of her thought; you must be an element of that popular energy which is entirely called forth for the freeing, the progress and the happiness of Africa. There is no place outside that fight for the artist or for the intellectual who is not himself concerned with completely at one with the people in the great battle of Africa and of suffering humanity.[918]

At the beginning of this book, the Court was described as a child in its teens trying to find its feet in a very complex international system which is already rooted in well-established principles such as state sovereignty and immunity, and where politics is omnipotent. In the African oral tradition, there is a saying that despair and fear have a nullifying effect upon a man's activity and throw him into confusion. That is why the initiation process in many African societies contains a test of courage. It is an exercise of the will, a struggle with oneself. The saying captures what the Court has been through since its establishment when the Rome Statute entered into force in 2002. It has been thrown into confusion, when those who had first supported it turned their backs on it and continue to threaten it with withdrawal and even decided not to cooperate with it. In Darfur, the Office of Prosecutor had to decide to suspend new investigations due to a lack of foresight from the UN Security Council. The Court is undergoing some form of initiation process to test its resolve and to shake some of the relics of international systems such that humanity can at least actually strike back when confronted with the evil of genocide, crimes against humanity, war crimes and hopefully aggression.

In Africa, the Kenyan President Uhuru Kenyatta captured the effect that the existence of the Court was having on some of the continent's ruling elite – it

[918] Sékou Touré, the first President of Guinea, as quoted in Frantz Fanon, *The Wretched of the Earth* (Penguin, Harmondsworth, 1963), p. 166.

was giving them nightmares. It seems that it never occurred to them that the Court would actually investigate and prosecute them; as such, those who fear the Court and its possible prosecutions for committing international crimes have mobilised state resources and have lobbied their international allies into not only resisting the Court, but also delegitimising it. Of course, there is some degree of merit in some of the issues that they raise against the Court, but this author is content that such criticisms can equally be levelled against states themselves, as they are the ones that can actually address them. One of the main criticisms of the Court is that it is targeting Africa and African individuals, and the observer may concede that, yes, the Court has a broader jurisdiction to also address impunity in other parts of the world, but as discussed in this book, the majority of the situations where the Court ended up opening investigations were brought to it by either the states parties or the UN Security Council. The Office of the Prosecutor only triggered investigations in two African states: Kenya and Cote d'Ivoire. It has been suggested that the Office of the Prosecutor could have opened investigations *proprio motu* in other parts of the world. Still, one would observe that those potential situations, such as Syria, Israel and Sri Lanka, involve non-states parties to the Rome Statute, so the Office of the Prosecutor cannot act alone and trigger their jurisdictions.

On a practical note, it is known that the Court relies on state cooperation to enforce its mandate, so if the Office of the Prosecutor were to intervene in situations without a clear strategy of gaining and sustaining state cooperation throughout the judicial cycle, the chances are that such interventions would not deliver tangible results for the victims. State cooperation in arresting and surrendering suspects continues to be unpredictable for the Court, including in cases where states parties and the UN Security Council triggered the jurisdiction of the Court.

At the same time, humanity continues to wait with the hope that there will actually be courageous and sufficient consensus within the UN Security Council, regional bodies such as the AU and state authorities to deliver on the 'Never Again' promise. The reality seems to be that although the international community is ready and prepared to prevent the spread of diseases such as Ebola or Zika, it is still no better at preventing and punishing those responsible for atrocity crimes in a predictable and systematic manner. The disservice shown by the international community to humanity continues to manifest itself in areas such as Syria, Darfur, South Sudan, Ethiopia, North Korea and Ukraine and the Democratic Republic of the Congo.

There are two components in this chapter. The first is the presentation of some of the key lessons to be learned from studying the Court and its engagement with Africa, which can help us in understanding the complex nature of enforcing international criminal justice both from a legal and a political point of view. The second component considers the future scenarios for international criminal justice as enforced by the Court. Any attempt to assess any future developments relating to the Court is risky and is like trying to be a fortune-teller, as there are many unknowns involved. Still, it is an exercise that is worth the risk, considering that the potential that the Court has in at least signalling to powerful tyrants and brutal rebel or terrorist movements that targeting civilians and violating international humanitarian law that it is not business as usual, as there is now a permanent institution that will investigate and hold them to account.

8.1. LESSONS LEARNT

8.1.1. AFRICAN SITUATIONS ARE POISONED CHALICE AND NOT SOFT LANDING FOR THE NEW COURT

The situation in which the Court finds itself in Africa of being pushed back is to some extent an analogy of what happened to the US soldiers after the invasion of Iraq back in 2003, when they faced surging resistance. The image of the Court, as at least portrayed in the documentary 'The Prosecutor' where Chief Prosecutor Moreno Ocampo is presented dressed in angelic white suit and a hero for victims, landing in a military helicopter somewhere, which appears to be in Eastern Congo, is not much different from how Donald Rumsfeld viewed the US troops being 'welcomed' in Iraq as liberators by the Shia and Kurdish ethnic minorities. The reality turned out to be more complex than what both Moreno Ocampo and Rumsfeld had imagined in Africa and in Iraq respectively. The dynamics leading up to the adoption of the Rome Statute, the anti-Court stance taken by the US, and the rise of the EU as the main dominant and powerful supporter of the Court in particular meant that the Office of the Prosecutor had no free hand to act. The influence of the US and also the Court's reliance on the EU meant that the Office of the Prosecutor had to avoid any action that could have put the Court on a collision course with any of these two politically and economically powerful entities. Africa seemed to provide a soft landing for the Court, primarily because some African states were willing to remove the veil of sovereignty and allowed the Court to intervene in their territories through state referrals.

What the Office of the Prosecutor appeared to have missed is that some of the African states that ended up referring their situations to the Court had ulterior and political interests for doing so. For example, in 2004, out of concern that the Court's involvement in the Ituri region might end up implicating some of the Ugandan troops, President Yoweri Museveni, whose country was already facing judicial action at the International Court of Justice, wrote to Kofi Annan requesting provisional immunity from prosecution for Ituri armed group leaders and the suspension of investigations by the Court.[919] It is reported that Annan replied that he had no power to interfere with the Court. Still, President Museveni managed to draw the Court away from Ituri by referring the situation in North Uganda to the Court.

The Office of the Prosecutor had considered state referrals to be synonymous with state cooperation, which of course turned out to be an incorrect assumption. It seems that the states that referred their own situations did so in order to also ensure that they could exercise control over the Prosecutor's actions within their territories. This compromised the independence of the Court, as it could only act within the confines of what the states allowed it to do. In the Democratic Republic of the Congo, President Joseph Kabila took his time in cooperating with the Court in relation to the arrest and surrender to Bosco Ntaganda, who was on the Court's international arrest warrant. Kabila's 2010 speech to the media with regard to the Congolese government's failure to arrest Ntaganda addressed this. He pointed out that his government had a choice between 'expedited international justice or peace and security for [his] people in the east', and his choice was stability and security.[920] In a reflection of how political alliances quickly change in the context of the Democratic Republic of the Congo, Ntanganda resumed military operations against government forces in Eastern Congo and temporarily took over Goma. In 2012, when Ntaganda's military and political chances were becoming more narrow, he handed himself in at the US Embassy in Rwanda before he was subsequently surrendered to the Court, where he is now facing trial. The main point here is that although the African political leaders wanted to shape the discourse of selective enforcement, as being practised by the Court to serve Western interests in Africa, the reality is that Africa's ruling elite also wanted to use the Court against their political enemies. Either way this compromised the image of the Court as an independent institution.

The UN Security Council's commitment to international criminal justice requires serious review. Its referral of Sudan and Libya and the lack of follow-up actions suggest that its priorities are somewhere distant from achieving accountability. In Sudan, it seems to be more convincing that the referral was applied as a stick in order to ensure that the Khartoum government ensured the peaceful secession of South Sudan. This is because before the secession of South Sudan, Sudan was under considerable pressure from the Security Council to implement the Comprehensive Peace Agreement and to address the conflict in Darfur; however, such pressure appears to have significantly reduced since the

---

919 Human Rights Watch, *The Curse of Gold: Democractic Republic of Congo* (New York, Human Rights Watch, 2005), p. 123.

920 Eddy Isango, 'Congo: Rwanda, Uganda Troops to Leave in February' *Associated Press* (31 January 2009).

creation of South Sudan. Political support for the Court dwindled to such an extent that the Office of the Prosecutor rightfully decided to reduce her office's activities in Darfur.

On its part, Sudan proved to be a dark horse in African affairs. Back in 1884, General Gordon described it as a 'useless possession', yet in the face of diplomatic and political pressure from powerful states such as the US and the EU, it has demonstrated credible staying power. Regarding the Court, it successfully managed to rope in the support of both the AU and the Arab League. As a member of the AU, it is guaranteed the voices and support of more than 40 member states. The Arab League provides both numerical advantage and also financial support in the face of economic sanctions imposed by the US. As such, Sudan managed to avoid the Arab Spring, which toppled regimes in its neighbours Libya and Egypt. Comparatively, both politically and economically, Sudan appears to be more stable than most of its neighbours – as such, it receives the majority of refugees and economic migrants from Ethiopia, Eritrea, Chad, Libya, Central African Republic and South Sudan. Contrary to the perception that Sudan is becoming a failed state, it actually managed to commit some of its military to join the Saudi coalition in Yemen. This happened against the background of intensive fighting in some parts of Sudan, such as Darfur, South Kordofan and Blue Nile States. Still, it seems that the Sudanese administration is not so affected by such internal strife that it cannot commit some of its troops to fight in Yemen. The point is that, assuming that when the Prosecutor indicted President al-Bashir, the intention was that he would be weakened and eventually removed from power, the opposite seems to have happened. He has become national symbol against foreign interventions in the internal affairs of Sudan.

In Kenya, the slogan 'Do not be vague, let's go to The Hague' might have misled the Office of the Prosecutor into believing that there was unwavering and nationwide support for the Court to intervene. Furthermore, one of the AU institutions, the AU Panel of Eminent African Personalities, chaired by Kofi Annan, had handed over evidence and list of potential suspects to the Prosecutor, which could have suggested that even the AU was at some point behind the Court's actions in Kenya. However, and as discussed in this book, the Court's role became very complicated after the singling out of specific prominent Kenyan figures as key suspects. The Court appeared to have been caught off-guard when some of the summoned figures were actually allowed by the Kenyan judiciary to contest in presidential election in 2013 and won. In fact, Uhuru Kenyatta and Samoei Ruto used the Court's investigations and prosecutions as part of their campaign, claiming that their principals, President Mwai Kibaki and Prime Minister Raila Odinga, had sacrificed them. Their claims were boosted by the fact that the Court did not indict the two principals, although they were the senior to Uhuru Kenyatta and Samoei Ruto. As soon as they assumed the reins of power, President Uhuru and Deputy Ruto had the state legal and financial recourses at their command to challenge the Court's intervention. Slowly but surely, they seem to have implemented a strategy that weakened their cases at the Court. Some witnesses retracted their evidence in unclear circumstances. Consequently, their cases virtually collapsed due to a lack of evidence.

Before Deputy Ruto's case had collapsed, the Kenyan government had in 2015 sent about 90 delegates to The Hague to ensure that the Assembly of States Parties weighed in its support against the retroactive use of retracted evidence in the Deputy President's case. Although this was an unnecessary stunt, one wonders whether an ordinary suspect would have managed to mobilise such a level of political support.

8.1.2. THE COURT'S INTERNAL CONTROL MECHANISMS SHOULD BE A SOURCE OF CONFIDENCE FOR THE STATES

One of the thorny issues that caused nations such as the US to oppose an independent prosecutor was their perception of a lack of external control. The concern was that it would result in the creation of an independent self-initiating prosecutor accountable to no government or institution for his or her actions. As it turned out, in reality, the crucial actions of the Office of the Prosecutor have been constantly subject to judicial review by the Chambers. The Office of the Prosecutor had to file requests under Article 15 for authorisation to open investigations *proprio muto* in Kenya, Cote d'Ivoire and Georgia. The applications gave the Pre-Trial Chamber an opportunity to review and establish whether there were reasonable grounds for the Office of the Prosecutor to proceed.

The introduction of this layer of judicial control over the Office of the Prosecutor was crucial in persuading some sceptical delegates to accept the role of an independent prosecutor in the Rome Statute. It should therefore be a relief to see that over the last 14 years, the Pre-Trial Chamber actually scrutinised the Office of the Prosecutor's application prior to granting it authorisation to open investigations. It should be pointed out that, just like in any other court, the judges still do not always come up with the same conclusion as to whether to grant authorisation or not. In the situation in Kenya, Judge Hans-Peter Kaul could not agree with the majority that the Court had subject-matter jurisdiction over the post-election violence. In his view, the crimes committed in Kenya did not meet the necessary threshold to justify the Office of the Prosecutor's intervention.

Judicial control over the Office of the Prosecutor's decisions also extends to the stage when, after conducting preliminary investigations, the decision is made not to proceed. We have seen how the Union of the Comoros challenged the decision of the Office of the Prosecutor not to open formal investigations in the situation involving the Israel Defence Forces and the ship *Mavi Marmara*, which was flying the Union of the Comoros' flag. The Pre-Trial Chamber was not impressed by the Office of the Prosecutor's legal reasoning leading up to the decision not to proceed. However, since the review process was initiated by the Union of the Comoros, a state party, and not by the Pre-Trial Chamber, all the judges could do was to ask the Prosecutor to reconsider her decision. This is the case in order to maintain the separation of powers between the two organs of the Court. There is definitely a need to strengthen the accountability of the Office of the Prosecutor to ensure that in future, there would be no situations in which the Office of the Prosecutor would decide not to proceed for ulterior motives and without providing sound legal reasoning.

For example, when the Office of the Prosecutor decided not to proceed with the investigations into the invasion of Iraq by using a very unconvincing justification of gravity, an external mechanism, such as the Pre-Trial Chamber could have intervened asking the Prosecutor to review his decision or at least asked him to provide sound legal justifications. In any case, the point is that the Office of the Prosecutor has been under judicial review and such external mechanisms have helped us to understand how and why certain situations were picked and others were not. In addition, the Assembly of States Parties established an Independent Oversight Mechanism to boost its own role in providing management oversight to the Presidency, the Prosecutor and the Register regarding the administration of the Court.[921]

The Independent Oversight Mechanism is not yet operational, but its mandate will include: first, conducting unscheduled/*ad hoc* inspections of any premises or processes as requested by the Assembly of States Parties; second, providing evaluations of any programme, project or policy as requested by the Assembly or Head of any organ of the Court; and, third, receiving and investigating reports of misconduct or serious misconduct, including possible unlawful acts by elected officials, including the Prosecutor and the staff members of the Court. The Independent Oversight Mechanism's investigative mandate does not 'impede the authority of independence granted by the Rome Statute to the Presidency, judges, Register or the Prosecutor of the Court.'[922] How it will relate to other organs of the Court in practice is likely to generate considerable interest, if not tension. This is because there is a real risk that there could be perceptions that the Mechanism is either eroding the independence of some of the organs, such as the Office of the Prosecutor, or that such organs would become too overly protective of their mandates and would resist any form of accountability.

---

921 Assembly of States Parties (ICC-ASP/8/Res.1) Establishment of an Independent Oversight Mechanism, 2009.

922 Assembly of States Parties (ICC-ASP/12/Res.6) Independent Oversight Mechanism, 27 November 2013.

8.1.3. THE COURT'S CONTRIBUTION TOWARDS PROMOTING THE INTERNATIONAL RULE OF LAW

Critics of the application of the rule of law at an international level often point to the absence of a central authority and coercive sanctions at an international level to ensure compliance. Hans J. Morgenthau considered international law to be primitive and weak due to its decentralised nature.[923] Indeed, the establishment of the Court as a permanent international criminal court, always available to states and victims of international crimes, provides a mechanism for ending impunity by means of adjudication.[924] However, the Court's effectiveness in the adjudication process and in ending impunity relies on state cooperation, since it does not have its own forces with which to apprehend suspects.[925] One commentator pointed out that the most pressing external problem facing international tribunals has been the varying preparedness of states to support them.[926]

As already discussed, a lack of cooperation with the Court is not necessarily a reflection on the nature of a state's internal governance system. It can be argued that the attitude of democratic states like the US, Israel, France and the UK towards the Court cannot be hugely differentiated from that of Kenya, Russia, China, Sudan or Libya. The US, Libya, Sudan and Israel are not states parties to the Court, despite them having different governance systems. In addition, when the Rome Statute was established, the US campaigned against the Court's existence. As has been highlighted in this book, the position of the US has since shifted, with it even offering support to the efforts to arrest Joseph Kony. Having said that, despite the overall support given by the US to the rule of law concept in international affairs, it has not ratified the Rome Statute and does not seem likely to do so in the near future.

---

923 Hans J. Morgenthau, *Poltics among Nations: The Struggle for Power and Peace* (New York, Alfred A. Knopf, 1948), p. 229.

924 For this purpose of war trials, see the opening speech given by Robert H Jackson as the Chief Prosecutor for the United States at the Nuremburg Trial when he stated that: 'The privilege of opening the first trial in history for crimes against the peace of the world imposes a grave responsibility ... That four great nations, flushed with victory and stung with injury, stay the hand of vengeance and voluntarily submit their captive enemies to the judgment of the law is one of the most significant tributes that Power has ever paid to Reason ... We must never forget that the record on which we judge these defendants is the record on which history will judge us tomorrow.' See Telford Taylor, *The Anatomy of the Nuremburg Trials: A Personal Memoir* (New York, Alfred A. Knopf, 1992).

925 Antonio Cassese, *International Criminal Law* (2nd edn, Oxford, Oxford University Press, 2008), p. 441.

926 Gideon Boas, 'What is International Criminal Justice?' in Gideon Boas, William A. Schabas and Michael P. Scharf (eds.), *International Criminal Justice: Legitimacy and Coherence* (Cheltenham, Edward Elgar, 2012), p. 8.

Similarly, the debates in the House of Commons and House of Lords in the UK pertaining to the Court indicate that the existence of the Court generated anxiety among certain sections of the British ruling and military elite. This is despite the UK being one of the main financial supporters of the Court. The strength of Britain's commitment to international criminal justice and the international rule of law is likely to be tested, since the Prosecutor decided to officially open investigations related to war crimes committed in Iraq following the submission of a new file with evidence to support the allegations that the British military was involved in widespread torture during the invasion of Iraq in 2003.

The evidence for a lack of unflinching support for international justice from the liberal democracies (the US, the UK and France) was evident in Libya. As already discussed, Libya was unanimously referred to the Court by the UN Security Council, which was a positive sign, in that it demonstrated that the Court had gained some acceptance as a tool for the international rule of law in the global system. Speaking after the referral, Gerald Araudd, the French Ambassador to the UN, stated that: 'The International Criminal Court in this matter once again finds justification for its existence.'[927] The referral was followed up by an op-ed article written by President Barack Obama, President Nicolas Sarkozy and Prime Minister David Cameron, in which they stated that the Court was 'rightly investigating the crimes committed against civilians and the grievous violations of international law'. It also pointed out that Gaddafi must go, and go for good. The problem, as one commentator observed, is that they did not say where he was supposed to go.[928] They did not specifically suggest The Hague.

However, in July 2011, when the NATO military campaign against Gaddafi had reached a stalemate (the rebels had started to show signs of internal divisions and Gaddafi had proven his resilience), the leaders of France and the UK struck a reconciliatory tune, entertaining the possibility of Gaddafi staying in Libya if he was ready to leave power. This suggests that the Court (or international justice) was being viewed as an option rather than as an inevitable outcome.

At the same time, even critics of international law like Hans Morgenthau acknowledge that in general, states observe the rules of international law.[929] In general terms, states tend to observe international rules pertaining to diplomatic affairs and involving commercial treaties, as they are reciprocal in nature. For example, it is easy for a state whose diplomatic rights are violated to reciprocate with similar treatment; this is often not the case with human rights or international criminal law, due to the sacrosanct principle of sovereignty. The

[927] UN Doc. S/PV.6491, p. 5.
[928] Amann, 'Politics and Prosecutions', note 186, p. 43.
[929] Morgenthau, *Poltics among Nations*, note 907, p. 229; see also Louis Henkin, *How Nations Behave: Law and Foreign Policy* (New York, Columbia University Press, 1979).

principle of sovereignty has always been used to protect the right of a sovereign state to determine how to treat its nationals. The importance of respecting state sovereignty and prohibitions against the use of threats or force against the territorial integrity or political independence of any state is a well-guarded principle of the UN Charter.[930] The Rome Statute reaffirms this principle, meaning a member of the UN cannot use force to intervene in another state in order to arrest and surrender an international criminal suspect to the Court.[931]

There have been a few cases where states have intervened in the affairs of other states on the basis of the very controversial concept of humanitarian intervention.[932] This concept is marred by controversy both in practical and philosophical terms.[933] It borders on being a crime of aggression, as states often tend to invoke humanitarian intervention to cover their real intentions. During the Review Conference in Kampala, the US unsuccessfully attempted to include a clause justifying aggression for humanitarian purposes.[934]

As regards the enforcement of international criminal law, state records were unimpressive at the time of the establishment of the Court. There had already been several international treaties that provided substantive law for the prosecution of international crimes at the domestic level; however, the record was still weak. The establishment of the Court was expected to address this enforcement problem.

It seems that the establishment of a permanent international criminal court has had an impact as far as creating a benchmark for how states and non-state actors are expected to behave. Since the establishment of the Court, senior military members of powerful states, such as Lord Michael Boyce of the UK, and high-profile militia leaders, such as Laurent Nkunda of Eastern Congo (who is reported to have regularly called Human Rights Watch's Congo researcher Anneke Van Wounderberg to discuss his concern that the Court might target him because of abuses committed by his troops) appear to have realised that their behaviour may come under the scrutiny of the Court.

---

930 UN Charter, Chapter 1, Arts (2)(1) and (2)(4).

931 Rome Statute, Preamble, para. 7 states that: 'Reaffirming the Purposes and Principles of the Charter of the United Nations, and in particular that all States shall refrain from the threat or use of force against the territorial integrity of political independence of any State, or in any other manner inconsistent with the Purposes of the United Nations.'

932 The precedent can be traced as far back as 1827, when Great Britain, France and Russia intervened to prevent the complete subjugation of the Greek people and to advance the Greek claim to self-determination against the Ottoman Empire. The Tanzanian government, between 1978–79 supported the overthrow of President Idi Amin of Uganda based on the cruelties of Amin's regime and recently in 2011. See Thomas Al. Franck and Nigel S. Rodley, 'After Bangladesh: The Law of Humanitarian Intervention by Military Force' (1973) 67 *American Journal of International Law* 275. Lastly, in 2011 NATO forces justified their use of force in Libya on the basis of humanitarian intervention.

933 Thomas M. Franck, 'Humanitarian Intervention' in Samntha Besson and John Tasioulas (eds.), *The Philosophy of International Law* (Oxford, Oxford University Press, 2010), p. 536.

934 Schabas, *An Introduction to the International Criminal Court*, note 3, p. 150.

On 22 March 2013, another high-profile rebel leader in Eastern Congo, Bosco Ntanganda, surrendered in Rwanda before being taken to The Hague, while Gaddafi preferred to face trial at the Court over Libya. These two examples suggest that some suspects prefer to face trial at the Court rather than face the wrath of their national justice system, where trial conditions would likely be poor and marred by violations of suspects' human rights and where in some states those convicted could face the death penalty. In this regard, it is fair to say that although the Court is still in its early days, its existence is now a reality and it reinforces the international values and rules that the international community seeks to preserve. This view is in line with what Schabas noted when he said: 'The influence of the Rome Statue will extend deep into domestic law, enriching the jurisprudence of national courts and challenging prosecutors and judges to greater zeal in the repression of serious human rights.'[935]

8.1.4. AFRICAN STATES PARTIES TAKING THE LEAD IN THE FINE-TUNING OF THE ROME STATUTE SYSTEM

Amidst the adversity that has arisen in the relationship between the AU and the Court, one positive outcome is that the African States Parties have been able to come up with proposals that sought to improve the efficiency of the Court and complete the operationalisation of some of the articles in the Rome Statute. This was inevitable considering that much of the Court's work has been focussed on African situations. For example, in 2015, during the Assembly of States Parties Session, South Africa raised the need to develop procedures for the implementation of Article 97 of the Rome Statute.[936] Article 97 outlines the consultations that a state party may have to undertake with the Court in the event that it identifies problems that may impede or prevent it from cooperating with the Court.

The Assembly of States Parties has already agreed to consider, the issue of Article 97 that was triggered following what appeared to have been a misunderstanding on the status of a consultation that had taken place between the South Africa Embassy in The Hague and the Pre-Trial Chamber over the obligations of South African government just before President al-Bashir's visit to South Africa in 2015. The Office of the Prosecutor considered the meeting to have been a consultation on Article 97, and that this was communicated to the South African Embassy.[937] However, the South African Embassy viewed the

---

935 Ibid, p. 19.

936 *Official Records*, Assembly of States Parties to the Rome Statute of the International Criminal Court, Fourteenth Session, 2015 (ICC ASP/14/20), vol. 1, para. 59.

937 *Omar Hassan Ahmad Al-Bashir* (ICC-02/05-01/09), Prosecution Request for it to Be Heard Should the Domestic Legal Proceedings in the Republic of South African Not Be Finalised by

meeting to have just been 'a preliminary meeting between the Government and the Court',[938] suggesting that there was no definitive guidance given to South Africa on its obligations to the Court. As discussed already, this prompted the Prosecutor to make a request for the confidential filings related to the meetings and the entire travel of President al-Bashir to the South Africa to be made public.

This did not go down well with South Africa, which suggested that such a move would 'only serve to undermine confidence between a state party and the Court'. The South African Legal Counsellor Thanisa Naidu-Lewin explained that South Africa was the first state party to avail itself of the possibility of consultations and experienced first-hand the challenges created for states parties resulting from the absence of clear procedures to guide them in implementing the right to consultations.[939]

The proposal to amend rule 100 on the change of place of proceedings coincided with the pressure from the joint application by the defence teams of both President Uhuru Kenyatta and Deputy President Samoei Ruto. Although the consultations had started earlier, one cannot completely disassociate the urgency with which the amendments were made from the pressure exerted by Kenya, especially after President Kenyatta's inauguration in 2013. This makes a lot of sense if one considers the other amendments adopted during the same period. For instance rule 68 was amended to facilitate the use of prior recorded testimony during a trial. In addition, there were amendments to rule 134 where rules 134 *bis*, 134 *ter* and 134 *quarter* were added to allow an accused subject to a summons to be present at the trial through the use of video technology; this also applies if the accused is mandated to fulfil extraordinary public duties at the highest national level. The amendments related to the physical presence of the accused are subject to judicial review and the Pre-Trial Chamber has already insisted that some of the suspects attend the hearings in person. Still, this does not take away from the fact that Kenya has been a catalyst either directly or indirectly in effecting such amendments.

However, there is a very thin line between initiating genuine legal amendments and trying to compel an independent institution to suit the needs of certain individuals, especially when the amendments are made against the background of tension between a state party and the Court, as was the case with Kenya. The risk is that states parties might seek to employ intimidatory and bullying tactics,

---

31 December 2015, and for Confirmation of South Africa's Continuing Obligations to Arrest and Surrender Omar al-Bashir and for Reclassification of Filings, Office of the Prosecutor, 26 October 2015, para. 9.

938 Ibid.

939 *Omar Hassan Ahmad Al-Bashir* (ICC-02/05-01/09), Decision on the Request of the Republic of South Africa for an Extension of the Limit for Submitting their Views for the Purposes of Proceedings under Article 87(7) of the Rome Statute of 15 October 2015 (ICC-02/05-01/09), Embassy of the Republic of South Africa, 21 December 2015, para. 2.9.

which contradicts the ethos of fairness and independence of the Court. Such actions could amount to interference in the Court's judicial work. For instance, in 2015, although Kenya had submitted an agenda item to be considered by the Fourteenth Session of the Assembly of States Parties for the clarification on resolution on the application of rule 68,[940] it brought with it around 90 delegates to attend the Assembly of States Parties.

One of the Kenyan delegate's main objectives was to ensure that the Office of the Prosecutor was not permitted to use the retracted evidence in Ruto's and his co-accused Joshua Sang's trial. The presence of dozens of Kenyan Members of Parliament, researchers and so on might have been permissible as it could not have occurred without the approval of the accreditation team for the Assembly of States Parties Session, but was perhaps unwarranted considering that the issue was seized and reviewed by the Appeals Chamber. The Appeals Chamber reversed the Trial Chamber V decision,[941] holding that using prior recorded testimony would be to the detriment of the accused. The decision strengthened Ruto's and Sang's defence. As such, there might have been no need for the Kenyan delegation to take the issue to the Assembly of States Parties or to travel to The Hague in large numbers. It is better that the Court is left alone when conducting its judicial work free from political pressure.

Elsewhere, Kenya and South Africa have made proposals for the amendment of the Rome Statute. As already discussed, Kenya proposed the inclusion of regional criminal jurisdictions as part of a complementary regime. This proposal is in line with the AU resolution, which seeks to fast-track the establishment of the African Court of Justice and Human and Peoples' Rights. The proposal is to ensure that once the African Court of Justice and Human and Peoples' Rights is established, the AU would be able to challenge the admissibility of the cases through making references to the role and actions of the regional court.

There are two observations that could be noted if this indeed is the logic behind the Kenyan proposal. Before delving into such observations, it is important to state from the outset that there should be nothing wrong in the establishment of a regional court, even if it shares the same jurisdiction as the Court. The first observation is that the Chambers and the Office of the Prosecutor have demonstrated that they are conservative in their review of the assessment of admissibility. Their standard is that those challenging the admissibility of a case have to demonstrate that they are investigating the same person and for the

940 Official Records of the Assembly of States Parties to the Rome Statute of the International Criminal Court, Fourteenth Session, The Hague, 18–26 November 2015 (ICC-ASP/14/20) vol. 1, ICC-ASP/14/35/Add.2 provides the list of supplementary items requested for inclusion in the agenda of the fourteenth session of the Assembly, Annex III; it includes a submission by Kenya on 3 November 2015.

941 *Ruto and Sang* (ICC-01/09-01/11 OA 10) Judgment on the Appeals of Mr Samoei Ruto and Mr Joshua Arap Sang against the Decision of (A) of 19 August 2015 Entitled 'Decision on Prosecution Request for Admission of Prior Recorded Testimony', 12 February 2016.

same crimes as the Court. If this conservative approach is to be maintained, then the AU will have the huge task of demonstrating that it is actually investigating some of the leaders who might be wanted by the Court. That on its own could be a tall order for the AU, as it is likely to upset the tradition of long-established solidarity among the African ruling elite. It is curious if not doubtful that the regional court will be able to do what national courts would have demonstrated to be incapable of doing, that is, investigating and prosecuting sitting heads of state and senior government officials. The unintended impact of establishing such a regional court could be that it justifies the existence of the Court. Since the regional court would not have jurisdication over the sitting heads of state and state officials the appropriate forum for their trial will be the Court.

The second observation is that the record of the role of the existing African regional or sub-regional courts does not inspire confidence that a new justice and human rights court will be effective to the level of meeting the criterion for challenging admissibility. In March 2016, the African Court on Human and Peoples' Rights was supposed to have a hearing in the case *Ingabire Victoire Umuhoza v. The Republic of Rwanda.*[942] Ms Ingabire Victoire Umuhoza is the head of a Rwandan political party, Forces Democratiques Unifiees (FDU Inkingi), and is serving a prison sentence of 15 years after having been convicted by the Supreme Court of Rwanda of crimes including spreading the ideology of genocide, aiding and abetting terrorism and the establishment of an armed branch of a rebel movement. She alleges that the Rwandan government violated her civil and political rights.[943]

Rwanda gave a standard response stating that the application was inadmissible before the Court and that Ms Ingabire had not exhausted local remedies before approaching the African Court. The hearing could not proceed as scheduled and, according to media reports, Rwanda pulled out of the African Court on Human and Peoples' Rights. It justified its withdrawal on the grounds that it had competent courts to investigate and prosecute all cases, including those involving human rights.[944] Rwanda is one of the few of the states that made a Declaration required under Article 34(6) of the Protocol to the African Charter on Human and Peoples' Rights on the Establishment of the African Court on Human and Peoples' Rights which allows individuals and NGOs to bring cases directly before the Court.[945] The withdrawal report suggests that Rwanda is backtracking on its commitment and the leadership it had demonstrated when it made the declaration. One is tempted to conclude that this action reveals that

942 Application No. 003/2014 *Ingabire Victoire Umuhoza v. Republic of Rwanda*, African Court on Human and Peoples' Rights.

943 Ibid.

944 Ivan R. Mugisha and Mohammed M. Mupenda, 'No Recourse in African Court for Rwandan Victoire Ingabire' *The East African* (5 March 2016).

945 There are only seven states that have made the same Declaration: Burkina Faso, Cote d'Ivoire, Ghana, Malawi, Mali, Rwanda and Tanzania.

in Africa, some states are strong on promise and short on delivery when it comes to the accountability of those in power. This could be an isolated case, but it still raises doubts as to the effectiveness of the yet to be established African Court of Justice and Human and Peoples' Rights as an alternative to the Court.

8.1.5 THE PITFALLS OF LIMITED PROMOTION OF INSTITUTIONS ROOTED IN PROGRESSIVE AFRICAN VALUES, HISTORY AND PHILOSOPHY

The dynamic relationship between the AU and the Court exposes a deep-seated weakness common to post-colonial African states. That is, upon attaining independence, instead of demonstrating that before the arrival of the Europeans, Africa had its own history and institutions, which could contribute to the wellbeing of humanity, they uncritically inherited the institutions of the colonial states. Instead of reshaping Africa's own awakening, those who took over from the colonial rulers appeared not to have the intellectual courage to vigorously challenge the structure of Africa that was created by the colonial masters, or at least to vigorously blend the Western notion of statehood with progressive African values and ethos. This was a missed opportunity as it cemented the view that Africa had no history, and confirmed how Europeans had restructured Africa to fit the idea of how it should be. As such, it seems that African states became a mirror image of Europe, with a few exceptions, primarily in North Africa, where the Arab Enlightenment was so powerful that a distinct Arabic civilisation emerged to push back the encroachment of Western civilisation.

How then does this relate to the relationship between the AU and the Court? In this book, some of the inconsistencies shown by some African states' commitment to the Court have been highlighted. For example, the majority of the states that ratified the Rome Statute also signed Bilateral Agreements with the US, which effectively stop them from cooperating with the Court in arresting and surrendering US citizens to the Court. In addition, African states like Kenya are pushing for the amendment of Article 27 on immunity for serving heads of state, their deputies and anybody acting or who is entitled to act as such from prosecution during their current term of office. This is a complete change in position from that held at the time of the negotiation and the ratification of the Rome Statute. There are possible explanations for this. One could be that the African states somehow misunderstood the implications that the Rome Statute and the Court were going to have on them as sovereign states. Maybe they were blackmailed into accepting the Rome Statute – for instance, the EU made the ratification of the Court one of the conditions for African states to continue receiving aid. At the same time, it seems that the issue could be much complex than that of aid and misunderstanding the obligations that the Rome Statute brought with it.

It could be that the inconsistencies reflect profound differences in terms of how the concept of law is viewed in Africa and in the West. One trait of Western civilisation that was uncritically embraced at independence in Africa is that of the modern state. In Europe, where the concept of the modern state evolved, the state was based on law and existed to enforce it; therefore, rulers were both morally and politically bound by the law. In addition, it must be recalled that the law in Europe is an outcome of political struggles between dominant and competing groups – the Magna Carta was a result of the struggles between the king and the barons. The same European model was superimposed on Africa. This probably made it easy for the European states and the majority of the African states to form alliances during the Rome Conference on specific issues and proposals, including the removal of immunity.

However, as we have seen when it came to delivering on the obligations created by the Rome Statute, the African states consciously or unconsciously fell back into what seems to be their natural and perhaps pre-colonial conceptualisation of law – that is, law is not primarily a contractual undertaking endowed with binding force, but rather is a means of exercising social control and should not be separated from the kinship systems. It should therefore not come as a surprise that the level of state cooperation with the Court is dependent on the state of relations between the states parties and Sudan, for instance. We have seen this with regard to Chad's changing position. Perhaps had the positions and proposals of the African states during the Rome Conference been rooted in African value systems and approach to governance, Africa would not have jumped on the bandwagon and supported a treaty that they knew they were going to struggle to support and abide by or that was alien to their philosophy.

Arab states, and those practising Islam, ensured that they made their positions known. These positions, especially those related to the teaching of their religion, played a crucial role in their decision as to whether they were to ratify the Rome Statute or not. Rightly or wrongly, the Arab stance on the applicable penalties helped in safeguarding the right of sovereign states to apply penalties as they deemed fit.[946] The African proposals appear to have been informed by either the colonial history or the desire for justice. This is fair enough, considering that modern European human rights movements are also influenced by the events leading to both the First and Second World Wars. The emerging challenge for Africa's approach is that its desire to redress colonial justice makes it embrace an outward-looking approach to accountability. The desire to get 'them' – those who abused them (Africans)– seems to be at the root of the African states' approach to the Rome Statute justice system. It is hardly inward-looking to ensure that those in power should be held accountable. There is no appetite to ensure that officer bearers are answerable to electorate

946 Rome Statute, Art. 80.

This book has highlighted and supported the establishment of an African Court of Justice and Human and Peoples' Rights. However, there are already signs that since such an institution is modelled on the paradigm that was used to design the Court, its compatibility with African values and ethos is causing headaches for those in favour of such an institution. The question of the immunity of heads of state and governmental officials emerges again in the framework of the African Court of Justice and Human and Peoples' Rights. Human rights defenders and European states are critical of the inclusion of immunity for government officials. We have seen that such criticism comes naturally to them, as it is informed by their conceptualisation of the law.

The challenge seems to be for African leaders, intellectuals and researchers to at least avoid trying to mimic European institutions and transplanting them into the African context. Such an approach does not seem to be working. The reality is that just like the model of the European states, which Africa has embraced, such institutions were developed outside Africa's full knowledge, history and realities and this makes it hard to successfully mimic them.

Instead of trying to mimic Western models, African states may have to invest in coming up with their own models informed by their own traditions, values and history.

New concepts and innovations would benefit not only Africa but also Europe and humanity as a whole. This was evident with regard to the African Peer Review Mechanism, which was established in 2003. It lies at the core of the New Partnership for Africa's Development (NEPAD), which was initiated by former Presidents Thabo Mbeki, Abdoulaye Wade, Abdelaziz Bouteflika and Olusegun Obasanjo. The concept of peer review is an Africa self-monitoring mechanism, whose unique feature is that it is non-adversarial and relies heavily on mutual trust and clear rules of procedure.[947] President Museveni captured this uniqueness and its African roots when he said the following about the mechanism:

> Africans are very polite people with very polite cultures. We cannot go to somebody's home and tell him to do this or that. That is never done in our cultures. However, it does not seem to be a problem in other cultures ... The African Peer Review Mechanism is based on the principle of fellowship, unlike this other one of the other people where the other people come to review you and you do not review them. How can an adult review another adult and the other one does not review him? What sort of arrangement is this?[948]

The resemblances between the African Peer Review Mechanism and the UN Universal Periodical Review, which was established in 2006, suggest that the

[947] Adebayo Adedeji, 'NEPAD's African Peer Review Mechanism: Progress and Prospects' in John Akokpari, Angela Ndinga- Muvumba and Time Murithi (eds.)(eds.) *The Africa Union and its Institutions* (Fanele, Johannesburg, 2008), pp. 241–69.

[948] President Yoweri Museveni, 'State of the Nation Address', Ugandan Parliament, 6 June 2007.

drafters of the latter were aware of the African model and adopted it for application at the level of the UN. Therefore, there is the potential that if the African states turn to their heritage, they might come up with effective mechanisms to address their own problems, especially regarding accountability. This includes finding sustainable solutions to the challenge of political exclusion, which seems to be the main cause of turmoil and instability in many post-independence African states. The majority of atrocity crimes committed in Africa, including the Rwanda genocide of 1994, the conflict in Darfur, South Sudan and the post-election violence in Kenya, are directly or indirectly linked to the problem of political exclusion.

That said, and for Africa to achieve real action and be taken seriously on the global stage, it is imperative that ordinary African people are put at the heart of any regional initiative. As such, those concerned about Africa, including its political leaders, must be, as Sékou Touré, first President of Guinea, said, 'living part of Africa and of her thought'. So far, there is a great divide that separates the views and aspirations of ordinary African citizens and their eloquent political and intellectual leaders. Such a gap weakens the positions of African leaders as they attempt to speak in the name of Africans. In a hypothetical scenario, it would be interesting to see how many of the policy positions adopted by the AU, such as non-cooperation with the Court, would receive overwhelming support in a referendum.

8.2. PROSPECTS

8.2.1. THE COURT'S FORTUNES ARE LIKELY TO DEPEND ON THE POLITICAL AND ECONOMIC SITUATION IN THE EU

The EU's ability to sustain its dominant presence in providing political and economic support to the Court is crucial for the latter's future. As long as the EU considers the fight against impunity to be a fundamental feature of its approach to building and maintaining lasting international justice and the rule of law as part of its external policy, the Court is likely to continue demonstrating resilience in the face of adversity. The strong links existing between the EU former colonial powers such as France, Belgium and the UK and some African States Parties may mean that the latter may find it hard to come up with radical positions against the Court. In addition, the chances are that once the Court begins to have, and exercise, jurisdiction over the crime of aggression, militarily weaker African states might increase their support for the Court in order to have some form of protection from potential aggressors.

The worst-case scenario for the Court, is that the EU gets distracted by other priorities, including worsening relations with Russia, the migration crisis and the economic challenges that might put its free market economy and integration into question, such that promotion of human rights and support for international criminal justice becomes secondary on its foreign policy agenda. In such a situation, the Court's presence might decline. In 2008, we already saw how the major financial providers for the Court reduced their funding due to the global economic downturn. In Sudan, the EU has demonstrated that finding lasting solution to the migration crisis (majority of the migrants transit through Sudan to the Mediterranean Sea to Europe) was its top priority and started to work closely with Government of Sudan. This was a shift from its position when President Bashir was indicted in 2009. In this event, the Court might have to diversify its sources of financial support. Perhaps more resources will find their way to the Court as the existing *ad hoc* tribunals for Rwanda and Yugoslavia complete their mandates. However, the likelihood of similar *ad hoc* tribunals being established is very high, as is already being contemplated for South Sudan and Syria.

8.2.2. THE REGIONALISATION OF THE COURT FOR VISIBILITY AND EFFICIENCY

The current status quo of having The Hague as the seat of the Court and also the place where all proceedings take place might be financially unsustainable, and the Court is likely to streamline its activities, including opening regional offices as cost-cutting measures. There are already field offices around Africa such as those in Uganda and Kenya; however, additional regional offices are also likely to be established to cater for complete trials sessions or just part of the trials, especially during the pre-trial phase. Some potential locations for such regional offices include South Africa, Tanzania and Senegal. The measures could reduce the running costs of the Court, but would also bring the proceedings closer to the affected communities. It might take a while before the AU permits the opening of a Liaison Office in Addis Ababa, but this should not stop the Court from approaching regional economic committees such as the Southern African Development Community (SADC), the East African Community and ECOWAS in order to open its regional offices. In fact, the chances are high that such regional economic committees might be more receptive than the AU.

8.2.3. THE OFFICE OF THE PROSECTOR LIKELY TO CONCENTRATE ON SUSPECTS LACKING PROTECTION FROM AND CONTROL OF STATE INSTITUTIONS

The trend that is currently being observed where the Court has managed to secure the custody of heads of state who have lost political power or rebel leaders is likely to continue. The chances of the Court gaining custody of a sitting head of state are very slim simply because these individuals can easily use their state's legal, political and financial resources to protect themselves and avoid being arrested and surrendered to the Court. The irony is that in the event that they unceremoniously lose their grip on power and would have to choose between being prosecuted by their successors or the Court, they are likely to prefer the latter. We have already witnessed this with regard to Gaddafi's family, who supported the Court in putting Saif Gaddafi on trial instead of the post Gaddafi government in Libya. The main driver for this trend is the knowledge by suspects that they stand a better chance of a fair trial and better conditions if they go to the Court than through their own national justice system.

8.2.4. INTERNATIONAL COURT OF JUSTICE INTERVENTION TO SETTLE HEAD OF STATE OF IMMUNITY IN THE CONTEXT OF THE ROME STATUTE

The recurring legal debates on the status of immunity of head of state and governments of non-states parties indicted by the Court are likely to end up at the International Court of Justice. The issue could be either taken by a non-state party or could be in the form of a request of an Advisory Opinion from the UN General Assembly. The South African Supreme Court judgment in 2016 on the case involving President al-Bashir's visit to South Africa in 2015, where it held that the South African government has legal obligations under the Rome Statute to arrest and surrender al-Bashir, suggests that it prefers a restrictive theory of immunity. Still, there appears to be no consensus among scholars of international criminal law on the issue. The emerging trend from the UN Security Council referral suggests that it assumes that its resolutions referring non-states parties remove any immunity of the potential suspects. This observation is supported by the fact that since the referral of the situation in Darfur to the Court and the debates on al-Bashir's immunity, the Security Council did not change the wording of its resolutions referring Libya and also in the vetoed draft resolution on Syria. This suggests that the scale seems to be tilting towards a restrictive application of immunity of sitting heads of state. However, an opinion or judgment from the International Court of Justice in the matter could be more authentic.

BIBLIOGRAPHY

BOOKS

Allen, T., *Trial Justice: The International Criminal Court and the Lord's Resistance Army* (Zed Books, 2006)

Ambos, K., *The Colombian Peace Process and the Principle of Complementarity of the International Criminal Court: An Inductive, Situation-Based Approach* (Springer, 2010)

Annan, K. with N. Mousavizadeh, *Interventions: A Life in War and Peace* (Penguin Books, 2012)

Arendt, H., *Eichmann in Jerusalem: A Report on Banality of Evil* (Penguin Books, 1964)

Armstrong, D., T. Farrell and H. Lambert, *International Law and International Relations* (Cambridge University Press, 2007)

Bass, G.J., *Stay the Hand of Vengeance: The Politics of War Crimes Tribunals* (Princeton University Press 2000)

Boot, M., *Genocide, Crimes against Humanity and War Crimes: Nullum Crimen Sine Lege and the Subject Matter Jurisdiction of the ICC* (Intersentia, 2002)

Broomhall, B., *International Justice and the International Criminal Court: Between Sovereignty and the Rule of Law* (Oxford University Press, 2003)

Brownlie, I., *The Principles of Public International Law* (7th edn, Oxford University Press, 2008)

Bushra, M.A., *Criminal Justice and Crime Problem in Sudan: A Comparative Study* (Khartoum University Press, 1998)

Cassese, A., *International Criminal Law* (Oxford University Press, 2003)

—— *International Criminal Law* (2nd edn, Oxford University Press, 2005)

Cassese, A. et al. (eds.), *International Criminal Law: Cases & Commentary* (Oxford University Press, 2011)

Clarke, K.M., *Fictions of Justice: The International Criminal Court and the Challenge of Legal Pluralism in Sub-Saharan Africa* (Cambridge University Press, 2009)

Cryer, R., *Prosecuting International Crimes: Selectivity and the International Criminal Law Regime* (Cambridge University Press, 2005)

Cryer, R. et al., An Introduction to International Criminal Law and Procedure (Cambridge University Press, 2007)

Dicey, AV, *Lectures Introductory to the Study of the Law of the Constitution* (Macmillan, 1885)

Doyle, A.C., *The Crime of the Congo* (4th edn, Hutchinson & Co, 1909)

Drumbl, M.A., *Atrocity, Punishment and International Law* (Cambridge University Press, 2007)

Englebert, E., *Africa: Unity, Sovereignty, and Sorrow* (Lynne Rienner, 2009)

Finnstrom, S., *Living with Bad Surroundings: War, History, and Everyday Moments in Northern Uganda* (Duke University Press, 2008)

Glasius, A., *The International Criminal Court: A Global Civil Society Achievement* (Routledge, 2006)

Goldstone, R., *For Humanity: Reflections of a War Crimes Investigator* (Yale University Press, 2002)

Goldstone, R. and A.M. Smith, *International Judicial Institutions: The Architecture of International Justice at Home and Abroad* (Routledge, 2009)

Henkin, L., *How Nations Behave: Law and Foreign Policy* (Columbia University Press, 1979)

Hochschild, A., *King Leopold's Ghost: A Story of Greed Terror and Heroism in Colonial Africa* (Mariner Books, 1998)

Huntington, S.P., *The Clash of Civilizations and the Remaking of World Order* (Free Press, 2002)

Ifeonu, E., *From Consent to Suspicion: Understanding the African Union's Emerging Resistance to the Enforcement of International Criminal Justice in the African Region* (Saarbrucken VDM Verlag Dr. Muller Aktiengesellschaft & Co. KG, 2009)

Mamdani, M., *Saviors and Survivors: Darfur, Politics and the War on Terror* (Verso, 2009)

Mazrui, A.A. and A. Mazrui, *The Power of Babel: Language and Governance in the African Experience* (James Currey, 1998)

McCormick, N., *Rhetoric and the Rule of Law: A Theory of Legal Reasoning* (Oxford University Press, 2009)

Melvern, L., *A People Betrayed: The Role of the West in Rwanda's Genocide* (2nd edn, Zed Books, 2009)

Mendes, E.P., *Peace and Justice at the International Criminal Court: A Court of Last Resort* (Edward Elgar, 2010)

Morgenthau, H.J., *Politics among Nations: The Struggle for Power and Peace* (Alfred A Knopf, 1948)

Murungu, C. and J. Biegon (eds.), Prosecuting International Crimes in Africa (Pretoria University Law Press, 2011)

Mutua, M., *Human Rights: A Political and Cultural Critique* (Bert B. Lockwood Jr. ed., University of Pennsylvania Press 2002)

Nouwen, S.M.H., Co*mplementarity in the Line of Fire: The Catalysing Effect of the International Criminal Court in Uganda and Sudan* (Cambridge University Press, 2013)

Peters, R., *Crime and Punishment in Islamic Law: Theory and Practice from the Sixteenth to the Twenty-First Century* (Cambridge University Press, 2005)

Plessis, M., *The International Criminal Court that Africa Wants* (Institute of Security Studies, 2010)

Posner, E.A., *The Perils of Global Legalism* (University of Chicago Press, 2009)

Prunier, G., *From Genocide to Continental War: The 'The Congolese' Conflict and the Crisis of Contemporary Africa* (Hurst & Company, 2009)

—— *Darfur: The Ambiguous Genocide* (Hurst, 2010)

Raz, J., *The Authority of Law: Essay on Law and Morality* (Oxford University Press, 1983)

Rice, C., *No Higher Honour: A Memoir of My Years in Washington* (Simon & Schuster, 2011)

Robertson G., *Crimes against Humanity: The Struggle for Global Justice* (3rd edn, Penguin Books, 2006)

Schabas, W., *The International Criminal Court: A Commentary on the Rome Statute* (Oxford University Press, 2010)

—— *An Introduction to the International Criminal Court* (4th edn, Cambridge University Press, 2011)

—— *Unimaginable Atrocities: Justice, Politics, and Rights as the World Crimes Tribunals* (Oxford University Press, 2012)

Scheffer, D., *All the Missing Souls: A Personal History of the War Crimes Tribunals* (Princeton University Press, 2012)

Stegmiller, I., *The Pre-investigation Stage of the ICC: Criteria for Situation Selection* (Duncker & Humblot, 2011)

Stigen, J., *The Relationship between the International Criminal Court and National Jurisdictions: The Principle of Complementarity* (Martinus Nijhoff, 2008)

Taylor, T., *The Anatomy of the Nuremburg Trials: A Personal Memoir* (Alfred A. Knopf, 1992)

Zeidy, M.M., *The Principle of Complementarity in International Criminal Law: Origin, Development and Practice* (Martinus Nijhoff Publishers, 2008)

BOOK CHAPTERS

Amann, D.M., 'Politics and Prosecutions: Form Katherine Fite to Fatou Bensouda' in E. Andersen and D.M. Crane (eds.), *Proceedings of the Fifth International Humanitarian Law Dialogs* (American Society of International Law, 2012)

Bassiouni, M.C., 'International Criminal Justice in Historical Perspective: The Tension between States' Interests and Pursuit of International Justice' in A. Cassese (ed), *The Oxford Companion to International Criminal Justice* (Oxford University Press, 2009)

—— 'Revisiting the Architecture of Crimes against Humanity: Almost a Century in the Making, with Gaps and Ambiguities Remaining – The Need for a Specialised Convention' in L.N. Sadat (ed), *Forging a Convention for Crimes against Humanity* (Cambridge Press University, 2011)

Boas, G., 'What is International Criminal Justice?' in G. Boas, W.A. Schabas and M.P. Scharf (eds.), *International Criminal Justice: Legitimacy and Coherence* (Edward Elgar, 2012)

Brown, B.S., 'The Statute of the ICC: From The Hague to Rome and Back Again' in S.B. Sewall and C. Kaysen (eds.), *The United States and the International Criminal Court: National Security and International Law* (Rowman & Littlefield, 2000)

Cassese, A., 'The Rationale for International Criminal Justice' in A. Cassese (ed), *The Oxford Companion to International Criminal Justice* (Oxford University Press, 2009)

Cerone, J.P., 'U.S. Attitudes Towards International Criminal Courts and Tribunals' in C.P.R. Romano (ed), *The Sword and the Scales the United States and International Courts and Tribunals* (Cambridge University Press, 2009)

Clark, P., 'Law, Politics and Pragmatism: The ICC and Case Selection in Uganda and the Democratic Republic of Congo' in N. Waddell and P. Clark (ed), *Courting Conflict? Justice, Peace and the ICC in Africa* (Royal African Society, 2008)

Condorelli, L. and S. Villalpando, 'Referral and Deferral by the Security Council' in A. Cassese, P. Gaeta and J.R.W.D. Jones (eds.), *The Rome Statute of the International Criminal Court: Commentary* (Oxford University Press, 2002)

Crane, DM, 'The Bright Red Thread: The Politics of International Criminal Law – Do We Want Peace or Justice? The West African Experience' in LN Sadat (ed), *Forging a Convention for Crimes against Humanity* (Cambridge University Press, 2011)

Cryer, R., 'The Philosophy of International Criminal Law' in A. Orakhelashvili (ed), *Research Handbook on the Theory and History of International Law* (Edward Elgar, 2011)

Franck, T.M., 'Humanitarian Intervention' in S. Besson and J. Tasioulas (eds.), *The Philosophy of International Law* (Oxford University Press, 2010)

Garsky, S., 'Strong, Independent, and Effective: The European Union's Promotion of the International Criminal Court' in A. Boening, J.F. Kremer and A. Loon (eds.), *Global Power Europe: Vol 2: Policies, Actions and Influence of the EU's External Relations* (Springer, 2013)

Gewald, J.-B., 'Imperial Germany and the Herero of Southern Africa: Genocide and the Quest for Recompense' in A. Jones (ed), *Genocide, War Crimes and the West* (Zed Books, 2004)

Gomes, S., 'The Peacemaking Role of the OAU and the AU: A Comparative Analysis' in J. Akokpari, A. Ndinga-Muvumba and T. Murithi (eds.), *The African Union and its Institutions* (Fanele, 2002)

Holmes, J.T., 'Complementarity: National Courts versus the ICC' in A. Cassese, P. Gaeta and J.R.W.D. Jones (eds.), *The Rome Statute of the International Criminal Court: A Commentary* (Oxford University Press, 2002)

Kaul, H.-P., 'Preconditions to the Exercise of Jurisdiction' in A. Cassese, P. Gaeta and J.R.W.D. Jones (eds.), *The Rome Statute of the International Criminal Court: A Commentary* (Oxford University Press, 2002)

—— 'The International Criminal Court – Its Relationship to Domestic Jurisdictions' in C. Stahn and G. Sluiter (eds.), *The Emerging Practice of the International Criminal Court* (Martinus Nijhoff, 2009)

Kirsch, P. and D. Robinson, 'Initiation of Proceedings by the Prosecutor' in A. Cassese, P. Gaeta and J.R.W.D. Jones (eds.), *The Rome Statute of the International Criminal Court: A Commentary* (Oxford University Press, 2002)

Lerace, M., 'Complexities in Prosecuting International Crime: The ICC Libyan Warrants' in G. Boas, W. Schabas and M.P. Scharf (eds.), *International Criminal Justice: Legitimacy and Coherence* (Edward Elgar, 2012)

McCormack, T.L.H., 'Their Atrocities and Our Misdemeanours: The Reticence of States to Try Their "Own Nationals" for International Crimes' in M. Lattimer and P. Sands (eds.), *Justice for Crimes against Humanity* (Hart Publishing, 2003)

Mwanasali, M., 'From Non-interference to Non-indifference: The Emerging Doctrine of Conflict Prevention in Africa' in J. Akokpari, A. Ndinga-Muvumba and T. Murithi (eds.), *The African Union and its Institutions* (Fanele, 2008)

Obura, K., 'Duty to Prosecute International Crimes under International Law' in C. Murungu and J. Biegon (eds.), *Prosecuting International Crimes in Africa* (Pretoria University Law Press, 2011)

Ocampo, L.M., 'Building a Future on Peace and Justice: The International Criminal Court' in K. Ambos, J. Large and M. Wierda (eds.), *Building a Future on Peace and Justice* (Springer, 2007)

Ohlin, J.D., 'Peace, Security, and Prosecutorial Discretion' in C. Stahn and G. Sluiter (eds.), *The Emerging Practice of the International Criminal Court* (Martinus Nijhoff, 2009)

Pace, W.R. and R. Ripanganiban, 'The Power of Global Activist Networks: The Campaign for an International Criminal Court' in P.I. Hajnal (ed), *Civil Society in the Information Age* (Ashgate, 2002)

Popovski, V., 'Legality and Legitimacy of International Criminal Tribunals' in R. Falk, M. Juergensmeyer and V. Popovski (eds.), *Legality and Legitimacy in Global Affairs* (Oxford University Press, 2012)

Reydams, L. and J. Wouters, 'The Politics of Establishing International Criminal Tribunals' in L. Reydams, J. Wouters and C. Ryngaert (eds.), *International Prosecutors* (Oxford University Press, 2012)

Rodrigues, A., 'Undue Delay and the ICTY's Experience of Status Conferences: A Judge's Personal Annotations' in J. Doria, H.P. Gasser and M.C. Bassiouni (eds.), *The Legal Regime of the International Criminal Court: Essays in Honour of Professor Igor Blishchenko* (Martinus Nijhoff, 2009)

Schabas, W.A., 'Prosecutorial Discretion and Gravity' in C. Stahn and G. Sluiter (eds.), *The Emerging Practice of the International Criminal Court* (Martinus Nijhoff, 2009)

Simpson, G.J., 'War Crimes: A Critical Introduction' in T.L.H. McCormack (ed), *The Law of War Crimes: National and International Approaches* (Kluwer Law International, 1997)

Sloan, J., 'The ICC and Domestic Enforcement in Canada and the UK' in C.P.M. Waters (ed), *British and Canadian Perspectives on International Law* (Martinus Nijhoff, 2006)

Snidal, D., 'International Political Economy Approaches to International Institutions' in J.S. Bhandari and A.O. Sykes (eds.), *Economic Dimensions in International Law: Comparative and Empirical Perspectives* (Cambridge University Press. 1997)

Stahn, C., 'Judicial Review of Prosecutorial Discretion: Five Years on' in C. Stahn and G. Sluiter (eds.), *The Emerging Practice of the International Criminal Court* (Martinus Nijhoff, 2009)

Townsend, G., 'Structure and Management' in L. Reydams, J. Wouters and C. Ryngaert (eds.), *International Prosecutors* (Oxford University Press, 2012)

Wierda, M. and M. Otim, 'Justice at Juba: International Obligations and Local Demands in Northern Uganda' in N. Waddell and P. Clark (eds.), *Courting Conflict? Justice, Peace and the ICC in Africa* (Royal African Society, 2008)

Zappala, S., 'Prosecutorial Discretion' in A. Cassese (ed), *The Oxford Companion to International Criminal Justice* (Oxford University Press, 2008)

Zeidy, M.M., 'Admissibility in International Criminal Law' in W.A. Schabas and N. Bernaz (eds.), *Routledge Handbook of International Criminal Law* (Routledge, 2011)

JOURNAL ARTICLES

Abass, A., 'The Proposed International Criminal Jurisdiction for the African Court: Some Problematical Aspects' [2013] *Netherlands International Law Review* 27

Akhavan, P., 'The International Criminal Tribunal for Rwanda: The Politics and Pragmatics of Punishment' (1996) 90 *American Journal of International Law* 501

Bassiouni, M.C., 'International Crimes: *Jus Cogens* and *Obligatio Erga Omnes*' (1996) 59 *Law and Contemporary Problems* 1

—— 'Negotiating the Treaty of Rome on the Establishment of an International Criminal Court' (1999) 32 *Cornell International Law Journal* 443
—— 'Combating Impunity for International Crimes' (2000) 71 *University of Colorado Law Review* 409
Benedetti, F. and J.L. Washburn, 'Drafting the International Criminal Court Treaty: Two Years to Rome and an Afterword on the Rome Diplomatic Conference' (1999) 5 *Global Governance* 1
Benzing, M., 'The Complementarity Regime of the International Criminal Court: International Criminal Justice between State Sovereignty and the Fight against Impunity' (2003) 7 *Max Planck Yearbook of United Nations Law* 591
Bergsmo, M., 'The Jurisdictional Regime of the International Criminal Court (Part II, Articles 11–19)' (1998) 6 *European Journal of Crime, Criminal Law and Criminal Justice* 345
Bishop, A., 'Failure of Complementarity: The Future of the International Criminal Court Following the Libyan Admissibility Challenge' (2013) 22 *Minnesota Journal of International Law* 388
Bratza, N., 'The Relationship between the UK Courts and Strasbourg' (2011) 5 *European Human Rights Law Review* 505
Broomhall, B., 'Toward US Acceptance of the International Criminal Court' (2001) 64 *Law and Contemporary Problems* 141
Burke-White, W.W. and S. Kaplan, 'Shaping the Contours of Domestic Justice: The International Criminal Court and an Admissibility Challenge in the Uganda Situation' (2009) 7 *Journal of International Criminal Justice* 257
Caban, P., 'Preliminary Examinations by the Office of the Prosecutor of the International Criminal Court' (2011) 2 *Czech Yearbook of Public & Private International Law* 199
Cayley, A.T., 'The Prosecutor's Strategy in Seeking the Arrest of Sudanese President Al Bashir on Charges of Genocide' (2008) 6 *Journal of International Criminal Justice* 829
Cote, L., 'Reflections on the Exercise of Prosecutorial Discretion in International Criminal Law' (2005) 3 *Journal of International Criminal Justice* 162
Crawford, J., 'The ILC Adopts a Statute for an International Criminal Court' (1995) 89 *American Journal of International Law* 404
Crook, J.R., 'US Proposes New Regional Court to Hear Charges Involving Darfur, Others Urge ICC' (2005) 99 *American Journal of International Law* 501
Danner, A.M., 'Enhancing the Legitimacy and Accountability of Prosecutorial Discretion at the International Criminal Court' (2003) 97 *American Journal of International Law* 510
De Guzman, M.M., 'Gravity and the Legitimacy of the International Criminal Court' (2009) 32 *Fordham International Law Journal* 1400
Eftekhari, S., 'France and the Algerian War: From a Policy of "Forgetting" to a Framework for Accountability' (2003) 34 *Colombian Human Rights Law Review* 413
Fehl, C., 'Explaining the International Criminal Court: A "Practice Test" for Rationalist and Constructivist Approaches' (2004) 10 *European Journal of International Relations* 357
Franck, T.A.L. and N.S. Rodley, 'After Bangladesh: The Law of Humanitarian Intervention by Military Force' (1973) 67 *American Journal of International Law* 275
Groenleer, M.L.P. and L.G.V. Schaik, 'United We Stand? The European Union's International Actorness in the Cases of the International Criminal Court and the Kyoto Protocol' (2007) 45 *Journal of Common Market Studies* 969

Guruk, J., 'United States Opposition to the 1998 Rome Statute Establishing an International Criminal Court: Is the Court's Jurisdiction Truly Complementary to National Criminal Jurisdictions?' (2002) 35 *Cornell International Law Journal* 592

Hall, C.K., 'The First Five Sessions of the UN Preparatory Commission for the International Criminal Court' (2000) 94 *American Journal of International Law* 773

Hirsch, F., 'The Soviets at Nuremberg: International Law, Propaganda, and the Making of the Postwar Order' (2008) 113 *American Historical Review* 701

Hunt, A., 'The Theory of Critical Legal Studies' (1986) 6 *Oxford Journal of Legal Studies* 1

Hutchinson, A. and P. Monahan, 'Law Politics and the Critical Legal Scholars' (1984) 36 *Stanford Law Review* 199

Jalloh, C.C., 'Regionalizing International Criminal Law' (2009) 9 *International Criminal Law Review* 445

—— 'Universal Jurisdiction, Universal Prescription? A Preliminary Assessment of the African Union Perspective on Universal Jurisdiction' (2010) 21 *Criminal Law Forum* 1

—— 'Situation in the Republic of Kenya. No ICC-01/09-02/11-274. Judgement on Kenya's Appeal of Decision Denying Admissibility' (2012) 106 *American Journal of International Law* 118

Jalloh, C.C., D. Akande and M. Plessis, 'Assessing the African Union Concerns about Article 16 of the Rome Statute of the International Criminal Court' (2011) 4 *African Journal of Legal Studies* 5

Johansson, P., 'The Humdrum Use of Ultimate Authority: Defining and Analysing Chapter VII Resolutions' (2009) 78 *Nordic Journal of International Law* 309

Kaul, H.P., 'Construction Site for More Justice: The International Criminal Court after Two Years' (2005) 99 *American Journal of International Law* 370

Kennedy, D., 'Critical Labour Theory: A Comment' (1981) 4 *Industrial Relations Law Journal* 503

Kirsch, P. and J.T. Holmes, 'The Rome Conference on an International Criminal Court: The Negotiating Process' (1999) 93 *American Journal of International Law* 2

Kissinger, H.A., 'The Pitfalls of Universal Jurisdiction: Risking Judiciary Tyranny' (2001) 80 *Foreign Affairs* 86

Koskenniemi, M., 'Between Impunity and Show Trials' (2002) 6 *Max Plank Yearbook of United Nations Law* 1

Leckie, S., 'The Inter-state Complaint Procedure in International Human Rights Law: Hopeful Prospects or Wishful Thinking' (1988) 10 *Human Rights Quarterly* 249

Lowe, A.V. and C. Warbrick, 'The Lockerbie Affair' (1992) 41 *International and Comparative Law Quarterly* 907

McCormack, T.L.H., 'Selective Reaction to Atrocity: War Crimes and the Development of International Law' (1997) 60 *Albany Law Review* 681

Megret, F., 'The Politics of International Criminal Justice' (2002) 13 *European Journal of International Law* 1261

Meron, T., 'International Criminalization of Atrocities' (1995) 89 *American Journal of International Law* 554

Morris, M., 'High Crimes and Misconceptions: The ICC and Non-states Parties' (2001) 64 *Law and Contemporary Problems* 13

Murphy, S.D., 'American Servicemembers' Protection Act' (2002) 96 *American Journal of International Law* 975

Mutua, M., 'From Nuremberg to the Rwanda Tribunal: Justice or Retribution' (2000) 6 *Buffalo Human Rights Law Review* 77
Nouwen, S.M.H. and W.G. Werner, 'Doing Justice to the Political: The International Criminal Court in Uganda and Sudan' (2011) 21 *European Journal of International Law* 941
Nsereko, D.D.N., 'Prosecutorial Discretion before National Courts and International Tribunals' (2005) 3 *Journal of International Criminal Justice* 124
Orentlicher, D., 'Setting Accounts the Duty to Prosecute Human Rights Violations of a Prior Regime' (1991) 100 *Yale Law Journal* 2537
Pichon, J., 'The Principle of Complementarity in the Cases of the Sudanese National Ahmad Harun and Ali Kushayb before the International Criminal Court', 8 *International Criminal Law Review* 185
Posch, A., 'The Kadi Case: Rethinking the Relationship between EU Law and International Law' (2009) 15 *Columbia Journal of European Law Online* 1
Posner, D.N. and D.J. Young, 'The Institutionalization of Political Power in Africa' (2007) 18 *Journal of Democracy* 126
Reydams, L., 'Belgium's First Application of Universal Jurisdiction: the Butare Four Case' (2003) 1 *Journal of International Criminal Justice* 428
Richardson, I., 'The Privy Council as the Final Court for the British Empire' (2012) 43 *Victoria University of Wellington Law Review* 103
Robinson, D., 'Serving the Interest of Justice: Amnesties: Truth Commissions and the International Criminal Court' (2003) 14 *European Journal of International Law* 481
— 'The Controversy over Territorial State Referrals and Reflections on ICL Discourse' (2011) 9 *Journal of International Criminal Justice* 355
Rowlinson, S.P., 'The British System of Military Justice' (2002) 52 *Air Force Law Review* 17
Schabas, W.A., 'Complementarity in Practice: Some Uncomplimentary Thoughts' (2008) 19 *Criminal Law Forum* 5
— 'Prosecutorial Discretion v. Judicial Activism at the International Criminal Court' (2008) 6 *Journal of International Criminal Justice* 731
— 'State Policy as an Element of International Crimes' (2008) 98 *Journal of Criminal Law and Criminology* 953
— 'The Banality of International Justice' (2013) 11 *Journal of International Criminal Justice* 545
Scheffer, D., 'The United States and the International Criminal Court' (1999) 93 *American Journal of International Law* 12
— 'Symposium on 'The ICTY 10 Years on: The View from Inside' – Three Memories from the Year of Origin, 1993' (2004) 2 *Journal of International Criminal Justice* 353
— 'Article 98(2) of the Rome Statute: America's Original Intent' (2005) 3 *Journal of International Criminal Justice* 333
Simpson, G., 'The Death of Baha Mousa' (2007) 8 *Melbourne Journal of International Law* 340
Stahn, C., 'The Ambiguities of Security Council Resolution 1422' (2002) 14 *European Journal of International Law* 85
— 'Between "Faith" and "Facts": By What Standards Should We Assess International Criminal Justice?' (2012) 25 *Leiden Journal of International Law* 251
Stuart, H.V., 'The ICC in Trouble' (2000) 6 *Journal of International Criminal Justice* 409

Tabak, S., 'Article 124, War Crimes, and the Development of the Rome Statute' (2009) 40 *Georgetown Journal International Law* 1096

Tladi, D., 'The African Union and the International Criminal Court: The Battle for the Soul of International Law' (2009) 34 *South African Yearbook of International Law* 57

Vanteginste, S., 'Bypassing the Prohibition of Amnesty for Human Rights Crimes: Lessons Learned from Burundi Peace Process' (2011) 29 *Netherlands Quarterly of Human Rights* 189

Whitaker, B.E., 'Soft Balancing among Weak States in Africa' (2010) 86 International Affairs 1109

OFFICIAL PUBLICATIONS

Council on Foreign Relations, 'Koh and Rapp's Remarks on U.S. Engagement in the International Criminal Court and the Outcome of the ICC Assembly of States Parties Conference' (Harold Hongju Koh, Legal Advisor US Department of State, and Stephen J. Rapp, Ambassador-at Large for War Crimes Issues Remarks at a Press Conference, Washington DC, 15 June 2010)

UKICC-Communication to the Prosecutor -The Responsibility of Officials of the United Kingdom for War Crimes Involving Systematic Detainee Abuse in Iraq from 2003–2008 submitted by the European Centre for Constitutional and Human Rights (ECCHR) and the Public Interest Lawyers (PIL)

EU, Press Release (EU 19/06/845), 'The European Commission Contributes to the Restoration of Justice in the East of the Democratic Republic of the Congo' (Brussels 26 June 2006)

Goodluck, J., 'Statement by President Goodluck Jonathan at the Extraordinary Session of African Union Heads of State and Government in Addis Ababa, 12 October 2013'

Hall, C.K., Suggestions Concerning International Criminal Court Prosecutorial Policy and Strategy and External Relations (Expert consultation process on general issues relevant to the ICC Office of the Prosecutor, ICC Prosecutorial Policy and Strategy and External Relations 2003)

Human Rights Watch, *Making Justice Work: Restoration of the Legal System in Ituri, DRC: A Human Rights Watch Briefing Paper* (Human Rights Watch, 2004)

—— *The Curse of Gold: Democratic Republic of the Congo* (Human Rights Watch, 2005)

Kaul, H.-P., 'The ICC of the Future' (6th Annual International Humanitarian Law Dialogues 2012 'Hybrid International Court: A Tenth Anniversary Retrospective on the Special Court of Sierra Leone', Chautauqua Institution, Robert H Jackson Centre, 28 August 2012)

Kenyatta, U., 'Speech by His Excellency Hon. Uhuru Kenyatta, C.G.H., President and Commander in Chief of the Defence Forces of the Republic of Kenya' (Extraordinary Session of the Assembly of Heads of State and Government of the African Union, Addis Ababa, 12 October 2013)

AUPD (2009) Darfur: The Quest for Peace, Justice and Reconciliation. Report of the African High-Level Panel on Darfur (AUPD), African Union

Mugabe, R., 'Statement by His Excellency the President of the Republic of Zimbabwe Comrade Robert Gabriel Mugabe, During the General Debate of the 66th Session of the United Nations General Assembly New York, 22nd September 2011'

Museveni, Y.K., 'Statement by H.E Yoweri Kaguta Museveni President of the Republic of Uganda' (Inauguration of HE Uhuru Kenyatta, Kenya's President-Elect, Nairobi, 9 April 2013)

Rice, C., Press Release, Trip Briefing, State Government Website, 10 March 2006

United Nations, Official Records Volume II Summary Records of the Plenary Meetings and of the Meetings of the Committee of the Whole 6th Plenary Meeting, A/CONF.183/SR.6 (United Nations 1998)

ONLINE ARTICLES

'African Countries Back away from ICC Withdrawal Demand' *Sudan Tribune* http://www.sudantribune.com/spip.php?article31443 (8 June 2009)

'African Union Refuses Arrest against Rwandans' *Rwanda Focus* (7 July 2008)

BBC, 'World Reaction: Bashir Warrant' http://news.bbc.co.uk/2/hi/africa/7923797.stm (4 March 2009)

—— 'Sudan to Expel Ambassador after Kenya's Bashir Warrant' (29 November 2011)

—— 'Kenya asks UN to halt ICC charges against Kenyatta' *BBC World News* http://www.bbc.com/news/world-africa-15932019 (9 May 2013)

—— 'Sudan's President Bashir Leaves AU Summit in Nigeria' http://www.bbc.com/news/world-africa-23327830 *BBC News* (16 July 2013)

—— 'William Hague Rejects Iraq "Abuse" Complaint to ICC' http://www.bbc.com/news/uk-25703723 *BBC News* (12 January 2014)

Boisvert, Y., 'La fragile justice internationale fragilisée' *La Presse* (17 June 2013)

Borger, J., 'Commonwealth Chief admonished by ICC over "War Crimes" Remarks' *The Guardian* (27 October 2010)

Bravin, J., 'US Warms to Hague Tribunal: New Stance Reflects Desire to Use Court to Prosecute Darfur Crimes' *Wall Street Journal* (7 February 2014)

—— 'Justice Delayed for Global Court, Uganda, Rebels Prove Tough Test; African Politics, http://www.wsj.com/articles/SB114971481626174102 ((8 June 2006)'

Burgis, T., 'Uganda Disputes ICC Charges against Kony' *Financial Times* (11 March 2008)

'Chad Rolls Red Carpet for Sudanese President, Says Bashir is Safe from Arrest' *Sudan Tribune* (22 July 2010)

Chothia, F., 'African's Fatou Bensouda is New ICC Chief Prosecutor' (2011) http://www.bbc.co.uk/news/world-africa-16029121

Corcoran, B., 'Days of Reckoning for Criminal Court as African Union Members Convene' *Irish Times* (9 October 2013)

Crossette, B., 'Helms Vows to Make War on UN Court' *New York Times* (27 March 1998)

—— '10 Years after Lockerbie, Still No Trial' *New York Times* (22 December 1998)

'Ethiopian Leader Accuses International Court of Racial Bias' *Reuters* (12 November 2013)

Flint, J. and A. de Waal, 'Case Closed: A Prosecutor without Borders' *World Affairs* (2 February 2009)

Gettleman, J., 'Rebel Leader in Congo is Flown to The Hague' *New York Times* (22 March 2013)

Goldstone, R., 'Does the ICC Target Africa?' EQ: Equality of Arms Review March 2009 www.ibanet.org/Document/Default.aspx?DocumentUid accessed 04 May 2012

Henley, J., 'Why is the European Ccourt of Hhuman Rrights Hhated by the UK Right? Court designed to protect the vulnerable is respected in Europe but despised by many Tories and UK newspapers' The Guardian (22 December 2013)
Hope, C., 'Archbishop Desmond Tutu Pulls out of Event with Tony Blair Because of Iraq War' *Daily Telegraph* (28 August 2012)
Kambale, P., 'The ICC and Lubanga: Missed Opportunities' *African Futures* (20 May 2013)
'Kid gloves are off' *News Africa* (20 May 2011)
Laing, A., 'International Criminal Court is "Hunting" Africans' *The Telegraph* (27 May 2013)
Lough, R., 'African Union Accuses ICC Prosecutor of Bias' *Reuters* (30 January 2011)
MacAskill, E., 'Clinton: It is a "Great Regret" that the US is not in International Criminal Court' *The Guardian* (6 August 2009)
Malone, B., 'Africans Push UN to Call off "Racist" Court' *Al Jazeera* (15 November 2013)
Meldrum, A., 'African Union refuses to arrest Gaddafi' (2011) http://www.globalpost.com/dispatches/globalpost-blogs/africa-emerges/african- union-refuses-arrest-gaddafi
Ngarmbassa, M., 'Sudan's al-Bashir Defies ICC with Chad Visit' *Mail and Guardian* (22 July 2010)
Obama, B., D. Cameron and N. Sarkozy, 'Libya's Pathway to Peace' *New York Times* (14 April 2011)
Owino, W., 'Botswana Faults Gaddafi over "Hasty" AU Decisions' *Kenya Daily Nation* http://www.nation.co.ke/News/africa/-/1066/620312/-/138uiegz/- /index.html
Pincus, W., 'Clinton's Goals Detailed' *Washington Post* (6 August 2009)
'President Uhuru Hits out at the West over ICC' *Kenya Daily Nation* (12 October 2013)
Roth, K., 'Africa Attacks the International Criminal Court' *New York Review of Books* (14 January 2014)
Rozenberg, J., 'Why Britain's Top Soldier Would Not End up in the Dock over Iraq' *Daily Telegraph* (2 May 2005)
Schabas, W, 'Britain, France Flirting with Letting Gaddafi Avoid Prosecution by the ICC' (PhD Studies in Human Rights, 28 July 2011)
Scharf, M., 'Results of the Rome Conference for an International Criminal Court' *ASIL Insights* (11 August 1998)
Scheffer, D., 'The Security Council's Struggle over Darfur and International Justice' *Jurist Legal News and Research* http://jurist.law.pitt.edu/forumy/2008/08/security-councils-struggle-over-darfur.php
Sherwell, P., 'WikiLeaks: Sudan's President Stashed $9 billion' *Daily Telegraph* (17 December 2010)
Slack, J., 'Europe's War on British on British: UK Loses Three out of Four Human Rights Cases, Damning Report Reveals' *Daily Mail* (11 January 2012)
Smith, D., Kofi Annan: 'African Justice is Weak' *The Guardian* (10 October 2013)
'South Sudan's Kiir Backs Kenya's Uhuru against ICC Charges' *Sudan Tribune* (24 May 2013)
Stearns, S., 'African Union Says ICC Prosecutions are Discriminatory' *Voice of America* (4 July 2011)
'Sudan Reiterates Rejection of Darfur Hybrid Courts' *Sudan Tribune* (31 October 2009)
'Sudan to Request ICJ Opinion on UN Security Council Authority to Refer Case to ICC' *Sudan Tribune* (29 July 2008)

Swaine, J., Libya: African Mercenaries 'Immune from Prosecution for War Crimes' *Daily Telegraph* (27 February 2011) http://www.telegraph.co.uk/news/worldnews/africaandindianocean/libya/8350968/Libya-African-mercenaries-immune-from-prosecution-for-war-crimes.html

Igihe 'Rwanda Supports AU position on ICC', http://en.igihe.com/news/rwanda-supports-au-position-on-icc.html 15 October 2013) accessed 24 February 2014

Tutu, D., 'Why I Had No Choice But to Spurn Tony Blair' *The Observer* (2 September 2012)

—— 'In Africa, Seeking a License to Kill' *New York Times* (10 October 2013)

INDEX

www.ingramcontent.com/pod-product-compliance
Ingram Content Group UK Ltd.
Pitfield, Milton Keynes, MK11 3LW, UK
UKHW051926100926
8556IPUK00022B/1397

9 781780 683874